D0319695

REGIMENTS AND CORPS OF THE BRITISH ARMY

REGIMENTS AND CORPS OF THE BRITISH ARMY

IAN S. HALLOWS

NEW
ORCHARD

To the memory of
EDGAR HADDON HALLOWS, DCM
2/Lt Royal Field Artillery

First published in 1991 by **Arms and Armour Press**
A Cassell Imprint
Villiers House, 41–47 Strand, London WC2N 5JE.

This edition published in 1994
by **New Orchard Editions**
(A Cassell Imprint)
and distributed by **Bracken Books**,
an imprint of Studio Editions Ltd,
Princess House, 50 Eastcastle Street, London W1N 7AP, England

British Library Cataloguing in Publication Data
Hallows, Ian S.
Regiments and corps of the British Army.
1. Great Britain. Army, history
I. Title
355. 310941
ISBN 1–85891–237–7

Designed and edited by DAG Publications Ltd.
Designed by David Gibbons; edited by Michael Boxall;
typeset by Typesetters (Birmingham) Ltd, Warley,
West Midlands; printed and bound in Great Britain by
Mackays of Chatham PLC, Chatham, Kent

CONTENTS

6   CONTENTS

PREFACE

The history of the regiments and corps of the British army is a long and complicated one, often extending over two or three centuries. The regimental system has always been the backbone of the army, providing deep regional roots and a sense of historical identity which men in battle have found to be a source of strength. Over the years, changes have been inevitable and many of the benefits issuing from such a sense of identity have been watered down as a result of amalgamations. Nevertheless, regimental pride remains at the heart of the British army. With massive changes taking place in the world's political landscape, the consequent review of Britain's defence requirements should make this book a timely one. It is hoped that a new generation will be able to appreciate the richness of our tradition.

8

ACKNOWLEDGMENTS

The author wishes to express his gratitude to the following military attachés and advisers of Commonwealth countries for confirming and correcting the present titles of their countries' units that are allied to or associated with British regiments and corps: Col D. R. Lawrence AM, Australia; Maj J. M. Hartland, Barbados; Maj R. S. Wilson CD, Canada; Maj S. A. Mulumbi, Kenya; Maj D. B. A. Rahman, Malaysia; Mr B. M. Dilmahood, Mauritius; Mr J. A. B. Crawford, New Zealand; Mr R. Nithiandum, Singapore; Maj V. R. L. Anthonisz, Democratic Socialist Republic of Sri Lanka; and the Military Attaché, Zambia. He is also grateful for information on alliances in 1914 from Col Lawrence, Australia; Maj Wilson, Canada; Mr Crawford, New Zealand; and Maj-Gen P. Pretorius, South Africa.

He also wishes to thank the following regimental, corps and museum officers and staff for their help in compiling and correcting data on the units listed: Maj J. F. Ainsworth, Royal Sussex Regiment; Mr S. Anglim, Parachute Regiment; Capt D. J. Archibald, Scots Guards; Maj A. F. W. Astle, Cheshire Regiment; Mr B. S. Baxter, Corps of Royal Electrical and Mechanical Engineers; Maj W. E. G. Beldham, Royal Army Veterinary Corps; Maj R. C. H. Berry MBE, The Light Infantry; Dr S. Bull, 14th/20th King's Hussars, Queen's Lancashire Regiment; Maj J. Carroll, Devonshire and Dorset Regiment, Dorset Regiment; Brig J. K. Chater, Royal Warwickshire Fusiliers; Maj A. G. B. Cobbold, Suffolk Regiment; Lt-Col R. A. Costain, Corps of Royal Military Police; Col J. S. Cowley, King's Own Yorkshire Light Infantry; Brig J. M. Cubiss CBE MC, Prince of Wales's Own Regiment of Yorkshire; Lt-Col C. D. Darroch DL, Royal Hampshire Regiment; Maj M. A. Easey, Royal Army Chaplains' Department; Lt-Col A. W. Scott Elliot, Argyll and Sutherland Highlanders (Princess Louise's); Lt-Col R. Eyeions OBE, Royal Army Medical Corps; Lt-Col A. A. Fairrie, Queen's Own Highlanders (Seaforth and Camerons); Maj D. J. H. Farquharson, 16th/5th The Queen's Royal Lancers; Maj M. J. Fogwell, Small Arms School Corps; Mr D. Fraser MA, 9th/12th Royal Lancers (Prince of Wales's); Mr G. S. Gill BA Cert Ed, 1st The Queen's Dragoon Guards; Mr F. Hackett BA AMA FGS, Bedfordshire and Hertfordshire Regiment; Maj J. McQ. Hallam, Lancashire Fusiliers; Capt C. Harrison, Gordon Highlanders; Mr T. L. Hewitson, Royal Northumberland Fusiliers; Mr T. F. J. Hodgson, Queen's Own Buffs, The Royal Kent Regiment, and The Buffs (Royal East Kent Regiment); Mr N. Holme, Royal Welch Fusiliers; Mr G. Holmes, Royal Tank Regiment; Mr I. Hook, Essex Regiment; Capt D. D. Horn MISM, Guards Museum; Maj R. J. Jeffreys MBE, 4th/7th Royal Dragoon Guards; Maj A. W. Kersting MISM, Household Cavalry; Maj J. S. Knight, The Queen's Own Hussars; Maj J. E. G. Lamond, Brigade of Gurkhas; Maj E. W. Leask, Oxfordshire and Buckinghamshire Light Infantry; Maj K. D. Lewis MBE, Welsh Guards; Lt-Col P. Love, Worcestershire and Sherwood Foresters Regiment; Maj A. J. Maher MBE, The Loyal Regiment (North Lancashire); Col R. K. May FMA, King's Own Royal Border Regiment, Border Regiment; Lt-Col N. D. McIntosh, Green Howards (Alexandra, Princess of Wales's Own Regiment of Yorkshire); Maj R. D. W. McLean, Staffordshire

Regiment (The Prince of Wales's), South Staffordshire Regiment, North Staffordshire Regiment; Lt-Col R. B. Merton, The Royal Hussars (Prince of Wales's Own); Mr L. J. Murphy, Devonshire and Dorset Regiment, Devonshire Regiment; Maj M. B. Murphy, Royal Irish Rangers, Royal Ulster Rifles; Lt Bryn Owen RN FMA, Royal Regiment of Wales (24th/41st Foot), Welch Regiment; Mr G. Archer Parfitt FMA, FCII, King's Shropshire Light Infantry; LSgt L. Pearce, Coldstream Guards; Lt-Col C. E. Penn, Royal Corps of Transport; Lt-Col W. G. Pettifar MBE JP, Royal Regiment of Fusiliers, Royal Fusiliers (City of London Regiment); Lt-Col C. E. Potts OBE, Worcestershire and Sherwood Foresters Regiment (29th/45th Foot), Worcestershire Regiment; Mr G. Preece, Manchester Regiment; Caroline N. Reed BA AMA, Corps of Royal Engineers; Mr S. D. Shannon, Durham Light Infantry; Capt A. R. Smith, Royal Lincolnshire Regiment; Lt-Col J. L. Wilson Smith OBE, The Royal Scots (The Royal Regiment); Maj C. D. Spears, Royal Pioneer Corps; Mr J. Spencer, Duke of Wellington's Regiment (West Riding); Maj G. E. M. Stephen MBE, Royal Inniskilling Fusiliers; Mr R. Thompson, 15th/19th The King's Royal Hussars; Dr P. Thwaites BA MSc PhD, Royal Corps of Signals; Brig K. A. Timbers, Royal Regiment of Artillery; Maj S. Tipping, South Lancashire Regiment, Lancashire Regiment (The Prince of Wales's Volunteers); Maj V. W. Ward, Royal Army Dental Corps; Col H. B. H. Waring OBE, Queen's Own Royal West Kent Regiment; Lt-Col R. M. H. Weeks, Prince of Wales's Own Regiment of Yorkshire; Maj W. H. White DL, Duke of Cornwall's Light Infantry; Mr D. Whybrow, Middlesex Regiment (Duke of Cambridge's Own); Lt-Col L. M. B. Wilson MBE, Queen's Regiment, Queen's Royal Regiment (West Surrey), East Surrey Regiment; Mr S. Wood, National Museums of Scotland; Lt-Col R. G. Woodhouse DL, Somerset Light Infantry (Prince Albert's); Maj M. Wright, Royal Irish Fusiliers; Lt-Col M. H. G. Young, R. Corps of Transport.

Gratitude is also expressed to Regimental Secretaries and to Keepers, Curators and Assistant Curators of the museums of the following regiments and corps: 5th Royal Inniskilling Dragoon Guards; 17th/21st Lancers; Royal Lincolnshire Regiment; King's Own Scottish Borderers; Army Air Corps; Royal Army Pay Corps; Royal Army Educational Corps; Royal Army Dental Corps; Army Physical Training Corps; Queen Alexandra's Royal Army Nursing Corps; Women's Royal Army Corps. In a very few cases, it has not been possible to have a unit's entry checked.

Permission to include short extracts in the chapter on regimental anniversaries has been generously given by the following publishers of the books concerned: Bailey Bros and Swinfen Ltd; The Bodley Head; Bullfinch Publications; Jonathan Cape Ltd; Hamish Hamilton Ltd; Harrap Publishing Group Ltd; Ian Henry Publications; International Thomson Publishing Services Ltd (Routledge and Kegan Paul); Michael Joseph Ltd; John Murray (Publishers) Ltd; Osprey Publishing Group Ltd; Oxford University Press.

Much use has been made of the Bromley and Lewisham central reference libraries. The help of the librarians involved is gratefully acknowledged.

The advice and encouragement of Mr Roderick Dymott and Mr Christopher Westhorp of Arms & Armour Press in the preparation of this book has been much appreciated, and the author wishes also to thank Mr Brian Wells and Mr Anthony Sibblies for help in various ways. However, any errors of fact or of judgment are the responsibility of the author alone.

INTRODUCTION

The British regular army can be broadly divided into cavalry regiments – now part of the Royal Armoured Corps – infantry regiments and support corps, but a closer examination will show greater differences. The Household Cavalry, for example, are not part of the RAC though having mechanized squadrons; armoured former cavalry regiments are joined in the RAC by the Royal Tank Regiment; the five Guards regiments are in a division separate from the five divisions of the infantry of the line; and the Parachute Regiment, the Brigade of Gurkhas and the Special Air Service Regiment are in no division. Several support corps have active service roles – though they were originally raised to overcome the commissariat disasters of the Crimean, Boer and Great Wars, but more recently they have tended to specialize in particular aspects of supply and maintenance of the greatly increased complexity of military weapons and communications.

Although supporting corps troops now far outnumber the fighting soldiers, regiments retain a corporate identity. From 1660 to 1881, British infantry regiments were usually raised for particular overseas campaigns and were given numerical titles ('raised' always indicates the origin of a regiment; 'formed' indicates one that has been amalgamated). From 1751, however, territorial titles were gradually introduced, a process which ended in 1881. In this book, regimental history before 1881 (infantry) or 1922 (cavalry) is given in outline only. Before those years, many changes took place, particularly with the junior regiments, which will only be of interest to specialists. For example, the 96th Foot (later the Manchester Regiment) and the 99th (later the Wiltshire Regiment) were disbanded and re-formed six times before 1881; the 98th (later the North Staffordshire Regiment) five times; and the 97th (later the Queen's Own Royal West Kent Regiment) four times. The 19th Hussars, 20th Hussars and 21st Lancers were re-formed three times before 1922.

When widespread amalgamations were carried out in 1881, resulting in eighty-three infantry regiments becoming the 1st and 2nd battalions of forty-one regiments, there must have been some unhappy combinations at first. This may well have been the case with some of the 1958–1971 amalgamations also.

Those post-war amalgamations also led to the formation under new titles of seven cavalry regiments (there had been eight amalgamations in 1922) and sixteen infantry regiments. As a result, no cavalry regiment now exists under its original title – the 1st and 2nd Life Guards became The Life Guards in 1922. However, the five regiments of the Guards Division and five infantry regiments – the Royal Scots, the Green Howards, the Cheshire Regiment, the Royal Welch Fusiliers and the King's Own Scottish Borderers – still keep their titles and have never been amalgamated. Also, six regiments retain the titles they were given in 1881: the Gloucestershire Regiment, the Duke of Wellington's Regiment, the Royal Hampshire Regiment, the Black Watch, the Gordon

Highlanders and the Argyll and Sutherland Highlanders. But the Queen's Regiment is now made up of eleven previous regiments, and the Light Infantry and the Royal Anglian Regiment each of nine. Details of the parents of such amalgamated regiments have also been included, so that the reader can refer to their operational history. The index serves as a guide to these and makes such a task easier.

The new titles after the amalgamations, though unpopular at first, appear now to have been reasonably well chosen. Some lack of imagination may perhaps be seen in the titles of the new cavalry regiments. The 9th/12th Lancers (Prince of Wales's Own) gives the parentage in the title – as did all the 1922 cavalry amalgamations – but the Queen's Own Hussars, the Queen's Royal Irish Hussars and the Royal Hussars seem too similar in name. Although yeomanry regiments are only mentioned here with their associated regular regiments, the Queen's Own Yeomanry, the Queen's Own Mercian Yeomanry the Queen's Own Yorkshire Yeomanry and the Royal Yeomanry could have been given more distinctive names. What happened to Hussars, Dragoons, Horse or Scouts?

Most regiments and some corps have Colonels-in-Chief. HM The Queen is Col-in-C of fifteen regiments and two corps – and of eighteen Common-wealth units. Two members of European royal families are Cols-in-C: of the Queen's Regiment: the only non-royal Col-in-C is the Duke of Wellington. Only one Gurkha regiment – 2nd King Edward VII's Own Gurkha Rifles (The Sirmoor Rifles) – has a Col-in-C, and only twelve corps. Some regiments have been given titles associating them with royalty, but only one survives with its original title – the Green Howards (Alexandra, Princess of Wales's Own Regiment of Yorkshire).

At present, each infantry regiment belongs to one of six divisions: Guards, Scottish, Queen's, King's, Prince of Wales's and Light. The hated brigade system did not last for long. It should be remembered that the Army List, though giving cavalry regiments in order of precedence, lists infantry regiments by division, the senior regiment of each division determining that division's seniority. Thus the Scottish Division comes next to the Guards Division through the Royal Scots (The Royal Regiment). Infantry regiments appear in the main text in order of precedence, but, for easy reference they also appear in alphabetical order in the index.

CAP BADGES

Cap badges illustrated in the text are those of soldiers, because officers' cap badges differ in some units – such as the Coldstream and Scots Guards and the Royal Scots. 'King's' crowns on badges should have been replaced by 'Queen's' crowns after the accession of HM The Queen, but some had not been altered before amalgamations took place. Some pre-amalgamation badges are still worn, however – the Austrian double-headed eagle of 1st King's Dragoon Guards by 1st The Queen's Dragoon Guards; the Prussian eagle of 14th (King's) Hussars by the 14th/20th King's Hussars; and the skull and crossbones of 17th (Duke of Cambridge's Own) Lancers by 17th/21st Lancers. It should be remembered that the absence of a Royal crown does not necessarily mean that the regiment lacks a Royal title – such as the Royal Anglian Regiment or the Royal Welch Fusiliers – although all Royal corps cap badges do carry the crown. Nor are King's and Queen's crowns the only ones used. For example, the badges of the Green Howards and of Queen Alexandra's Royal Army Nursing Corps bear the Dannebrog; the Royal Regiment of Wales, the Staffordshire Regiment and 2nd King Edward VII's Own Gurkha Rifles the coronet of HRH The Prince of Wales; the Duke of Edinburgh's Royal Regiment and 7th Duke of Edinburgh's Own Gurkha Rifles the coronet of HRH Prince Philip The Duke of Edinburgh; and 10th Princess Mary's Own Gurkha Rifles the coronet of HRH The Princess Royal. And, of former regiments, the Royal Irish Fusiliers had the coronet of the Princess Victoria; the Wiltshire Regiment that of the Prince Consort; the Rifle Brigade a Guelphic crown; the Somerset Light Infantry and the Somerset and Cornwall Light Infantry a mural crown; and the short-lived Mercian Brigade a Saxon crown.

REGIMENTAL ANNIVERSARIES

Most regiments celebrate the anniversaries of their most noted engagements. These were not always victories – Arnhem, Balaklava, Gallipoli and Maiwand are among those that were not. The earliest regimental anniversary is Blenheim (2 August 1704): it is celebrated by the King's Regiment and the Royal Anglian Regiment, descendants of the 8th Foot, later the King's Regiment (Liverpool), and of the 16th Foot, later the Bedfordshire and Hertfordshire Regiment.

BATTLE HONOURS

Battle honours were originally authorized to be emblazoned on regimental standards, guidons or colours – King's colours and 2nd colours having been established for foot regiments by Royal Warrant in 1745. Standards are carried by the Household Cavalry, Dragoon Guards and the Royal Tank Regiment; guidons by Lancers and Hussars; and colours by Foot Guards (who also have company colours) and infantry of the line (except the Royal Green Jackets, for rifle regiments have no colours). The first honour – by Royal Warrant in 1768 – was Emsdorff (1760) to the 15th Light Dragoons in the Seven Years War, only a year after the regiment had been raised: this honour still appears on the guidon of 15th/19th The King's Royal Hussars. Often, however, it was many years before an honour was awarded. Tangier 1662–80 and Namur 1695 were not awarded until 1910; Gibraltar 1704–5 not until 1909; Blenheim (1704) not until 1882; and Belleisle (1761) not until 1951. Yet most Peninsular War honours were awarded before 1825; and Waterloo in 1815, the year of the battle.

Since many battle honours were awarded for the Great War, it was ordered in 1922 that regiments should not have more than twenty-five honours emblazoned on their standards, guidons or colours, of which no more than ten should be Great War honours; in 1956 a limit of ten was applied to Second World War honours; and in 1958 a limit of two to Korean War honours. After the 1958–71 amalgamations, regiments were authorized to emblazon up to forty honours on each of the Queen's and regimental colours. The average number of honours so chosen is forty-six: the large regiments, with the greatest choice, have selected most. The names of the wars or campaigns in which honours were gained are, as a matter of historical interest, given in bold type although those names do not actually appear on colours. Honours that have not been chosen to appear on colours – usually Great War and Second World War honours, but some earlier ones with the large amalgamated regiments – are listed as 'accredited' honours, having still been earned by the regiment. A few examples of lesser-known honours that have been passed on to successor regiments may be mentioned here. Detroit (War of 1812) was awarded to the 41st, or Welsh Regiment, and is still borne by the Royal Regiment of Wales. Koosh-ab (Persian War of 1857) was awarded to the Prince of Wales's (North Staffordshire Regiment), the 78th (Ross-shire Buffs) and the 106th (Bombay Light Infantry): it is still carried on the colours of two of their successor regiments, the Staffordshire Regiment (The Prince of Wales's) and the Queen's Own Highlanders (Seaforth and Camerons) but not on those of the Light Infantry. But Moro (Seven Years War), though awarded to the 56th Foot, is not carried by the Royal Anglian Regiment. Some honours summarize much of British military history: Blenheim, Dettingen, Plassey, Waterloo, Balaklava, Cambrai, El Alamein, for example. Others show world-wide campaigns of the past: Abyssinia, Afghanistan, Archangel, Ava (Burma), Kilimanjaro, Monte Video, New Zealand, Niagara, Norway, Persia, Tangier, Taku Forts (China). Studying all battle honours and without passing judgement on imperial expansions of the past, it would seem that only Rome and Britain have engaged in such widespread campaigns from such small bases.

THE VICTORIA CROSS AND THE GEORGE CROSS

The Victoria Cross was instituted on 29 January 1856 (the title of 'The Military Order of Victoria' had been first suggested) and the George Cross on 24 September 1940. Living holders in 1940 of the Empire Gallantry Medal (founded 1922) were instructed to exchange it for the George Cross, as were living holders in 1971 of the Albert Medal (founded 1866) and the Edward Medal (founded 1907).

Former members of the Boys' Brigade have been awarded more VCs than those of any other organization; next are former pupils of Eton College. Perhaps the author may mention a personal interest, as he believes he is the only survivor of those who attended the Distinguished Conduct Medal centenary service at St Martin-in-the-Fields in 1954 and the VC centenary service at Westminster Abbey in 1956 (the DCM League was founded in 1928, the VC Association – now the VC and GC Association – in 1956): eighteen VCs were awarded during the Great War to men who already held the DCM. There is even one case (during the Second World War) where the award of a DCM was cancelled and the award of a VC made in its place at the insistence of King George VI: sadly, the recipient died recently.

On the inception of the VC, its award was accompanied by a pension of £10 a year. In 1897, Piper G. Findlater of the Gordon Highlanders was awarded the VC for his bravery during the Tirah Campaign, but was subsequently discharged from the service on account of his wounds. When he tried to earn a living by playing the pipes at an Aberdeen music hall, the military authorities requested that the appearance should not take place and forbade the officers and pipers of the Aberdeen Depot to attend. Questions were then asked in Parliament, and it was agreed (in 1898) that the Secretary of State for War should, at his discretion, grant a pension of £50 a year to holders of the VC. More recently, a flat-rate tax-free annuity of £100 was granted to surviving holders of the VC in 1959 and to surviving holders of the GC in 1965 by the efforts of Brigadier Sir John Smyth, VC: the annuity was back-dated to the date of the award.

Eight VCs have been forfeited for offences that cannot be considered particularly serious: sadly, one holder later committed suicide but, more happily, the pauper's grave at Darlington of another holder was refurbished and re-dedicated in 1985 by his old corps. A later offence should surely not allow such forfeiture, since the original act of gallantry still stands. The current Warrant (SAO 65 of 1961) allows the Sovereign to cancel and annul the award of a VC, although this has not happened since 1908. Restoration can only be made if the original recommendation for cancellation has been withdrawn. King George V maintained that, even if the holder of a VC were to be hanged for murder, he should be allowed to wear the VC on the scaffold. Although none who has forfeited the VC is still alive, it must be time that the awards were posthumously restored and the power to cancel and annul surrendered. Details of VC and GC awards are given with the regiments in which the recipients served. Where a first award was made before 1881, the number of the regiment concerned is given.

MEMORIALS

There are many regimental and corps war memorials in Britain, well maintained by their parent units. However, there are many more local memorials and it is only recently that a central register is being compiled by the Imperial War Museum: it is hoped that the names commemorated on these memorials will also be included, as they would be of great assistance in demographic, local history and genealogical studies.

MILITARY MARCHES

At the end of 1989, it was reported that the Ministry of Defence spent £62 million in 1988–9 on maintaining military bands, 56 per cent of all centrally funded expenditure on music. These figures are difficult to accept: with about 2,500 military musicians in the three services, the average cost of a single musician would appear to be nearly £30,000 a year or £70 a day. Since musicians are soldiers first and musicians second, acting as medical orderlies in wartime, their military pay – apart from their extra costs as musicians – would surely be part of normal defence expenditure. And it should be remembered, as Rudyard Kipling said at a Mansion House meeting in 1915 promoted by the Recruiting

Bands Committee: 'A band revives memories, it quickens associations, it opens and unites the hearts of men more surely than any other appeal can, and in this respect aids recruiting perhaps more than any other agency.'

It should be noted that quick marches were not officially authorized for infantry regiments until 1882 or slow marches for cavalry regiments until 1903, although many had been used long previously. In some cases, their origin cannot be traced with certainty, but some are two or three centuries old. The earliest would appear to be *Lilliburlero*, a tune ascribed to Purcell and first appearing in 1685. Next, there is *Hielan* (or *Highland*) *Laddie*, which was first published in the Black MS of 1692. The last 17th-century march is *Trumpet Tune*, which was composed by Jeremiah Clark.

Only four marches are named after battles: *Balaklava*, *Barrosa*, *Dettingen March* and *Minden March*. Perhaps *Thin Red Line* should be added as commemorating the deeds of the Argyll and Sutherland Highlanders in the Crimea – the only foot regiment to have been awarded the battle honour of Balaclava.

Some titles of later marches seem at first sight to have little military connection. Examples are *Aupres de ma Blonde*; *Here's to the Maiden of Bashful Fifteen*; *Off, Off, Said the Stranger*; *Rusty Buckles*; and *Whistle o'er the Lave o't*.

Although many marches are of traditional origin, the works of classical composers have often been used as the basis for military band arrangements. These composers include Elgar, Gounod, Handel, Haydn, Meyerbeer, Mozart, Purcell, Rossini, Johann Strauss the elder, von Suppé, Verdi, Wagner and Weber. Bandmasters have composed many marches and arranged many more: some have come from serving officers.

There are some marches that seem less appropriate than others – such as the slow march of the Royal Army Medical Corps or the quick march of the Royal Army Dental Corps. An odd march was used when Major-General V. A. Vasiliev, then head of the Russian Military Mission, took a passing-out parade at Sandhurst during the last war: *The Volga Boatmen* was played for the march past – though the author cannot now remember whether it was in slow or quick time. Before the Second World War, the pipe band of the Scottish Horse – a yeomanry regiment not then mechanized – played on horseback; after the war, the Cambrai band of the Royal Tank Regiment was known to perform from scout cars.

Regimental Mascots

Nine regiments have mascots sanctioned by the Ministry of Defence: they are entitled to movement and quarantine at public expense and to receive veterinary facilities and services without payment. The Royal Scots Dragoon Guards and The Queen's Own Hussars each have a drum horse as mascot; the Irish Guards have a wolfhound; the Royal Regiment of Fusiliers has an Indian black buck; the Royal Welch Fusiliers and the Royal Regiment of Wales each has a goat; the Worcestershire and Sherwood Foresters have a ram; and the Argyll and Sutherland Highlanders and the Parachute Regiment each has a Shetland pony. In most cases, mascots were adopted many years ago: for example, the Irish Guards adopted their first wolfhound in 1902; the Royal Warwickshire

Regiment (now the Royal Regiment of Fusiliers) have had black bucks since 1871; the Royal Welch Fusiliers a goat since the late 18th Century; the Welch Regiment (now the Royal Regiment of Wales) a goat since the Crimean War; the Sherwood Foresters (now the Worcestershire and Sherwood Foresters Regiment) a ram since the Indian Mutiny; and the Argyll and Sutherland Highlanders a Shetland pony since 1929. Unofficial mascots in the past have included a hen and a goose (Royal Dragoons), a bear (17th Lancers), cows (Scots Guards), a fox terrier (South Wales Borderers), a pig (Royal Inniskilling Fusiliers), a deer (Black Watch), a donkey and a panther (King's Own Yorkshire Light Infantry) and even an elephant (Seaforth Highlanders).

THE COUNTY REGIMENTS 1751–1958

As mentioned earlier, foot regiments were identified by numbers alone before 1751 – and numbers still appear in the present-day titles of the Royal Regiment of Wales (24th/41st Foot), the Royal Irish Rangers (27th (Inniskilling) 83rd and 87th) and the Worcestershire and Sherwood Foresters (29th and 45th Foot). By Royal Warrant dated 1 July 1751, two regiments were given territorial affiliations: the 23rd the Royal Welch Fusiliers and the 27th Enniskillen Regiment. The Royal Welch Fusiliers have never been amalgamated and retain their title to this day.

The majority of territorial affiliations before 1881, however, result from two lists issued by the Commander-in-Chief on 31 August 1782, one directing 'the Rank of Regiments as attached to Counties' and the other directing 'Counties as assigned to Regiments' (there are a few discrepancies between these two lists). The Cheshire Regiment, affiliated in 1782, retains that title, and the 28th North Gloucestershire still exists as the Gloucestershire Regiment, though amalgamated with the 61st South Gloucestershire Regiment in 1881. The 84th York and Lancaster Regiment, amalgamated with the 65th 2nd Yorkshire, North Riding Regiment in the same year, retained their affiliation until disbandment in 1968. A few further affiliations took place between 1783 and 1866.

In 1881, eighty-three regiments were amalgamated into the 1st and 2nd Battalions of forty-one regiments (The Queen's Own Cameron Highlanders had only one battalion until 1897), leaving only the first twenty-five regiments of foot, the King's Royal Rifle Corps and the Rifle Brigade untouched (the last two with four battalions each). Although almost all amalgamations were between geographical neighbours and kept the titles of the 1st Battalions, it will be seen that the 30th Cambridgeshire and the 59th Nottinghamshire Regiments became the 1st and 2nd Battalions of the East Lancashire Regiment; other major changes can also be followed. In a few cases, regiments that had been given territorial affiliations between 1792 and 1825 became 2nd Battalions in the amalgamations. Only the King's Royal Rifle Corps, the Rifle Brigade and the Scottish regiments were not given territorial affiliations in 1881.

COMMONWEALTH ALLIANCES

Many British regiments and corps have alliances with the regiments and corps of Commonwealth countries. The guidelines for these alliances are broadly similar in each country: in Canada, for example, the formation of an alliance is suggested when 'close ties and personal relationships have developed . . . through combined participation in operations or training, regular exchange of personnel on exercise, special meets, parades, competitions or [where] there is commonality of history, traditions, or similarity of titles'. (CFAO 99-7, 30 November 1984).

These alliances cover a very wide field. They include such units as the 12th/16th Hunter River Lancers, of Australia; the Barbados Regiment; the Queen's York Rangers (1st American Regiment), of Canada; the Falklands Islands Defence Force; the Fiji Artillery; the Gibraltar Regiment; the Hong Kong Regiment (The Volunteers); Skinner's Horse (1st Duke of York's Own Cavalry), of India; the Jamaican Regiment; the Kenya Rifles; the Antigua and Barbuda Defence Force, of the Leeward Islands; the Royal Malay Regiment; the Mauritius Special Mobile Force; Queen Alexandra's (Waikato/Wellington East Coast) Squadron RNZAC, of New Zealand; the 9th Battalion (Wilde's) Frontier Force Regiment, of Pakistan; the Pacific Island Regiment New Guinea; the Singapore Voluntary Artillery; the 1st Reconnaissance Regiment, of Sri Lanka; and the Zambia Armoured Car Regiment.

There were also overseas regiments and corps allied to British units in 1914. Some are still the same and others have only been renamed. For example, the 1914 allied regiment of the Gordon Highlanders was the 48th Highlanders of Canada; the alliance remains, under the same titles. With one change, the 3rd (Auckland) Regiment (Countess of Ranfurly's Own), of New Zealand, in 1914 the allied regiment of the Royal Norfolk Regiment, is still an alliance of its successor, the Royal Anglian Regiment. And the Royal Canadian Artillery, though now the Royal Regiment of Canada Artillery, continues to be allied to the Royal Regiment of Artillery.

ASSOCIATIONS

Unit associations exist so that former members can keep in touch and can be helped in civilian life and with financial problems. Former regular soldiers are often members of their unit's association; wartime soldiers and post-war national servicemen very seldom.

JOURNALS AND MUSEUMS

Regimental and corps journals are usually named after their units, but there are some exceptions. Examples are *The Acorn* (Life Guards), *Eagle and Carbine* (Royal Scots Dragoon Guards (Carabiniers and Greys)), *Cross Belts* (Queen's Royal Irish Hussars), *The Delhi Spearmen* (9th/12th Royal Lancers (Prince of Wales's)), *The Hawk* (14th/20th King's Hussars) and *The Scarlet and Green* (16th/5th The Queen's Royal Lancers).

Addresses of museums and hours of opening are correct at the time of writing. However, these should be confirmed by telephone before a visit. In recent years, many military museums have been considerably improved – not only the largest, such as the Imperial War Museum, the National Army

Museum and the Tank Museum, but also the smaller ones devoted to one or two regiments. It has in fact been claimed that military museums have probably seen greater improvement than any other class of museum.

UNIT HISTORIES

The very large numbers of unit histories – including the most recent ones – that are listed should be of value to serious researchers and serving soldiers alike. In general, histories before 1914 have been omitted unless they were part of a series that runs to recent years or refer to cavalry regiments that were amalgamated in 1922. The most recent history appears first followed by all others in chronological order.

ABBREVIATIONS

It should be noted that the names of regiments and corps are given in full in their histories, but that abbreviations are used elsewhere. Abbreviations for regiments that have been amalgamated are in the *1939–1945 Field Service Pocket Book* and those of present-day regiments and corps come from the current *Army List*. Those for regiments and corps whose titles have not been changed since 1958 remain the same in most cases, though A & SH is now A AND SH, R Tks now RTR, R Sigs now R SIGNALS and Para Regt now PARA. Other changes result from the conferment of royal titles – CMP is now RMP, AD Corps now RADC, HAMPS now R HAMPS and Pnr Corps now RPC. QUEENS is now used for the Queen's Regiment though previously for the Queen's Royal Regiment (West Surrey) and KINGS for the King's Regiment though previously for the King's (Liverpool) Regiment. As some of these abbreviations are not immediately obvious – D AND D, PWO, DERR, for example – an alphabetical list has been included.

REGIMENTS AMALGAMATED OR DISBANDED SINCE 1958

(Royal Armoured Corps regiments appear under Dragoons, Dragoon Guards, Hussars or Lancers in order of precedence)

PART ONE:
REGIMENTS AND CORPS
IN ORDER OF PRECEDENCE

THE LIFE GUARDS
Colonel-in-Chief: HM The Queen

History
Formed in 1922 as The Life Guards (1st and 2nd), becoming The Life Guards by the amalgamation of the 1st and 2nd Life Guards in 1928.
MOTTO: *Honi soit qui mal y pense* (Evil be to him who evil thinks).
HEADQUARTERS: Horse Guards, Whitehall, London.
RECRUITMENT AREA: Nationwide.

Emblazoned Battle Honours
War of Austrian Succession (1740–8): Dettingen. **Peninsular War** (1808–14): Peninsula. **Hundred Days** (1815): Waterloo. **Revolt of Arabi Pasha** (1882): Tel-el-Kebir. **First Sudan War** (1882–4): Egypt 1882. **South African War** (1899–1902): Relief of Kimberley; Paardeburg; South Africa 1899–1900. **Great War:** Mons; Le Cateau; Marne 1914; Aisne 1914; Messines 1914; Ypres 1914, 1915, 1917; Somme 1916, 1918; Arras 1917, 1918; Hindenburg Line; France and Flanders 1914–18. **Second World War:** Souleuvre; Brussels; Nederrijn; North-West Europe 1944–5; Iraq 1941; Palmyra; Syria 1941; El Alamein; North Africa 1942–3; Italy 1944.

Accredited Battle Honours
Great War: Retreat from Mons; Armentières 1914; Langemarck 1914; Gheluvelt; Nonne Bosschen; St Julien; Frezenberg; Albert 1916; Scarpe 1917, 1918; Broodseinde; Poelcapelle; Passchendaele; Bapaume 1918; Epéhy; St Quentin Canal; Beaurevoir; Cambrai 1918; Selle. **Second World War:** Mont Pinçon; Noireau Crossing; Amiens 1944; Neerpelt; Nijmegen; Lingen; Bentheim; Baghdad 1941; Arezzo; Advance to Florence; Gothic Line.

Memorials
Chapel (Egyptian Campaign 1882); Memorial (South Africa 1899–1902); Screen and altar rails (Great War); eight-bell carillon and roll of honour (Second World War); two plaques (Cyprus 1956–9, 1964): Holy Trinity Church, Windsor. Memorial book and cloister: Guards' Chapel, Wellington Barracks, London. Memorial (First Battle of Ypres 1915): Zandvoorde, Belgium. Two pews (Second World War): chapel, Royal Military Academy, Sandhurst. Plaque (Great War): Scottish National War Memorial, Edinburgh. Monument (Waterloo 1815, Major R. C. Packe): St George's Chapel, Windsor.

Dress
DIFFERENCES: Blue dress cap, scarlet band and piping, gold braid edging on peak

according to rank; blue side cap, scarlet top, piped yellow.
REGIMENTAL TIE: Dull red and navy stripes.

Marches
Trot past: *Keel Row*. Quick: *Milanollo* and *Men of Harlech*. Slow: *The Life Guards Slow March* and *Men of Harlech*.

Alliances
The President's Bodyguard, of Pakistan. (Household Cavalry) Associated regular regiment of C (Kent and Sharpshooters Yeomanry) Sqn, The Royal Yeomanry; Band (Inns of Court and City Yeomanry), The Royal Yeomanry.

Journal
The Acorn (once a year).

Associations
The Life Guards Association.

Museum
Household Cavalry Museum, Combermere Barracks, St Leonard's Rd, Windsor, Berkshire (tel 0753 868222 ext 203); open Monday–Friday 1000–1300, 1400–1700.

Record Office
Except officers: Horse Guards, Whitehall, London; officers: MS(AODO), London Rd, Stanmore, Middlesex.

Regimental Histories
Hills, R. J. T. *The Life Guards,* Leo Cooper, 1971. Arthur, Sir George. *History of the Household Cavalry* (3 vols), Constable, 1909, 1909, 1926. Hills, R. J. T. *A Short History of the Life Guards,* Gale & Polden, 1933.

Predecessors

THE 1st LIFE GUARDS

History
Raised in 1661 as the 1st or His Majesty's Own Troop of Guards (1st Life Guards in 1788).

Emblazoned Battle Honours
War of Austrian Succession (1740–8): Dettingen. **Peninsular War** (1808–14): Peninsula. **Hundred Days** (1815): Waterloo. **Revolt of Arabi Pasha** (1882): Tel-el-Kebir. **First Sudan War** (1882–4): Egypt 1882. **South African War** (1899–1902): Relief of Kimberley; Paardeburg; South Africa 1899–1900. **Great War**: Mons; Le Cateau; Marne 1914; Aisne 1914; Messines 1914; Ypres 1914, 1915, 1917; Somme 1916, 1918; Arras 1917, 1918;

Hindenburg Line; France and Flanders 1914–18.

Accredited Battle Honours
Great War: Retreat from Mons; Armentières 1914; Langemarck 1914; Gheluvelt; Nonne Bosschen; St Julien; Frezenberg; Albert 1916; Scarpe 1917, 1918; Broodseinde; Poelcapelle; Passchendaele; Bapaume 1918; Epéhy; St Quentin Canal; Beaurevoir; Cambrai 1918; Selle.

Memorial
Chapel (South African War 1899–1902): Holy Trinity Church, Windsor.

Marches
Quick: *Milanollo*. Slow: *The Slow March of the 1st Life Guards.*

Museum
Household Cavalry Museum, Combermere Barracks, St Leonard's Rd, Windsor, Berkshire (tel 0753 868222 ext 203): open Monday–Friday 1000–1300, 1400–1700.

Regimental Histories
Arthur, Sir George. *History of the Household Cavalry* (3 vols), Constable, 1909, 1909, 1926. Bell, C. W. *The Story of the First Life Guards*, Harrap, 1922.

THE 2ND LIFE GUARDS

History
Raised in 1660 as the 3rd, or Duke of Albemarle's, Troop of Guards (2nd Life Guards in 1788).

Emblazoned Battle Honours
War of Austrian Succession (1740–8): Dettingen. **Peninsular War (1808–14):** Peninsula. **Hundred Days (1815):** Waterloo. **Revolt of Arabi Pasha (1882):** Tel-el Kebir. **First Sudan War (1882–4):** Egypt 1882. **South African War (1899–1902):** Relief of Kimberley; Paardeburg; South Africa 1899–1900. **Great War:** Mons; Le Cateau; Marne 1914; Aisne 1914; Messines 1914; Ypres 1914, 1915, 1917; Somme 1916, 1918; Arras 1917, 1918; Hindenburg Line; France and Flanders 1914–18.

Accredited Battle Honours
Great War: Retreat from Mons; Armentières 1914; Langemarck 1914; Gheluvelt; Nonne Bosschen; St Julien; Frezenberg; Albert 1916; Scarpe 1917, 1918; Broodseinde; Poelcapelle; Passchendaele; Bapaume 1918; Epéhy; St Quentin Canal; Beaurevoir; Cambrai 1918; Selle.

Marches
Quick: *Men of Harlech*. Slow: *The Slow March of the 2nd Life Guards.*

Museum
Household Cavalry Museum, Combermere Barracks, St Leonard's Rd, Windsor, Berkshire (tel 0753 868222 ext 203): open Monday–Friday 1000–1300, 1400–1700.

THE BLUES AND ROYALS (ROYAL HORSE GUARDS AND 1st DRAGOONS)
Colonel-in-Chief: HM The Queen

History
Formed in 1969 by the amalgamation of The Royal Horse Guards (The Blues) and The Royal Dragoons (1st Dragoons).
MOTTO: *Honi soit qui mal y pense* (Evil be to him who evil thinks).
HEADQUARTERS: Horse Guards, Whitehall, London.
RECRUITMENT AREA: Nationwide.
REGIMENTAL ANNIVERSARY: Waterloo Day (18 June).

Emblazoned Battle Honours
Defence of Tangier (1662–80): Tangier 1662–80. War of Austrian Succession (1740–8): Dettingen; Warburg. French Revolutionary Wars (1793–1802): Beaumont; Willems. Peninsular War (1808–14): Fuentes d'Onor; Peninsula. Hundred Days (1815): Waterloo. Crimean War (1854–5): Balaklava; Sevastopol. Revolt of Arabi Pasha (1882): Tel-el-Kebir. First Sudan War (1882–4): Egypt 1882. South African War (1899–1902): Relief of Kimberley; Paardeburg; Relief of Ladysmith; South Africa 1899–1902. Great War: Le Cateau; Marne 1914; Messines 1914; Ypres 1914, 1915, 1917: Gheluvelt; Frezenberg; Loos; Arras 1917; Somme 1918; Amiens; Hindenburg Line; Cambrai 1918; Sambre; Pursuit to Mons; France and Flanders 1914–18. Second World War: Souleuvre; Brussels; Nederrijn; Rhine; North-West Europe 1944–5; Iraq 1941; Palmyra; Syria 1941; Knightsbridge; El Alamein; Advance on Tripoli; North Africa 1941–3; Sicily 1943; Italy 1943–4. Falklands War (1982): Falklands Islands 1982.

Accredited Battle Honours
Great War: Mons; Retreat from Mons; Aisne 1914; Armentières 1914; Langemarck 1914; Nonne Bosschen; St Julien; Scarpe 1917; St Quentin; Avre; Broodseinde; Poelcapelle; Passchendaele; Beaurevoir. Second World War: Mont Pinçon; Noireau Crossing; Amiens 1944; Neerpelt; Veghel; Nijmegen; Lingen; Bentheim; Baghdad 1941; Msus; Gazala; Defence of Alamein Line; El Agheila; Arezzo; Advance to Florence; Gothic Line.

Memorials
Memorial (South African War 1899–1902); screen and altar rails (Great War); eight-bell carillon and roll of honour (Second World War); two plaques (Cyprus 1956, 1964): Holy Trinity Church, Windsor. Memorial book and cloister; Guards' Chapel, Wellington Barracks, London. Memorial (First Battle of Ypres, 1915): Zandvoorde, Belgium. Two pews (Second World War): Royal

Military Academy, Sandhurst. Plaque (Great War): Scottish National War Memorial, Edinburgh. Monument (Waterloo, 1815 Major R. C. Packe): St George's Chapel, Windsor.

Dress
DIFFERENCES: Blue dress cap, scarlet band and piping. Blue/scarlet/blue striped stable belt. White lanyard for soldiers, red lanyard for officers. Blue cloth-backed Eagle badge on upper left sleeve.
REGIMENTAL TIE: Dull red and navy stripes.

Marches
Trot past: *Keel Row*. Quick: *Regimental Quick March of the Blues and Royals* (*Grand March* from *Aida* and *The Royals*). Slow: *Slow March of the Blues and Royals*.

Alliances
The Royal Canadian Dragoons; The Governor-General's Horse Guards, of Canada.

Journal
The Blue and Royal (once a year).

Museum
Household Cavalry Museum, Combermere Barracks, St Leonard's Rd, Windsor, Berkshire (tel 0753 868222 ext 203): open Monday–Friday 1000–1300, 1400–1700.

Record Office
Except officers: Horse Guards, Whitehall, London; officers: MS(AODO), London Rd, Stanmore, Middlesex.

Predecessors

THE ROYAL HORSE GUARDS (THE BLUES)

History
Raised in 1661 as the Royal Regiment of Horse (The Royal Regiment of Horse Guards in 1689).

MOTTO: *Honi soit qui mal y pense* (Evil be to him who evil thinks).

Emblazoned Battle Honours
War of Austrian Succession (1740–8): Dettingen. Seven Years War (1756–63): Warburg. French Revolutionary Wars (1793–1802): Beaumont. Peninsular War (1808–14): Peninsula. Hundred Days (1815): Waterloo. Revolt of Arabi Pasha (1882): Tel-el-Kebir. First Sudan War (1882–4): Egypt 1882. South African War (1899–1902): Relief of Kimberley;

Paardeburg; South Africa 1899–1900. **Great War:** Le Cateau; Marne 1914; Messines 1914; Ypres 1914, 1915, 1917; Gheluvelt; Frezenberg; Loos; Arras 1917; Sambre; France and Flanders 1914–18. **Second World War:** Souleuvre; Brussels; Nederrijn; North-West Europe 1944–5; Iraq 1941; Palmyra; Syria 1941; El Alamein; North Africa 1942–3; Italy 1944.

Accredited Battle Honours

Great War: Mons; Retreat from Mons; Aisne 1914; Armentières 1914; Langemarck 1914; Nonne Bosschen; St Julien; Scarpe 1917; Broodseinde; Poelcapelle; Passchendaele; Hindenburg Line; Cambrai 1918. **Second World War:** Mont Pinçon; Noireau Crossing; Amiens 1944; Neerpelt; Nijmegen; Lingen; Bentheim; Baghdad 1941; Arezzo; Advance to Florence; Gothic Line.

Marches

Quick: *The Royal Horse Guards March* and *March of the Priests* from *Aida*.

Journal

The Blues.

Museum

Household Cavalry Museum, Combermere Barracks, St Leonard's Rd, Windsor, Berkshire (tel 0753 868222 ext 203): open Monday–Friday 1000–1300, 1400–1700.

Regimental Histories

Hills, R. J. T. *The Royal Horse Guards*, Leo Cooper, 1970. Arthur, Sir George. *A History of the Household Cavalry* (3 vols), Constable, 1909, 1909, 1926. *His Majesty's Royal Regiment of Horse Guards (The Blues)*, Gale & Polden, 1929.

THE ROYAL DRAGOONS (1st DRAGOONS)

History

Raised in 1661 as the Tangier Troop of Horse (The Royal Regiment of Dragoons in 1690).
MOTTO: *Spectemur agendo* (Let us be judged by our actions).

Emblazoned Battle Honours

Defence of Tangier (1662–80): Tangier 1662–80. War of Austrian Succession (1740–8): Dettingen. Seven Years War (1756–63): Warburg. **French Revolutionary Wars** (1793–1802): Beaumont; Willems. **Peninsular War** (1808–14): Fuentes d'Onor; Peninsula. **Hundred Days** (1815): Waterloo. **Crimean War** (1854–5): Balaklava; Sevastopol. **South African War** (1899–1902): Relief of Ladysmith; South Africa 1899–1902. **Great War:** Ypres 1914, 1915; Frezenberg; Loos; Arras 1917; Somme 1918; Amiens; Hindenburg Line; Cambrai 1918; Pursuit to Mons; France and Flanders 1914–18. **Second World War:** Nederrijn; Rhine; North-West Europe 1944–5; Syria 1941; Knightsbridge; El Alamein; Advance on Tripoli; North Africa 1941–3; Sicily 1943; Italy 1943.

Accredited Battle Honours

Great War: Langemarck 1914; Gheluvelt; Nonne Bosschen; Scarpe

1917; St Quentin, Avre; Beaurevoir. **Second World War:** Veghel; Msus; Gazala; Defence of Alamein Line; El Agheila.

Awards
Second Lieutenant J. S. Dunville (1896–1917) was awarded the Victoria Cross near Epéhy, France, 24/25 June 1917: gazetted posthumously 2 August 1917.

Marches
Quick and slow: *The Royals*.

Museum
Household Cavalry Museum, Com-bermere Barracks, St Leonard's Rd, Windsor, Berkshire (tel 0753 868222 ext 203): open Monday–Friday 1000–1300, 1400–1700.

Regimental Histories
Hills, R. J. T. *The Royal Dragoons*, Leo Cooper, 1972. Atkinson, C. T. *History of the Royal Dragoons, 1661–1934*, printed for the regiment by Hale, 1934. Pitt-Rivers, J. A. *The Story of the Royal Dragoons, 1938–1945*, Clowes, 1956.

1st THE QUEEN'S DRAGOON GUARDS
Colonel-in-Chief: HM Queen Elizabeth The Queen Mother

History
Formed in 1959 by the amalgamation of 1st King's Dragoon Guards and The Queen's Bays (2nd Dragoon Guards).
MOTTO: *Pro rege et patria* (for King and country).
HOME HEADQUARTERS: Maindy Barracks, Whitchurch Rd, Cardiff, South Glamorgan.
RECRUITMENT AREA: Wales, Shropshire and (old) Herefordshire.
REGIMENTAL ANNIVERSARY: Waterloo/Gazala Day, 18 June.

Emblazoned Battle Honours
War of Spanish Succession (1701–15): Blenheim; Ramillies; Oudenarde; Malplaquet. **War of Austrian Succession** (1740–8): Dettingen. **Seven Years War** (1756–63): Warburg. **French Revolutionary Wars** (1793–1802): Beaumont; Willems. **Hundred Days** (1815): Waterloo. **Crimean War** (1854–5): Sevastopol. **Indian Mutiny** (1857–8): Lucknow. **Second China War** (1857–60): Taku Forts; Pekin 1860. **Zulu and Basuto War** (1877–9): South Africa 1879. **South African War** (1899–1902): South Africa 1901–2. **Great War:** Mons; Le Cateau; Marne 1914; Messines 1914; Ypres 1914, 1915; Somme 1916, 1918; Morval; Scarpe 1917; Cambrai 1917, 1918; Amiens; Pursuit to Mons; France and Flanders 1914–18. **Third Afghan War** (1919): Afghanistan 1919. **Second World War:** Somme 1940; Beda Fomm; Defence of Tobruk; Gazala; Defence of Alamein Line; El Alamein; Advance on Tripoli; Tebaga Gap; El Hamma; Tunis; North Africa 1941–3; Monte Camino; Gothic Line; Coriano; Lamone Crossing; Rimini Line; Argenta Gap; Italy 1943–4.

Accredited Battle Honours
Great War: Retreat from Mons; Aisne 1914; Armentières 1914; Frezenberg; Bellewaarde; Flers-Courcelette; Arras 1917; St Quentin; Bapaume 1918; Rosières; Albert 1918; Hindenburg Line; St Quentin Canal; Beaurevoir. **Second World War:** Withdrawal to Seine; North-West Europe 1940; Tobruk 1941; Tobruk Sortie; Relief of Tobruk; Msus; Bir el Aslagh; Bir Hacheim; Cauldron; Knightsbridge; Via Balbia; Mersa Matruh; Alam el Halfa; El Agheila; Point 201 (Roman Wall); Akarit; El Kourza; Djebel Kournine; Creteville Pass; Capture of Naples; Scafati Bridge; Garigliano Crossing; Capture of Perugia; Arezzo; Carpineta; Defence of Lamone Bridgehead; Ceriano Ridge; Cesena; Athens; Greece 1944–5.

Dress
DIFFERENCES: Blue dress cap. Royal blue stable belt.
REGIMENTAL TIE: Equal dull red and navy stripes with thin silver line.

Marches
Quick: *Regimental March of 1st The Queen's Dragoon Guards (Radetsky* and *Rusty Buckles).* Slow: *1st Dragoon Guards and 2nd Dragoon Guards Slow March.*

Alliances
Governor-General's Horse Guards, of Canada; 1st/15th Royal New South Wales Lancers, of Australia; 11th Cavalry (Frontier Force), of Pakistan; 1st Reconnaissance Regiment, of Sri Lanka. Associated regular regiment of the (Shropshire Yeomanry) Sqn, The Queen's Own Mercian Yeomanry.

Journal
The Journal of The Queen's Dragoon Guards (once a year).

Association
QDG Regimental Association, c/o HHQ, QDG, Maindy Barracks, Whitchurch Rd, Cardiff, South Glamorgan.

Museum
Cardiff Castle, Cardiff, South Glamorgan (tel 0222 229367): open summer daily 1000–1800; winter daily 1000–1600.

Record Office
Except officers: Queen's Park, Chester. Officers: MS(AODO), London Rd, Stanmore, Middlesex.

Regimental History
Belfield, E. *The Queen's Dragoon Guards*, Leo Cooper, 1978.

Predecessors

1ST KING'S DRAGOON GUARDS

History
Raised in 1685 as the Queen's, or 2nd, Regiment of Horse (1st King's Dragoon Guards in 1746).

Emblazoned Battle Honours
War of Spanish Succession (1701–15): Blenheim; Ramillies; Oudenarde; Malplaquet. **War of Austrian Succession** (1740–8): Dettingen. **Seven Years War** (1756–63): Warburg. **French Revolutionary Wars** (1793–1802): Beaumont. **Hundred Days** (1815): Waterloo. **Crimean War** (1854–5): Sevastopol. **Second Chinese War** (1857–60): Taku Forts; Pekin 1860. **Zulu and Basuto War** (1877–9): South Africa 1879. **South African War** (1899–1902): South Africa 1901–2. **Great War:** Somme 1916;

Morval; France and Flanders 1914–17. **Third Afghan War** (1919): Afghanistan 1919. **Second World War:** Beda Fomm; Defence of Tobruk; Defence of Alamein Line; Advance on Tripoli; Tebaga Gap; Tunis; North Africa 1941–3; Monte Camino; Gothic Line; Italy 1943–4.

Accredited Battle Honours
Second World War: Tobruk 1941; Tobruk Sortie; Relief of Tobruk; Gazala; Bir Hacheim; Alam el Halfa; El Agheila; Point 201 (Roman Wall); El Hamma; Akarit; Capture of Naples; Scafati Bridge; Garigliano Crossing; Capture of Perugia; Arezzo; Athens; Greece 1944–5.

Awards
Private J. Doogan (1853–1940) was awarded the Victoria Cross at Laing's Nek, Boer War, 28 January 1881: gazetted 14 March 1882.

Memorials
Bushman's Kop, South Africa (South African War 1899–1902); Nery, France (Great War); San Martini, Venti, Italy (Second World War).

Marches
Quick: *Radetsky*. Slow: *The King's Dragoons Guards*.

Journal
Regimental Journal of 1st King's Dragoon Guards.

Museum
Cardiff Castle, Cardiff, South Glamorgan (tel 0222 229367): open summer daily 1000–1800; winter daily 1000–1600.

Regimental Histories
McCorquodale, D., Hutchings, B. L. B. and Woozley, A. D. *A History of the King's Dragoon Guards, 1938–1945*, printed for the regiment, 1950. *A Short History of the 1st King's Dragoon Guards, 1685–1929*, Gale & Polden, 1929.

THE QUEEN'S BAYS
(2nd DRAGOON GUARDS)

History
Raised in 1685 as the Earl of Peterborough's Horse (2nd, or Queen's, Dragoon Guards in 1746).
MOTTO: *Pro rege et patria* (For King and country).

Emblazoned Battle Honours
Seven Years War (1756–63): Warburg. **French Revolutionary Wars** (1793–1802): Willems. **Indian Mutiny** (1857–8): Lucknow. **South African War** (1899–1902): South Africa 1901–2. **Great War:** Mons; Le Cateau; Marne 1914; Messines 1914; Ypres 1914, 1915; Somme 1916, 1918; Scarpe 1917: Cambrai 1917, 1918; Amiens; Pursuit to Mons. **Second World War:** Somme 1940; Gazala; El Alamein; El Hamma; Tunis; North Africa 1941–3; Coriano; Lamone Crossing; Rimini Line; Argenta Gap.

Accredited Battle Honours
Great War: Retreat from Mons; Aisne 1914; Armentières 1914; Frezenberg; Bellewaarde; Flers-Courcelette; Arras 1917; St Quentin; Bapaume 1918; Rosières; Albert 1918; Hindenburg Line; St Quentin Canal; Beaurevoir; France and Flanders 1914–18. **Second World War:** Withdrawal to Seine; North-West Europe 1940; Msus; Bir el Aslagh; Cauldron; Knightsbridge; Via Balbia;

Mersa Matruh; Tebaga Gap; El Kourzia; Djebel Kournine; Creteville Pass; Carpineta; Lamone Bridgehead; Ceriano Ridge; Cesena; Italy 1944–5.

Awards
Four members of the regiment have been awarded the Victoria Cross: three in the Indian Mutiny (1857–8) and one at Khartoum (1898). First award: Lieutenant R. Blair, later Captain (1834–58) Bolundshadur, India, 28 September 1857: gazetted 18 June 1858.

Marches
Quick: *Rusty Buckles*. Slow: *The Queen's Bays*.

Journal
Regimental Journal of The Queen's Bays (2nd Dragoon Guards).

Museum
Cardiff Castle, Cardiff, South Glamorgan (tel 0222 229367): open summer daily 1000–1800; winter daily 1000–1600.

Regimental Histories
Beddington, W. R. *A History of the Queen's Bays (2nd Dragoon Guards), 1929–1945*, Warren, 1954. Whyte, F. and Atteridge, A. H. *A History of the Queen's Bays (2nd Dragoon Guards) 1685–1929*, Cape, 1930.

THE ROYAL SCOTS DRAGOON GUARDS (CARABINIERS AND GREYS)
Colonel-in-Chief: HM The Queen

History
Formed in 1971 by the amalgamation of the Royal Scots Greys (2nd Dragoons) and 3rd Carabiniers (Prince of Wales's Dragoon Guards).
MOTTO: Second to none.
HOME HEADQUARTERS: The Castle, Edinburgh.
RECRUITMENT AREA: Scotland.
REGIMENTAL ANNIVERSARIES: Nunshigum Day (13 April); Waterloo Day (18 June); Regimental Birthday (2 July).

Emblazoned Battle Honours
War of Spanish Succession (1701–15): Blenheim; Ramillies; Oudenarde; Malplaquet. **War of Austrian Succession** (1740–8): Dettingen. **Seven Years War** (1756–63): Warburg. **French Revolutionary Wars** (1793–1802): Beaumont; Willems. **Peninsular War** (1808–14): Talavera; Albuhera; Vittoria; Peninsula. **Hundred Days** (1815): Waterloo (1815). **Crimean War** (1854–5): Balaklava; Sevastopol. **Indian Mutiny** (1857–8): Delhi 1857. **Abyssinian War** (1867–8): Abyssinia. **Second Afghan War** (1878–80): Afghanistan 1879–80. **South African War** (1899–1902): Relief of Kimberley; Paardeburg; South Africa 1899–1902. **Great War:** Retreat from Mons; Marne 1914; Aisne 1914; Messines 1914; Ypres 1914, 1915; Arras 1917; Cambrai 1917, 1918; Somme 1918; Amiens; Hindenburg Line; Canal du Nord; Pursuit to Mons. **Second World War:** Hill 112; Falaise; Hochwald; Aller; Merjayun; Alam el Halfa; El Alamein; Nofilia; Salerno; Imphal; Nunshigum; Bishenpur; Kanglatongbi; Kennedy Peak; Sagaing; Mandalay; Ava; Irrawaddy.

Accredited Battle Honours
Great War: Mons; Le Cateau; Armentières 1914; Nonne Bosschen; Gheluvelt; Neuve Chapelle; St Julien; Frezenberg; Bellewaarde; Loos; Scarpe 1917; Lys; Hazebrouck; St Quentin; Avre; Albert 1918; Bapaume 1918; St Quentin Canal; Beaurevoir; Selle; Sambre; France and Flanders 1914–18. **Second World War:** Caen; Venlo Pocket; Bremen; North-West Europe 1944–5; Syria 1941; El Agheila; Advance on Tripoli; North Africa 1942–3; Battipaglia; Volturno Crossing; Italy 1943; Tamu Road; Shwebo; Yenangyaung 1945; Burma 1944–5.

Dress
DIFFERENCES: Blue dress cap, yellow vandyke band, yellow piping, black-

backed badge, gold braid on peak for officers. Blue side cap, yellow vandyke. Blue stable belt, grey/yellow/red stripes. Prince of Wales's plume and motto on left sleeve.

Marches
Band, quick: *3 DGs*, slow: *Garb of Old Gaul*. Pipes and drums, quick: *Hielan' Laddie*, slow: *My Home*.

Regimental Mascot
Drum horse.

Alliances
The Windsor Regiment (RCAC), of Canada; 12/16th Hunter River Lancers (RAAC), of Australia; 1st and 2nd Squadrons, New Zealand and Scottish (RNZAC), of New Zealand. Associated regular regiment of A (Ayrshire) Squadron, The Queen's Own Yeomanry.

Journal
Eagle and Carbine.

Museum
The Castle, Edinburgh (tel 031 225 7534): open May–September Monday–Saturday 0930–1800, Sunday 1100–1800; October–April Monday–Saturday 0930–1715, Sunday 1230–1630.

Regimental History
Wood, S. *In The Finest Tradition*, Mainstream, 1988.

Record Office
Except officers: Queen's Park, Chester; officers: MS(AODO), London Rd, Stanmore, Middlesex.

Predecessors

THE ROYAL SCOTS GREYS (2nd DRAGOONS)

History
Raised in 1678 as the Royal Regiment of Scots Dragoons (2nd Royal North British Dragoons in 1751).

MOTTO: Second to none.
REGIMENTAL ANNIVERSARY: Waterloo Day (18 June).

Emblazoned Battle Honours
War of Spanish Succession (1701–15): Blenheim; Ramillies; Oudenarde; Malplaquet. War of Austrian Succession (1740–8): Dettingen. Seven Years War (1756–63): Warburg. French Revolutionary Wars (1793–1802): Willems. Hundred Days (1815): Waterloo. Crimean War (1854–5): Balaklava; Sevastopol. South African War (1899–

1902): Relief of Kimberley; Paardeburg; South Africa 1899–1902. **Great War:** Retreat from Mons; Marne 1914; Aisne 1914; Ypres 1914, 1915; Arras 1917; Amiens; Somme 1918; Hindenburg Line; Pursuit to Mons; France and Flanders 1914–18. **Second World War:** Hill 112; Falaise; Hochwald; Aller; Bremen; Merjayun; Alam el Halfa; El Alamein; Nofilia; Salerno; Italy 1943.

Accredited Battle Honours
Great War: Mons; Messines 1914; Gheluvelt; Neuve Chapelle; St Julien; Bellewaarde; Scarpe 1917; Cambrai 1917, 1918; Lys; Hazebrouck; Albert 1918; Bapaume 1918; St Quentin Canal; Beaurevoir. **Second World War:** Caen; Venlo Pocket; North-West Europe 1944–5; Syria 1941; El Agheila; Advance on Tripoli; North Africa 1942–3; Battipaglia; Volturno Crossing.

Awards
Three members of the regiment have been awarded the Victoria Cross: two in the Crimean War and one in the Second World War. First award: Sergeant-Major J. Grieve, later Lieutenant and Adjutant (1822–73) Balaclava 25 October 1854: gazetted 24 February 1857.

Marches
Trot and canter: *The Keel Row* and *Bonnie Dundee.* Quick: *Highland Laddie.* Slow and walk: *Garb of Old Gaul.*

Journal
The Journal of the Royal Scots Greys.

Museum
The Royal Scots Greys Room, Scottish United Services Museum, The Castle, Edinburgh (tel 031 225 7534): open May–September Monday–Saturday 0930–1800, Sunday 1100–1800; October–April Monday–Saturday 0930–1715, Sunday 1230–1630.

Regimental Histories
Blacklock, M. *The Royal Scots Greys,* Leo Cooper, 1971. Pomeroy, R., Collins, W. F., Duguid-McCombie, W. M., Hardy, J. S., MacDougall, A. I., and Gibbs, A. D. *History of The Royal Scots Greys (The Second Dragoons), August 1914–March 1919,* 1928. Lord Carver. *Second to None: The Royal Scots Greys, 1919–1945,* printed for the regiment, 1954.

3rd CARABINIERS (PRINCE OF WALES'S DRAGOON GUARDS)

History
Formed in 1922 as the 3rd/6th Dragoon Guards (3rd Carabiniers (Prince of Wales's Dragoon Guards) in 1928) by the amalgamation of 3rd Dragoon Guards (Prince of Wales's) and The Carabiniers (6th Dragoon Guards).
REGIMENTAL ANNIVERSARY: Nunshigum Day (13 April).

Emblazoned Battle Honours
War of Spanish Succession (1701–15): Blenheim; Ramillies; Oudenarde; Malplaquet. **Seven Years War (1756–63):** Warburg. **French Revolutionary Wars (1793–1802):** Beaumont; Willems. **Peninsular War (1808–14):** Talavera; Albuhera; Vittoria; Peninsula. **Abyssinian War (1867–8):** Abyssinia. **South African War (1899–1902):** South Africa 1901–2. **Great War:** Retreat from Mons; Marne 1914; Aisne 1914; Messines 1914; Ypres 1914, 1915; Arras 1917; Cambrai 1917, 1918; Amiens; Hindenburg Line. **Second World War:** Imphal; Nunshigum; Bishenpur; Kanglatongbi; Kennedy Peak; Shwebo; Sagaing; Mandalay; Ava; Irrawaddy.

Marches
Quick: *Third Dragoon Guards*. Slow: *Sixth Dragoon Guards*.

Journal
Feather and Carbine.

Museum
The Castle, Chester (tel 0244 327617): open daily 0900–1700.

Predecessors of 3rd Carabiniers

Regimental History
Oatts, L. B. *I Serve: Regimental History of the 3rd Carabiniers*, The Dale, Chester, 1966.

(Prince of Wales's Dragoon Guards) 3rd DRAGOON GUARDS (PRINCE OF WALES'S)

History
Raised in 1685 as the Earl of Plymouth's Regiment of Horse (3rd Regiment of Dragoon Guards in 1746).
FORMER MEMBER: Field Marshal Sir William Robertson (1860–1933), commissioned 1888.

Emblazoned Battle Honours
War of Spanish Succession (1701–15): Blenheim; Ramillies; Oudenarde; Malplaquet. Seven Years War (1756–63): Warburg. French Revolutionary Wars (1793–1802): Beaumont; Willems. Peninsular War (1808–14): Talavera; Albuhera; Vittoria; Peninsula. Abyssinian War (1867–8): Abyssinia. South African War (1899–1902): South Africa 1901–2. Great War: Ypres 1914, 1915; Loos; Arras 1917; Scarpe 1917; St Quentin; Avre; Amiens; Hindenburg Line; Pursuit to Mons; France and Flanders 1914–18.

Accredited Battle Honours
Great War: Nonne Bosschen; Frezenberg; Somme 1918; Beaurevoir; Cambrai 1918.

Marches Quick: *God Bless the Prince of Wales*. Slow: *Men of Harlech*.

Museum
The Castle, Chester (tel 0244 327617): open daily 0900–1700.

Regimental History
Holt, H. P. *The History of the Third (Prince of Wales's) Dragoon Guards, 1914–1918*, privately printed, 1937.

THE CARABINIERS (6th DRAGOON GUARDS)

History
Raised in 1685 as the Queen Dowager's Horse (6th Dragoon Guards (Carabiniers) in 1788).

Emblazoned Battle Honours

War of Spanish Succession (1701–15): Blenheim; Ramillies; Oudenarde; Malplaquet. **Seven Years War** (1756–63): Warburg. **French Revolutionary Wars** (1793–1802): Willems. **Crimean War** (1854–5): Sevastopol. **Indian Mutiny** (1857–8): Delhi 1857. **Second Afghan War** (1878–80): Afghanistan 1879–80. **South African War** (1899–1902): Relief of Kimberley; Paardeburg; South Africa 1899–1902. **Great War:** Retreat from Mons; Marne 1914; Aisne 1914; Messines 1914; Ypres 1915; Cambrai 1917, 1918; Somme 1916; Amiens; Sambre; France and Flanders 1914–18.

Accredited Battle Honours

Great War: Mons; Le Cateau; Armentières; St Julien; Bellewaarde; Arras 1917; Scarpe 1917; St Quentin; Lys; Hazebrouck; Bapaume 1918; Hindenburg Line; Canal du Nord; Selle.

Memorial

Chelsea Embankment, London, by Adrian Jones (South African War 1899–1902).

Museum

The Castle, Chester (tel 0244 327617: open daily 0900–1700.

Regimental History

Sprot, A. *A Continuation of the Historical Record of the VI DG Carabiniers*, Gale & Polden, 1888.

4th/7th ROYAL DRAGOON GUARDS
Colonel-in-Chief: Hon Major-General HRH The Duchess of Kent GCVO

History
Formed in 1922 as 4th/7th Dragoon Guards (Royal in 1936) by the amalgamation of 4th Royal Irish Dragoon Guards and 7th Dragoon Guards (Princess Royal's).
MOTTO: *Quis separabit* (Who shall separate us?)
HOME HEADQUARTERS: 3 Tower St, York.
RECRUITMENT AREA: North and West Yorkshire.
REGIMENTAL ANNIVERSARIES: Normandy Day (6 June); Dettingen Day (27 June).

Emblazoned Battle Honours
War of Spanish Succession (1701–15): Blenheim; Ramillies; Oudenarde; Malplaquet. **War of Austrian Succession** (1740–8): Dettingen. **Seven Years War** (1756–63): Warburg. **Peninsular War** (1808–14): Peninsula. **Seventh Kaffir War** (1846–7): South Africa 1846–7. **Crimean War** (1854–5): Balaklava; Sevastopol. **Revolt of Arabi Pasha** (1882): Tel-el-Kebir. **First Sudan War** (1882–4): Egypt 1882. **South African War** (1899–1902): South Africa 1900–02. **Great War:** Marne 1914; Aisne 1914; La Bassée 1914; Ypres 1914, 1915; Somme 1916; Amiens; Hindenburg Line; Pursuit to Mons. **Second World War:** Dyle; Dunkirk 1940; Normandy Landing; Odon; Mont Pinçon; Nederrijn; Geilenkirchen; Rhineland; Cleve; Rhine.

Accredited Battle Honours
Great War: Mons; Le Cateau; Retreat from Mons; Messines 1914; Armentières 1914; Ypres 1914, 1915; Givenchy 1914; St Julien; Frezenberg; Bellewaarde; Somme 1918; Bazentin; Flers-Courcelette; Arras 1917; Scarpe 1917; Cambrai 1917, 1918; St Quentin; Rosières; Avre; Lys; Hazebrouck; Albert 1918; St Quentin Canal; Beaurevoir; France and Flanders 1914–18. **Second World War:** Seine 1944; Roer; Bremen; North-West Europe 1940, 1944–5.

Dress
DIFFERENCES: Blue dress cap; red side cap, blue flaps piped yellow. Dark red stable belt, narrow yellow over blue stripes.
REGIMENTAL TIE: Alternate maroon and black stripes with thin gold line between.

Marches
Quick: *St Patrick's Day.* Slow: *4th Dragoon Guards Slow March* and *7th Dragoon Guards Slow March.*

Alliances

The Fort Garry Horse, of Canada; 4th/19th Prince of Wales's Light Horse, of Australia; Waikato/Wellington East Coast Squadron RNZAC, of New Zealand; 15 Lancers, of Pakistan. Associated regular regiment of Y (Yorkshire) Squadron, The Queen's Own Yorkshire Yeomanry.

Journal

4th/7th Royal Dragoon Guards Regimental Magazine.

Museum

3 Tower St, York (tel 0904 642036): open Monday–Saturday 0930–1630.

Regimental Histories

Brereton, J. M. *A History of the 4th/7th Royal Dragoon Guards and Their Predecessors, 1685–1980*, Catterick, 1982. Stirling, J. D. P. *The First and Last: The Story of the 4th/7th Royal Dragoon Guards, 1939–1945*, Art and Educational, 1946. d'Avigdor-Goldsmith, J. A. *Short History of the 4th Royal Irish Dragoon Guards 1685–1922, 7th (Princess Royal's) Dragoon Guards 1688–1922 and 4th/7th Royal Dragoon Guards 1922–1939*. Gale & Polden, 1949.

Predecessors

4th ROYAL IRISH DRAGOON GUARDS

History

Raised in 1685 as the 6th Horse or the Earl of Arran's Cuirassiers (4th Royal Irish Regiment of Dragoon Guards in 1788).

MOTTO: *Quis separabit* (Who shall separate us?)

Emblazoned Battle Honours

Peninsular War (1808–14): Peninsula. Crimean War (1854–5): Balaklava Sevastopol. Revolt of Arabi Pasha (1882): Tel-el-Kebir (1882). First Sudan War (1882–4): Egypt 1882. Great War (1914–18): Mons; Le Cateau; Retreat from Mons; Marne 1914; Aisne 1914; Messines 1914; Ypres 1914, 1915; Somme 1916, 1918; Cambrai 1917, 1918; Pursuit to Mons.

Accredited Battle Honours

Great War: Armentières 1914; St Julien; Frezenberg; Bellewaarde; Flers-Courcelette; Arras 1917; Scarpe 1917; St Quentin; Rosières; Amiens; Albert 1918; Hindenburg Line; France and Flanders 1914–18.

Awards

Captain A. Carton de Wiart, later Lieutenant-General Sir Carton de Wiart KBE CB CMG DSO (1880–1963) was awarded the Victoria Cross La Boiselle, France, 2 and 3 July 1916: gazetted 9 September 1916.

Marches

Quick: *St Patrick's Day*. Slow: *4th Royal Irish Dragoons Slow March*.

Journal

4th Royal Irish Dragoon Guards Regimental Record.

Museum
3 Tower St, York (tel 0904 64206): open Monday–Saturday 0930–1630.

Regimental History
Gibb, H. *Records of the 4th Royal Irish Dragoon Guards in the Great War, 1914–1918*, privately printed, 1925.

7th DRAGOON GUARDS (PRINCESS ROYAL'S)

History
Raised in 1688 as the Earl of Devonshire's Horse, or 10th Horse (7th (The Princess Royal's) Dragoon Guards in 1788).

Emblazoned Battle Honours
War of Spanish Succession (1701–15): Blenheim; Ramillies; Oudenarde; Malplaquet. War of Austrian Succession (1740–8): Dettingen. Seven Years War (1756–63): Warburg. Seventh Kaffir War: South Africa 1846–7. Revolt of Arabi Pasha (1882): Tel-el-Kebir. First Sudan War (1882–84): Egypt 1882. South African War (1899–1902): South Africa 1900–2. Great War: La Bassée 1914; Givenchy 1914; Somme 1916, 1918; Bazentin; Cambrai 1917, 1918; St Quentin; Avre; Amiens; Hindenburg Line; Pursuit to Mons.

Accredited Battle Honours
Great War: Flers-Courcelette; Lys; Hazebrouck; St Quentin Canal; Beaurevoir; France and Flanders 1914–18.

Marches
Slow: *7th (Princess Royal's) Dragoon Guards*.

Journal
The Black Horse Gazette.

Museum
3 Tower St, York (tel 0904 642036): open Monday–Saturday 0930–1630.

Regimental Histories
Scott, J. F. *Records of the Seventh Dragoon Guards (Princess Royal's) during the Great War*, Bennett, 1929. Thompson, C. W. *Seventh (Princess Royal's) Dragoon Guards: The Story of the Regiment, 1688–1882*, Daily Post, 1913. Campbell, N. D. H., Whetherly, W. S., and Holland, J. E. D. *Seventh (Princess Royal's) Dragoon Guards: With the Regiment in South Africa, 1900–1902*, Daily Post, 1913.

5th ROYAL INNISKILLING DRAGOON GUARDS

Colonel-in-Chief: HRH The Prince of Wales KG KT GCB AK QSO ADC

History
Formed in 1922 as 5th/6th Dragoons (5th Inniskilling Dragoon Guards in 1927, Royal in 1935) by the amalgamation of 5th Dragoon Guards (Princess Charlotte of Wales's) and The Inniskillings (6th Dragoons).
MOTTO: *Vestigia nulla retrorsum* (We do not retreat).
HOME HEADQUARTERS: The Castle, Chester, Cheshire.
RECRUITMENT AREA: Northern Ireland, Cumbria and Cheshire.
REGIMENTAL ANNIVERSARIES: Oates Sunday (Sunday nearest 17 March); Waterloo Day (18 June); Salamanca Day (22 July); Balaklava Day (23 October).

Emblazoned Battle Honours
War of Spanish Succession (1701–15): Blenheim; Ramillies; Oudenarde; Malplaquet. **War of Austrian Succession** (1740–8): Dettingen. **Seven Years War** (1756–63): Warburg. **French Revolutionary Wars** (1793–1802): Beaumont; Willems. **Peninsular War** (1808–14): Salamanca; Vittoria; Toulouse; Peninsula. **Hundred Days** (1815): Waterloo. **Crimean War** (1854–5): Balaklava; Sevastopol. **South African War** (1899–1902): Defence of Ladysmith; South Africa 1899–1902. **Great War:** Mons; Le Cateau; Marne 1914; Somme 1916; Cambrai 1917; Amiens; Hindenburg Line; Pursuit to Mons. **Second World War:** Withdrawal to Escaut; St Omer–La Bassée; Dunkirk 1940; Mont Pinçon; Lower Maas. **Korean War** (1950–3): The Hook 1952; Korea 1951–2.

Accredited Battle Honours
Great War: Retreat from Mons; Aisne 1914; La Bassée 1914; Messines 1914; Armentières 1914; Ypres 1914, 1915; Frezenberg; Bellewaarde; Somme 1918; Flers-Courcelette; Morval; Arras 1917; Scarpe 1917; Cambrai 1918; St Quentin; Rosières; Avre; Lys; Hazebrouck; Albert 1918; St Quentin Canal; Beaurevoir; France and Flanders 1914–18. **Second World War:** St Pierre La Vieille; Lisieux; Risle Crossing; Roer; Ibbenburen; North-West Europe 1940, 1944–5.

Dress
DIFFERENCES: Dark green dress cap, primrose yellow band and striping; primrose and green side hat, dark green flaps piped yellow. Red, yellow and green stable belt.
REGIMENTAL TIE: Red, yellow and green diagonal stripes.

Marches
Quick: *Fare ye well Inniskilling.* Slow: *The Soldiers' Chorus* from Gounod's *Faust.*

Alliances
The British Columbia Dragoons, of Canada; 3rd/9th South Australian Mounted Rifles. Associated regular regiment of D (North Irish Horse) Squadron, The Royal Yeomanry; C (Cheshire) Squadron, The Queen's Own Yeomanry.

Journal
The Regimental Journal of the 5th Inniskilling Dragoon Guards (once a year).

Museum
The Chester Military Museum, The Castle, Chester (tel 0244 347203): open daily 1000–1700.

Record Office
Except officers: Queen's Park, Chester; officers: MS(AODO), London Rd, Stanmore, Middlesex.

Regimental Histories
Boardman, C. J. *Tracks in Europe*, privately printed (from Home HQ), 1980.
Evans, R. *The Story of the Fifth Royal Inniskilling Dragoon Guards*, London, 1951.
Blacker, C., and Woods, H. *Change and Challenge: 5th Royal Inniskilling Dragoon Guards, 1928–1978*, privately printed, 1978.

Predecessors

5th DRAGOON GUARDS (PRINCESS CHARLOTTE OF WALES'S)

History
Raised in 1685 as the Duke of Shrewsbury's Regiment of Horse (5th Dragoon Guards in 1784).
MOTTO: *Vestigia nulla retrorsum* (We do not retreat),
REGIMENTAL ANNIVERSARY: Salamanca Day (22 July).

Emblazoned Battle Honours
War of Spanish Succession (1701–15): Blenheim; Ramillies; Oudenarde; Malplaquet. **French Revolutionary Wars** (1793–1802): Beaumont. **Peninsular War** (1808–14): Salamanca; Vittoria; Toulouse; Peninsula. **Crimean War** (1854–5): Balaklava; Sevastopol. **South African War** (1899–1902): Defence of Ladysmith; South Africa 1899–1902. **Great War**: Mons; Le Cateau; Marne 1914; Messines 1914; Ypres 1914, 1915; Bellewaarde; Somme 1916, 1918; Cambrai 1917, 1918; Amiens; Pursuit to Mons.

Accredited Battle Honours
Great War: Retreat from Mons; Aisne 1914; La Bassée 1914; Armentières 1914; Frezenberg; Flers-Courvellette; Arras 1917; Scarpe 1917; St Quentin; Rosières;

Albert 1918; Hindenburg Line; St
Quentin Canal; Beaurevoir; France and
Flanders 1914–18.

Awards
Second Lieutenant J. Norwood, later
Captain (1876–1914) was awarded the
Victoria Cross Ladysmith 30 October
1899: gazetted 20 July 1900. He was
killed in France 8 September 1914.

Memorial
Aldershot.

Marches
Quick: *The Gay Cavalier*. Slow: *Soldiers'
Chorus* from Gounod's *Faust*.

THE INNISKILLINGS
(6th DRAGOONS)

History
Raised in 1689 as [Albert] Cunningham's Dragoons (6th (Inniskilling)
Dragoons in 1751).
MOTTO: *Inniskilling.*
FORMER MEMBERS: Field Marshal Viscount Allenby (1861–1936), commissioned 1882; Captain L. E. G. Oates
(1880–1912).

Emblazoned Battle Honours
War of Austrian Succession (1740–8):
Dettingen. **Seven Years War** (1756–
63): Warburg. **French Revolutionary
Wars** (1793–1802): Willems. **Hundred
Days** (1815): Waterloo. **Crimean War**
(1854–5): Balaklava; Sevastopol. **South
African War** (1899–1902): South Africa.
Great War: Somme 1916, 1918; Morval;
Cambrai 1917, 1918; St Quentin; Avre;
Amiens; Hindenburg Line; St Quentin
Canal; Pursuit to Mons; France and
Flanders 1914–18.

Journal
The Green Horse.

Museum
The Chester Military Museum, The
Castle, Chester (tel 0244 347203): open
daily 1000–1700.

Regimental History
Pomeroy, R. L. *The Story of a Regiment
of Horse (5th Princess of Wales's Dragoon
Guards) 1685–1922* (2 vols), Blackwood,
1924.

Accredited Battle Honours
Great War: Lys; Hazebrouck; Beaurevoir.

Awards
Surgeon J. Mouat, later Surgeon-
General Sir James Mouat KCB (1815–
99) was awarded the Victoria Cross
Balaclava 26 October 1854: gazetted 2
July 1858.

Marches
Quick: *Fare ye well Inniskillings*. Slow:
The Inniskilling Dragoons.

Allied Regiment in 1914
25th Brant Dragoons, of Canada.

Journal
The Inniskilliner.

Museum
Chester Military Museum, The Castle,
Chester (tel 0244 347203): open daily
1000–1700.

Regimental History
Jackson, E. S. *The Inniskilling Dragoons*,
Humphreys, 1909.

THE QUEEN'S OWN HUSSARS
Colonel-in-Chief: HM Queen Elizabeth The Queen Mother

History
Formed in 1958 by the amalgamation of 3rd The King's Own Hussars and 7th Queen's Own Hussars.
MOTTO: *Nec aspera terrent* (Nor do difficulties deter).
HOME HEADQUARTERS: 28 Jury St, Warwick, Warwickshire.
RECRUITMENT AREA: Warwickshire, West Midlands and (old) Worcestershire.
REGIMENTAL ANNIVERSARIES: Waterloo Day (18 June); Dettingen Day (27 June); Colonel-in-Chief's Birthday (4 August); El Alamein Day (2 November).

Emblazoned Battle Honours
War of Austrian Succession (1740–8): Dettingen. **Seven Years War** (1756–63): Warburg. **French Revolutionary Wars** (1793–1802): Beaumont; Willems. **Peninsular War** (1808–14): Salamanca; Vittoria; Orthes; Toulouse; Peninsula. **Hundred Days** (1815): Waterloo. **First Afghan War** (1839–42): Cabool 1842. **First Sikh War** (1839–42): Moodkee; Ferozeshah; Sobraon. **Second Sikh War** (1848–9): Chillianwallah; Goojerat; Punjaub. **Indian Mutiny** (1857–8): Lucknow. **South African War** (1899–1902): South Africa 1901–2. **Great War:** Retreat from Mons; Marne 1914; Ypres 1914, 1915; Cambrai 1917, 1918; Somme 1918; Amiens; France and Flanders 1914–18; Khan Baghdadi; Sharqat; Mesopotamia 1917–18. **Second World War:** Egyptian Frontier 1940; Buq Buq; Beda Fomm; Sidi Rezegh 1941; El Alamein; North Africa 1940–2; Citta della Piave; Ancona; Italy 1944–5; Crete; Burma 1942.

Accredited Battle Honours
South African War (1899–1902): South Africa 1902. **Great War:** Mons; Le Cateau; Aisne 1914; Messines 1914; Armentières 1914; Gheluvelt; St Julian; Bellewaarde; Arras 1917; Scarpe 1917; St Quentin; Lys; Hazebrouck; Bapaume 1918; Hindenburg Line; Canal du Nord; Selle; Sambre. **Second World War:** Sidi Barrani; Sidi Suleiman; North Africa 1940–1; Pegu; Paungde; Citta di Castello; Rimini Line; Italy 1944.

Memorial
Flag Pole (3H); Statue (7H) (Second World War); Brass Gong (3H) (Great War).

Dress
DIFFERENCES: Scarlet dress cap; scarlet side cap piped yellow. Blue/yellow/blue striped stable belt, scarlet line on blue stripe; leather cross-belt embossed with

regimental cipher for officers. Silver and scarlet Maid of Warsaw badge on left sleeve.

REGIMENTAL TIE: Gold and blue stripes with thin red, Garter blue and yellow lines on the blue.

Marches
Gallop: *The Campbells are coming*. Trot: *Encore*. Quick: (Regimental) *Light Cavalry, Robert the Devil* and *Bannocks of Barley Meal*. (Inspection) *The Dettingen March*. Slow: *The 3rd Hussars Slow March* and *The Garb of Old Gaul*.

Regimental Mascot
Drum horse.

Alliances
The Sherbrook Hussars, of Canada; 3rd/9th South Australian Mounted Rifles; Queen Alexandra's (Waikato/Wellington East Coast) Squadron RNZAC, of New Zealand. Affiliated TA Squadron: A (QOWWY) Squadron, The Queen's Own Mercian Yeomanry.

Journal
The Journal of the Queen's Own Hussars (once a year).

Associations
The Queen's Own Hussars Regimental Association and The Queen's Own Hussars Aid Society, 28 Jury St, Warwick, Warwickshire (tel 0926 492035).

Museum
Lord Leycester Hospital, High St, Warwick, Warwickshire (tel 0926 492755): open April–September Monday–Saturday 1000–1800; October–March closing 1600.

Record Office
Except officers: Queen's Park, Chester; officers: MS(AODO), London Rd, Stanmore, Middlesex.

Predecessors

3rd THE KING'S OWN HUSSARS

History
Raised in 1685 as the Queen Consort's Own Regiment of Dragoons (3rd (King's Own) Hussars in 1861).

MOTTO: *Nec aspera terrent* (Nor do difficulties deter).

REGIMENTAL ANNIVERSARIES: Dettingen Day (27 June); El Alamein Day (2 November).

Emblazoned Battle Honours
War of Austrian Succession (1740–8): Dettingen. Peninsular War (1808–14): Salamanca; Vittoria; Toulouse; Peninsula. First Afghan War (1839–42):

Cabool 1842. **First Sikh War** (1845–6): Moodkee; Ferozeshah; Sobraon. **Second Sikh War** (1848–9): Chillianwallah; Goojerat; Punjaub. **South African War** (1899–1902): South Africa 1902. **Great War:** Retreat from Mons; Marne 1914; Aisne 1914; Messines 1914; Ypres 1914, 1915; Arras 1917; Cambrai 1917, 1918; Somme 1918; Amiens; France and Flanders 1914–18. **Second World War:** Sidi Barrani; Buq Buq; Beda Fomm; Sidi Suleiman; El Alamein; North Africa 1940–2; Citta della Piave; Citta di Castello; Italy 1944; Crete.

Accredited Battle Honours

Great War: Mons; Le Cateau; Armentières 1914; Gheluvelt; St Julien; Bellewaarde; Scarpe 1917; St Quentin; Lys; Hazebrouck; Bapaume 1918; Hindenburg Line; Canal du Nord; Selle; Sambre.

Marches

Quick: *Robert the Devil.* Slow: *The 3rd Hussars Slow March.*

Journal

3rd The King's Own Hussars Regimental Journal.

Museum

Lord Leycester Hospital, Warwick, Warwickshire (tel 0926 492755): open April–September Monday–Saturday 1000–1800; October–March closing 1600.

Regimental Histories

Bolitho, H. *The Galloping Third: The Story of the 3rd King's Own Hussars,* John Murray, 1962. Willcox, W. T. *The 3rd King's Own Hussars in the Great War (1914–1919),* John Murray, 1925. *Historical Records of 3rd The King's Own Hussars,* Gale & Polden, 1927.

7th QUEEN'S OWN HUSSARS

History

Raised in 1689 as the Queen's Own Dragoons, or [Robert] Cunningham's Dragoons (7th (Queen's Own) Hussars in 1807).

REGIMENTAL ANNIVERSARY: Waterloo Day (18 June).

FORMER MEMBERS: Field Marshal Earl Haig (1861–1928), commissioned 1885 – statue Whitehall, London; Field Marshal Sir John Stanier (*b*1925) commissioned 1946.

Emblazoned Battle Honours

War of Austrian Succession (1740–8): Dettingen. **Seven Years War** (1756–63): Warburg. **French Revolutionary Wars** (1793–1802): Beaumont; Willems. **Peninsular War** (1808–14): Orthes; Peninsula. **Hundred Days** (1815): Waterloo. **Indian Mutiny** (1857–8): Lucknow. **South African War** (1899–1902): South Africa. **Great War:** Khan Baghdadi; Sharqat; Mesopotamia 1917–18. **Second World War:** Egyptian Frontier 1940; Beda Fomm; Sidi Rezegh 1941; North Africa 1940–1; Ancona; Rimini Line; Italy 1944–5; Pegu; Paungde; Burma 1942.

Awards

Two members of the regiment have been awarded the Victoria Cross – both in the Indian Mutiny (1857–8). First award: Cornet W. G. H. Bankes (1836–58) Lucknow, 19 March 1858; gazetted 24 December 1858.

Marches

Canter: *The Campbells are Coming.* Quick: *Bannocks o'Barley Meal (The Kynegad Slashers).* Slow: *Garb of Old Gaul.*

Journal

The Regimental Journal of the 7th (Queen's Own) Hussars.

Museum

Lord Leycester Hospital, High St, Warwick, Warwickshire (tel 0926 492755): open April–September Monday–Saturday 1000–1800; October–March closing 1600.

Regimental Histories

Brereton, J. M. *The Seventh Queen's Own Hussars,* Leo Cooper, 1975. Evans, R. *The Years Between: The Story of the 7th Queen's Own Hussars, 1911–1937,* Gale & Polden, 1965. Davy, G. M. O. *The Seventh and Three Enemies: The Story of World War II and the 7th Queen's Own Hussars,* Heffer, 1953. Barrett, C. R. B. *The 7th (Queen's Own) Hussars* (2 vols), RUSI, 1914.

THE QUEEN'S ROYAL IRISH HUSSARS
Colonel-in-Chief: Field Marshall HRH The Prince Philip
Duke of Edinburgh KG KT OM GBE AC QSO

History
Formed in 1958 by the amalgamation of 4th Queen's Own Hussars and 8th (King's Royal Irish) Hussars.
MOTTOES: *Mente et manu* (With heart and hand); *Pristinae virtutis memores* (The memory of former valour).
HOME HEADQUARTERS: Regent's Park Barracks, Albany St, London.
RECRUITMENT AREA: Northern Ireland.
REGIMENTAL ANNIVERSARY: Balaklava Day (25 October).

Emblazoned Battle Honours
War of Austrian Succession (1740–8): Dettingen. **Second Maratha and Pindari War** (1816–18): Leswarree. **India** (1802–22): Hindoostan. **Peninsular War** (1808–14): Talavera; Albuhera; Salamanca; Vittoria; Toulouse; Peninsula. **First Afghan War** (1839–42): Ghuznee 1839; Affghanistan 1839. **Crimean War** (1854–5): Alma; Balaklava; Inkerman; Sevastopol. **Indian Mutiny** (1857–8): Central India. **Second Afghan War** (1878–80): Afghanistan 1879–80. **South African War** (1899–1902): South Africa 1900–2. **Great War:** Mons; Le Cateau; Marne 1914; Aisne 1914; Ypres 1914, 1915; Givenchy 1914; St Julien; Somme 1916, 1918; Arras 1917; Cambrai 1917, 1918; Bapaume 1918; Rosières; Amiens; Albert 1918; Beaurevoir; Pursuit to Mons; France and Flanders 1914–18. **Second World War:** Villers Bocage; Lower Maas; Roer; Rhine; North-West Europe 1944–5; Buq Buq; Sidi Rezegh 1941; Gazala; Ruweisat; Alam el Halfa; El Alamein; North Africa 1940–2; Coriano; Senio Pocket; Rimini Line; Argenta Gap; Proasteion; Corinth Canal; Greece 1941. Korean War (1950–3): Imjin; Korea 1950–1.

Accredited Battle Honours
Great War: Retreat from Mons; Messines 1914; Armentières 1914; Langemarck 1914; Gheluvelt; Bellewaarde; Bazentin; Flers-Courcelette; Arras 1917; Scarpe 1917; St Quentin; Hindenburg Line; Canal du Nord; St Quentin Canal. **Second World War:** Mont Pinçon; Dives Crossing; Nederrijn; Best; Egyptian Frontier 1940; Sidi Barrani; Relief of Tobruk; Bir el Igela; Defence of Alamein Line; San Clemente; Conventello-Comacchio; Senio; Salerno Crossing; Italy 1944–5; Proasteion. **Korean War** (1950–3): Seoul; Hill 327; Kowang-San.

Dress
DIFFERENCES: Scarlet dress cap; green side cap piped yellow. Brown bandolier

and silver pouch for officers. Yellow lanyard. Two chevrons for lance-coporals.

Marches
Quick: *St Patrick's Day. Berkeley's Dragoons* and *A Galloping 8th Hussar.* Slow: *Loretto* and *March of the Scottish Archers.*

Alliances
The Royal Canadian Hussars (Montreal); 8th Canadian Hussars (Princess Louise's); 2nd/14th Light Horse (QMI), of Australia; 8th/13th Victorian Mounted Rifles, of Australia; 3rd Battalion The Royal Australian Regiment. Associated regular regiment of D (North Irish Horse) Squadron, The Royal Yeomanry.

Journal
Cross-Belts.

Museums
Museum of Irish Cavalry Regiments, Carrickfergus, Co Antrim, Northern Ireland (tel 023 83 62273): open April–September Monday–Saturday 1000–1800, Sunday 1400–1800; October–March closing 1600. Sussex Combined Services Museum, The Redoubt Fortress, Royal Parade, Eastbourne, East Sussex (tel 0323 460300): open seasonally and other times by appointment.

Record Office
Except officers: Queen's Park, Chester; officers: MS(AODO), London Rd, Stanmore, Middlesex.

Predecessors

4th QUEEN'S OWN HUSSARS

History
Raised in 1685 as the Princess of Denmark's Dragoons (4th (Queen's Own) Hussars in 1861).
MOTTO: *Mente et manu* (With heart and hand).
REGIMENTAL ANNIVERSARY: Balaklava Day (25 October).
FORMER MEMBERS: Field Marshal Lord Raglan (1788–1855), commissioned 1804 – plaque 5 Stanhope Gate, London; Sir Winston Churchill (1874–1965), commissioned 1895 – statue Parliament Square, London.

Emblazoned Battle Honours
War of Austrian Succession (1740–8): Dettingen. **Peninsular War (1808–14):** Talavera; Albuhera; Salamanca; Vittoria; Toulouse; Peninsula. **First Afghan War (1839–42):** Ghuznee 1839; Affghanistan 1839. **Crimean War (1854–5):** Alma; Balaklava; Inkerman; Sevastopol. **Great War:** Mons; Le Cateau; Marne 1914; Aisne 1914; Ypres 1914, 1915; St Julien; Arras 1917; Cambrai 1917; Somme 1918; Amiens. **Second World War:** Ruweisat; Alam el Halfa; El Ala-

mein; Coriano; Senio Pocket; Rimini Line; Argenta Gap; Proasteion; Corinth Canal; Greece 1941.

Accredited Battle Honours
Great War: Retreat from Mons; Messines 1914; Armentières 1914; Langemarck 1914; Gheluvelt; Bellewaarde; Scarpe 1917; Hindenburg Line; Canal du Nord; Pursuit to Mons; France and Flanders 1914–18. **Second World War:** Gazala; Defence of Alamein Line; North Africa 1942; San Clemente; Conventello-Comacchio; Senio; Santerno Crossing; Italy 1944–5.

Awards
Private S. Parkes (1813–64) was awarded the Victoria Cross Balaklava, 25 October 1854: gazetted 24 February 1857.

Marches
Quick: *Berkeley's Dragoons*. Slow: *Litany of Loretto*.

Journal
IV Hussars Journal.

Museum
Museum of Irish Cavalry Regiments, Carrickfergus, Co Antrim, Northern Ireland (tel 023 83 62273): open April–September Monday–Saturday 1000–1800, Sunday 1400–1800; October–March closing 1600.

Regimental Histories
Daniell, D. S. *4th Hussar: The Story of the 4th Queen's Own Hussars, 1685–1958*, Gale & Polden, 1959. Evans, H. K. D., and Laing, N. D. *The 4th (Queen's Own) Hussars in the Great War*, Gale & Polden, 1920. Edwards, *A Short History of the 4th Queen's Own Hussars*, Thomas (Canterbury), 1935.

8th (KING'S ROYAL IRISH) HUSSARS

History
Raised in 1693 as [Robert] Cunningham's Dragoons (8th (King's Royal Irish) Hussars in 1822).
MOTTO: *Pristinae virtutis memores* (The memory of former valour).
REGIMENTAL ANNIVERSARY: Salamanca Day (22 July).
FORMER MEMBER: Field Marshal, The Earl of Ypres (1852–1925), commissioned 1874.

Emblazoned Battle Honours
Second Maratha and Pindari War (1816–18): Leswarree. **India** (1802–22): Hindoostan. **Crimean War** (1854–5): Alma; Balaklava; Inkerman; Sevastopol. **Indian Mutiny** (1857–8): Central India. **Second Afghan War** (1878–80): Afghanistan. **South African War** (1899–1902): South Africa 1900–02. **Great War:** Givenchy 1914; Somme 1916, 1918; Cambrai 1917, 1918; Bapaume 1918; Rosières; Amiens; Albert 1918; Beaurevoir; Pursuit to Mons; France and Flanders 1914–18. **Second World War:** Villers Bocage; Lower Maas; Rhine; North-West Europe 1944–5; Buq Buq; Sidi Rezegh 1941; Gazala; El Alamein; North Africa 1940–2. **Korean War** (1950–3): Imjin; Korea 1950–1.

Accredited Battle Honours
Great War: Bazentin; Flers-Courcelette; St Quentin; Hindenburg Line; St Quentin Canal. **Second World War:** Mont Pinçon; Dives Crossing; Nederrijn; Best; Egyptian Frontier 1940; Sidi Barrani; Relief of Tobruk; Bir el Igela; Mersa Matruh; Alam el Halfa.

Awards

Five members of the regiment have been awarded the Victoria Cross, all during the Indian Mutiny (1857–8). First awards: Captain C. W. Heneage (1831–1901); Farrier G. Hollis (1833–79); Private J. Pearson, later Sergeant (1822–1900) and Sergeant J. Ward (1832–72) Gwalior 17 June 1858; gazetted 26 January 1859 – all elected by the regiment.

Marches

Quick: *The Galloping 8th Hussar.* Slow: *The Scottish Archers.*

Journal

Cross-Belts.

Museum

Museum of Irish Cavalry Regiments, Carrickfergus, Co Antrim, Northern Ireland (tel 023 83 62273): open April–September Monday–Saturday 1000–1800, Sunday 1400–1800; October–March closing 1600.

Regimental Histories

Fitzroy, O. *Men of Valour, 1927–1958,* Tinling, 1961. Murray, R. H. *The History of the VIII King's Royal Irish Hussars, 1693–1927* (2 vols), Heffer, 1928.

9th/12th ROYAL LANCERS (PRINCE OF WALES'S)

Colonel-in-Chief: HM Queen Elizabeth The Queen Mother

History
Formed in 1960 by the amalgamation of 9th Queen's Royal Lancers and 12th Royal Lancers (Prince of Wales's).
HOME HEADQUARTERS: TA Centre, Wigston, Leicestershire.
RECRUITMENT AREA: Leicestershire, Derbyshire, Northamptonshire and Greater London.
REGIMENTAL ANNIVERSARY: Mons/Moy Day (weekend in August or September).

Emblazoned Battle Honours
Peninsular War (1808–14): Salamanca; Peninsula. Hundred Days (1815): Waterloo. Gwalior Campaign (1843): Punniar. First Sikh War (1845–6): Sobraon. Second Sikh War (1848–9): Chillianwallah; Goojerat; Punjaub. Eighth Kaffir War (1851–3): South Africa 1851–3. Crimean War (1854–5): Sevastopol. Indian Mutiny (1857–8): Delhi 1857; Central India; Lucknow. Second Afghan War (1878–80): Charasiah; Kabul 1879; Kandahar 1880; Afghanistan 1878–80. South African War (1899–1902): Modder River; Relief of Kimberley; Paardeburg; South Africa 1899–1902. Great War: Mons; Retreat from Mons; Marne 1914; Aisne 1914; Messines 1914; Ypres 1914, 1915; Somme 1916, 1918; Arras 1917; Cambrai 1917, 1918; Rosières; Sambre; Pursuit to Mons. Second World War: Dyle; Dunkirk 1940; Somme 1940; North-West Europe 1940; Chor es Sufan; Gazala; Ruweisat; El Alamein; El Hamma; Tunis; North Africa 1941–3; Defence of Lamone Bridgehead; Argenta Gap; Bologna; Italy 1944–5. The Sphinx superscribed 'Egypt' is also borne on the guidon.

Accredited Battle Honours
Great War: Le Cateau; La Bassée 1914; Armentières 1914; Neuve Chapelle; Gravenstafel; St Julien; Frezenberg; Bellewaarde; Pozières; Flers-Courcelette; Scarpe 1917; St Quentin; Avre; Lys; Hazebrouck; Amiens; Albert 1918; Hindenburg Line; St Quentin Canal; Beaurevoir; France and Flanders 1914–18. Second World War: Defence of Arras; Arras Counter-attack; Withdrawal to Seine; Saunnu; Bir el Aslagh; Sidi Rezegh 1942; Defence of Alamein Line; Ruweisat Ridge; Alam el Halfa; Advance on Tripoli; Tebaga Gap; Akarit; El Kourzia; Djebel Kournine; Creteville Pass; Citerna; Gothic Line; Coriano; Capture of Forli; Lamone Crossing; Pideura; Conventello-Comacchio; Sillaro Crossing; Idice Bridgehead.

Dress

DIFFERENCES: Scarlet dress cap, blue piping and quarter welts; scarlet side cap piped yellow, blue side cap piped gold for officers. Yellow stable belt edged in red, wider central stripe. Red and yellow lanyard.

REGIMENTAL TIE: Gold stripes on deep red ground.

Marches

Quick: *God Bless the Prince of Wales*. Slow: *Men of Harlech*.

Alliances

The Prince Edward Island Regiment, of Canada; 12th Cavalry, of Pakistan. Associated regular regiment of NH (Northumberland Hussars) Squadron, The Queen's Own Yeomanry.

Journal

The Delhi Spearmen: The Regimental Journal of the 9th/12th Royal Lancers (once a year).

Museum

Derby Museum and Art Gallery, The Strand, Derby, Derbyshire (tel 0332 255581): open Monday 1100–1700, Tuesday–Saturday 1000–1700, Sunday 1400–1700.

Record Office

Except officers: Queen's Park, Chester; officers: MS(AODO), London Rd, Stanmore, Middlesex.

Predecessors

9th QUEEN'S ROYAL LANCERS

History

Raised in 1715 as Wynne's Dragoons (9th (Queen's Royal) Lancers in 1822).

Emblazoned Battle Honours

Peninsular War (1808–14): Peninsula. Gwalior Campaign (1843): Punniar. First Sikh War (1845–6): Sobraon. Second Sikh War (1848–9): Chillianwallah; Goojerat; Punjaub. Indian Mutiny (1857–8): Delhi 1857; Lucknow. Second Afghan War (1878–80): Charasiah; Kabul; Kandahar 1880; Afghanistan 1878–80. South African War (1899–1902): Modder River; Relief of Kimberley; Paardeburg; South Africa 1899–1902. Great War: Retreat from Mons; Marne 1914; Aisne 1914; Messines 1914; Ypres 1914, 1915; Somme 1916, 1918; Arras 1917; Cambrai 1917, 1918; Rosières; Pursuit to Mons. Second World War: Somme 1940; North-West Europe 1940; Gazala; Ruweisat; El Alamein; El Hamma; North Africa 1942–3; Defence of Lamone Bridgehead; Argenta Gap; Italy 1944–5.

Accredited Battle Honours

Great War: Mons; Le Cateau; La Bassée

1914; Armentières 1914; Gravenstafel; St Julien; Frezenberg; Bellewaarde; Pozières; Flers-Courcelette; Scarpe 1917; St Quentin; Avre; Amiens; Albert 1918; Hindenburg Line; France and Flanders 1914–18. **Second World War:** Withdrawal to Seine; Saunnu; Bir el Aslagh; Sidi Rezegh 1942; Defence of Alamein Line; Ruweisat Ridge; Tebaga Gap; El Kourzia; Tunis; Creteville Pass; Coriano; Capture of Forli; Lamone Crossing; Pideura.

Awards
Fourteen members of the regiment have been awarded the Victoria Cross: twelve in the Indian Mutiny (1857–8), one in the Zulu and Basuto War (1879–80) and one in the Great War. First awards: Lieutenant A. S. Jones, later Lieutenant-Colonel (1832–1920) Badle-ke-Serai 8 June 1857, gazetted 18 June 1858; Sergeant H. Hartigan (1826–86) Badle-ke-Serai 8 June 1857 and Agra 10 October 1857: gazetted 19 June 1858.

Memorials
Canterbury Cathedral, wall by Warriors' Chapel and in cloisters (Great War); Royal Garrison Church, Aldershot (Second Afghan War 1878–80); Exeter Cathedral (India 1843–58).

Marches
Quick: *Soldiers' Chorus* from Gounod's *Faust*. Slow: *Men of Harlech*.

Journal
The Delhi Spearmen.

Museum
Derby Museum and Art Gallery, The Strand, Derby, Derbyshire (tel 0332 255581): open Monday 1100–1700, Tuesday–Saturday 1000–1700, Sunday 1400–1700.

Regimental Histories
Bright, J. (ed.) *The Ninth Queen's Royal Lancers, 1936–1945*, Gale & Polden, 1951. Sheppard, E. W. *The Ninth Queen's Royal Lancers, 1715–1936*, Gale & Polden, 1939.

12th ROYAL LANCERS (PRINCE OF WALES'S)

History
Raised in 1715 as Bowles' Dragoons (12th (The Prince of Wales's) Royal Lancers in 1817).
FORMER MEMBER: Field Marshal Lord Birdwood (1865–1951), commissioned 1885.

Emblazoned Battle Honours
Peninsular War (1808–14): Salamanca; Peninsula. **Hundred Days** (1815): Waterloo. **Eighth Kaffir War** (1851–3): South Africa 1851–2. **Crimean War** (1854–5): Sevastopol. **Indian Mutiny** (1857–8): Central India. **South African War** (1899–1902): Relief of Kimberley; Paardeburg; South Africa 1899–1902. **Great War:** Mons; Retreat from Mons; Marne 1914; Aisne 1914; Messines 1914; Ypres 1914, 1915; Arras 1917; Cambrai 1917, 1918; Somme 1918; Sambre. **Second World War:** Dyle; Dunkirk 1940; North-West Europe 1940; Chor es Sufan; Gazala; El Alamein; Tunis; North Africa 1941–3; Bologna; Italy 1944–5. The Sphinx superscribed 'Egypt' was also borne on the drum banners.

Accredited Battle Honours
Great War: Neuve Chapelle; St Julien; Bellewaarde; Scarpe 1917; St Quentin; Lys; Hazebrouck; Amiens; Albert 1918; Hindenburg Line; St Quentin Canal; Beaurevoir; France and Flanders 1914–18. **Second World War:** Defence of Arras; Arras Counter-attack; Alam el Halfa; Advance on Tripoli; Tebaga Gap; El Hamma; Akarit; El Kourzia; Djebel

Kournine; Creteville Pass; Citerna; Gothic Line; Capture of Forli; Conventello-Comacchio; Sillaro Crossing; Idice Bridgehead.

Memorial
Royal Garrison Church, Aldershot (South Africa 1899–1902).

Marches
Quick: *God Bless the Prince of Wales.*
Slow: *Coburg.*

Allied Regiment in 1914
12th Manitoba Dragoons, of Canada.

Journal
The Twelfth Royal Lancers Journal.

Museum
Derby Museum and Art Gallery, The Strand, Derby, Derbyshire (tel 0332 255581): open Monday 1100–1700, Tuesday–Saturday 1000–1700, Sunday 1100–1700.

Regimental History
Stewart, P. F. *The History of the XII Royal Lancers (Prince of Wales's)*, OUP, 1950.

THE ROYAL HUSSARS
(PRINCE OF WALES'S OWN)
Colonel-in-Chief: HRH Princess Alice, Duchess of Gloucester
GCB CI GCVO GBE

History
Formed in 1969 by the amalgamation of 10th Royal Hussars (Prince of Wales's Own) and 11th Hussars (Prince Albert's Own).
Motto: *Ich dien* (I serve).
Home Headquarters: Peninsula Barracks, Winchester, Hampshire.
Recruitment Area: Oxfordshire, Buckinghamshire, Berkshire, Hampshire, Wiltshire and Gloucestershire.
Regimental Anniversary: El Alamein Day (23 October).

Emblazoned Battle Honours
Seven Years War (1756–63): Warburg. **French Revolutionary Wars** (1793–1802): Beaumont; Willems. **Peninsular War** (1808–14): Salamanca; Peninsula. **Hundred Days** (1815): Waterloo. **Revolt of Rajah of Bhurtpore** (1826): Bhurtpore. **Crimean War** (1854–5): Alma; Balaklava; Inkerman; Sevastopol. **Second Afghan War** (1878–80): Ali Masjid; Afghanistan 1878–9. **First Sudan War** (1882–4): Egypt 1884. **South African War** (1899–1902): Relief of Kimberley; Paardeburg; South Africa 1899–1902. **Great War:** Le Cateau; Retreat from Mons; Marne 1914; Aisne 1914; Messines 1914; Frezenberg; Loos; Somme 1916, 1918; Arras 1917, 1918; Cambrai 1917, 1918; Amiens; Drocourt-Queant; Selle; Pursuit to Mons; France and Flanders 1914–18. **Second World War:** Somme 1940; Villers Bocage; Roer; Rhine; North-West Europe 1940, 1944–5; Egyptian Frontier 1940; Sidi Barrani; Beda Fomm; Sidi Rezegh 1941; Saunnu; Gazala; El Alamein; El Hamma; Tunis; Coriano; Santarcangelo; Valli di Comacchio; Argenta Gap; Italy 1943–5. The Sphinx superscribed 'Egypt' is also borne on the guidon.

Accredited Battle Honours
Great War: Mons; Armentières 1914; Ypres 1914, 1915; Langemarck 1914; Gheluvelt; Nonne Bosschen; Bellewaarde; Flers-Courcelette; Scarpe 1917; St Quentin; Rosières; Avre; Albert 1918; Hindenburg Line; St Quentin Canal; Beaurevoir. **Second World War:** Bourguébus Ridge; Mont Pinçon; Jurques; Dives Crossing; La Vie Crossing; Lisieux; Le Touquet Crossing; Risle Crossing; Ibbenburen; Aller; Withdrawal to Matruh; Bir Enba; Buq Buq; Bardia 1941; Capture of Tobruk; Halfaya 1941; Sidi Suleiman; Tobruk 1941; Gubi I, II; Gabr Saleh; Taieb el Essem; Relief of Tobruk; Msus; Bir el Aslagh;

Defence of Alamein Line; Alam el Halfa; Advance on Tripoli; Enfidaville; El Kourzia; Djebel Kournine; North Africa 1940–3; Capture of Naples; Volturno Crossing; Cosina Canal Crossing; Senio Pocket; Cesena.

Memorial
Garrison Church, Aldershot, Hampshire.

Dress
DIFFERENCES: Crimson dress cap; crimson side cap piped yellow; reddish brown beret, crimson patch behind badge. Crimson stable belt bordered gold, edged black. Crimson trousers.

Marches
Quick: *The Merry Month of May*. Slow: *Coburg*.

Alliances
1st Hussars, of Canada; 10th Light Horse, of Australia; The Guides Cavalry, of Pakistan. Associated regular regiment of A (Royal Wiltshire Yeomanry) Squadron, The Royal Yeomanry; and A (Royal Gloucestershire Hussars), B (Royal Wiltshire Yeomanry) and C (Royal Gloucestershire Hussars) Squadrons, The Royal Wessex Yeomanry.

Journal
The Royal Hussars' Journal (once a year – May).

Associations
Old Comrades' Association and Benevolent Fund: Peninsular Barracks, Winchester, Hampshire (tel 0962 863751).

Museum
Peninsula Barracks, Winchester, Hampshire (tel 0962 863751): open Tuesday–Friday 1000–1600, Saturday, Sunday, Bank Holidays 1200–1600.

Record Office
Except officers: Queen's Park, Chester; officers: MS(AODO), London Rd, Stanmore, Middlesex.

Predecessors

10th ROYAL HUSSARS
(PRINCE OF WALES'S OWN)

History
Raised in 1715 as Gore's Dragoons (10th Dragoons in 1751, Hussars in 1806).
MOTTO: *Ich dien* (I serve).
REGIMENTAL ANNIVERSARY: El Alamein Day (23 October).

FORMER MEMBERS: Field Marshal Viscount Byng of Vimy (1862–1935), commissioned 1883; HRH The Duke of Gloucester (1900–74), commissioned 1920.

Emblazoned Battle Honours

Seven Years War (1756–63): Warburg. Peninsular War (1808–14): Peninsula. Hundred Days (1815): Waterloo. Crimean War (1854–5): Sevastopol. Second Afghan War (1878–80): Ali Masjid; Afghanistan 1878–9. First Sudan War (1882–4): Egypt 1884. South African War (1899–1902): Relief of Kimberley; Paardeburg; South Africa 1899–1902. Great War: Ypres 1914, 1915; Frezenberg; Loos; Arras 1917, 1918; Somme 1918; Avre; Amiens; Drocourt-Quéant; Selle; Cambrai 1918; Pursuit to Mons; France and Flanders 1914–18. Second World War: Somme 1940; Saunnu; Gazala; El Alamein; El Hamma; Tunis; Coriano; Santarcangelo; Valli di Comacchio; Argenta Gap.

Accredited Battle Honours

Great War: Langemarck 1914; Gheluvelt; Nonne Bosschen; Scarpe 1917; St Quentin; Hindenburg Line; Beaurevoir; Cambrai 1918. Second World War: North-West Europe 1940; Bir el Aslagh; Alam el Halfa; El Kourzia; Djebel Kournine; North Africa 1942–3; Cosina Canal Crossing; Senio Pocket; Cesena; Italy 1944–5.

Awards

Two members of the regiment have been awarded the Victoria Cross, both in the South African War (1899–1902). First award: Lieutenant Sir J. P. Millbanke Bt, later Lieutenant-Colonel (1872–1915) Colesburg 5 January 1900: gazetted 6 July 1900. He was killed at Gallipoli.

Marches

Quick: *The Merry Month of May*. Slow: *God Bless the Prince of Wales*.

Journal

The Tenth Royal Hussars Gazette.

Museum

Peninsula Barracks, Winchester, Hampshire (tel 0962 863751): open Tuesday–Friday 1000–1600, Saturday, Sunday, Bank Holidays 1200–1600.

Regimental Histories

Brander, M. *The 10th Royal Hussars (1715–1969)*, Leo Cooper, 1969. Liddell, R. S. *Memoires of the 10th Royal Hussars (PWO) (1715–1890)*, Longmans Green, 1891. Whitmore, F. H. D. C. *The 10th (PWO) Royal Hussars and Essex Yeomanry during the European War 1914–1918*, Benham, 1920. *The 10th Royal Hussars in the Second World War 1939–1945*, ed. by Committee, Gale & Polden, 1948.

11th HUSSARS (PRINCE OF ALBERT'S OWN)

History

Raised in 1715 as Honywood's Dragoons (11th Dragoons in 1751, Hussars in 1840).

MOTTO: *Treu und fest* (Loyal and steadfast).
REGIMENTAL ANNIVERSARY: El Alamein Day (23 October).
FORMER MEMBER: HRH Prince Michael of Kent (b1942), commissioned 1962.

Emblazoned Battle Honours

Seven Years War (1756–63): Warburg. French Revolutionary Wars (1793–1802): Beaumont; Willems. Peninsular War (1808–14): Salamanca; Peninsula. Hundred Days (1815): Waterloo. Revolt of Rajah of Bhurtpore (1826):

Bhurtpore. **Crimean War** (1854–5): Alma; Balaklava; Inkerman; Sevastopol. **Great War:** Le Cateau; Retreat from Mons; Marne 1914; Aisne 1914; Messines 1914; Ypres 1914, 1915; Somme 1916, 1918; Cambrai 1917, 1918; Amiens; France and Flanders 1914–18. **Second World War:** Villers Bocage; Roer; Rhine; Egyptian Frontier 1940; Sidi Barrani; Beda Fomm; Sidi Rezegh 1941; El Alamein; Tunis; Italy 1943. The Sphinx superscribed 'Egypt' was also borne on the drum banners.

Accredited Battle Honours
Great War: Mons; Armentières 1914; Frezenberg; Bellewaarde; Flers-Courcelette; Arras 1917; Scarpe 1917; St Quentin; Rosières; Albert 1918; Hindenburg Line; St Quentin Canal; Beaurevoir; Selle. **Second World War:** Bourguébus Ridge; Mont Pinçon; Jurques; Dives Crossing; La Vie Crossing; Lisieux; Le Touques Crossing; Risle Crossing; Ibbenburen; Aller; North-West Europe 1944–5; Withdrawal to Matruh; Bir Enba; Buq Buq; Bardia 1941; Capture of Tobruk; Halfaya 1941; Sidi Suleiman; Tobruk 1941; Gubi I, II; Gabr Saleh; Taieb el Essom; Relief of Tobruk; Saunnu; Msus; Defence of Alamein Line; Alam el Halfa; Advance on Tripoli; Enfidaville; North Africa 1940–3; Capture of Naples; Volturno Crossing.

Awards
Lieutenant A. R. Dunn, later Colonel (1833–68) was awarded the Victoria Cross Balaklava 25 October 1854: gazetted 24 February 1857.

Memorial
Royal Garrison Church, Aldershot.

Marches
Quick: *Moses in Egypt.* Slow: *Coburg.*

Journal
The 11th Hussars Journal.

Museum
Peninsula Barracks, Winchester, Hampshire (tel 0962 863751): open Tuesday–Friday 1000–1600, Saturday, Sunday, Bank Holidays 1200–1600.

Regimental Histories
Brett-Smith, H. *The 11th Hussars (1715–1969),* Leo Cooper, 1969. Williams, G. T. *The Historical Records of the 11th Hussars, Prince Albert's Own (1715–1908),* Newnes, 1908. Lumley, L. R. (Earl of Scarborough) *History of the 11th Hussars (Prince Albert's Own) 1908–1934,* RUSI, 1936. Clarke, D. *Story of the 11th Hussars 1934–1945: The Eleventh at War,* Michael Joseph, 1952.

13th/18th ROYAL HUSSARS (QUEEN MARY'S OWN)
Colonel-in-Chief: HRH The Princess of Wales

History
Formed in 1922 as 13th/18th Hussars (13th/18th Royal Hussars (Queen Mary's Own) in 1935) by the amalgamation of 13th Hussars and 18th Royal Hussars (Queen Mary's Own).

MOTTOES: *Viret in aeternum* (It shall flourish for ever); *Pro rege, pro lege, pro patria conamur* (We strive for our King, our law and our country).

HOME HEADQUARTERS: 3 Tower St, York.

RECRUITMENT AREA: South Yorkshire.

REGIMENTAL ANNIVERSARIES: Laji Day (5 March); Normandy Day (6 June); Balaklava Day (25 October).

Emblazoned Battle Honours
Peninsular War (1808–14): Albuhera; Vittoria; Orthes; Toulouse; Peninsula. **Crimean War** (1854–5): Alma; Balaklava; Sevastopol. **South African War** (1899–1902): Defence of Ladysmith; South Africa 1899–1902. **Great War**: Mons; Marne 1914; Aisne 1914; Messines 1914; Ypres 1915, 1916; Somme 1916, 1918; Cambrai 1917, 1918; Amiens; Hindenburg Line; France and Flanders 1914–18; Kut al Amara 1917; Baghdad; Sharqat; Mesopotamia 1916–18. **Second World War**: Ypres-Comines Canal; Normandy Landing; Caen; Mont Pinçon; Geilenkirchen; Roer; Rhineland; Goch; North-West Europe 1940, 1944–5.

Accredited Battle Honours
Great War: Le Cateau; Retreat from Mons; La Bassée 1914; Armentières 1914; Gravenstafel; St Julien; Frezenberg; Bellewaarde; Flers–Courcelette; Arras 1917; Scarpe 1917; St Quentin; Rosières; Albert 1918; Pursuit to Mons. **Second World War**: Dyle; Withdrawal to Escaut; Bretteville; Bourguébus Ridge; St Pierre la Vieille; Waal Flats; Rhine; Bremen.

Dress
DIFFERENCES: White dress cap, blue band; white side cap, piped yellow, blue flaps and peak. Blue and white stable belt.

REGIMENTAL TIE: blue, silver and green stripes.

Marches
Quick: *Balaklava*. Slow: *13th Hussars Slow March* and *18th Hussars Slow March*.

Alliances

The Royal Canadian Hussars (Montreal); Skinner's Horse (1st Duke of York's Own Cavalry), of India; 6 Lancers, of Pakistan; 2nd Regiment, Royal Malaysian Armoured Corps. Associated regular regiment of Y (Yorkshire) Squadron, The Queen's Own Yeomanry.

Journal

13th/18th Journal.

Museum

Cannon Hall, Barnsley, South Yorkshire (tel 0226 790270): open Monday–Saturday 1030–1700, Sunday 1430–1700.

Record Office

Except officers: Queen's Park, Chester; officers; MS(AODO), London Rd, Stanmore, Middlesex.

Regimental History

Miller, C. H., *History of the 13th/18th Royal Hussars, 1922–1947*, Chisman & Bradshaw, 1949.

Predecessors

13th HUSSARS

History

Raised in 1715 as Munden's Dragoons (13th Hussars in 1861).

MOTTO: *Viret in aeternum* (May it flourish for ever).

REGIMENTAL ANNIVERSARIES: Laji Day (5 March); Balaklava Day (25 October).

FORMER MEMBER: Field Marshal Sir Evelyn Wood VC (1838–1919), commissioned 1855.

Emblazoned Battle Honours

Peninsular War (1808–14): Albuhera; Vittoria; Orthes; Toulouse; Peninsula. Hundred Days (1815): Waterloo. Crimean War (1854–5): Alma; Balaklava; Inkerman; Sevastopol. South African War (1899–1902): Relief of Ladysmith; South Africa 1899–1902. Great War: France and Flanders 1914–16; Kut al Amara 1917; Baghdad; Sharqat; Mesopotamia 1916–18.

Awards

Sergeant J. Malone, later Captain and Riding Master (1833–83) was awarded the Victoria Cross Balaklava 25 October 1854: gazetted 25 September 1857.

Marches

Quick: *The Regimental March of the 13th Hussars.* Slow: *13th Hussars Slow March.*

Museum

Cannon Hall, Cawthorne, Barnsley, South Yorkshire (tel 0226 790270): open Monday–Saturday 1030–1700, Sunday 1430–1700.

Regimental Histories

Mortimer Durand, Sir H. *The Thirteenth Hussars in the Great War*, Blackwood, 1921. Barrett, C. R. B. *History of the XIII Hussars*, Blackwood, 1911.

18th ROYAL HUSSARS (QUEEN MARY'S OWN)

History
Raised in 1759 as the 19th Light Dragoons (18th Light Dragoons in 1763, 18th (Queen Mary's Own) Hussars in 1910).
MOTTO: *Pro rege, pro lege, pro patria conamur* (We strive for our King, our laws and our country.

Emblazoned Battle Honours
Peninsular War (1808–14): Peninsula. Hundred Days (1815): Waterloo. South African War (1899–1902): Defence of Ladysmith; South Africa 1899–1902. Great War: Mons; Marne 1914; Aisne 1914; Messines 1914; Ypres 1914, 1915; Somme 1916, 1918; Cambrai 1917, 1918; Amiens; Hindenburg Line; France and Flanders 1914–18.

Accredited Battle Honours
Great War: Le Cateau; Retreat from Mons; La Bassée 1914; Armentières 1914; Gravenstafel; St Julien; Frezenberg; Bellewaarde; Flers-Courcelette; Arras 1917; Scarpe 1917; St Quentin; Rosières; Albert 1918; Pursuit to Mons.

Awards
Private H. G. Crandon, later Corporal (1874–1953) was awarded the Victoria Cross at Springbok Laagte, South Africa, 4 July 1901: gazetted 18 October 1901.

Marches
Slow: *The Regimental March of the 18th Hussars*. Slow: *18th Hussars Slow March.*

Allied Regiment in 1914
18th Mounted Rifles, of Canada.

Museum
Cannon Hall, Cawthorne, Barnsley, South Yorkshire (tel 0226 790270): open Monday–Saturday 1030–1700, Sunday 1430–1700.

Regimental History
Burnett, C. *The Memoirs of the 18th (Queen Mary's Own) Royal Hussars, 1906–1922*, Warren, 1922.

14th/20th KING'S HUSSARS
Colonel-in-Chief: HRH The Princess Royal GCVO

History
Formed in 1922 as 14th/20th Hussars (14th/20th King's Hussars in 1936) by the amalgamation of 14th King's Hussars and 20th Hussars.
HOME HEADQUARTERS: Fulwood Barracks, Preston, Lancashire.
RECRUITMENT AREA: Lancashire, Greater Manchester and the Isle of Man.
REGIMENTAL ANNIVERSARIES: Ramadi Day (28 September); Ramnuggur Day (22 November).

Emblazoned Battle Honours
Peninsular War (1808–14): Vimiera; Douro; Talavera; Fuentes d'Onor; Salamanca; Vittoria; Pyrenees; Orthes; Peninsula. **Second Sikh War** (1848–9): Chillianwallah; Goojerat; Punjaub. **Persian War** (1856–7): Persia. **Indian Mutiny** (1857–8): Central India. **Egyptian Campaign** (1885): Suakin 1885. **South African War** (1899–1902): Relief of Ladysmith; South Africa 1900–02. **Great War:** Mons; Retreat from Mons; Marne 1914; Aisne 1914; Messines 1914; Ypres 1914, 1915; Cambrai 1917, 1918; Somme 1918; Amiens; Sambre; Tigris 1916; Kut al Amara 1917; Baghdad; Mesopotamia 1915–18; Persia 1918. **Second World War:** Bologna; Medecina; Italy 1945.

Accredited Battle Honours
Great War: Neuve Chapelle; St Julien; Bellewaarde; Arras 1917; Scarpe 1917; St Quentin; Lys; Hazebrouck; Albert 1918; Bapaume 1918; Hindenburg Line; St Quentin Canal; Beaurevoir; France and Flanders 1914–18.

Dress
DIFFERENCES: Scarlet dress cap; scarlet side cap piped yellow; diagonal blue over yellow patch behind beret badge. Blue/yellow/blue stable belt. Crossed kukri arm badge.
REGIMENTAL TIE: Blue and primrose stripes.

Marches
Quick: *Royal Sussex*. Slow: *The Eagle*.

Alliances
2nd/14th Queensland Mounted Infantry, of Australia; 8th/13th Victorian Mounted Rifles, of Australia; Queen Alexandra's Squadron RNZAC, of New Zealand; Zambia Armoured Car Regiment.

Affiliated Regiment
6th Queen Elizabeth's Own Gurkha Rifles. Associated regular regiment of The Duke of Lancaster's Own Yeomanry.

Journal
The Hawk (once a year – November).

Museum
County and Regimental Museum, Stanley St, Preston, Lancashire (tel 0772 264075): open Monday, Wednesday–Saturday 1000–1700.

Record Office
Except officers: Queen's Park, Chester; officers: MS(AODO), London Rd, Stanmore, Middlesex.

Regimental History
Oatts, L. B. *Emperor's Chambermaids: History of the 14th/20th King's Hussars*, Lock, 1973.

Predecessors

14th KING'S HUSSARS

History
Raised in 1715 as Dormer's Dragoons (14th (King's) Hussars in 1861).
REGIMENTAL ANNIVERSARIES: Ramadi Day (28 September); Ramnuggur Day (22 November).

Emblazoned Battle Honours
Peninsular War (1808–14): Douro; Talavera; Fuentes d'Onor; Salamanca; Vittoria; Pyrenees; Orthes; Peninsula. Second Sikh War (1848–9): Chillianwalla; Goojerat. Persian War (1856–7): Persia. Indian Mutiny (1857–8): Central India. South African War (1899–1902): Relief of Ladysmith; South Africa 1900–02. Great War: Tigris 1916; Kut al

Amara 1917; Baghdad; Mesopotamia 1915–18; Persia 1918.

Awards
Two members of the regiment have been awarded the Victoria Cross: one in the Indian Mutiny (1857–8) and one in the South African War (1899–1902). First award: Lieutenant J. Leith, later Major (1826–69) Betwah, India, 1 April 1858: gazetted 24 December 1858.

Marches
Quick: *Royal Sussex*. Slow: *King of Prussia*.

Allied Regiment in 1914
16th Light Horse, of Canada.

Museum
County and Regimental Museum, Stanley St, Preston, Lancashire (tel 0772 264075): open Monday, Wednesday–Saturday 1000–1700.

Regimental History
Hamilton, H. B. *Historical Records of the 14th (King's) Hussars, 1900–1922*, RUSI, 1932.

20th HUSSARS

History
Raised in 1759 as the 20th Inniskilling Light Dragoons (20th Hussars in 1861, disbanded in 1921 but reconstituted in 1922).

Emblazoned Battle Honours
Peninsular War (1808–14): Vimiera; Peninsula. Egyptian Campaign (1885): Suakin 1885. **South African War** (1899–1902): South Africa 1901–02. **Great War:** Mons; Retreat from Mons; Marne 1914; Aisne 1914; Messines 1914; Ypres 1914, 1915; Cambrai 1917, 1918; Somme 1918; Amiens; Sambre.

Accredited Battle Honours
Great War: Neuve Chapelle; St Julien; Bellewaarde; Arras 1917; Scarpe 1917; St Quentin; Lys; Hazebrouck; Albert 1918; Bapaume 1918; Hindenburg Line; St Quentin Canal; Beaurevoir; France and Flanders 1914–18.

Journal
The Yellow Plume.

Museum
County and Regimental Museum, Stanley St, Preston, Lancashire (tel 0772 264075): open Monday, Wednesday–Saturday 1000–1700.

Regimental History
Darling, C. J. *20th Hussars in the Great War*, privately printed, 1923.

15th/19th THE KING'S ROYAL HUSSARS
Colonel-in-Chief: HRH The Princess Margaret Countess of Snowdon
CI DCVO

History
Formed in 1922 as 15th/19th Hussars (15th The King's Royal Hussars in 1932, 15th/19th The King's Royal Hussars in 1933) by the amalgamation of 15th The King's Hussars and 19th (Queen Alexandra's Own Royal) Hussars.
MOTTO: *Merebimur* (We shall be worthy).
HOME HEADQUARTERS: Fenham Barracks, Newcastle-upon-Tyne.
RECRUITMENT AREA: Northumberland, Durham, Tyne and Wear, Cleveland.
REGIMENTAL ANNIVERSARIES: Esla Day (31 May); Sahagun Day (21 December).

Emblazoned Battle Honours
Seven Years War (1756–63): Emsdorff. **Third Mysore War** (1789–91): Mysore. **French Revolutionary Wars** (1793–1802): Villers-en-Cauchies; Willems; Egmont op Zee. **Fourth Mysore War** (1799): Seringapatam. **Peninsular War** (1808–14): Sahagun; Vittoria. **War of 1812** (1812–14): Niagara. **Peninsular War** (1808–14): Peninsula. **Hundred Days** (1815): Waterloo. **Second Afghan War** (1878–80): Afghanistan 1878–80. **Revolt of Arabi Pasha** (1882): Tel-el-Kebir. **First Sudan War** (1882–4): Egypt 1882, 1884. **Egyptian Campaign** (1885): Abu Klea; Nile 1884–5. **South African War** (1899–1902): Defence of Ladysmith; South Africa 1899–1902. **Great War**: Le Cateau; Retreat from Mons; Marne 1914; Aisne 1914; Armentières 1914; Ypres 1914, 1915; Bellewaarde; Somme 1916, 1918; Cambrai 1917, 1918; Rosières; Amiens; Pursuit to Mons; France and Flanders 1914–18. **Second World War**: Withdrawal to Escaut; Seine 1944; Nederrijn; Rhineland; Hochwald; Rhine; Ibbenburen; Aller; North-West Europe 1940, 1944–5. An elephant superscribed 'Assaye' is also borne on the guidon.

Accredited Battle Honours
Great War: Mons; Langemarck 1914; Gheluvelt; Nonne Bosschen; Frezenberg; Flers-Courcelette; St Quentin; Albert 1918; Bapaume 1918; Hindenburg Line; St Quentin Canal; Beaurevoir; Hechtel; Venraij.

Memorials
Brass Gong inscribed with names of those who died during the Second World War – with the regiment. Garrison Church of All Saints, Aldershot, Hampshire: individual memorials (1939–45). Leazes Park, Newcastle-upon-Tyne: memorial rose garden.

Dress

DIFFERENCES: Scarlet dress cap; scarlet side cap piped with tubular gold braid for officers, RSM and Bandmaster, scarlet side cap with yellow piping for SNCOs and other ranks. Embroidered badge for officers and warrant officers.

REGIMENTAL TIE: Dark blue with narrower yellow and red diagonal stripes.

Marches

Quick: *The Bold King's Hussars*. Slow: *Eliott's Light Horse* and *Denmark*.

Alliances

The South Alberta Light Horse, of Canada; 1st/15th Royal New South Wales Lancers, of Australia; 19 Lancers, of Pakistan. Associated regiment of D (Northumberland Hussars) Squadron and HQ (Northumberland Hussars) Squadron, The Queen's Own Yeomanry.

Journal

15th/19th The King's Royal Hussars (once a year).

Association

15th/19th The King's Royal Hussars Regimental Association, Fenham Barracks, Newcastle-upon-Tyne.

Museums

John George Joicey Museum, City Rd, Newcastle-upon-Tyne (tel 091 2324562): open Tuesday–Friday, Saturday 1000–1730. Fenham Barracks, Newcastle-upon-Tyne (tel 091 2611046 ext 3142): open Monday–Friday 0830–1600 (ring first).

Record Office

Except officers: Queen's Park, Chester; officers: MS(AODO), London Rd, Stanmore, Middlesex.

Regimental Histories

Thompson, R. *The 15th/19th The King's Royal Hussars: A Pictorial History*, Quoin Publishing, 1989. Courage, G. *The History of 15/19 The King's Royal Hussars, 1939–1945*, Gale & Polden, 1949. Bastin, J. *The 15th/19th The King's Royal Hussars, 1945–1980*, Keats House, 1981.

Predecessors

15th THE KING'S HUSSARS

History

Raised in 1759 as the 15th Light Dragoons or Eliott's Light Horse (15th (King's) Hussars in 1807, 15th The King's Hussars in 1901).

MOTTO: *Merebimur* (We shall be worthy).

REGIMENTAL ANNIVERSARIES: Esla Day (31 May); Sahagun Day (21 December).

Emblazoned Battle Honours
Seven Years War (1756–63): Emsdorff. French Revolutionary Wars (1793–1802): Villers-en-Cauchies; Willems; Egmont op Zee. Peninsular War (1808–14): Sahagun; Vittoria; Peninsula. Hundred Days (1815): Waterloo. Second Afghan War (1878–80): Afghanistan 1878–80. Great War: Retreat from Mons; Marne 1914; Aisne 1914; Ypres 1914, 1915; Bellewaarde; Somme 1916, 1918; Cambrai 1917, 1918; Rosières; Pursuit to Mons; France and Flanders 1914–18.

Accredited Batttle Honours
Great War: Mons; Langemarck 1914; Gheluvelt; Nonne Bosschen; Frezenberg; Flers-Courcelette; St Quentin; Amiens; Albert 1918; Bapaume 1918; Hindenburg Line; St Quentin Canal; Beaurevoir.

Memorial
Brass Gong inscribed with names of those who died in the Great War – with the 15th/19th The King's Royal Hussars.

Awards
Corporal C. E. Garforth (1891–1973) was awarded the Victoria Cross Harmignies, France, 23 August 1914: gazetted 16 November 1914.

Marches
Quick: *The Bold King's Hussars.* Slow: *Eliott's Light Horse.*

Allied Regiment in 1914
15th Light Horse, of Canada.

Museum
John George Joicey Museum, City Rd, Newcastle-upon-Tyne (tel 091 2324562) open Tuesday–Friday, Saturday 1000–1730. Fenham Barracks, Newcastle-upon-Tyne (tel 091 2611046 ext 3142): open Monday–Friday 0830–1600 (ring first).

Regimental Histories
Carnock, Lord. *The History of the 15th The King's Hussars, 1914–1922*, Crypt House, 1932. Wylly, H. C. *XVth (The King's) Hussars, 1759–1913*, Caxton Publishing, 1914.

19th (QUEEN ALEXANDRA'S OWN ROYAL) HUSSARS

History
Raised in 1759 as the 19th Light Dragoons (19th Hussars in 1861, disbanded in 1921 but reconstituted in 1922).

FORMER MEMBERS: Field Marshal French, The Earl of Ypres (1852–1925) gazetted to 8th Hussars but transferred in 1874; Field Marshal Lord Chetwode (1869–1950), commissioned 1889.

Emblazoned Battle Honours
Third Mysore War (1789–91): Mysore. Fourth Mysore War (1799): Seringapatam. War of 1812 (1812–14): Niagara. Revolt of Arabi Pasha (1882): Tel-el-Kebir. First Sudan War (1882–4): Egypt 1882, 1884. Egyptian Campaign (1885): Nile 1884–5; Abu Klea. South African War (1899–1902): Defence of Ladysmith; South Africa 1899–1902. Great War: Le Cateau; Retreat from Mons; Marne 1914; Aisne 1914; Armentières 1914; Ypres 1915; Somme 1916, 1918; Cambrai 1917, 1918; Amiens; Pursuit to Mons. An elephant superscribed

'Assaye' was also borne on the drum banners.

Accredited Battle Honours
Great War: Frezenberg; Bellewaarde; Flers-Courcelette; St Quentin; Rosières; Albert 1918; Bapaume 1918; Hindenburg Line; St Quentin Canal; Beaurevoir; France and Flanders 1914–18.

Awards
Three members of the regiment have been awarded the Victoria Cross: one in the Indian Mutiny (1857–8), one in the First Sudan War (1882–4) and one in the Great War. First award: Lieutenant H. H. Gough, later General Sir Hugh Gough GCB (1833–1909) Alumbagh, India, 12 November 1857 and Jellalabad 25 February 1858: gazetted 24 December 1858. His brother and nephew were also awarded the Victoria Cross.

Memorials
Garrison Church of All Saints, Aldershot, Hampshire: stained glass window and tablet (Sudan and Egypt 1882–6); memorial (Great War); individual memorials.

Marches
Quick: *Haste to the Wedding.* Slow: *Denmark.*

Museum
John George Joicey Museum, City Rd, Newcastle-upon-Tyne (tel 091 2324562): open Tuesday–Saturday 1000–1730. Fenham Barracks, Newcastle-upon-Tyne (tel 091 2611046 ext 3142): open Monday–Friday 0830–1600 (ring first).

Regimental History
Biddulph, J. *The Nineteenth and their Times,* John Murray, 1900.

16th/5th THE QUEEN'S ROYAL LANCERS
Colonel-in-Chief: HM The Queen

History
Formed in 1922 as 16th/5th Lancers (16th/5th The Queen's Royal Lancers in 1954) by the amalgamation of 16th The Queen's Lancers and 5th Royal Irish Lancers.
MOTTO: *Aut cursu aut cominus armis* (Either in the charge or hand to hand).
HOME HEADQUARTERS: Kitchener House, Lammascote Rd, Stafford, Staffordshire.
RECRUITMENT AREA: Staffordshire.
REGIMENTAL ANNIVERSARY: Aliwal Day (28 January).

Emblazoned Battle Honours
War of Spanish Succession (1701–15): Blenheim; Ramillies; Oudenarde; Malplaquet. **French Revolutionary Wars** (1793–1802): Beaumont; Willems. **Peninsular War** (1808–14): Talavera; Fuentes d'Onor; Salamanca; Vittoria; Nive; Peninsula. **Hundred Days** (1815): Waterloo. **Revolt of Rajah of Bhurtpore** (1826): Bhurtpore. **First Afghan War** (1839–42): Ghuznee 1839; Affghanistan 1839. **Gwalior Campaign** (1843): Maharajpore. **First Sikh War** (1845–6): Aliwal; Sobraon. **Egyptian Campaign** (1885): Suakin 1885. **South African War** (1899–1902): Defence of Ladysmith; Relief of Kimberley; Paardeburg; South Africa 1899–1902. **Great War:** Mons; Le Cateau; Retreat from Mons; Marne 1914; Aisne 1914; Messines 1914; Ypres 1914, 1915; Bellewaarde; Arras 1917; Cambrai 1917; Somme 1918; St Quentin; Pursuit to Mons. **Second World War:** Fondouk; Bordj; Djebel Kournine; Tunis; North Africa 1942–3; Cassino II; Liri Valley; Advance to Florence; Argenta Gap; Italy 1944–5.

Accredited Battle Honours
Great War: Armentières 1914; Gheluvelt; St Julien; Scarpe 1917; Amiens; Hindenburg Line; Canal du Nord; France and Flanders 1914–18. **Second World War:** Kasserine; Kairouan; Gromballa; Bou Ficha; Monte Piccolo; Capture of Perugia; Arezzo; Traghetto.

Dress
DIFFERENCES: Scarlet dress cap, blue piping and quarter welts; scarlet side cap, blue flaps and peak. Red/yellow/blue striped stable belt, officers' Sam Brownes worn reversed.
REGIMENTAL TIE: Equal red and dark blue stripes, with thin yellow stripes.

Marches
Quick: *Scarlet and Green*. Slow: *The Queen Charlotte.*

Journal
The Scarlet and Green (once a year).

Museum
Kitchener House, Lammascote Rd, Stafford, Staffordshire (tel 0785 45840 ext 4519): open Monday–Friday 0930–1300, 1400–1600 except public holidays.

Regimental Histories
Lunt, J. *The 16th/5th The Queen's Royal Lancers*, Leo Cooper, 1973. Barclay, C. N. *A History of the 16th/5th The Queen's Royal Lancers, 1925–1961*, Gale & Polden, 1963.

Predecessors

16th THE QUEEN'S LANCERS

History
Raised in 1759 as the 16th Light Dragoons, or Burgoyne's Light Horse (16th (The Queen's) Lancers in 1861).
Motto: *Aut cursu aut cominus armis* (Either in the charge or hand to hand).
Regimental Anniversary: Aliwal Day (28 January).
Former Members: Field Marshal Earl Harcourt (1743–1830), commissioned 1759. Field Marshal Sir William Robertson (1860–1935), joined 1877.

Emblazoned Battle Honours
French Revolutionary Wars (1793–1802): Beaumont; Willems. Peninsular War (1808–14): Talavera; Fuentes d'Onor; Salamanca; Vittoria; Nive; Peninsula. Hundred Days (1815): Waterloo. Revolt of Rajah of Bhurtpore (1826): Bhurtpore. First Afghan War (1839–42): Ghuznee 1839; Affghanistan 1839. Gwalior Campaign (1843): Maharajpore. First Sikh War (1845–6): Aliwal; Sobraon. South African War (1899–1902): Relief of Kimberley; Paardeburg; South Africa 1899–1902. Great War: Mons; Le Cateau; Marne 1914; Aisne 1914; Messines 1914; Ypres 1914, 1915; Bellewaarde; Arras 1917; Cambrai 1917; Somme 1918.

Accredited Battle Honours
Great War: Retreat from Mons; Armentières 1914; Gheluvelt; St Julien; Scarpe 1917; Amiens; Hindenburg Line; Canal du Nord; Pursuit to Mons; France and Flanders 1914–18.

Awards
Lieutenant Viscount Fincastle, later Major The Earl of Dunmore DSO MVO (1871–1962) was awarded the Victoria Cross, Tirah Campaign 17 August 1897: gazetted 9 November 1896.

Marches
Quick: *English Patrol*. Slow: *Slow March of the 16th Lancers (Queen Charlotte).*

Allied Regiment in 1914
16th Light Horse, of Canada.

Museum
Kitchener House, Lammascote Rd,

Stafford, Staffordshire (tel 0785 45840 ext 4519): open Monday–Friday 0930–1300, 1400–1600 except public holidays.

Regimental History
Graham, H. *History of the 16th The* *Queen's Light Dragoons (Lancers) 1912–1925*, privately printed, 1926. Graham, H. *History of the 16th The Queen's Light Dragoons (Lancers), 1759–1912*, privately printed, 1912.

5th ROYAL IRISH LANCERS

History
Raised in 1689 as Wynne's Dragoons (disbanded 1799–1858, 5th (Royal Irish) Lancers in 1861, disbanded in 1921 but reconstituted in 1922).
Motto: *Quis separabit* (Who will separate us?)

Emblazoned Battle Honours
War of Spanish Succession (1701–15): Blenheim; Ramillies; Oudenarde; Malplaquet. **Egyptian Campaign** (1885): Suakin 1885. **South African War** (1899–1902): Defence of Ladysmith; South Africa 1899–1902. **Great War:** Mons; Le Cateau; Retreat from Mons; Marne 1914; Aisne 1914; Messines 1914; Ypres 1914, 1915; Cambrai 1917; St Quentin; Pursuit to Mons.

Accredited Battle Honours
Great War: Gheluvelt; St Julien; Bellewaarde; Arras 1917; Scarpe 1917; Somme 1918; Amiens; Hindenburg Line; Canal du Nord; France and Flanders 1914–18.

Awards
Two members of the regiment have been awarded the Victoria Cross: one in the South African War (1899–1902) and one in the Great War. First award: Lieutenant F. B. Dugdale (1877–1901) Derby, South Africa, 3 March 1901: gazetted 17 September 1901.

Marches
Quick: *St Patrick's Day*. Slow: *Let Erin Remember* and *The Harp that once through Tara's Halls*.

Museum
Kitchener House, Lammascote Rd, Stafford, Staffordshire (tel 0785 45840 ext 4519): open Monday–Friday 0930–1300, 1400–1600, except public holidays.

Regimental Histories
Harvey, J. R. *The History of the 5th (Royal Irish) Regiment of Dragoons from 1689 to 1799, afterwards the 5th Royal Irish Lancers from 1858–1921* (completed by H. A. Cape), privately printed, 1923. Willcox, W. T. *Historical Records of the 5th (Royal Irish) Lancers 1689–1906*, privately printed, 1908.

17th/21st LANCERS
Colonel-in-Chief: HRH Princess Alexandra, The Hon Lady Ogilvy GCVO

History
Formed in 1922 by the amalgamation of 17th Lancers (Duke of Cambridge's Own) and 21st Lancers (Empress of India's).
MOTTO: *Or Glory.*
HOME HEADQUARTERS: Prince William of Gloucester Barracks, Grantham, Lincolnshire.
RECRUITMENT AREA: Nottinghamshire, Lincolnshire and South Humberside.
REGIMENTAL ANNIVERSARIES: Khartoum Day (2 September); Balaklava Day (25 October).
FORMER MEMBERS: Field Marshal Sir Richard Hull (1907–89), commissioned 1928.

Emblazoned Battle Honours
Crimean War (1854–5): Alma; Balaklava; Inkerman; Sevastopol. **Indian Mutiny** (1857–8): Central India. **Zulu and Basuto War** (1877–9): South Africa 1879. **Reconquest of the Sudan** (1896–8): Khartoum. **South African War** (1899–1902): South Africa 1900–02. **Great War:** Festubert 1914; Somme 1916, 1918; Morval; Cambrai 1917, 1918; St Quentin; Avre; Hazebrouck; Amiens; Pursuit to Mons; France and Flanders 1914–18; NW Frontier India 1915, 1916. **Second World War:** Tebourba Gap; Kasserine; Fondouk; El Kourzia; Tunis; North Africa; Cassino II; Capture of Perugia; Argenta Gap; Italy 1944–5.

Accredited Battle Honours
Great War: Lys; Hindenburg Line; St Quentin Canal; Beaurevoir. **Second World War:** Bou Arada; Thala; Hammam Lif; Monte Piccolo; Advance to Florence; Argenta Gap; Fossa Cembalina.

Dress
DIFFERENCES: Blue dress cap, white band, piping and quarter welts; white side cap, blue flaps piped yellow. Blue stable belt, twin narrow white stripes.
REGIMENTAL TIE: Blue stripes, thinner silver stripes with central blue line.

Marches
Quick: *The White Lancer.* Slow: *Rienzi.*

Alliances
Lord Strathcona's Horse (Royal Canadians). Associated regular regiment of B (Sherwood Rangers Yeomanry) Squadron, The Royal Yeomanry.

Journal
The White Lancer and the Vedette (once a year – May).

Museum
Belvoir Castle, near Grantham, Lincolnshire (tel 0476 870262): open mid-March to early October Tuesday–Saturday 1100–1800, Sunday 1100–1900; Bank Holiday Mondays 1100–1900.

Record Office
Except officers: Queen's Park, Chester; officers: MS(AODO), London Rd, Stanmore, Middlesex.

Regimental Histories
Blake, F. *The 17th/21st Lancers*, Hamish Hamilton, 1968. ffrench-Blake, R. L. V. *A History of the 17th/21st Lancers, 1922–1929*, Macmillan, 1962.

Predecessors

17th LANCERS
(DUKE OF CAMBRIDGE'S OWN)

History
Raised in 1759 as the 18th Light Dragoons (17th (Duke of Cambridge's Own) Lancers in 1876).
MOTTO: *Or Glory*.
REGIMENTAL ANNIVERSARY: Balaklava Day (25 October).

Emblazoned Battle Honours
Crimean War (1854–5): Alma; Balaclava; Inkerman; Sevastopol. Indian Mutiny (1857–8): Central India. Zulu and Basuto War (1877–9): South Africa 1879. South African War (1899–1902): South Africa 1900–1902. Great War: Festubert 1914; Somme 1916, 1918; Morval; Cambrai 1917, 1918; St Quentin; Avre; Hazebrouck; Amiens; Pursuit to Mons; France and Flanders 1914–18.

Accredited Battle Honours
Great War: Lys; Hindenburg Line; St Quentin Canal; Beaurevoir.

Awards
Five members of the regiment have been awarded the Victoria Cross: three in the Crimean War (1854–5), one in the Indian Mutiny (1857–8) and one in the South African War (1899–1902). First award: Troop-Sergeant-Major J. Berryman, later Major (1825–1896), Balaklava 25 October 1854: gazetted 24 February 1857.

Marches
Quick: *The White Lancer*. Slow: *Occasional Overture*.

Journal
The White Lancer.

Museum
Belvoir Castle, near Grantham, Lincolnshire (tel 0476 870262): open mid-March to early October Tuesday–Saturday 1100–1800, Sunday 1100–1900; Bank Holiday Mondays 1100–1900.

Regimental Histories

Micholls, G. *A History of the 17th Lancers, 1895–1924*, Macmillan, 1931.

Fortescue, Sir John. *A History of the 17th Lancers (Duke of Cambridge's Own)*, Macmillan, 1895 and 1931.

21st LANCERS (EMPRESS OF INDIA'S)

History

Raised in 1759 as the 21st Light Dragoons, or Royal Windsor Foresters (21st Lancers in 1897).

REGIMENTAL ANNIVERSARY: Khartoum Day (2 September).

Emblazoned Battle Honours

Reconquest of the Sudan (1896–8): Khartoum. **Great War:** NW Frontier India 1915, 1916.

Awards

Four members of the regiment have been awarded the Victoria Cross: three at Khartoum (1898) and one in the Great War. First awards: Private T. Byrne (1866–1944), Lieutenant the Hon R. H. L. J. De Montmorency, later Captain (1867–1900) and Captain P. A. Kenna, later Brigadier-General P. A. Kenna DSO (1862–1915), Khartoum 2 September 1898; gazetted 15 November 1898. Brigadier-General Kenna was killed at Gallipoli.

Marches

Quick: *Coburg*. Slow: *The Merry Month of May*.

Journal

The Vedette.

Museum

Belvoir Castle, near Grantham, Lincolnshire (tel 0476 870262): open mid-March to early October Tuesday–Saturday 1100–1800, Sunday 1100–1900; Bank Holiday Mondays 1100–1900.

THE ROYAL TANK REGIMENT
Colonel-in-Chief: HM The Queen

History
Formed in 1917 as the Tank Corps (previously the Heavy Branch of the Machine Gun Corps) (Royal Tank Corps in 1922, Royal Tank Regiment in 1939).

MOTTO: *Fear naught.*

HEADQUARTERS: Bovington Camp, Wareham, Dorset.

RECRUITMENT AREA: See individual regiments (designated battalions to 1939 – some units retained designations until after 1945).

REGIMENTAL ANNIVERSARY: Cambrai Day (20 November).

FORMER MEMBER: Field Marshal Lord Carver (*b*1915), commissioned 1935.

Emblazoned Battle Honours
Great War: Somme 1916, 1918; Arras 1917, 1918; Messines 1917; Ypres 1917; Cambrai 1917; Villers Bretonneux; Amiens; Bapaume 1918; Hindenburg Line; France and Flanders 1916–18. **Second World War:** Rhine; North-West Europe 1940, 1944–5; Abyssinia 1940; Tobruk 1941; El Alamein; North Africa 1940–3; Sicily 1943; Italy 1943–5; Greece 1941; Burma 1942. **Korean War** (1950–3): Korea 1951–3.

Accredited Battle Honours
Great War: St Quentin; Epéhy; Selle; Gaza; Somme 1918. **Second World War:** Arras Counter-attack; Calais 1940; St Omer-La Bassée; Somme 1940; Odon; Caen; Bourguébus Ridge; Mont Pinçon; Falaise; Nederrijn; Scheldt; Venlo Pocket; Rhineland; Bremen; Sidi Barrani; Beda Fomm; Sidi Suleiman; Sidi Rezegh 1941; Belhamed; Gazala; Cauldron; Knightsbridge; Defence of Alamein Line; Alam el Halfa; Mareth; Akarit; Fondouk; El Kourzia; Medjez Plain; Tunis; Primosole Bridge; Gerbini; Adrano; The Sangro; Salerno; Volturno Crossing; Garigliano Crossing; Anzio; Advance to Florence; Gothic Line; Coriano; Lamone Crossing; Rimini Line; Argenta Gap.

Awards
Six members of the regiment have been awarded the Victoria Cross: four in the Great War and two in the Second World War. First award: Captain C. Robertson (1890–1917) Ypres 30 September and 4 October 1917: gazetted posthumously 18 December 1917. Lieutenant St J G. Young (1921–44) was awarded the George Cross Italy 24 July 1944: gazetted posthumously 20 July 1945. Private F. Naughton, later Captain (*b*1915) was awarded the Empire Gallantry Medal (later exchanged for the George Cross) Moshii, River Indrayani, 5 August 1936: gazetted 1 February 1937.

Memorials

Hyde Park Corner, London, by F. Derwent Wood RA (Machine Gun Corps 1914–18); Pozières, France, first use of tanks in war (Flers-Courcelette, September 1916).

Dress

DIFFERENCES: Black beret, brown/red/green hackle behind badge for ceremonials. Brown/red/green striped stable belt. White tank emblem on upper right arm. Black overalls, footwear, and webbing. Black Sam Browne and ash walking-stick for officers. Different colour shoulder flash for each regiment.
REGIMENTAL TIE: Equal brown/red/green stripes (at one time, unequal stripes for other ranks).

Marches

Quick: *My Boy Willie*. Slow: *Royal Tank Regiment*.

Alliances

12e Régiment Blindé du Canada; 1st Armoured Regiment RAAC, of Australia; Royal New Zealand Armoured Corps; 2nd Lancers, of India; 13 Lancers, of Pakistan.

Journal

Tank (four times a year).

Museum

The Tank Museum, Bovington Camp, Wareham, Dorset, Dorsetshire (tel 0929 462721 ext 3329 and 3463): open daily 1000–1700 (closed two weeks over Christmas and the New Year).

Benevolent Fund

RTR Benevolent Fund, HQ RAC Centre, Bovington Camp, Wareham, Dorset.

Record Office

Except officers: Queen's Park, Chester; officers: MS(AODO), London Rd, Stanmore, Middlesex.

Regimental Histories

Forty, G. *A Pictorial History Royal Tank Regiment*, Spellmount, 1988. Macksey, K. *The Tanks: The History of the Royal Tank Regiment 1945–1975*, Arms & Armour Press, 1979. Liddell Hart, B. H. *The Tanks: The History of the Royal Tank Regiment 1914–1945* (2 vols), Cassell, 1959. Macksey, K. *To the Green Fields Beyond*, RHQ, 1965. Chadwick, K. *The Royal Tank Regiment*, Leo Cooper, 1970.

1st ROYAL TANK REGIMENT

History

Raised in 1916 as A Company, Heavy Branch, Machine Gun Corps (1st Royal Tank Regiment in 1939).
RECRUITMENT AREA: Merseyside, Blackburn, Burnham, Oldham, Leeds, Halifax and Wakefield.

March
Quick: *Lippe Detmold.*

Regimental History
The First Royal Tank Regiment in Hong Kong, 1957–1958, Cathay.

2nd ROYAL TANK REGIMENT

History
Raised in 1916 as B Company, Heavy Branch, Machine Gun Corps (2nd Royal Tank Regiment in 1939).
RECRUITMENT AREA: Cambridgeshire, Bedfordshire, Norfolk, Suffolk, East Kent and London.

March
Quick: *Saffron.*

Association
Associated regular regiment of HQ (Westminster Dragoons) Squadron, The Royal Yeomanry.

Regimental History
Chadwick, K. *Seconds Out!*, published privately, TPDW, HQ RAC Centre, n.d.

3rd ROYAL TANK REGIMENT

History
Raised in 1916 as C Company, Heavy Branch, Machine Gun Corps (3rd Royal Tank Regiment in 1939, amalgamated with 6th Royal Tank Regiment in 1960).
RECRUITMENT AREA: Cornwall, Devon, Dorset, Somerset and Avon.

March
Quick: *On the Quarterdeck.*

Association
Associated regular regiment of (Royal Devon Yeomanry) Squadron, The Royal Wessex Yeomanry.

4th ROYAL TANK REGIMENT

History
Raised in 1916 as D Company, Heavy Branch, Machine Gun Corps (4th Royal Tank Regiment in 1939, amalgamated with 7th Royal Tank Regiment in 1960).
RECRUITMENT AREA: Scotland.

March
Quick: *Blue Flash.*

Association
Associated regular regiment of NH (Northumberland Hussars) Squadron, The Queen's Own Yeomanry.

Regimental Histories
Jolly, A. *Blue Flash: The Story of an Armoured Regiment*, privately printed, 1952.
Burges-Short, H. G. R. *A Historical Record of the 4th Battalion Royal Tank Corps*, Gale & Polden, 1925.

ROYAL REGIMENT OF ARTILLERY
Captain-General: HM The Queen

History

Raised in 1716 (Royal Horse Artillery raised in 1793).

MOTTOES: *Ubique* (Everywhere); *Quo fas et gloria ducunt* (Wherever right and glory lead).

HEADQUARTERS: Government House, Woolwich New Road, London.

RECRUITMENT AREA: Nationwide.

REGIMENTAL ANNIVERSARY: Foundation Day (26 May).

FORMER MEMBERS: Field Marshal Sir Hew Ross (1779–1868), commissioned 1795; Field Marshal Sir George Pollock (1786–1872), commissioned 1803; Field Marshal Sir Richard Dacres (1799–1886), commissioned 1817; Field Marshal Earl Roberts VC (1832–1914), commissioned 1851; Field Marshal HRH The Duke of Connaught and Strathearn (1850–1942), commissioned 1868; Field Marshal Lord Milne (1866–1948), commissioned 1885; Field Marshal Sir Archibald Montgomery-Massingberd (1871–1947), commissioned 1891; Field Marshal Lord Ironside (1880–1959), commissioned 1899; Field Marshal Viscount Alanbrooke (1883–1963), commissioned 1902; Field Marshal Sir Geoffrey Baker (1912–80), commissioned 1932.

Battle Honours

The regiment does not display honours, but on parade the guns are accorded the same ceremony as the colours of a regiment. Many individual batteries have been awarded honour titles: these mainly commemorate actions in which the battery concerned played a particularly notable part – for example, 19 (Gibraltar 1779–83) Battery, which is the oldest battery still serving in the regiment and was awarded this honour title for its part in the great siege of Gibraltar. There are also honour titles linking the battery concerned with a famous commander during a period or an incident of exceptional service – for example, G Battery (Mercer's Troop) RHA – and others linked with a special honour – for example, the grant of the title 'The Chestnut Troop' to A Battery RHA by the late King Edward VII in 1902 to mark its distinguished service.

Awards

Sixty-two members of the regiment have been awarded the Victoria Cross: nine in the Crimean War (1854–5), eighteen in the Indian Mutiny (1857–8), three in the Third Maori War (1863–6), two in the Second Afghan War (1878–80), one in the Sudan (1885), nine in the South African War (1899–1902), seventeen in the Great War and three in the Second World War. First award: Brevet Lieutenant-Colonel C. Dickson CB (1807–1904) Sevastopol 17 October 1854: gazetted 23 June 1857. Three members of the regiment have been awarded the George Cross: all in the Second World War. First award: Gunner H. H.

Reed (1911–41), North Sea 21 June 1941: gazetted posthumously 23 September 1941. Bombadier A. Lungley, later Battery Sergeant-Major (1905–89) was awarded the Empire Gallantry Medal (later exchanged for the George Cross), Quetta earthquake 31 May–1 June 1935: gazetted 19 November 1935.

Memorials
Beside the parade ground of the RA Barracks, Woolwich, London, by John Bell (Crimean War 1854–5); Repository Rd, Woolwich, London, by Count Gleichen (Zulu and Afghan Wars); The Mall, St James's Park, London, by W. R. Colton (South African War 1899–1902); Hyde Park Corner, London, by C. S. Jagger (Great War, Second World War); Larkhill Garrison Church, Wiltshire (1946–68).

Dress
DIFFERENCES: Blue dress cap, scarlet band. Red stable belt, blue central band and yellow centre stripe (RHA light blue stable belt, narrow yellow centre stripe). REGIMENTAL TIES: Crimson zig-zags on navy ground.

Marches
Quick: *The RA Quick March*. Slow: *Royal Artillery Slow March*. Trot past: *The Keel Row*. Canter past: *Bonnie Dundee*.

Alliances
The Royal Regiment of Canadian Artillery; The Royal Regiment of Australian Artillery; The Royal Regiment of New Zealand Artillery; Regiment of Artillery of India; Artillery of Pakistan; The Sri Lanka Artillery; Malaysian Artillery; The Singapore Voluntary Artillery; The Fiji Artillery.

Allied Regiment in 1914
The Royal Canadian Artillery.

Journals
Gunner (twelve times a year); *Royal Artillery Journal* (twice a year).

Museums
RA Regimental Museum, Old Royal Military Academy, Woolwich, London (tel 081-854 2242 ext 5628): open Monday–Friday 1230–1630, weekends 1400–1600. The Museum of Artillery in The Rotunda, Repository Rd, Woolwich, London (tel 081-316 5402): open April–September Monday–Friday 1200–1700, Saturday, Sunday 1300–1700; October–March closing 1600; closed Good Friday, Christmas and New Year's Day.

Record Office
Except officers: RA Manning and Records Office, Imphal Barracks, York; officers: MS(AODO), London Rd, Stanmore, Middlesex.

Regimental Histories

Hughes, Major-General B. P. (ed.) *The History of the Royal Artillery 1919–1939*, Royal Artillery Institution, 1978; Brassey's, 1991. Duncan, Captain F. *The History of the Royal Regiment of Artillery* (2 vols.); vol. 1, to the Peace of 1783; vol. 2, to 1815, John Murray, 1872 and 1873. Hime, Lieutenant-Colonel H. W. L. *History of the Royal Regiment of Artillery 1815–1853*, Longmans Green, 1908. Jocelyn, Colonel J. R. J. *The History of the Royal Artillery (Crimean Period)*, John Murray, 1911. Jocelyn, Colonel J. R. J. *The History of the Royal and Indian Artillery in the Mutiny of 1857*, John Murray, 1915. *History of the Royal Artillery from the Indian Mutiny to the Great War* (3 vols.); vol. 1, *1860–99*, Sir Charles Calwell; vol. 2, *1899–1914*, Sir John Headlam; vol. 3, *campaign maps*; Royal Artillery Institution, 1931 and 1937. Farndale, General Sir Martin. *History of the Royal Regiment of Artillery: Western Front 1914–1918*, Royal Artillery Institution, 1986. Farndale, General Sir Martin. *The Forgotten Fronts and the Home Base, 1914–1918*, Royal Artillery Institution, 1989.

CORPS OF ROYAL ENGINEERS
Colonel-in-Chief: HM The Queen

History
Raised: Officers: 1716 Royal Artillery and Corps of Engineers constituted on
separate establishments, 1787 Corps of Royal Engineers. Soldiers: 1772 Soldier
Artificers, 1812–13 Royal Sappers and Miners, 1856 incorporated into Corps
of Royal Engineers.
Mottoes: *Ubique* (Everywhere); *Quo fas et gloria ducunt* (Where right and glory
lead).
Headquarters: Brompton Barracks, Chatham, Kent.
Recruitment Area: Nationwide.
Former Members: Field Marshal Sir John Lintorn Simmons (1823–1903),
commissioned 1837; Major-General Charles Gordon (1833–85); Field Marshal
Lord Napier of Magdala (1810–90), commissioned 182?; Field Marshal Lord
Nicholson (1845–1918), commissioned 1865; Field Marshal Earl Kitchener of
Khartoum (1850–1916), commissioned 1871 – statue Horse Guards Parade,
London; plaque 2 Carlton Gardens, London.

Awards
Forty-six members of the corps have been awarded the Victoria Cross: eight
in the Crimean War (1854–5), eight in the Indian Mutiny (1857–8), two in the
Bhutan Campaign (1865), one in the Ashantee Campaign (1874), one in the
Zulu and Basuto War (1878–9), two in the Second Afghan War (1878–80), one
in the Hunza Campaign (1891), two in the Mohmand Campaign (1898), two
in the South African War (1899–1902), seventeen in the Great War and two in
the Second World War. First award: Lieutenant W. O. Lennox, later
Lieutenant-General Sir Wilbraham Lennox KCB (1830–97), Rifle Pits, Crimea,
20 November 1854: gazetted 24 February 1857. Eleven members of the corps
have been awarded the George Cross: ten in the Second World War and one
in 1958. First awards: Lieutenant R. Davies (1900–1975) and Sapper G. Wylie
(*b* 1908): both gazetted 30 September 1940. Six members of the corps have been
awarded the Empire Gallantry Medal (later exchanged for the George Cross):
one in 1914, one in 1928 and four in 1940. First award: Major H. E. Burton
(1864–1944) North Sea 1 November 1914: gazetted 26 June 1924.

Dress
Corps Tie: Thin/thick/thin dark red stripes on navy ground.

March
Quick: *Wings*.

Alliances

Military Engineering Branch, of Canada; The Corps of Royal Australian Engineers; The Corps of Royal New Zealand Engineers; Indian Engineers; Pakistan Engineers; The Sri Lanka Engineers; Malaysian Engineer Corps; Zambia Corps of Engineers; The Corps of Fiji Engineers.

Affiliated Regiment

The Queen's Gurkha Engineers.

Journals

The Royal Engineers Journal (three times a year); *The Sapper* (six times a year).

Museum

Prince Arthur Rd, Gillingham, Kent (tel 0634 406397): open Tuesday–Friday 1000–1700, Sunday 1130–1700: postal address Royal Engineers Museum, Brompton Barracks, Chatham, Kent ME4 4UG.

Record Office

Except officers: Kentigern House, Brown St, Glasgow; officers: MS(AODO), London Rd, Stanmore, Middlesex.

Corps Histories

Boyd, D. *The Royal Engineers*, Leo Cooper, 1975. *History of the Corps of Royal Engineers* (10 vols.): vol. 1 (*up to 1860*) and vol. 2 (*1860–85*), Major-General W. Porter, Longmans Green, 1889; vol. 3 (*1885–1912*), Colonel Sir Charles Watson, Royal Engineers Institution, 1914; vol. 4 (*1885–1902*), Brigadier-General W. B. Brown, 1952, Royal Engineers Institution; vol. 5 (*1914–19*), 1952, Royal Engineers Institution; vol. 6 (*1914–1919*), 1952, Royal Engineers Institution; vol. 7 (*1918–1938*), 1952, Royal Engineers Institution; vol. 8 (*1938–48*), R. P. Pakenham-Walsh, Royal Engineers Institution; vol. 10 (*1948–60*), Royal Engineers Institution.

ROYAL CORPS OF SIGNALS
Colonel-in-Chief: HRH The Princess Royal GCVO

History
Formed in 1920 from the Signals Service of the Corps of Royal Engineers.
MOTTO: *Certa cito* (Swift and sure).
HEADQUARTERS: 56 Regency St, London, SW1.
RECRUITMENT AREA: Nationwide.

Awards
Signalman K. Smith (1920–45) was awarded the George Cross Ist Island, Adriatic, 10 January 1945: gazetted posthumously 19 October 1945.

Dress
DIFFERENCES: Dark blue dress cap, dark blue beret; narrow light blue and dark green stripes on dark blue stable belt.
CORPS TIE: Thin silver and green stripes on navy ground.

Marches
Quick: *The Royal Signals March* based on *Begone Dull Care* and *Newcastle*. Slow: *HRH The Princess Royal*.

Alliances
Communications and Electronics Branch, of Canada; The Royal Australian Corps of Signals; Royal New Zealand Corps of Signals; Corps of Signals, of India; Signal Corps, of Pakistan; The Signal Corps, of Sri Lanka; Malaysian Signal Corps; Zambia Corps of Signals.

Affiliated Regiment
Queen's Gurkha Signals.

Journals
The Royal Signals Journal (three times a year); *The Wire* (six times a year).

Association
Royal Signals Association.

Museum
Blandford Camp, Blandford Forum, Dorset (tel 0258 452581 ext 2248): open Monday–Friday 1000–1700, June–September Saturday, Sunday 1000–1600.

Record Office
Except officers: Kentigern House, Brown St, Glasgow; officers: MS(AODO), London Rd, Stanmore, Middlesex.

Corps Histories
Warner, P. *The Vital Link: The Story of the Royal Signals, 1945–1985*, Leo Cooper, 1985. Nalder, R. F. H. *The History of British Army Signals in the Second World War*, Royal Signals Institution, 1953. Priestley, R. E. *The Signal Service in the European War, 1914–1918*, Mackay, 1921. Nalder, R. F. H. *The Royal Corps of History: A History of its Antecedents and Development (c1800–1955)*, Royal Signals Institution, 1958.

GRENADIER GUARDS
(The Guards Division)
Colonel-in-Chief: HM The Queen

History
Raised in 1656 as His Majestie's Regiment of Guards (Wentworth's Regiment) (Grenadier Guards in 1815). Two battalions.
HEADQUARTERS: Wellington Barracks, Birdcage Walk, London.
RECRUITMENT AREA: England.
FORMER MEMBERS: Field Marshal The Earl of Cavan (1865–1946), commissioned 1885; Field Marshal Viscount Gort VC (1886–1946), commissioned 1905.
REGIMENTAL ANNIVERSARY: St George's Day (23 April).

Emblazoned Battle Honours
Defence of Tangier (1662–80): Tangier 1680. War of the League of Augsburg (1689–97): Namur 1695. War of Spanish Succession (1701–15): Gibraltar 1704–5; Blenheim; Ramillies; Oudenarde; Malplaquet. War of Austrian Succession (1740–48): Dettingen. French Revolutionary Wars (1793–1802): Lincelles; Egmont op Zee. Peninsular War (1808–14): Corunna; Barrosa; Nive; Peninsula. Hundred Days (1815): Waterloo. Crimean War (1854–5): Alma; Inkerman; Sevastopol. Revolt of Arabi Pasha (1882): Tel-el-Kebir. First Sudan War (1882–4): Egypt. Egyptian Campaign (1885): Suakin 1885. Reconquest of the Sudan (1896–8): Khartoum. South African War (1899–1902): Modder River; South Africa 1899–1902. Great War: Marne 1914; Aisne 1914; Ypres 1914, 1917; Loos; Somme 1916, 1918; Cambrai 1917, 1918; Arras 1918; Hazebrouck; Hindenburg Line; France and Flanders 1914–18. Second World War: Dunkirk 1940; Mont Pinçon; Nijmegen; Rhine; Mareth; Medjez Plain; Salerno; Monte Camino; Anzio; Gothic Line.

Accredited Battle Honours
Great War: Mons; Retreat from Mons; Langemarck 1914; Gheluvelt; Nonne Bosschen; Neuve Chapelle; Aubers; Festubert 1915; Ginchy; Flers-Courcelette; Morval; Pilckem; Menin Road; Poelcapelle; Passchendaele; St Quentin; Bapaume 1918; Lys; Albert 1918; Scarpe 1918; Havrincourt; Canal du Nord; Selle; Sambre. Second World War: Dyle; Cagny; Reichswald; North-West Europe 1940, 1944–5; North Africa 1942–3; Volturno Crossing; Battaglia; Italy 1943–5.

Awards
Thirteen members of the regiment have been awarded the Victoria Cross: four

in the Crimean War (1854–5), seven in the Great War and two in the Second World War. First awards: Private A. Palmer (1819–92) and Brevet Major Sir Charles Russell (1826–83), Inkerman 5 November 1854: gazetted 24 February 1857. Captain R. L. Nairac (1948–77) was awarded the George Cross Republic of Ireland 15 May 1977: gazetted posthumously 13 February 1979.

Dress

DIFFERENCES: Bearskin with white plume on left; blue dress cap, red band and piping. Blue/red/blue striped stable belt. Buttons worn singly.
REGIMENTAL TIE: Dull red and navy stripes.

Marches

Quick: *The British Grenadiers* and *The Grenadiers' March*. Slow: *Scipio* and *The Duke of York*.

Alliances

The Canadian Grenadier Guards; 1st Battalion The Royal Australian Regiment.

Journal

The Grenadier Gazette (once a year).

Museum

Guards Museum, Wellington Barracks, Birdcage Walk, London (tel 071-930 4466 ext 3271): open daily except Friday 1000–1600.

Record Office

Except officers: Imphal Barracks, York; officers: MS(AODO), London Rd, Stanmore, Middlesex.

Regimental Histories

Whitworth, R. H. *The Grenadier Guards*, Leo Cooper, 1974. Ponsonby, Sir Frederick. *The Grenadiers Guards in the Great War of 1914–1918*, Macmillan, 1920. Nicholson, N., and Forbes, P. *The Grenadier Guards in the War of 1939–1945* (2 vols.), Gale & Polden, 1949.

COLDSTREAM GUARDS
(The Guards Division)
Colonel-in-Chief: HM The Queen

History
Raised in 1650 as Monck's Regiment of Foot (2nd or Coldstream Guards in 1670). Two battalions.

MOTTO: *Nulli Secundus* (Second to None).

REGIMENTAL HEADQUARTERS: Wellington Barracks, Birdcage Walk, London.

RECRUITMENT AREA: England, with a preference for those counties passed through during the Regiment's march in 1660 from Coldstream to London.

PATRON SAINT: St George (George's Day, 23 April).

Emblazoned Battle Honours
Defence of Tangier (1662–80): Tangier 1680. **War of the League of Augsburg** (1689–97): Namur 1695. **War of Spanish Succession** (1701–15): Gibraltar 1704–5; Oudenarde; Malplaquet. **War of Austrian Succession** (1740–8): Dettingen. **French Revolutionary Wars** (1793–1802): Lincelles. **Peninsular War** (1808–14): Talavera; Barrosa; Fuentes d'Onor; Salamanca; Nive; Peninsula. **Hundred Days** (1815): Waterloo. **Crimean War** (1854–5): Alma; Inkerman; Sevastopol. **Revolt of Arabi Pasha** (1882): Tel-el-Kebir. **First Sudan War** (1882–4): Egypt 1882. **Egyptian Campaign** (1885): Suakin 1885. **South African War** (1899–1902): Modder River; South Africa 1899–1902. **Great War:** Retreat from Mons; Marne 1914; Aisne 1914; Ypres 1914, 1917; Loos; Somme 1916, 1918; Cambrai 1917, 1918; Arras 1918; Hazebrouck; Hindenburg Line. **Second World War:** Dunkirk 1940; Mont Pinçon; Rhineland; North-West Europe 1940, 1944–5; Sidi Barrani; Tobruk 1941, 1942; Tunis; Salerno; Monte Ornito; Italy 1943–5. The Sphinx superscribed 'Egypt' is also borne on the Queen's and Regimental Colours.

Accredited Battle Honours
Great War: Mons; Langemarck 1914; Gheluvelt; Nonne Bosschen; Givenchy 1914; Neuve Chapelle; Aubers; Festubert 1915; Mount Sorrel; Flers-Courcelette; Morval; Pilckem; Menin Road; Poelcapelle; Passchendaele; St Quentin; Bapaume 1918; Lys; Albert 1918; Scarpe 1918; Drocourt-Quéant; Havrincourt; Canal du Nord; Selle; Sambre; France and Flanders 1914–18. **Second World War:** Dyle; Defence of Escaut; Cagny; Quarry Hill; Estry; Heppen; Nederrijn; Venraij; Meihel; Roer; Reichswald; Cleve; Goch; Moyland; Hochwald; Rhine; Lingen; Uelzen; Egyptian Frontier 1940; Halfaya 1941; Msus; Knightsbridge; Defence of Alamein Line; Medenine; Mareth; Longstop

Hill 1942; Sbiba; Steamroller Farm; Hammam Lif; North Africa 1940–3; Battipaglia; Cappezano; Volturno Crossing; Monte Piccolo; Monte Camino; Calabretto; Garigliano Crossing; Capture of Perugia; Arezzo; Advance to Florence; Monte Domini; Catarelto Ridge; Argenta Gap.

Awards

Thirteen members of the regiment have been awarded the Victoria Cross: four in the Crimean War (1854–5), seven in the Great War and two in the Second World War. First award: Brevet Major G. L. Goodlake, later Lieutenant-General (1832–90), Windmill Corner, Crimea, 28 October 1854: gazetted 24 February 1857. Acting Brigadier A. F. C. Nicholls (1911–44) was awarded the George Cross Albania 11 February 1944: gazetted posthumously 1 March 1946.

Dress

DIFFERENCES: Bearskin with red plume on right; forage cap, white band and piping. Blue/red/blue striped stable belt. Buttons worn in pairs.
BRIGADE TIE: Guards red and navy stripes.

Marches

Quick: *Milanollo*. Slow: *Figaro*.

Alliances and Affiliations

Governor-General's Foot Guards, of Canada; 2nd/4th Battalion, The Royal Australian Regiment; HMS *Brilliant*.

Journal

Coldstream Gazette (once a year).

Museums

Guards Museum, Wellington Barracks, Birdcage Walk, London (tel 071-930 4466 ext 3271): open daily except Friday, 1000–1600; also a small museum in Coldstream.

Record Office

Except officers: Imphal Barracks, York; officers: MS(AODO), London Rd, Stanmore, Middlesex.

Regimental Histories

Crichton, Colonel R. J. V. *The Coldstream Guards 1946–70.* MacKinnon, Colonel. *Origin and Services of The Coldstream Guards* (2 vols.). Davies, G. *The Early History of The Coldstream Guards.* Ross-of-Bladensburg CB, Lieutenant-Colonel. *A History of The Coldstream Guards.* Hall, Sir John. *The Coldstream Guards 1885–1914,* Clarendon Press, 1929. Ross-of-Bladensburg, Sir John. *The Coldstream Guards 1914–1918* (2 vols.), OUP, 1928. Howard, M. E., and Sparrow, J. *The Coldstream Guards, 1920–1946,* OUP, 1951.

SCOTS GUARDS
(The Guards Division)
Colonel-in-Chief: HM The Queen

History
Raised in 1642 as Argyle's Regiment (re-raised as Scottish Footguards 1661), brought on to English establishment as Scotch Guards in 1686, (Scots Fusilier Guards in 1831, Scots Guards in 1877). Two battalions.
HEADQUARTERS: Wellington Barracks, Birdcage Walk, London.
RECRUITMENT AREA: Nationwide.
REGIMENTAL ANNIVERSARY: St Andrew's Day (30 November).
FORMER MEMBER: Field Marshal Lord Methuen (1843–1932), commissioned 1864.

Emblazoned Battle Honours
War of the League of Augsburg (1689–97): Namur 1695. **War of Austrian Succession** (1740–8): Dettingen. **French Revolutionary Wars** (1793–1802): Lincelles. **Peninsular War** (1808–14): Talavera; Barrosa; Fuentes d'Onor; Salamanca; Nive; Peninsula. **Hundred Days** (1815): Waterloo. **Crimean War** (1854–5): Alma; Inkerman; Sevastopol. **Revolt of Arabi Pasha** (1882): Tel-el-Kebir. **First Sudan War** (1882–4): Egypt 1882. **Egyptian Campaign** (1885): Suakin 1885. **South African War** (1899–1902): Modder River; South Africa 1899–1902. **Great War:** Retreat from Mons; Marne 1914; Aisne 1914; Ypres 1914, 1917; Festubert 1915; Loos; Somme 1916, 1918; Cambrai 1917, 1918; Hindenburg Line; France and Flanders 1914–18. **Second World War:** Quarry Hill; Rhineland; North-West Europe 1944–5; Gazala; Medenine; Djebel Bou Aoukaz 1943; North Africa 1941–3; Monte Camino; Anzio; Italy 1943–5. **Falklands War** (1982): Falkland Islands 1982. The Sphinx superscribed 'Egypt' is also borne on the Queen's and regimental colours.

Accredited Battle Honours
Great War: Langemarck 1914; Gheluvelt; Nonne Bosschen; Givenchy 1914; Neuve Chapelle; Aubers; Flers-Courcelette; Morval; Pilckem; Poelcapelle; Passchendaele; St Quentin; Albert 1918; Bapaume 1918; Arras 1918; Drocourt-Quéant; Havrincourt; Canal du Nord; Selle; Sambre. **Second World War:** Stien; Norway 1940; Mont Pinçon; Estry; Venlo Pocket; Reichswald; Cleve; Moyland; Hochwald; Rhine; Lingen; Uelzen; Halfaya 1941; Sidi Suleiman; Tobruk 1941; Knightsbridge; Defence of Alamein Line; Tadjera Khir; Medjez Plain; Grich el Oued; Salerno; Battipaglia; Volturno Crossing; Rochetta e Croce; Campoleone; Carroceto; Trasimene Line; Advance to Florence; Monte

San Michele; Catarelto Ridge; Argenta Gap; Falklands War (1982): Tumbledown Mountain.

Awards
Eleven members of the regiment have been awarded the Victoria Cross: five in the Crimean War (1854–5), five in the Great War and one in the Second World War. First award: Brevet Major R. J. Loyd-Lindsay, later Brigadier-General Lord Wantage KCB (1832–1901), Alma 20 September 1854 and Inkerman 5 November 1854: gazetted 24 February 1857.

Dress
DIFFERENCES: Bearskin without plume; blue dress cap red/white/blue diced band. Blue/red/blue striped stable belt. Buttons worn in threes. Feather bonnet and Royal Stuart tartan for pipers. Order of the Thistle rank stars for officers. REGIMENTAL TIE: Dull red and navy stripes.

Marches
Quick: *The Highland Laddie* (known by regimental custom as *Hielan' Laddie*). Slow: *The Garb of Old Gaul*. There is also a pipe march for each company.

Alliance
3rd Battalion The Royal Australian Regiment.

Journal
Scots Guards' Magazine (once a year).

Museum
Wellington Barracks, Birdcage Walk, London (tel 071-930 4466 ext 3271): open daily except Friday 1000–1600.

Record Office
Except officers: Imphal Barracks, York; officers: MS(AODO), London Rd, Stanmore, Middlesex.

Regimental Histories
Goodings, A. *The Scots Guards*, Leo Cooper, 1960. Petre, F. L., Ewart, W. and Lowther, Sir Cecil. *The Scots Guards in the Great War*, John Murray, 1925. Maurice, Sir Frederick. *The History of the Scots Guards* (2 vols.), Chatto & Windus, 1934. Erskine, the Hon. N. H. *The Scots Guards 1919–1955*.

IRISH GUARDS
(The Guards Division)
Colonel-in-Chief: HM The Queen

History
Raised in 1900.
HEADQUARTERS: Wellington Barracks, Birdcage Walk, London.
RECRUITMENT AREA: Ireland.
REGIMENTAL ANNIVERSARY: St Patrick's Day (17 March).
FORMER MEMBER: Field Marshal Earl Alexander of Tunis (1891–1969), commissioned 1917.

Emblazoned Battle Honours
Great War: Retreat from Mons; Marne 1914; Aisne 1914; Ypres 1914, 1917; Festubert 1915; Loos; Somme 1916, 1918; Cambrai 1917, 1918; Hazebrouck; Hindenburg Line. **Second World War:** Norway 1940; Boulogne 1940; Mont Pinçon; Neerpelt; Nijmegen; Rhineland; North-West Europe 1944–5; Djebel Bou Aoukaz 1943; North Africa 1943; Anzio.

Accredited Battle Honours
Great War: Mons; Langemarck 1914; Gheluvelt; Nonne Bosschen; Flers-Courcelette; Morval; Pilckem; Poelcapelle; Passchendaele; St Quentin; Lys; Albert 1918; Bapaume 1918; Arras 1918; Scarpe 1918; Drocourt-Quéant; Canal du Nord; Selle; Sambre; France and Flanders 1914–18. **Second World War:** Pothus; Cagny; Aam; Hochwald; Rhine; Bentheim; Medjez Plain; Aprilia; Carroceto; Italy 1943–4.

Awards
Six members of the regiment have been awarded the Victoria Cross: four in the Great War and two in the Second World War. First award: Lance-Corporal M. O'Leary, later Major (1888–1952), Cuinchy, France, 1 February 1915: gazetted 18 February 1915.

Dress
DIFFERENCES: Bearskin with St Patrick's plume on right side; blue dress cap, green band and piping. Blue/red/blue striped stable belt. Buttons worn in fours.
REGIMENTAL TIE: Dull red and navy stripes.

Mascot
Wolfhound.

Marches
Quick: *St Patrick's Day*. Slow: *Let Erin Remember*.

Alliance
2nd/4th Battalion The Royal Australian Regiment.

Journal
Irish Guards Journal (once a year).

Museum
Guards Museum, Wellington Barracks, Birdcage Walk, London (tel 071-930 4466 ext 3271): open daily except Friday 1000–1600.

Record Office
Except officers: Imphal Barracks, York; officers: MS(AODO), London Rd, Stanmore, Middlesex.

Regimental Histories
Verney, P. *The Micks: The Story of the Irish Guards*, Peter Davies, 1970. Kipling, R. *The Irish Guards in the Great War* (2 vols.), Macmillan, 1923. Fitzgerald, D. J. L. *History of the Irish Guards in the Second World War*, Gale & Polden, 1949.

WELSH GUARDS
(The Guards Division)
Colonel-in-Chief: HM The Queen

History
Raised in 1915. One battalion.
HEADQUARTERS: Wellington Barracks, Birdcage Walk, London.
RECRUITMENT AREA: Wales and Border Counties.
REGIMENTAL ANNIVERSARY: St David's Day (1 March).

Emblazoned Battle Honours
Great War: Loos; Ginchy; Flers-Courcelette; Morval; Pilckem; Poelcapelle; Cambrai 1917, 1918; Bapaume 1918; Canal du Nord; Sambre. **Second World War:** Defence of Arras; Boulogne 1940; Mont Pinçon; Brussels; Hechtel; Fondouk; Hammam Lif; Monte Ornito; Monte Piccolo; Battaglia. **Falklands War** (1982): Falkland Islands 1982.

Accredited Battle Honours
Great War: Somme 1916, 1918; Ypres 1917; Passchendaele; Arras 1918; Albert 1918; Drocourt-Quéant; Hindenburg Line; Havrincourt; Selle; France and Flanders 1915–18. **Second World War:** St Omer-La Bassée; Bourguébus Ridge; Cagny; Nederrijn; Rhineland; Lingen; North-West Europe 1940, 1944–5; Djebel el Rhorab; Tunis; North Africa 1943; Liri Valley; Capture of Perugia; Arezzo; Advance to Florence; Gothic Line; Italy 1944–5.

Awards
Two members of the regiment have been awarded the Victoria Cross: one in the Great War and one in the Second World War. First award: Sergeant R. Bye (1889–1962) Yser Canal, Belgium, 31 July 1917: gazetted 6 September 1917.

Dress
DIFFERENCES: Bearskin with white/green/white plume on left side; blue dress cap, black band. Blue/red/blue striped stable belt. Buttons worn in fives.
REGIMENTAL TIE: Blue/red/blue.

Marches
Quick: *Rising of the Lark*. Slow: *Men of Harlech*.

Affiliations
5th/7th Battalion The Royal Australian Regiment; HMS *Andromeda*.

Journal
Welsh Guards Regimental Magazine (once a year).

Museum
Guards Museum, Wellington Barracks, Birdcage Walk, London (tel 071-930 4466 ext 3271): open daily except Friday 1000–1600.

Record Office
Except officers: Imphal Barracks, York; officers: MS(AODO), London Rd, Stanmore, Middlesex.

Regimental Histories
Royle, T. *Anatomy of a Regiment*, Michael Joseph, 1990. Rettallack, J. *The Welsh Guards*, Warne, 1981. Dudley Ward, C. H. *History of the Welsh Guards*, John Murray, 1920. Ellis, L. F. *Welsh Guards at War*, Gale & Polden, 1946. All available from RHQ.

THE ROYAL SCOTS
(THE ROYAL REGIMENT)
(The Scottish Division)
Colonel-in-Chief: HRH The Princess Royal GCVO

History
Raised in 1633 by Sir John Hepburn by Royal Warrant granted by Charles I
for service in France, and returned to England in 1661 (known as Hepburn's
Douglas's and Dumbarton's Regiment until given the title The Royal Regiment
of Foot in 1679. One regular battalion.

MOTTO: *Nemo me impune lacessit* (No one provokes me with impunity).

HEADQUARTERS: The Castle, Edinburgh.

RECRUITMENT AREA: The Lothians and that part of Borders which was
Peebleshire.

REGIMENTAL ANNIVERSARY: Foundation Day (28 March).

Emblazoned Battle Honours
Defence of Tangier (1662–80): Tangier 1680. **War of the League of Augsburg**
(1689–97): Namur 1695. **War of Spanish Succession** (1701–15): Blenheim;
Ramillies; Oudenarde; Malplaquet. **Seven Years War** (1756–63): Louisburg;
Havannah. **French Revolutionary Wars** (1793–1802): Egmont op Zee; **Nap-
oleonic Wars** (1803–15): St Lucia 1803. **Peninsular War** (1808–14): Corunna;
Busaco; Salamanca; Vittoria; San Sebastian; Nive; Peninsula. **War of 1812**
(1812–14): Niagara. **Hundred Days** (1815): Waterloo. **Second Maratha and
Pindari War** (1816–18): Nagpore; Maheidpore. **First Burma War** (1824–6):
Ava. **Crimean War** (1854–5): Alma; Inkerman; Sevastopol. **Second China War**
(1857–60): Taku Forts; Pekin 1860. **South African War** (1899–1902): South
Africa 1899–1902. **Great War:** Le Cateau; Marne 1914, 1918; Ypres 1915, 1917,
1918; Loos; Somme 1916, 1918; Arras 1917, 1918; Lys; Struma; Gallipoli 1915–
16; Palestine 1917–18. **Second World War:** Defence of Escaut; Odon; Aart;
Flushing; Rhine; North-West Europe 1940, 1944–5; Gothic Line; Italy 1944–5;
Kohima; Burma 1943–5. The Sphinx superscribed 'Egypt' is also borne on the
colours.

Accredited Battle Honours
Great War: Mons; Retreat from Mons; Aisne 1914; La Bassée 1914; Neuve
Chapelle; Gravenstafel; St Julien; Frezenberg; Bellewaarde; Aubers; Festubert
1915; Albert 1916, 1918; Bazentin; Pozières; Flers-Courcelette; La Transloy;
Ancre Heights; Ancre 1916, 1918; Scarpe 1917, 1918; Arleux; Pilckem;
Langemarck 1917; Menin Road; Polygon Wood; Poelcapelle; Passchendaele;
Cambrai 1917; St Quentin; Rosières; Estaires; Messines 1918; Hazebrouck;

Bailleul; Kemmel; Béthune; Soissonais-Ourcq; Tardenois; Amiens; Bapaume 1918; Drocourt-Quéant; Hindenburg Line; Canal du Nord; St Quentin Canal; Beaurevoir; Courtrai; Selle; Sambre; France and Flanders 1914–18; Macedonia 1915–18; Helles; Landing at Helles; Krithia; Suvla; Scimitar Hill; Rumani; Egypt 1915–16; Gaza; El Mughar; Nebi Samwil; Jaffa; Archangel 1918–19. **Second World War:** Dyle; St Omer-La Bassée; Cheux; Defence of Rauray; Caen; Esquay; Mont Pinçon; Nederrijn; Best; Scheldt; Meijel; Venlo Pocket; Roer; Rhineland; Reichswald; Cleve; Goch; Uelzen; Bremen; Artlenberg; Marradi; Monte Gamberaldi; South-East Asia 1941; Donbaik; Relief of Kohima; Aradura; Shwebo; Mandalay.

Awards
Seven member of the regiment have been awarded the Victoria Cross: one in the Crimean War (1854–5) and six in the Great War. First award: Private J. Prosser (1828–69), Sevastopol 18 June 1855; gazetted 24 February 1857. Captain D. Ford (1918–43) was awarded the George Cross, Hong Kong Prison Camp 1943: gazetted posthumously 18 April 1946.

Memorials
The Royal Scots Club, Abercromby Place, Edinburgh (Great War); The Scottish National War Memorial, Edinburgh Castle (1914 to present); The Royal Scots Memorial Gates, Glencorse Barracks (Great War); Rosemount Cemetery, Leith (7th Bn Gretna rain disaster 22 May 1915).

Dress
DIFFERENCES: Blue glengarry with diced band and black cock's feather. Hunting Stewart tartan trews. Pipers Royal Stuart tartan, granted in 1933 by King George V to commemorate the regiment's 30th anniversary.
REGIMENTAL TIE: Thick red, navy and blue stripes.

Marches
Quick: *Dumbarton's Drums* (*The Daughter of the Regiment* when Royalty is present). Slow: *The Garb of Old Gaul*.

Alliances
The Canadian Scottish Regiment (Princess Mary's); The Royal Newfoundland Regiment.

Affiliated Regiment
10th Princess Mary's Own Gurkha Rifles.

Journal
The Thistle (twice a year).

Museum
The Castle, Edinburgh (tel 031 336 1761 ext 4265): open May–September Monday–Saturday 0930–1630, Sunday 1100–1630; October–April Monday–Friday 0930–1600.

Record Office
Except officers: Imphal Barracks, York; officers MS(AODO), London Rd, Stanmore, Middlesex.

Regimental Histories
Brander, A. M. *The Royal Scots (The Royal Regiment)*, Leo Cooper, 1976. McCance. *Records of the Royal Scots 1633–1911*, Alexander Thorn (Dublin). Ewing, J. *The Royal Scots 1914–1919* (2 vols.), Oliver & Boyd, 1925. Simpson, H. J. *Three Hundred Years: The Royal Scots (The Royal Regiment)*, Skinner, 1933. McBain. *A Regiment at War: The Royal Scots 1939–45*, Pentland. Muir, A. *The First of Foot: The History of the Royal Scots*, Edinburgh, 1961.

THE QUEEN'S REGIMENT
(The Queen's Division)
Allied Colonels-in-Chief: HRH Princess Juliana of the Netherlands;
HM Queen Margrethe II of Denmark

History
Formed in 1966 by the amalgamation of the Queen's Royal Surrey Regiment; the Queen's Own Buffs, the Royal Kent Regiment; the Royal Sussex Regiment; and the Middlesex Regiment (Duke of Cambridge's Own). Three regular battalions, three volunteer battalions (5th, 6th/7th and 8th Queen's Fusiliers).
MOTTO: *Unconquered I serve.*
HEADQUARTERS: Howe Barracks, Canterbury, Kent.
RECRUITMENT AREA: Greater London, Kent, Surrey and Sussex.
REGIMENTAL ANNIVERSARIES: Sobraon Day (10 February); Albuhera Day (16 May); Glorious First of June (1 June); Sevastopol Day (8 September); Salerno Day (9 September); Quebec Day (13 September); British Battalion Day (20 December).

Emblazoned Battle Honours
Defence of Tangier (1662–80): Tangier 1662–80. **War of the League of Augsburg** (1689–97): Namur 1695. **War of Spanish Succession** (1701–15): Gibraltar 1704–5; Blenheim; Ramillies; Malplaquet. **War of Austrian Succession** (1740–8): Dettingen. **Seven Years War** (1756–63): Louisburg; Guadaloupe 1759; Quebec 1759; Martinique 1762. **War of American Independence** (1775–8): St Lucia 1778. **Fourth Mysore War** (1799): Seringapatam. **Napoleonic Wars** (1803–15): Maida. **Peninsular War** (1808–14): Vimiera; Corunna; Douro; Talavera; Albuhera; Almaraz; Badajoz; Salamanca; Vittoria. **First Afghan War** (1839–42): Affghanistan 1839. **Gwalior Campaign** (1843): Punniar. **First Sikh War** (1845–6): Moodkee; Sobraon. **Crimean War** (1854–5): Inkerman; Sevastopol. **Indian Mutiny** (1857–8): Lucknow. **Second China War** (1857–60): Taku Forts. **Third Maori War** (1863–6): New Zealand. **Zulu and Basuto War** (1877–9): South Africa 1879. **Egyptian Campaign** (1885): Nile 1884–5. **Third Burma War** (1885–7): Burma 1885–7. **Chitral Campaign** (1895): Chitral. **South African War** (1899–1902): Relief of Ladysmith; Relief of Kimberley; South Africa 1899–1902. **Great War** (1914–18): Mons; Marne 1914, 1918; Aisne 1914; Ypres 1914, 1915, 1917, 1918; Hill 60; Festubert 1915; Somme 1916, 1918; Albert 1916, 1918; Vimy 1917; Cambrai 1917, 1918; Hindenburg Line; Italy 1917–18; Macedonia 1915–18; Gallipoli 1915; Gaza; Jerusalem; Palestine 1917–18; Defence of Kut al Amara 1917; Mesopotamia 1915–18; NW Frontier India 1915, 1916–17. **Second World War: Dunkirk 1940; Normandy Landing;**

North-West Europe 1940, 1944–5; Abyssinia 1941; Omars; Alam el Halfa; El Alamein; Longstop Hill 1943; North Africa 1940–3; Sicily 1943; Sangro; Salerno; Anzio; Cassino; Italy 1943–5; Malta 1940–2; Malaya 1941–2; Hong Kong; Defence of Kohima; Burma 1943–5. **Korean War** (1950–3): Korea 1950–1. A naval crown superscribed '1st June 1794' and the Sphinx superscribed 'Egypt' are also borne on the colours.

Accredited Battle Honours

War of Spanish Succession (1701–15): Oudenarde; Belleisle. **Seven Years War** (1756–63): Havannah. **Third Mysore War** (1789–91): Mysore. **French Revolutionary Wars** (1793–1802): Martinique 1794. **Napoleonic Wars** (1803–15): Guadaloupe 1810. **Peninsular War** (1808–14): Ciudad Rodrigo; Pyrenees; Nivelle; Nive; Orthes; Toulouse; Peninsula. **First Afghan War** (1839–42): Ghuznee 1839; Khelat; Cabool 1842. **First Sikh War** (1845–6): Ferozeshah; Aliwal. **Eighth Kaffir War** (1851–3): South Africa 1851–2. **Crimean War** (1854–5): Alma. **Second China War** (1857–60): Pekin 1860. **Second Afghan War** (1878–80); Afghanistan 1878–9. **First Sudan War:** Egypt 1882. **Egyptian Campaign** (1885): Abu Klea; Suakin 1885. **Tirah Campaign** (1897–8): Tirah. **South African War** (1899–1902): Paardeburg. **Great War:** Le Cateau; Retreat from Mons; La Bassée 1914; Messines 1914, 1917, 1918; Armentières 1914; Langemarck 1914, 1917; Gheluvelt; Nonne Bosschen; Givenchy 1914; Neuve Chapelle; Gravenstafel; St Julien; Frezenberg; Bellewaarde; Aubers; Hooge 1915; Loos; Bazentin; Delville Wood; Pozières; Guillemont; Ginchy; Flers-Courcelette; Morval; Thiepval; Le Transloy; Ancre Heights; Ancre 1916, 1918; Bapaume 1917, 1918; Arras 1917, 1918; Scarpe 1917, 1918; Arleux; Oppy; Bullecourt; Pilckem; Menin Road; Polygon Wood; Broodseinde; Poelcapelle; Passchendaele; St Quentin; Rosières; Avre; Villers Bretonneux; Lys; Estaires; Hazebrouck; Bailleul; Kemmel; Scherpenberg; Soissonais-Ourcq; Amiens; Drocourt-Quéant; Epéhy; Canal du Nord; St Quentin Canal; Beaurevoir; Courtrai; Selle; Valenciennes; Sambre; France and Flanders 1914–18; Piave; Vittorio Veneto; Struma; Doiran 1917, 1918; Suvla; Landing at Suvla; Scimitar Hill; Rumani; Egypt 1915–17; El Mughar; Nebi Samwil; Jericho; Jordan; Tell'Asur; Megiddo; Sharon; Aden; Tigris 1916; Kut al Amara 1917; Baghdad; Khan Baghdadi; Sharqat; Murman 1918–19; Dukhovskaya; Siberia 1918–19; .**Third Afghan War** (1919): Afghanistan 1919. **Second World War:** Dyle; Defence of Escaut; Amiens 1940; St Omer-La Bassée; Forêt de Nieppe; Ypres-Comines Canal; Withdrawal to Seine; Cambes; Breville; Villers Bocage; Odon; Caen; Orne; Hill 112; Bourguébus Ridge; Troarn; Mont Pinçon; Falaise; Seine 1944; Nederrijn; Le Havre; Lower Maas; Venraij; Meijel; Geilenkirchen; Venlo Pocket; Roer; Rhineland; Reichswald; Goch; Rhine; Lingen; Brinkum; Bremen; Karora-Marsa Taclai; Cub Cub; Mescelit Pass; Keren; Mt Englahat; Messawa; Syria 1941; Sidi Barrani; Sidi Suleiman; Tobruk 1941; Tobruk Sortie; Alem Hamza; Benghazi; Deir El Munassib; El Agheila; Advance on Tripoli; Medenine; Mareth; Tebaga Gap; El Hamma; Akarit; Djebel el Meida; Djebel Roumana; Djebel Abiod; Tebourba; Djebel Azzag 1942, 1943; Robaa Valley; Fort McGregor; Oued Zarga; Djebel Bech Chekaoui; Djebel Ang; Heidous; Djebel Djaffa Pass; Medjez Plain; Si Abdallah; Tunis; Montarnaud; Francofonte; Sferro; Adrano; Sferro Hills; Centuripe; Monte Rivoglia; Termoli; Trigno; San Salvo; Romagnoli; Impossible Bridge; Villa Grande; Monte Stella; Scafati Bridge; Volturno Crossing; Monte Camino; Garigliano Crossing; Damiano; Carroceto; Monastery Hill; Castle Hill; Liri Valley; Aquino; Piedimonte Hill; Rome; Trasimene Line; Arezzo; Advance to Florence; Monte Scalari; Gothic Line; Coriano; Pian di Castello; Gemmano Ridge; Monte Reggiano; Capture of Forli; Cassa Fortis; Senio Pocket; Senio Floodbank; Rimini Line; Casa Fabbri Ridge; Savio Bridgehead; Monte Pianoereno; Monte Spaduro; Monte Grande; Senio; Menate; Filo; Argenta Gap; Greece 1944–5; Leros; Middle East 1943; Kampar; South-East Asia 1941; North Arakan; Razabil; Mayu Tunnels; Kohima; Pinwe; Shweli; Myitson; Taungtha; Yenang-yaung 1945; Sittang 1945; Chindits 1944. **Korean War** (1950–3): Naktong Bridgehead; Chonju; Chongchon II; Chaum-Ni; Kapyong-chon; Kapyong.

Dress
DIFFERENCES: Blue dress cap, scarlet band and piping; blue side cap, scarlet piping. Blue stable belt. Different colour lanyard for each battalion.
REGIMENTAL TIE: Thin gold, thick Royal blue, thin gold, thick silver, thin gold stripes.

Marches
Quick: *The Soldiers of the Queen*. Slow: *The Caledonian*.

Alliances
The Queen's York Rangers (1st American Regiment) RCAC, of Canada; The South Alberta Light Horse (RCAC), of Canada; The Queen's Own Rifles of Canada; The Hastings and Prince Edward Island Regiment, of Canada; 1st Battalion The Royal New Brunswick Regiment (Carleton and York), of Canada; The Essex and Kent Scottish, of Canada; The Royal New South Wales Regiment, of Australia; The Royal Western Australia Regiment; The University of New South Wales Regiment, of Australia; 2nd Battalion (Canterbury Nelson Marlborough West Coast) RNZIR, of New Zealand; 5th Battalion (Wellington, West Coast and Taranki) RNZIR, of New Zealand; 12th, 14th, 15th and 17th Battalions The Punjab Regiment, of Pakistan; The Royal Hong Kong Regiment (The Volunteers).

Journal
The Journal of the Queen's Regiment (twice a year – June, December).

Museum
Dover Castle, Dover, Kent (tel 0304 240121): open daily Summer 0900–1800, Winter 0930–1600.

Record Office
Except officers: Higher Barracks, Exeter; officers: MS(AODO), London Rd, Stanmore, Middlesex.

Regimental History

Riley, J. *History of the Queen's Regiment*, RHQ, to be published 1992.

Predecessors

THE QUEEN'S ROYAL SURREY REGIMENT

History

Formed in 1959 by the amalgamation of the Queen's Royal Regiment (West Surrey) and the East Surrey Regiment.

Predecessors of the Queen's Royal Surrey Regiment

Memorial

Chapel Guildford Cathedral, Surrey.

Museum

Clandon Park, West Clandon, Guildford, Surrey (tel 0483 223419): open April–October   Tuesday–Thursday, Saturday, Sunday 1400–1800.

Regimental History

Riley, J. *The History of the Queen's Royal Surrey Regiment 1959–1970*, RHQ, 1970.

THE QUEEN'S ROYAL REGIMENT (WEST SURREY)

History

Raised in 1661 as the Old Tangier Regiment of Foot (Queen's Foot in 1684, 2nd or Queen's Royal Regiment in 1751).

MOTTOES: *Pristinae virtutis memor* (Mindful of the gallant actions of the past); *Vel exuviae triumphans* (Even in defeat there can be triumph).

REGIMENTAL ANNIVERSARIES: Glorious First of June (1 June); Salerno Day (9 September).

Emblazoned Battle Honours

Defence of Tangier (1662–80): Tangier 1662–80. **War of the League of Augsburg** (1689–97): Namur 1695. **Peninsular War** (1808–14): Vimiera; Corunna; Salamanca; Vittoria; Pyrenees; Nivelle; Toulouse; Peninsula. **First Afghan War** (1839–42): Ghuznee 1839; Affghanistan 1839; Khelat. **Sixth Kaffir War** (1835): South Africa 1851–1852–1853. **Second China War** (1857–60): Taku Forts; Pekin 1860. **Third Burma War** (1885–7): Burma 1885–7. **Tirah Campaign** (1897–8): Tirah. **South African War** (1899–1902): Relief of Ladysmith; South Africa 1899–1902. **Great War:** Retreat from Mons; Ypres 1914, 1917, 1918; Somme 1916, 1918; Messines 1917; Vittorio Veneto; Macedonia 1916–17; Gallipoli 1915; Palestine 1917–18; Mesopotamia 1915–18; NW Frontier India 1916–17. **Third Afghan War** (1919): Afghanistan 1919. **Second World War:** Villers Bocage; Tobruk 1941; El Alamein; Medenine; Salerno; Monte Camino; Anzio; Gemmano Ridge; North Arakan; Kohima. A naval crown superscribed '1st June 1794' and the Sphinx superscribed 'Egypt' were also borne on the colours.

Accredited Battle Honours

Great War: Mons; Marne 1914, 1918; Aisne 1914; Langemarck 1914; Gheluvelt; Aubers; Festubert 1915; Loos; Albert 1916, 1918; Bazentin; Delville Wood; Pozières; Guillemont; Flers-Courcelette; Morval; Thiepval; Le Transloy; Ancre Heights; Ancre 1916, 1918; Arras 1917, 1918; Scarpe 1917; Bullecourt; Pilckem; Menin Road; Polygon Wood; Broodseinde; Passchendaele; Cambrai 1917, 1918; St Quentin; Bapaume 1918; Rosières; Avre; Villers Bretonneux; Lys; Hazebrouck; Bailleul; Kemmel; Soissonais-Ourcq; Amiens; Epéhy; Hindenburg Line; St Quentin Canal; Courtrai; Selle; Sambre; France and Flanders 1914–18; Piave; Italy 1917, 1918; Suvla; Doiran 1917; Landing at Suvla; Scimitar Hill; Rumani; Egypt 1915, 1916; Gaza; El Mughar; Nebi Samwil; Jerusalem; Jericho; Jordan; Tell'Asur; Megiddo; Sharon; Khan Baghdadi. **Second World War:** Defence of Escaut; Mont Pinçon; Lower Maas; Roer; North-West Europe 1940, 1944–45; Syria 1941; Sidi Barrani; Tobruk Sortie; Deir el Munasib; Advance on Tripoli; Tunis; North Africa 1940–3; Monte Stella; Scafati Bridge; Volturno Crossing; Garigliano Crossing; Damiano; Gothic Line; Senio Pocket; Senio Floodbank; Casa Fabbri Ridge; Menate; Filo; Argenta Gap; Italy 1943–5; Yenangyaung 1945; Sittang 1945; Chindits 1944; Burma 1943–5.

Awards

Six members of the regiment have been awarded the Victoria Cross: one in West Africa (1903), four in the Great War and one in the Second World War. First award Lieutenant W. D. Wright, later Brigadier-General W. D. Wright CB, CMG, DSO (1875–1953) West Africa 26 February 1903: gazetted 11 September 1903. Two members of the regiment have been awarded the Empire Gallantry Medal (later exchanged for the George Cross): Lance-Corporal G. Henshaw (1910–72) and Private A. Brooks (1908–57) Quetta earthquake 31 May–1 June 1935: gazetted 19 November 1935.

Memorial

Chapel, Holy Trinity Church, Guildford, Surrey.

Marches

Quick: *Braganza*. Slow: *Scipio*.

Journal

The Journal of the Queen's Royal Regiment.

Museum

Clandon Park, West Clandon, Guildford, Surrey (tel 0483 223419): open April–October Tuesday, Saturday, Sunday 1400–1800.

Regimental Histories

Haswell, J. *The Queen's Royal Regiment*, Hamish Hamilton, 1967. *History of the 2nd Queen's Royal Regiment, now the Queen's (Royal West Surrey) Regiment* (9 vols.): vols. 1–3, by J. Davies, Bentley 1887–95; vols. 4–6, Eyre & Spottiswoode, 1902–6; vol. 7, by H. C. Wylly (comp), Gale & Polden, 1925; vol. 8 (1924–48), by R. C. G. Foster (comp), Gale & Polden, 1953; vol. 9 (1948–59), by R. C. G. Foster, Gale & Polden, 1961.

THE EAST SURREY REGIMENT

History

Raised in 1702 as Villiers' Regiment of Marines (31st Foot in 1751) and as the 2nd Battalion of the 31st Foot in 1756 (70th Foot in 1758). These two regiments became the 1st and 2nd Battalions of the East Surrey Regiment in 1881.

REGIMENTAL ANNIVERSARIES: Sobraon Day (10 February); Ypres Day (23 April).

FORMER MEMBER: Field Marshal Sir Charles Egerton (1848–1921), commissioned 1867.

Emblazoned Battle Honours

(awards before 1881 to 70th Foot★)
War of Spanish Succession (1701–15): Gibraltar 1704–5. War of Austrian Succession (1740–8): Dettingen. French Revolutionary Wars (1793–1802): ★Martinique 1794. Napoleonic Wars (1803–15): ★Guadaloupe 1810. Peninsular War (1808–14): Talavera; Albuhera; Vittoria; Pyrenees; Nivelle; Nive; Orthes; Peninsula. First Afghan War (1839–42): Cabool 1842. First Sikh War (1845–6): Moodkee; Ferozeshah; Aliwal; Sobraon. Crimean War (1854–5): Sevastopol. Second China War (1857–60): Taku Forts. Third Maori War (1863–6): ★New Zealand. Second Afghan War (1878–89): Afghanistan 1878–9. Egyptian Campaign (1885): Suakin 1885. South African War (1899–1902): Relief of Ladysmith; South Africa 1899–1902. Great War: Mons; Marne 1914; Somme 1916, 1918; Albert 1916, 1918; Cambrai 1917, 1918; Macedonia 1915–18. Second World War: Dunkirk 1940; Longstop Hill; Sicily 1943; Sangro; Cassino; Italy 1943–5.

Accredited Battle Honours

Great War: Le Cateau; Retreat from Mons; Aisne 1914; Armentières 1914; Hill 60; Gravenstafel; St Julien; Frezenberg; Bellewaarde; Bazentin; Delville Wood; Pozières; Guillemont; Flers-Courcelette; Morval; Thiepval; Le Transloy; Ancre Heights; Ancre 1916; Arras 1917, 1918; Vimy 1917; Scarpe 1917; Messines 1917; Pilckem; Langemarck 1917; Menin Road; Polygon Wood; Broodseinde; Poelcapelle; Passchendaele; St Quentin; Bapaume 1918; Rosières; Avre; Lys; Estaires; Hazebrouck; Amiens; Hindenburg Line; Epéhy; Canal du Nord; St Quentin Canal; Courtrai; Sambre; France and Flanders 1914–18; Italy 1917–18; Struma; Macedonia 1915–18; Egypt 1915; Aden; Mesopotamia 1917–18; Murman 1919; Second World War: Defence of Escaut; Tebourba; Fort McGregor; Djebel Ang; Djebel Djaffa Pass; Medjez Plain; Tunis; Montarnaud; Adrano; Centuripe; Trigno; Capture of Forli; Argenta Gap; Greece 1944–5; Kampar.

Awards

Nine members of the Regiment have been awarded the Victoria Cross: one in the South African War (1899–1902), seven in the Great War and one in the Second World War First award: Private A. E. Curtis, later Sergeant (1866–1900) Onderbank, South Africa, 23 February 1900: gazetted 15 January 1901.

Memorial

All Saints Church, Kingston-upon-Thames, Surrey.

Journal

The Journal of the East Surrey Regiment.

Marches

Quick: *A Southerly Wind and a Cloudy Sky.* Slow: *Lord Charles Montague's Huntingdonshire March.*

Allied Regiment in 1914
4th (Otago) Regiment, of New Zealand.

Museum
Clandon Park, West Clandon, Guildford, Surrey (tel 0483 223419): open April–October Tuesday–Thursday, Saturday, Sunday 1400–1800.

Regimental Histories
Langley, M. *The East Surrey Regiment*, Leo Cooper, 1972. *History of the 31st/70th Foot, East Surrey Regiment* (4 vols); vol. 1 (1702–1914), H. W. Pearse, Spottiswoode/Ballantyne, 1916; vols. 2 and 3 (1914–19), H. W. Pearse and H. S. Sloman, Medici Society, 1933 and 1934; vol. 4 (1920–52), D. S. Daniell, Benn, 1957.

THE QUEEN'S OWN BUFFS, THE ROYAL KENT REGIMENT

History
Formed in 1961 by the amalgamation of The Buffs (Royal East Kent Regiment)

Predecessors of the Queen's Own Buffs, The Royal Kent Regiment

and the Queen's Own Royal West Kent Regiment.

Museum
The Royal Museum and Art Gallery, High St, Canterbury, Kent (tel 0227 452747): open Monday–Saturday 1000–1700.

Association
The Queen's Regimental Association (The Queen's Own Buffs): tel 0227 763434 ext 4252.

THE BUFFS (ROYAL EAST KENT REGIMENT)

History
Raised in 1665 as the Holland Regiment (3rd Foot in 1751).

MOTTO: *Veteri frondescit honore* (It flourishes in ancient honour).

REGIMENTAL ANNIVERSARIES: Corunna Day (16 January); Albuhera Day (16 May).

Emblazoned Battle Honours
War of Spanish Succession (1701–15): Blenheim; Ramillies; Oudernarde; Malplaquet. **War of Austrian Succession** (1740–8): Dettingen. **Seven Years War** (1756–63): Guadeloupe 1759; Belleisle. **Peninsular War** (1808–14): Douro; Talavera; Albuhera; Vittoria; Pyrenees; Nivelle; Nive; Orthes; Toulouse; Peninsula. **Gwalior Campaign** (1843): Punniar. **Crimean War** (1854–5): Sevastopol. **Second China War** (1857–60): Taku Forts. **Zulu and Basuto War** (1877–9): South Africa 1879. **Chitral Campaign** (1895): Chitral. **South African War** (1899–1902): Relief of Kimberley; Paardeburg; South Africa 1900–02. **Great War:** Aisne 1914; Ypres

1915, 1917; Loos; Somme 1916, 1918; Arras 1917; Amiens; Hindenburg Line; Struma; Baghdad; Jerusalem. **Second World War:** North-West Europe 1940; Alem Hanza; El Alamein; Robaa Valley; Trigno; Anzio; Sicily 1943; Argenta Gap; Leros; Shweli.

Accredited Battle Honours

Great War: Armentières 1914; Gravenstafel; St Julien; Frezenberg; Bellewaarde; Hooge 1915; Albert 1916, 1918; Bazentin; Delville Wood; Pozières; Flers-Courcelette; Morval; Thiepval; Le Transloy; Ancre Heights; Ancre 1916–17; Scarpe 1917; Messines 1917; Pilckem; Passchendaele; Cambrai 1917, 1918; St Quentin; Avre; Bapaume 1918; Epéhy; St Quentin Canal; Selle; Sambre; France and Flanders 1914–18; Doiran 1918; Macedonia 1915–18; Gaza; Tell'Asur; Palestine 1917–18; Aden; Tigris 1916; Kut al Amara 1917; Mesopotamia 1915–18. **Second World War:** Defence of Escaut; St Omer-La Bassée; Withdrawal to Seine; Sidi Suleiman; Alam el Halfa; El Agheila; Advance on Tripoli; Tebaga Gap; El Hamma; Akarit; Djebel Azzag 1943; Djebel bech; Chekaoui; Heidows; Medjez Plain; Longstop Hill 1943; North Africa 1941–3; Centuripe; Monte Rivoglia; Termoli; Sangro; Cassino I; Liri Valley; Aquino; Rome; Trasimene Line; Coriano; Monte Spaduro; Senio; Italy 1943–5; Middle East 1943; Malta 1940–2; Myitson; Burma 1945.

Awards

Five members of the regiment have been awarded the Victoria Cross: three in the Crimean War (1854–5), one in the Mohmand Campaign (1897) and one in the Great War. First awards: Private J. Connors (1830–58) and Major F. F. Maude, later General Sir Frederick Maude GCB (1821–97) The Redan, Crimea, 8 September 1855: gazetted 24 February 1857. Lieutenant B. G. Ellis (1890–1979) was awarded the Albert Medal (later exchanged for the George Cross) Mesopotamia 21 August 1918: gazetted 18 July 1919.

Memorial

The Warriors' Chapel, Cathedral Church of Christ, Canterbury, Kent.

Marches

Quick: *The Buff.* Slow: *The Men of Kent.*

Allied Regiment in 1914

The Queen's Own Rifles of Canada.

Journal

The Dragon (twelve times a year – up to February 1961.)

Museum

The Royal Museum, High St, Canterbury, Kent (tel 0227 452747): open Monday–Saturday 1000–1700.

Regimental Histories

Blaxland, G. *The Buffs,* Leo Cooper, 1972. *Historical Records of the Buffs, East Kent Regiment* (4 vols); vol. 1 (1572–1704), H. R. Knight, Gale & Polden, 1905; vol. 2, C. R. B. Knight, Medici Society, 1935; vol. 3 (1914–19), R. S. Moody, Medici Society, 1922; vol. 4 (1919–48), C. R. B. Knight, Medici Society, 1951. Blaxland, G. *Final Records of The Buffs 1948–1967,* printed for the regiment, 1967.

THE QUEEN'S OWN ROYAL WEST KENT REGIMENT

History
Raised in 1756 as the 52nd Foot (50th Foot in 1757) and in 1824 as the 97th Foot. These two regiments became the 1st and 2nd Battalions of The Queen's Own (Royal West Kent Regiment) in 1881.

MOTTOES: *Quo fas et gloria ducunt* (Where right and glory lead); *Invicta* (Undefeated).

FORMER MEMBERS: Field Marshal Studholme John Hodgson (1708–98), commissioned 1728 (50th); Field Marshal Sir John Griffin Griffin (later Lord Howard de Walden) (1719–97), commissioned 1739 (50th); Field Marshal Viscount Hardinge of Lahore and King's Norton (1785–1856), commissioned 1798 (97th).

REGIMENTAL ANNIVERSARIES: Corunna Day (16 January); Sevastopol Day (8 September).

Emblazoned Battle Honours
(awards before 1881 to 97th*)
Peninsular War (1808–14): Vimiera; Corunna; Almaraz; Vittoria; Pyrenees; Nive; Orthes; Peninsula. **Gwalior Campaign** (1843): Punniar. **First Sikh War** (1845–6): Moodkee; Ferozeshah; Aliwal; Sobraon. **Crimean War** (1854–5): Alma; Inkerman; Sevastopol. **Indian Mutiny** (1857–8): *Lucknow. **Third Maori War** (1863–6): New Zealand. **First Sudan War** (1882–4): Egypt 1882. **Egyptian Campaign** (1885): Nile 1884–5. **South African War** (1899–1902): South Africa 1900–2. **Great War**: Mons; Ypres 1914, 1915, 1917, 1918; Hill 60; Somme 1916, 1918; Vimy 1917; Italy 1917–18; Gallipoli 1915; Gaza; Defence of Kut el Amara; Shargat. **Third Afghan War** (1919): Afghanistan 1919. **Second World War**: North-West Europe 1940; El Alamein; Medjez Plain; Centuripe; The Sangro; Cassino; Trasimene Line; Argenta Gap; Malta 1940–2; Defence of Kohima. The Sphinx superscribed 'Egypt' was also borne on the colours.

Accredited Battle Honours
Great War: Le Cateau; Retreat from Mons; Marne 1914; Aisne 1914; La Bassée 1914; Messines 1914, 1917; Gravenstafel; St Julien; Frezenberg; Loos; Albert 1916, 1918; Bazentin; Delville Wood; Pozières; Guillemont; Flers-Courcelette; Morval; Thiepval; Le Transloy; Ancre Heights; Ancre 1916, 1918; Arras 1917, 1918; Scarpe 1917; Oppy; Pilckem; Langemarck 1917; Menin Road; Polygon Wood; Broodseinde; Passchendaele; Cambrai 1917, 1918; St Quentin; Rosières; Avre; Villers Bretonneux; Lys; Hazebrouck; Kemmel; Amiens; Bapaume 1918; Hindenburg Line; Epéhy; Canal du Nord; St Quentin Canal; Courtrai; Selle; Sambre; France and Flanders 1914–18; Suvla; Landing at Suvla; Scimitar Hill; Rumani; Egypt 1915–16; El Mughar; Jerusalem; Jericho; Tell'Asur; Palestine 1917–18; Mesopotamia 1915–18. **Second World War**: Defence of Escaut; Forêt de Nieppe; Alam el Halfa; Djebel Abiod; Djebel Azzag 1942; Oued Zarga; Djebel Ang; Longstop Hill 1943; Si Abdallah; North Africa 1942–3; Monte Rivoglia; Sicily 1943; Termoli; San Salvo; Romagnoli; Impossible Bridge; Villa Grande; Castle Hill; Liri Valley; Piedimonte Hill; Arezzo; Advance to Florence; Monte Scalari; Casa Fortis; Rimini Line; Savio Bridgehead; Monte Planoereno; Monte Spaduro; Senio; Italy 1943–5; Greece 1944–5; Leros; North Arakan; Razabil; Mayu Tunnels; Taungtha; Sittang 1945; Burma 1943–5.

Memorials
Regimental Cenotaph (Great War and Second World War), Brenchley Gardens, Maidstone, by Sir Edwin Lutyens; Regimental Chapel (Regimental Colours and Books of Remembrance), All Saints Church, Maidstone; 50th Regimental Memorial (Sutlej Campaign 1845–6), Canterbury Cathedral.

Awards
Six members of the regiment have been awarded the Victoria Cross: two in the Crimean War (1854–5), three in the Great War and one in the Second World War. First award: Sergeant J. Coleman (1798–1858), Sevastopol 30 August 1855: gazetted 24 February 1857 (97th Foot). He is believed to be the only British soldier born in the 18th century to have been awarded the Victoria Cross.

Marches
Quick: *The Hundred Pipers*, Slow: *The Men of Kent*.

Allied Regiment in 1914
1st (Canterbury) Regiment, of New Zealand.

Association
The Queen's Past and Present Association now incorporated into The Queen's

Regimental Association (The Queen's Own Buffs), RHQ The Queen's Regiment, Howe Barracks, Canterbury, Kent CT1 1JU.

Museum
Maidstone Museum and Art Gallery, St Faith's St, Maidstone, Kent (tel 0622 754497): open Monday–Saturday 1000–1730; Bank Holidays 1100–1700.

Regimental Histories
Chaplin, Lieutenant-Colonel H. D. *The 97th or Earl of Ulster's Regiment 1824–1881*, The Queen's Own Royal West Kent Regiment Museum Committee, 1973. Fyler, Colonel A. E. *The History of the 50th (or The Queen's Own) Regiment*, Chapman & Hall, 1895. Atkinson, C. T. *The Queen's Own Royal West Kent Regiment 1914–1918*, Simpkin, Marshall, Hamilton, Kent, 1924. Chaplin, Lieutenant-Colonel H. D. *The Queen's Own Royal West Kent Regiment 1920–1950*, Michael Joseph, 1954. Chaplin, Lieutenant Colonel H. D. *The Queen's Own Royal West Kent Regiment 1881–1914*, The Queen's Own Regimental History Committee, 1959. Chaplin, Lieutenant-Colonel H. D. *The Queen's Own Royal West Kent Regiment 1951–1961*, The Queen's Own Museum Committee, 1964.

THE ROYAL SUSSEX REGIMENT

History
Raised in 1701 as the Earl of Donegal's Regiment (35th Foot in 1751) and in 1853 as the 3rd Bengal European Light

Infantry (HEICo) (107th Bengal Infantry in 1861). These two regiments became the 1st and 2nd Battalions of the Royal Sussex Regiment in 1881.
REGIMENTAL ANNIVERSARY: Quebec Day (13 September).

Emblazoned Battle Honours
War of Spanish Succession (1701–15): Gibraltar 1704–5. Seven Years War (1756–63): Louisburg; Quebec 1759; Martinique 1762; Havannah. War of American Independence (1775–8): St Lucia 1778. Napoleonic Wars (1803–15): Maida. First Sudan War (1882–4):

Egypt 1882. **Egyptian Campaign** (1885): Abu Klea; Nile 1884–5. **South African War** (1899–1902): South Africa 1900–02. **Great War:** Ypres 1914, 1915, 1917, 1918; Somme 1916, 1918; Pilckem; Hindenburg Line; Italy 1917–18; Gallipoli 1915; Palestine 1917–18; NW Frontier India 1915, 1916–17. **Second World War:** Abyssinia 1941; Omars; Alam al Halfa; El Alamein; Akarit; North Africa 1940–3; Cassino II; Italy 1944–5; Burma 1943–5.

Accredited Battle Honours

Great War: Mons; Aisne 1914; Gheluvelt; Nonne Bosschen; Givency 1914; Aubers; Loos; Albert 1916, 1918; Bazentin; Delville Wood; Pozières; Flers-Courcelette; Morval; Thiepval; Le Transloy; Ancre Heights; Ancre 1916, 1918; Arras 1917, 1918; Vimy 1917; Scarpe 1917; Arleux; Messines 1917; Langemarck 1917; Menin Road; Polygon Wood; Broodseinde; Poelcapelle; Passchendaele; Cambrai 1917; 1918; St Quentin; Bapaume 1918; Rosières; Avre; Lys; Kemmel; Scherpenberg; Soissonais-Ourcq; Amiens; Drocourt-Quéant; Epéhy; St Quentin Canal; Beaurevoir; Courtrai; Selle; Sambre; France and Flanders 1914–18; Piave; Vittorio Veneto; Suvla; Landing at Suvla; Scimitar Hill; Rumani; Egypt 1915–17; Gaza; El Mughar; Jerusalem; Jericho; Tell'Asur; Murman 1918–19. **Second World War:** Defence of Escaut; Amiens 1940; St Omer-La Bassée; Forêt de Nieppe; Karora-Marsa Taclai; Cub Cub; Mescelit Pass; Keren; Mt Engiahat; Massawa; Benghazi; Djebel el Meida; Tunis; Monastery Hill; Gothic Line; Pian di Castello; Monte Reggiano; North Arakan; Pinwe; Shweli.

Awards

Six members of the regiment have been awarded the Victoria Cross: one in the Third Maori War (1863–6), four in the Great War and one in the Second World War. First award: Lieutenant-Colonel J. C. McNeill, later Major-General Sir John McNeill GCVO KCB KCMG (1831–1904), New Zealand 30 March 1864: gazetted 16 August 1864 (107th Foot).

Memorial

St George's Chapel, Chichester Cathedral.

Marches

Quick: *The Royal Sussex.* Slow: *Roussillon.*

Journal

The Roussillon Gazette (once a year).

Association

The Royal Sussex Regimental Association (also representing The Queen's Regiment in Sussex), Roussillon Barracks, Chichester, Sussex PO19 4BL: Patron – HRH Princess Juliana of the Netherlands.

Museum

Sussex Combined Services Museum, The Redoubt Fortress, Royal Parade, Eastbourne, East Sussex (tel 0323 410300): open Easter–31 October daily 0930–1730: other times by appointment. Records at West Sussex Records Office, County Hall, Chichester.

Regimental History

The Last Twenty Years 1948–67, Moore & Tillyer, 1974. Fazan, E. A. C. *Cinq Ports Battalion,* 1971. Martineau, G. D. *A History of the Royal Sussex Regiment, 1701–1953,* Moore, 1955.

THE MIDDLESEX REGIMENT (DUKE OF CAMBRIDGE'S OWN)

History

Raised in 1755 as the 59th Foot (57th Foot in 1757) and in 1787 as the 77th Foot. These two regiments became the 1st and 2nd Battalions of the (Duke of Cambridge's Own) Middlesex Regiment in 1881.

REGIMENTAL ANNIVERSARY: Albuhera Day (16 May).

Emblazoned Battle Honours

(awards before 1881 to 77th★; awards to both 57th and 77th★★)
Third Mysore War (1789–91): ★Mysore. Fourth Mysore War (1799): ★Seringapatam. Peninsular War (1808–14): Albuhera; ★Ciudad Rodrigo; ★Badajos; Vittoria; Pyrenees; Nivelle; Nive; ★Peninsula. Crimean War (1854–5): Alma; ★★Inkerman; ★★Sevastopol. Second and Third Maori Wars (1860–1, 1863–6): New Zealand. Zúlu and Basuto War (1877–9): South Africa 1879. South African War (1899–1902): Relief of Ladysmith; South Africa 1900–02. Great War (1914–18): Mons; Marne 1914; Albert 1916, 1918; Cambrai 1917, 1918; Hindenburg Line; Macedonia 1915–18; Jerusalem. Second World War: Dunkirk 1940; Normandy Landing; North-West Europe 1940, 1944–5; El Alamein; Sicily 1943; Anzio; Hong Kong. Korean War (1950–3): Korea 1950–51.

Accredited Battle Honours

Great War: le Cateau; Retreat from Mons; Aisne 1914, 1918; La Bassée 1914; Messines 1914, 1917, 1918; Armentières 1914; Neuve Chapelle; Gravenstafel; St Julien; Frezenberg; Bellewaarde; Aubers; Hooge 1915; Loos; Somme 1916, 1918; Delville Wood; Pozières; Ginchy; Flers-Courcelette; Morval; Thiepval; Le Transloy; Ancre Heights; Ancre 1916, 1918; Bapaume 1917, 1918; Arras 1917, 1918; Vimy 1917; Scarpe 1917, 1918; Arleux; Pilckem; Langemarck 1917; Menin Road; Polygon Wood; Broodseinde; Poelcapelle; Passchendaele; St Quentin; Rosières; Avre; Villers Bretonneux; Lys; Estaires; Hazebrouck; Bailleul; Kemmel; Scherpenberg; Canal du Nord; St Quentin Canal; Courtrai; Selle; Valenciennes; Sambre; France and Flanders 1914–18; Italy 1917–18; Struma; Doiran 1918; Macedonia 1915–18; Landing at Suvla; Scimitar Hill; Gallipoli 1915; Rumani; Egypt 1915–17; Gaza; El Mughar; Jericho; Jordan; Tell' Asur; Palestine 1917–18; Murman 1919; Dukhovskaya; Siberia 1918–19. Second World War: Dyle; Defence of Escaut; Ypres-Comines Canal; Cambes; Breville; Odon; Orne; Hill 112; Bourguébus Ridge; Troarn; Falaise; Seine 1944; Nederrijn; Le Havre; Lower Maas; Venraij; Meijel; Geilenkirchen; Venlo Pocket; Rhineland; Reichswald; Goch; Lingen; Brinkum; Bremen; North-West Europe 1940, 1944–5; Advance on Tripoli; Mareth; Djebel Roumana; North Africa 1942–3; Francofonte; Sferro; Sferro Hills; Carroceto; Gothic Line; Monte Grande; Italy 1944–5; South-East Asia 1941.

Awards

Eleven members of the regiment have been awarded the Victoria Cross: four in the Crimean War (1854–5), two in the Third Maori War (1863–6) and five in the Great War. First awards: Sergeant G. Gardner, later Colour-Sergeant (1855–91) Sevastopol 22 June 1855: gazetted 2 June 1858 (57th Foot); Sergeant J. Park (1835–63) Alma 5 November 1854 and Inkerman 19 April 1855: gazetted 24 February 1857 (77th Foot). Colonel L. A. Newman MC (1889–1943) was awarded the George Cross, Hong Kong Prison Camp 18 December 1943: gazetted posthumously 18 April 1946.

Memorial
Chapel, St Paul's Cathedral, London.

Marches
Quick: *Sir Manley Power* and *Paddy's Resource*. Slow: *The Caledonian*.

Allied Regiments in 1914
57th Regiment 'Peterborough Rangers', of Canada; 77th Wentworth Regiment, of Canada; 11th Regiment (Taranaki Rifles), of New Zealand.

Museum
Bruce Castle, Lordship Lane; Tottenham, London (tel 081-808 8772): open Tuesday–Saturday 1300–1700.

Regimental Histories
Blaxland, G. *The Middlesex Regiment*, Leo Cooper, 1977. Kingsford, C. L. *The Story of the Duke of Cambridge's Own, Country Life*, 1916. Wyrall, E. *The Die-Hards in the Great War* (2 vols), Harrison, 1926 and 1930. Kemp, P. K. *The Middlesex Regiment (Duke of Cambridge's Own) 1919–1952*, Gale & Polden, 1956.

THE KING'S OWN
ROYAL BORDER REGIMENT
(The King's Division)
Colonel-in-Chief: HRH Princess Alexandra, The Hon Lady Ogilvy GCVO

History
Formed in 1959 by the amalgamation of the King's Own Royal Regiment (Lancaster) and the Border Regiment. One regular battalion, one volunteer battalion (4th).
HEADQUARTERS: The Castle, Carlisle, Cumbria.
RECRUITMENT AREA: Cumbria and Northern Lancashire.
REGIMENTAL ANNIVERSARIES: St George's Day (23 April); Arroyo dos Molinos Day (28 October).

Emblazoned Battle Honours
War of the League of Augsburg (1689–97): Namur 1695. **War of Spanish Succession** (1701–15): Gibraltar 1704–05. **Seven Years War** (1756–63): Guadaloupe 1759; Havana 1762. **War of American Independence** (1775–8): St Lucia 1778. **Peninsular War** (1808–14): Corunna; Albuhera; Arroyo dos Molinos; Badajos; Salamanca; Vittoria; Pyrenees; San Sebastian; Nivelle; Nive; Orthes; Peninsula. **War of 1812** (1812–14): Bladensburg. **Hundred Days** (1815): Waterloo. **Crimean War** (1854–5): Alma; Inkerman; Sevastopol. **Indian Mutiny** (1857–8): Lucknow. **Abyssinian War** (1867–8): Abyssinia. **Zulu and Basuto War** (1877–9): South Africa 1879. **South African War** (1899–1902): Relief of Ladysmith; South Africa 1899–1902. **Great War:** Marne 1914; Ypres 1914, 1915, 1917, 1918; Langemarck 1914, 1917; Somme 1916, 1918; Arras 1917, 1918; Messines 1917; 1918; Cambrai 1917, 1918; France and Flanders 1914–18; Vittorio Veneto; Macedonia 1915–18; Gallipoli 1915–16; Mesopotamia 1916–18. **Second World War:** Dunkirk 1940; Arnhem 1944; North-West Europe 1940, 1944; Defence of Habbaniya; Merjayun; Tobruk 1941; Tobruk Sortie; North Africa 1940–2; Landing in Sicily; Montone; Lamone Bridgehead; Malta 1941–2; Imphal; Myinmu Bridgehead; Meiktila; Chindits 1944; Burma 1943–5. A dragon superscribed 'China' is also borne on the colours.

Accredited Battle Honours
Great War: Le Cateau; Retreat from Mons; Aisne 1914; Armentières 1914; Gheluvelt; Neuve Chapelle; Gravenstafel; St Julien; Frezenberg; Bellewaarde; Aubers; Festubert 1915; Loos; Albert 1916, 1918; Bazentin; Delville Wood; Pozières; Guillemont; Ginchy; Flers-Courcelette; Morval; Thiepval; Le Transloy; Ancre Heights; Ancre 1916; Scarpe 1917, 1918; Arleux; Bullecourt; Pilckem; Menin Road; Polygon Wood; Broodseinde; Poelcapelle; Passchen-

daele; St Quentin; Rosières; Estaires; Hazebrouck; Bailleul; Kemmel; Béthune; Scherpenberg; Aisne 1918; Amiens; Bapaume 1918; Drocourt-Quéant; Hindenburg Line; Epéhy; Canal du Nord; St Quentin Canal; Beaurevoir; Courtrai; Selle; Valenciennes; Sambre; Piave; Italy 1917–18; Struma; Doiran 1917, 1918; Helles; Landing at Helles; Krithia; Suvla; Sari Bair; Landing at Suvla; Scimitar Hill; Egypt 1916; Kut al Amara 1917; Baghdad; NW Frontier India 1916–17; **Third Afghan War** (1919): Afghanistan 1919. **Second World War:** Defence of Escaut; St Omer-La Bassée; Somme 1940; Falluja; Iraq 1941; Jebel Mazar; Syria 1941; Citta di Castello; San Martino Sogliano; Italy 1944–5; Sakawng; Tamu Road; Shenam Pass; Kohima; Ukhrul; Mandalay; Rangoon Road; Pyabwe; Sittang 1945.

Dress
DIFFERENCES: Blue dress cap, scarlet band and piping; blue side cap, red flaps, yellow piped peak. Blue stable belt, gold centre stripe. Glider arm badge.

Marches
Quick: arrangement of *D'ye ken John Peel* and *Corn Rigs are Bonnie*; *Lass o'Gowrie*. Slow: *And shall Trelawny die*.

Alliances
The King's Own Calgary Regiment, of Canada; 31st Battalion The Royal Queensland Regiment, of Australia; 15th Battalion The Frontier Force Regiment, of Pakistan.

Journal
The Lion and the Dragon (once a year – March).

Association
King's Own Border Regiment Association, The Castle, Carlisle.

Museum
Border Regiment and King's Own Royal Border Regiment Museum, Queen Mary's Tower, The Castle, Carlisle, Cumbria (tel 0228 32774): open March–mid October daily 0930–1830; winter Monday–Saturday 0930–1600, Sunday 1400–1600.

Record Office
Except officers: Imphal Barracks, York; officers: MS (AODO), London Road, Stanmore, Middlesex.

Predecessors

THE KING'S OWN ROYAL REGIMENT (LANCASTER)

History
Raised in 1680 as the 2nd Tangier Regiment (4th Foot in 1751).

FORMER MEMBERS: Field Marshal Viscount Hardinge (1785–1856), commissioned 1802. Marshal of the Royal Air Force Sir John Salmond (1881–1968), commissioned 1901.

Emblazoned Battle Honours

War of the League of Augsburg (1689–97): Namur 1695; Gibraltar 1704–5. **Seven Years War** (1756–63): Guadaloupe 1759. **War of American Independence** (1775–8): St Lucia 1778. **Peninsular War** (1808–14): Corunna; Badajos; Salamanca; Vittoria; San Sebastian; Nive; Peninsula. **War of 1812** (1812–14): Bladensburg. **Hundred Days** (1815): Waterloo. **Crimean War** (1854–5): Alma; Inkerman; Sevastopol. **Abyssinian War** (1867–8): Abyssinia. **Zulu and Basuto War** (1877–9): South Africa 1879. South African War (1899–1902): Relief of Ladysmith; South Africa 1899–1902. **Great War:** Marne 1914; Ypres 1915, 1917; Somme 1916, 1918; Arras 1917, 1918; Messines 1917; Lys; France and Flanders 1914–18. **Second World War:** Dunkirk 1940; North-West Europe 1940; Defence of Habbiniya; Merjayun; Tobruk Sortie; Habbiniya (1941); Merjayun (1942); Tobruk Sortie (1942); North Africa 1940–2; Montone (1944); Lamone Bridgehead (1944); Malta 1941–2; Chindits 1944.

Accredited Battle Honours

Great War: Le Cateau; Retreat from Mons; Aisne 1914; Armentières 1914; Gravenstafel; St Julien; Frezenberg; Bellewaarde; Festubert 1915; Loos; Albert 1916, 1918; Bazentin; Delville Wood; Pozières; Guillemont; Ginchy; Flers-Courcelette; Morval; Le Transloy; Ancre Heights; Ancre 1916; Scarpe 1917, 1918; Arleux; Pilckem; Menin Road; Polygon Wood; Broodseinde; Poelcapelle; Cambrai 1917, 1918; St Quentin; Estaires; Hazebrouck; Béthune; Bapaume 1918; Drocourt-Quéant; Hindenburg Line; Canal du Nord; Selle; Valenciennes; Sambre; Struma; Doiran 1917, 1918; Suvla; Sari Bair; Egypt 1916; Tigris 1916; Kut al Amara 1917; Baghdad. **Second World War:** St Omer-La Bassée; Falluja; Iraq 1941; Jebel Mazar; Syria 1941; Tobruk 1941; Citta di Castello; San Martino Sogliano; Italy 1944–5; Burma 1944.

Awards

Nine members of the regiment have been awarded the Victoria Cross: one in the Crimean War (1854–5) and eight in the Great War. First award: Private T. Grady, later Sergeant (1835–91) siege operations, Crimea, 18 October and 27 November 1855; gazetted 23 June 1857.

THE BORDER REGIMENT

History

Raised in 1702 as Lucas's Regiment (34th Foot in 1751) and in 1755 as the 57th Foot (55th Foot in 1757). These two regiments became the 1st and 2nd Battalions of the Border Regiment in 1881.

REGIMENTAL ANNIVERSARY: Arroyo dos Molinos Day (28 October).

Emblazoned Battle Honours

(awards before 1881 to 55th*; awards to both 34th and 55th**)

Seven Years War (1756–63): Havannah. **War of American Independence** (1775–8): *St Lucia 1778. **Peninsular War** (1808–14): Albuhera; Arroyo dos Molinos; Vittoria; Pyrenees; Nivelle; Nive; Orthes; Peninsula. **Crimean War** (1854–5): *Alma; *Inkerman; **Sevastopol. **Indian Mutiny** (1857–8): Lucknow. **South African War** (1899–1902): Relief of Ladysmith; South Africa 1899–1902. **Great War:** Ypres 1914, 1915, 1917, 1918; Langemarck 1914, 1917; Somme 1916, 1918; Arras 1917, 1918; Cambrai 1917, 1918; Lys; France and Flanders 1914–18; Vittorio Veneto; Macedonia 1915–16; Gallipoli 1915–16. **Third Afghan War** (1919): Afghanistan 1919. **Second World War:** Dunkirk 1940; Arnhem 1944; North-West Europe 1940, 1944; Tobruk 1941; Landing in Sicily; Imphal; Myinmu Bridgehead; Meiktila; Chindits 1944; Burma 1943–5. A Dragon superscribed 'China' was also borne on the colours.

Accredited Battle Honours

Great War: Gheluvelt; Neuve Chapelle; Frezenberg; Bellewaarde; Aubers; Festubert 1915; Loos; Albert 1916, 1918; Bazentin; Delville Wood; Pozières; Guillemont; Flers-Courcelette; Morval; Thiepval; Le Transloy; Ancre Heights; Ancre 1916; Scarpe 1917; Bullecourt; Messines 1917, 1918; Pilckem; Polygon Wood; Broodseinde; Poelcapelle; Passchendaele; St Quentin; Rosières; Estaires; Hazebrouck; Bailleul; Kemmel; Scherpenberg; Aisne 1918; Amiens; Bapaume 1918; Hindenburg Line; Epéhy; St Quentin Canal; Beaurevoir; Courtrai; Selle; Sambre; Piave; Italy 1917–18; Doiran 1917, 1918; Helles; Landing at Helles; Krithia; Suvla; Landing at Suvla; Scimitar Hill; Egypt 1916, NW Frontier India 1916–17. **Second World War:** Defence of Escaut; Somme 1940; Sakawng; Tamu Road; Shenam Pass; Kohima; Ukhrul; Mandalay; Rangoon Road; Pyawbwe; Sittang 1945.

Awards

Ten members of the regiment have been awarded the Victoria Cross: four in the Crimean War (1854–5), one in the Indian Mutiny (1857–8) and five in the Great War. First awards: Private W. Coffey DCM, later Sergeant (1829–91) siege operations, Crimea, 29 March 1855: gazetted 24 February 1857 (34th). Private T. Beach (1824–64) Inkerman 5 November 1854: gazetted 24 February 1857 (55th Foot).

Memorial

Regimental Memorial Chapel, Carlisle Cathedral.

March

Quick: *John Peel*; *March of French 34e Régiment*; *Lass o'Gowrie*. Slow: *Horn of the Hunter*.

Museum

Border Regiment and King's Own Royal Border Regiment Museum, Queen Mary's Tower, The Castle, Carlisle, Cumbria (tel 0228 32774); open March–mid October daily 0930–1830; Winter Monday–Saturday 0930–1600, Sunday 1400–1600.

Regimental Histories

Sutherland, D. *Tried and Valiant*, Leo Cooper, 1972. Shears, P. J. *The Story of the Border Regiment 1939–1945*, Nisbet, 1948. Wylly, Colonel H. C. CB. *The Border Regiment in the Great War*, Gale & Polden, 1924.

THE ROYAL REGIMENT OF FUSILIERS
(The Queen's Division)
Colonel-in-Chief:
Major-General HRH The Duke of Kent KG GCMG GCVO ADC

History
Formed in 1968 by the amalgamation of the Royal Northumberland Fusiliers; the Royal Warwickshire Fusiliers; the Royal Fusiliers (City of London Regiment); and the Lancashire Fusiliers. Three regular battalions, two volunteer battalions (5th and 6th).
HEADQUARTERS: HM Tower of London.
RECRUITMENT AREA: Northumberland, Lancashire, Warwickshire, Midlands and Greater London.
REGIMENTAL ANNIVERSARIES: St George's Day (23 April); Minden Day (1 August).

Emblazoned Battle Honours
War of the League of Augsburg (1689–97): Namur 1695. **War of Austrian Succession** (1740–8): Dettingen. **Seven Years War** (1756–63): Minden; Wilhelmstael. **War of American Independence** (1775–8): St Lucia 1778. **French Revolutionary Wars** (1793–1802): Martinique 1794; Egmont op Zee. **Napoleonic Wars** (1803–15): Maida; Martinique 1809. **Peninsular War** (1808–14): Rolica; Vimiera; Corunna; Talavera; Busaco; Ciudad Rodrigo; Badajos; Albuhera; Salamanca; Vittoria; Pyrenees; Nivelle; Orthes; Toulouse; Peninsula. **War of 1812** (1812–14): Niagara. **Seventh Kaffir War** (1846–7): South Africa 1846–7. **Eighth Kaffir War** (1851–3): South Africa 1851–1852–1853. **Crimean War** (1854–5): Alma; Inkerman; Sevastopol. **Indian Mutiny** (1857–8): Lucknow. **Second Afghan War** (1878–80): Kandahar 1880; Afghanistan 1878–80. **Reconquest of the Sudan** (1896–8): Atbara; Khartoum. **South African War** (1899–1902): Modder River; Relief of Ladysmith; South Africa 1899–1902. **Great War:** Mons; Marne 1914; Aisne 1914, 1918; Ypres 1914, 1915, 1917, 1918: St Julien; Somme 1916, 1918; Arras 1917, 1918; Passchendaele; Cambrai 1917, 1918; Lys; Hindenburg Line; Piave; Struma; Macedonia 1915–18; Landing at Helles; Suvla; Sari Bair; Gallipoli 1915–16; Egypt 1915–17; Baghdad. **Second World War:** Defence of Escaut; Dunkirk 1940; Normandy Landing; Caen; Rhineland; Bremen; North-West Europe 1940, 1944–5; Keren; Defence of Tobruk; Medjez el Bab; North Africa 1940–3; Sangro; Mozzagrogna; Salerno; Anzio; Cassino II; Gothic Line; Malta 1941–2; Kohima; Burma 1943–5. **Korean War** (1950–3): Imjin; Korea 1950–3. The Sphinx superscribed 'Egypt' is also borne on the colours.

Accredited Battle Honours
Great War: Le Cateau; Retreat from Mons; La Bassée 1914; Messines 1914, 1917, 1918; Armentières 1914; Langemarck 1914, 1917; Gheluvelt; Nonne Bosschen; Neuve Chapelle; Gravenstafel; Frezenberg; Bellewaarde; Hooge 1915; Aubers; Festubert 1915; Loos; Albert 1916, 1918; Bazentin; Delville Wood; Pozières; Guillemont; Ginchy; Flers-Courcelette; Morval; Thiepval; Le Transloy; Ancre Heights; Ancre 1916, 1918; Vimy 1917; Scarpe 1917, 1918; Arleux; Bullecourt; Oppy; Pilckem; Menin Road; Polygon Wood; Broodseinde; Poelcapelle; St Quentin; Bapaume 1918; Rosières; Avre; Villers Bretonneux; Estaires; Hazebrouck; Bailleul; Kemmel; Béthune; Scherpenberg; Amiens; Drocourt-Quéant; Havrincourt; Epéhy; Canal du Nord; St Quentin Canal; Beaurevoir; Courtrai; Selle; Valenciennes; Sambre; France and Flanders 1914–18; Vittorio Veneto; Italy 1917–18; Doiran 1917; Helles; Krithia; Landing at Suvla; Scimitar Hill; Rumani; Megiddo; Nablus; Palestine 1918; Tigris 1916; Kut al Amara 1917; Mesopotamia 1916–18; Baku; Persia 1918; Troitsa; Archangel 1919; Kilimanjaro; Behobeho; Nyango; East Africa 1915–17. **Second World War:** Arras Counter-attack; St Omer-La Bassée; Wormhoudt; Ypres-Comines Canal; Odon; Bourguébus Ridge; Cagny; Mont Pinçon; Falaise; Nederrijn; Venraij; Lingen; Brinkum; Agordat; Syria 1941; Sidi Barrani; Tobruk 1941; Belhamed; Cauldron; Ruweisat Ridge; El Alamein; Advance on Tripoli; Medenine; Djebel Tebaga; Oued Zarga; Peter's Corner; Adrano; Sicily 1943; Termoli; Trigno; Caldari; St Lucia; Battipaglia; Teano; Volturno Crossing; Monte Camino; Garigliano Crossing; Damiano; Ripa Ridge; Trasimene Line; Gabbiano; Advance to Florence; Monte Scalari; Coriano; Croce; Monte Ceco; Casa Fortis; Monte Spaduro; Savio Bridgehead; Vall di Comacchio; Senio; Argenta Gap; Italy 1943–5; Athens; Greece 1944–5; Singapore Island; Rathedaung; Htizwe; Naga Village; Chindits 1944. **Korean War:** Seoul; Kowang-San.

DIFFERENCES: Blue beret, red over white hackle. Crimson/yellow/crimson stable belt.

Regimental Mascot
Indian black buck.

Marches
Quick: *The British Grenadiers.* Slow: *Rule Britannia, De Normandie,* including *St George* (Royal Northumberland Fusiliers); *Macbean's Slow March* (Royal Warwickshire Fusiliers); *De Normandie* (Royal Fusiliers); and *The Lancashire Fusiliers Slow March.*

Alliances
The Elgin Regiment, of Canada; The Royal Canadian Regiment; The Lorne Scots (Peel, Dufferin and Halton Regiment), of Canada; Les Fusiliers de St Laurent, of Canada; The Royal Westminster Regiment, of Canada; 5th/6th Battalion The Royal Victoria Regiment, of Australia; 6th Battalion (Hauraki) Royal New Zealand Infantry Regiment.

Journal
The Fusilier (twice a year – June, December).

Museum
HM Tower of London (tel 071-709 0765 ext 295): open March–October Monday–Saturday 1000–1700, Sunday summer only 1400–1700; November–February Monday–Saturday 1000–1615.

Record Office
Except officers: Higher Barracks, York; officers: MS(AODO), London Rd, Stanmore, Middlesex.

Predecessors

THE ROYAL NORTHUMBERLAND FUSILIERS

History
Raised in 1674 in the service of the Prince of Orange as the Irish Regiment. Placed on the English establishment in 1685, 5th Foot in 1751.

MOTTO: *Quo fata vocant* (Wherever fate calls).

REGIMENTAL ANNIVERSARY: St George's Day (23 April).

Emblazoned Battle Honours
Seven Years War (1756–63): Wilhelmstahl. **War of American Independence** (1775–8): St Lucia 1778. **Peninsular War** (1808–14): Rolica; Vimiera; Corunna; Busaco; Ciudad Rodrigo; Badajos; Salamanca; Vittoria; Nivelle; Orthes; Toulouse; Peninsula. **Indian Mutiny** (1857–8): Lucknow. **Second Afghan War** (1878–80): Afghanistan 1878–80. **Reconquest of Sudan** (1896–8): Khartoum. **South African War** (1899–1902): Modder River; South Africa 1899–1902. **Great War** (1914–18): Mons; Marne 1914; Ypres 1914, 1915, 1917, 1918; St Julien; Somme 1916, 1918; Scarpe 1917,

1918; Selle; Piave; Struma; Suvla. **Second World War:** Dunkirk 1940; Caen; Rhineland; Sidi Barrani; Defence of Tobruk; Tobruk 1941; Cauldron; El Alamein; Salerno; Cassino II. **Korean War** (1950–3): Imjin; Korea 1950–51.

Accredited Battle Honours
Great War: Le Cateau; Retreat from Mons; Aisne 1914, 1918; La Bassée 1914; Messines 1914, 1917, 1918; Armentières 1914; Nonne Bosschen; Gravenstafel; Frezenberg; Bellewaarde; Loos; Albert 1916, 1918; Bazentin; Delville Wood; Pozières; Flers-Courcelette; Morval; Thiepval; Le Transloy; Ancre Heights; Ancre 1916; Arras 1917, 1918; Arleux; Pilckem; Langemarck 1917; Menin Road; Polygon Wood; Broodseinde; Passchendaele; Cambrai 1917, 1918; St Quentin; Bapaume 1918; Rosières; Lys; Estaires; Hazebrouck; Bailleul; Kemmel; Béthune; Scherpenberg; Drocourt-Quéant; Hindenburg Line; Epéhy; Canal du Nord; St Quentin Canal; Beaurevoir; Courtrai; Valenciennes; Sambre; France and Flanders 1914–18; Vittorio Veneto; Italy 1917–18; Macedonia 1915–18; Landing at Suvla; Scimitar Hill; Gallipoli 1915; Egypt 1916–17. **Second World War:** Defence of Escaut; Arras Counter-attack; St Omer-La Bassée; Odon; Cagny; Falaise; Nederrijn; North-West Europe 1940, 1944–5; Belhamed; Ruweisat Ridge; Advance on Tripoli; Medenine; North

Africa 1940–3; Volturno Crossing; Monte Camino; Garigliano Crossing; Italy 1943–5; Singapore Island. **Korean War** (1950–3): Seoul; Kowang-San.

Awards

Ten members of the regiment have been awarded the Victoria Cross: three in the Indian Mutiny (1857–8), five in the Great War and two in the Second World War. First award: Sergeant R. Grant (1837–74) Alumbagh, India, 24 September 1857: gazetted 19 June 1860. Fusilier D. G. Kinne (b1930) was awarded the George Cross, Chinese POW Camp 1951–3: gazetted 13 April 1954.

Memorials

Alnwick Castle, Northumberland. St Nicholas Cathedral, Newcastle-upon-Tyne: Rolls of Honour for Great War, Second World War, Korea, Kenya and Aden; Colours of the four regular battalions; stained glass window for Indian Mutiny; marble panels for individuals and casualties of Omdurman, etc.

Marches

Quick: *The British Grenadiers* and *Blaydon Races.* Slow: *St George.*

Journal

St George's Gazette (1883–1968).

Museum

The Abbot's Tower, Alnwick Castle, Alnwick, Northumberland (tel 0665 602152): open May–September Monday –Friday, Sunday 1300–1700.

Regimental Histories

Peacock, B. *The Royal Northumberland Fusiliers,* Leo Cooper, 1970. Walker, H. M. *A History of the Northumberland Fusiliers 1674–1902,* London, 1919. Sandilands, H. R. *The Fifth in the Great War,* Grigg, 1938. Barclay, C. N. *The History of the Royal Northumberland Fusiliers in the Second World War,* Clowes, 1952.

THE ROYAL WARWICKSHIRE FUSILIERS

History

Raised in 1674 as Vane's Regiment (a Holland regiment). Placed on the English establishment in 1685 (1st Warwickshire in 1782, Royal in 1832, Fusiliers in 1963).

FORMER MEMBERS: Field Marshal The Earl of Lucan (1800–86), commissioned 1816; Marshal of the Royal Air Force Lord Newall (1886–1963), commissioned 1905; Field Marshal Viscount Montgomery (1887–1970), commissioned 1908 – statue opposite MOD, Whitehall, London; Field Marshal Viscount Slim (1891–1970), commissioned 1914 – statue Raleigh Green, Whitehall, London.

Emblazoned Battle Honours

War of the League of Augsburg (1689–97): Namur 1695. **French Revolutionary Wars** (1793–1802): Martinique 1794. **Peninsular War** (1808–14): Rolica; Vimiera; Corunna; Vittoria; Pyrenees; Nivelle; Orthes; Peninsula. **War of 1812** (1812–14): Niagara. **Seventh Kafir War** (1846–7): South Africa 1846–7. **Eighth Kafir War** (1851–3): South Africa 1851–1852–1853. **Reconquest of the Sudan** (1896–8): Atbara; Khartoum. **South African War** (1899–1902): South Africa 1899–1902. **Great War:** Le Cateau; Marne 1914; Ypres 1914, 1915, 1917; Somme 1916, 1918; Arras 1917, 1918; Lys; Hindenburg Line; Piave; Sari Bair; Baghdad. **Second World War:** Defence of Escaut; Wormhoudt; Ypres–Comines Canal; Normandy Landing; Caen; Mont Pinçon; Venraij; Bremen; North-West Europe 1940, 1944–5; Burma 1945.

Accredited Battle Honours
Great War: Retreat from Mons; Aisne 1914, 1918; Armentières 1914; Langemarck 1914, 1917; Gheluvelt; Neuve Chapelle; St Julien; Frezenberg; Bellewaarde; Aubers; Festubert 1915; Loos; Albert 1916, 1918; Bazentin; Delville Wood; Pozières; Guillemont; Flers-Courcelette; Morval; Le Transloy; Ancre Heights; Ancre 1916; Vimy 1917; Scarpe 1917, 1918; Arleux; Oppy; Bullecourt; Messines 1917, 1918; Pilckem; Menin Road; Polygon Wood; Broodseinde; Poelcapelle; Passchendaele; Cambrai 1917, 1918; St Quentin; Bapaume 1918; Rosières; Estaires; Hazebrouck; Bailleul; Kemmel; Béthune; Drocourt-Quéant; Epéhy; Canal du Nord; Beaurevoir; Selle; Valenciennes; Sambre; France and Flanders 1914–18; Vittorio Veneto; Italy 1917–18; Suvla; Gallipoli 1915–16; Tigris 1916; Kut al Amara 1917; Mesopotamia 1916–18; Baku; Persia 1918. **Second World War:** Bourguébus Ridge; Falaise; Rhineland; Lingen; Brinkum.

Awards
Six members of the regiment have been awarded the Victoria Cross – all in the Great War. First award: Private A. Vickers, later Lance-Corporal (1882–1944) Hulluch, France, 25 September 1915: gazetted 18 November 1915.

Marches
Quick: *The Warwickshire Lads*. Slow: *Macbean's Slow March*.

Journal
The Antelope (up to 1968).

Associations
Royal Regiment of Fusiliers Regiment Association, Warwickshire has seven branches. Royal Warwickshire Charitable Welfare Fund.

Museum
St John's House, Coten End, Warwick, Warwickshire (tel 0926 491653): open Tuesday–Saturday 1000–1230, 1330–1730, May–September Sunday 1430–1700.

Regimental Histories
Cunliffe, M. *History of the Royal Warwickshire Regiment, 1919–1955*, Clowes, 1956. Kingsford, C. L. *The Story of the Royal Warwickshire Regiment, County Life*, 1921.

THE ROYAL FUSILIERS (CITY OF LONDON REGIMENT)

History
Raised in 1685 as the Royal Regiment of Fusiliers (7th Foot in 1751).

Emblazoned Battle Honours
War of the League of Augsburg (1689–97): Namur 1695. **French Revolutionary Wars** (1793–1802): Martinique 1809. **Peninsular War** (1808–14): Talavera; Busaco; Albuhera; Badajos; Salamanca; Vittoria; Pyrenees; Orthes; Toulouse; Peninsula. **Crimean War** (1854–5): Alma; Inkerman; Sevastopol. **Second Afghan War** (1878–80): Kandahar 1880; Afghanistan 1879–80. **South African War** (1899–1902): Relief of Ladysmith; South Africa 1899–1902. **Great War:** Mons; Aisne 1914, 1918; Ypres 1914,

1915, 1917, 1918; Somme 1916, 1918; Arras 1917, 1918; Passchendaele; Cambrai 1917, 1918; Hindenburg Line; Macedonia 1915–18; Landing at Helles; Palestine 1918. **Second World War:** Dunkirk 1940; Keren; North Africa 1940, 1943; Mozzagrogna; Salerno; Garigliano Crossing; Anzio; Cassino II; Gothic Line; Coriano. **Korean War** (1950–3): Korea 1952–3.

Accredited Battle Honours
Great War: Le Cateau; Retreat from Mons; Aisne 1914; La Bassée 1914; Messines 1914, 1917; Armentières 1914; Nonne Bosschen; Gravenstafel; St Julien; Frezenberg; Bellewaarde; Hooge 1915; Loos; Albert 1916, 1918; Bazentin; Delville Wood; Pozières; Flers-Courcelette; Thiepval; Le Transloy; Ancre Heights; Ancre 1916; Vimy 1917; Scarpe 1917; Arleux; Pilckem; Langemarck 1917; Menin Road; Polygon Wood; Broodseinde; Poelcapelle; Passchendaele; St Quentin; Bapaume 1918; Rosières; Avre; Villers Bretonneux; Lys; Estaires; Hazebrouck; Béthune; Amiens; Drocourt-Quéant; Havrincourt; Epéhy; Canal du Nord; St Quentin Canal; Beaurevoir; Courtrai; Selle; Sambre; France and Flanders 1914–18; Italy 1917–18; Macedonia 1915–18; Helles; Krithia; Suvla; Scimitar Hill; Gallipoli 1915–16; Egypt 1916; Megiddo; Nablus; Troitsa; Archangel 1919; Kilimanjaro; Behobeho; Nyangao; East Africa 1915–17. **Second World War:** North-West Europe 1940; Agordat; Syria 1941; Sidi Barrani; Djebel Tebaga; Peter's Corner; Sangro; Caldari; St Lucia; Battipaglia; Teano; Monte Camino; Damiano; Ripa Ridge; Gabbiano; Advance to Florence; Monte Scalari; Croce; Casa Fortis; Savio Bridgehead; Valli di Comacchio; Senio; Argenta Gap; Italy 1943–5; Athens; Greece 1944–5.

Awards
Nineteen members of the regiment have been awarded the Victoria Cross: five in the Crimean War (1854–5), one in the Second Afghan War (1878–80), one in the South African War (1899–1902), ten in the Great War and two in North Russia (1919). First award: Private W. Norman, later Corporal (1832–96). White Horse Ravine, Crimea, 19 December 1854: gazetted 24 February 1857.

Marches
Quick: *The British Grenadiers* and *The Seventh Royal Fusiliers*.

Museum
HM Tower of London (tel 071-709 0765 ext 295): open March–October Monday–Saturday 1000–1700, Sunday summer only 1400–1700; November–February Monday–Saturday 1000–1615.

Regimental Histories
Foss, M. *The Royal Fusiliers*, Hamish Hamilton, 1967. O'Neill, H. C. *The Royal Fusiliers in the Great War*, Heinemann, 1922. Northcote Parkinson, C. *Always a Fusilier: The War History of the Royal Fusiliers*, Sampson Low, 1949.

THE LANCASHIRE FUSILIERS

History
Raised in 1688 as Peyton's 20th Regiment of Foot (XX Foot in 1751, XX The Lancashire Fusiliers in 1881). MOTTO: *Omnia audax* (Daring in all things).

REGIMENTAL DAYS: Gallipoli Day (25 April); Minden Day (1 August); Inkerman Day (5 November).

Emblazoned Battle Honours

War of Austrian Succession (1740–8): Dettingen. Seven Years War (1756–63): Minden. French Revolutionary Wars (1793–1802): Egmont op Zee. Napoleonic Wars (1803–15): Maida. Peninsular War (1808–14): Vimiera; Corunna; Vittoria; Pyrenees; Orthes; Toulouse; Peninsula. Crimean War (1854–5): Alma; Inkerman; Sevastopol. Indian Mutiny (1857–8): Lucknow. Reconquest of the Sudan (1896–8): Khartoum. South African War (1899–1902): Relief of Ladysmith; South Africa 1899–1902. Great War: Retreat from Mons; Aisne 1914, 1918; Ypres 1915, 1917, 1918; Somme 1916, 1918; Arras 1917, 1918; Passchendaele; Cambrai 1917, 1918; Hindenburg Line; Macedonia 1915–18; Landing at Helles. Second World War: Defence of Escaut; Caen; Medjez el Bab; Sangro; Cassino II; Argenta Gap; Malta 1941–2; Kohima; Chindits 1944; Burma 1943–5. The Sphinx superscribed 'Egypt' was also borne on the colours.

Accredited Battle Honours

Great War: Le Cateau; Marne 1914; Armentières 1914; St Julien; Bellewaarde; Albert 1916, 1918; Bazentin; Delville Wood; Pozières; Ginchy; Flers-Courcelette; Morval; Thiepval; Le Transloy; Ancre Heights; Ancre 1916, 1918; Scarpe 1917, 1918; Arleux; Messines 1917; Pilckem; Langemarck 1917; Menin Road; Polygon Wood; Broodseinde; Poelcapelle; St Quentin; Bapaume 1918; Rosières; Lys; Estaires; Hazebrouck; Bailleul; Kemmel; Béthune; Scherpenberg; Amiens; Drocourt-Quéant; Epéhy; Canal du Nord; St Quentin Canal; Courtrai; Selle; Sambre; France and Flanders 1914–18; Doiran 1917; Helles; Krithia; Suvla; Landing at Suvla; Scimitar Hill; Gallipoli 1915; Rumani; Egypt 1915–17. Second World War: St Omer-La Bassée; North-West Europe 1940, 1944; Oued Zarga; North Africa 1942–3; Adrano; Sicily 1943; Termoli; Trigno; Trasimene Line; Monte Ceco; Monte Spadura; Senio; Italy 1943–5; Rathedaung; Htizwe; Naga Village.

Awards

Nineteen members of the regiment have been awarded the Victoria Cross: eighteen in the Great War and one in the Second World War. First award: Private J. Lynn DCM (d 1915) Ypres 2 May 1915: gazetted posthumously 29 June 1915.

Marches

Quick: Minden March. Slow: The Lancashire Fusiliers Slow March.

Journal

The Lancashire Fusiliers' Annual (1891–1928); The Gallipoli Gazette (1928–1968).

Museum

Wellington Barracks, Bury, Lancashire (tel 061 764 2208): open Monday–Wednesday, Friday, Saturday 0900–1215, 1245–1630, Sunday 0900–1215, 1245–1700.

Regimental Histories

Ray, C. The Lancashire Fusiliers, Leo Cooper, 1971. Latter, J. C. The History of the Lancashire Fusiliers 1914–1918 (2 vols), Gale & Polden, 1949. Smythe, B. History of the Lancashire Fusiliers (XX Regiment) 1688–1903 (2 vols.) Sackville Press (Dublin), 1904. Surtees, G. A Short History of the Lancashire Fusiliers, Malcolm Page, 1955. Ray, C. Regiment of the Line: The Story of XX The Lancashire Fusiliers, Batsford, 1963.

THE KING'S REGIMENT
(the King's Division)
Colonel-in-Chief: HM Queen Elizabeth The Queen Mother

History
Formed in 1958 as the King's Regiment (Manchester and Liverpool) (The King's Regiment in 1968) by the amalgamation of the King's Regiment (Liverpool) and the Manchester Regiment. One regular battalion, one volunteer battalion (5th/8th).
HEADQUARTERS: TA Centre, Townsend Avenue, Liverpool.
RECRUITMENT AREA: Merseyside and Greater Manchester.
REGIMENTAL ANNIVERSARIES: Ladysmith Day (28 February); Kohima Day (15 May); Guadaloupe Day (10 June); Somme Day (1 July); Blenheim Day (13 August); Delhi Day (14 September); Inkerman Day (5 November).

Emblazoned Battle Honours
War of Spanish Succession (1701–15): Blenheim; Ramillies; Oudenarde; Malplaquet. **War of Austrian Succession** (1740–8): Dettingen. **Napoleonic Wars** (1803–15): Martinique 1809; Guadaloupe 1810. **War of 1812** (1812–14): Niagara (1813). **First Maori War** (1846–7): New Zealand 1846–7. **Crimean War** (1854–5): Alma; Inkerman; Sevastopol. **Indian Mutiny** (1857–8): Delhi 1857; Lucknow. **Second Afghan War** (1878–80): Peiwar Kotal; Afghanistan 1878–80. **First Sudan War** (1882–4): Egypt 1882. **Third Burma War** (1885–7): Burma 1885–7. **South African War** (1899–1902): Defence of Ladysmith; South Africa 1899–1902. **Great War:** Mons; Retreat from Mons; Marne 1914; Aisne 1914; Ypres 1914, 1915, 1917, 1918; Givenchy 1914; Festubert 1915; Loos; Somme 1916, 1918; Arras 1917, 1918; Scarpe 1917, 1918; Cambrai 1917, 1918; Hindenburg Line; Piave; Macedonia 1915–18; Gallipoli 1915; Megiddo; Baghdad. **Third Afghan War:** Afghanistan 1919. **Second World War:** Dyle; Defence of Arras; Normandy Landing; Caen; Scheldt; Lower Maas; Roer; Reichswald; Cassino II; Trasimene Line; Tuori; Gothic Line; Capture of Forli; Rimini Line; Malta 1940; Athens; Kohima; Chindits 1943; Chindits 1944. **Korean War** (1950–3): The Hook 1953; Korea 1952–3. The Sphinx superscribed 'Egypt' is also borne on the colours.

Accredited Battle Honours
Great War: Le Cateau; La Bassée 1914; Armentières 1914; Langemarck 1914, 1917; Gheluvelt; Nonne Bosschen; Neuve Chapelle; Gravenstafel; St Julien; Frezenberg; Bellewaarde; Aubers; Albert 1916, 1918; Bazentin; Delville Wood; Guillemont; Ginchy; Flers-Courcelette; Morval; Thiepval; Le Transloy; Ancre Heights; Ancre 1916, 1918; Bapaume 1917, 1918; Arleux; Bullecourt; Messines

1917, 1918; Pilckem; Menin Road; Polygon Wood; Broodseinde; Poelcapelle; Passchendaele; St Quentin; Rosières; Avre; Lys; Estaires; Bailleul; Kemmel; Béthune; Amiens; Scherpenberg; Drocourt-Quéant; Epéhy; Canal du Nord; St Quentin Canal; Beaurevoir; Courtrai; Selle; Sambre; France and Flanders 1914–18; Vittorio Veneto; Italy 1917–18; Doiran 1917; Helles; Krithia; Suvla; Landing at Suvla; Scimitar Hill; Rumani; Egypt 1915–17; Sharon; Palestine 1918; Tigris 1916; Kut al Amara 1917; Mesopotamia 1916–18; NW Frontier India 1915; Archangel 1918–19. **Second World War:** Withdrawal to Escaut; Defence of Escaut; St Omer-La Bassée; Ypres-Comines Canal; Esquay; Falaise; Nederrijn; Walcheren Causeway; Flushing; Venlo Pocket; Ourthe; Rhineland; Goch; Weeze; Rhine; Ibbenburen; Dreirwalde; Aller; Bremen; North-West Europe 1940, 1944–5; Monte Gridotto; Coriano; San Clemente; Gemmano Ridge; Montilgallo; Lamone Crossing; Defence of Lamone Bridgehead; Montescudo; Cesena; Italy 1944–45; Greece 1944–5; Singapore Island; Malaya 1941–2; North Arakan; Pinwe; Shwebo; Myinmu Bridgehead; Irrawaddy; Burma 1943–5.

Dress
DIFFERENCES: Blue dress cap, scarlet band and piping; maroon side cap, green tip. Deep green stable belt, maroon central stripe.
REGIMENTAL TIE: Thin blue/red/blue stripes on olive green.

Marches
Quick: *The Kingsman.* Slow: *Lord Ferrars March.*

Alliances
The Royal Regiment of Canada; 10th Battalion The Royal South Australia Regiment; 4th Battalion Otago and Southland Royal New Zealand Regiment; 1st Battalion (Scinde) The Frontier Force Regiment, of Pakistan.

Journal
The Kingsman (once a year: November/December).

Museum
County Museum. William Brown St, Liverpool (tel 051 207 0001 and 5451): open Monday–Saturday 1000–1700, Sunday 1400–1700.

Record Office
Except officers: Imphal Barracks, York; officers: MS(AODO), London Rd, Stanmore, Middlesex.

Predecessors

THE KING'S REGIMENT (LIVERPOOL)

History
Raised in 1685 as Princess Anne of Denmark's Regiment (8th Foot in 1751).

Motto: *Nec aspera terrent* (Nor do difficulties deter).

Regimental Anniversaries: Somme Day (1 July); Blenheim Day (13 August); Delhi Day (14 September).

Emblazoned Battle Honours

War of Spanish Succession (1701–15): Blenheim; Ramillies; Oudenarde; Malplaquet. **War of Austrian Succession** (1740–8): Dettingen. **Napoleonic Wars** (1803–15): Martinique 1809. **War of 1812** (1812–14): Niagara. **Indian Mutiny** (1857–8): Delhi 1857; Lucknow. **Second Afghan War** (1878–80): Peiwar Kotal; Afghanistan 1878–80. **Third Burma War** (1885–7): Burma 1885–7. **South African War** (1899–1902): Defence of Ladysmith. **Great War:** Retreat from Mons; Marne 1914; Aisne 1914; Ypres 1914, 1915, 1917; Festubert 1915; Loos; Somme 1916, 1918; Arras 1917, 1918; Scarpe 1917, 1918; Cambrai 1917, 1918. **Third Afghan War** (1919): Afghanistan 1919. **Second World War:** Normandy Landing; Cassino II; Trasimene Line; Tuori; Capture of Forli; Rimini Line; Athens; Chindits 1943; Chindits 1944. **Korean War** (1950–3): The Hook 1953; Korea 1952–3. The Sphinx superscribed 'Egypt' was also borne on the colours.

Accredited Battle Honours

Great War: Mons; Langemarck 1914, 1917; Gheluvelt; Nonne Bosschen; Neuve Chapelle; Gravenstafel; St Julien; Frezenberg; Bellewaarde; Aubers; Albert 1916, 1918; Bazentin; Delville Wood; Guillemont; Ginchy; Flers-Courcelette; Morval; Le Transloy; Ancre 1916; Bapaume 1917, 1918; Arleux; Pilckem; Menin Road; Polygon Wood; Poelcapelle; Passchendaele; St Quentin; Rosières; Avre; Lys; Estaires; Messines 1918; Bailleul; Kemmel; Béthune; Scherpenberg; Drocourt-Quéant; Hindenburg Line; Epéhy; Canal du Nord; St Quentin Canal; Selle; Sambre; France and Flanders 1914–18; Doiran 1917; Macedonia 1915–18; NW Frontier India 1915; Archangel 1918–19. **Second World War:** North-West Europe 1944; Italy 1944–5; Greece 1944–5; Burma 1943–4.

Awards

Nine members of the regiment have been awarded the Victoria Cross: three in the South African War (1899–1902) and six in the Great War. First awards: Sergeant H. Hampton, later Colour-Sergeant (1870–1920) and Corporal H. J. Knight (1875–1955), Van Wyk's Vlei, South Africa, 21 August 1900: gazetted 18 October 1901 and 4 January 1901.

Marches

Quick: *Here's to the Maiden of Bashful Fifteen.* Slow: *Zakhmi Dil.*

Allied Regiment in 1914

8th Australian Infantry.

Journal

The Kingsman.

Museum

County Museum, William Brown St, Liverpool (tel 051 207 0001 and 5451): open Monday–Saturday 1000–1700, Sunday 1400–1700.

Regimental Histories

Burke Gaffney, J. S. *The Story of the King's Regiment, 1914–1948*, Sharpe and Kellet, 1950. Threlfall, T. R. *The Story of the King's (Liverpool) Regiment, Country Life*, 1916. Wyrall, E. *A History of the King's Regiment, 1914–1919* (3 vols.), Arnold, 1928–35.

THE MANCHESTER REGIMENT

History

Raised in 1757 as the 2nd Battalion of the 8th Foot (King's) (63rd Foot in 1758) and in 1824 as the 96th Foot. These two regiments became the 1st and 2nd Battalions of the Manchester Regiment in 1881.

REGIMENTAL ANNIVERSARIES: Ladysmith Day (28 February); Kohima Day (15 May); Guadaloupe Day (10 June); Inkerman Day (5 November).

Emblazoned Battle Honours

(awards before 1881 to 96th★)

Seven Years War (1756–63): Guadaloupe 1759. **French Revolutionary Wars** (1793–1802): Egmont op Zee. **Napoleonic Wars** (1803–15): Martinique 1809; Guadaloupe 1810. **Peninsular War** (1808–14): Peninsula. **First Maori War** (1846–7): ★New Zealand. **Crimean War** (1854–5): Alma; Inkerman; Sevastopol. **Second Afghan War** (1878–80): Afghanistan 1879–80: **South African War** (1899–1902): Defence of Ladysmith; South Africa 1899–1902. **Great War:** Mons; Givenchy 1914; Ypres 1915, 1917, 1918; Somme 1916, 1918; Hindenburg Line; Piave; Macedonia 1915–18; Gallipoli 1915; Megiddo; Baghdad. **Second World War:** Dyle; Defence of Arras; Caen; Scheldt; Lower Maas; Roer; Reichswald; Gothic Line; Malta 1940; Kohima. The Sphinx superscribed 'Egypt' was also borne on the colours.

Accredited Battle Honours

Great War: Le Cateau; Retreat from Mons; Marne 1914; Aisne 1914; La Bassée 1914; Armentières 1914; Neuve Chapelle; Gravenstafel; St Julien; Frezenberg; Bellewaarde; Aubers; Albert 1916, 1918; Bazentin; Delville Wood; Guillemont; Flers-Courcelette; Thiepval; Le Transloy; Ancre Heights; Ancre 1916, 1918; Arras 1917, 1918; Scarpe 1917; Bullecourt; Messines 1917; Pilckem; Langemarck 1917; Menin Road; Polygon Wood; Broodseinde; Poelcapelle; Passchendaele; St Quentin; Bapaume 1918; Rosières; Lys; Kemmel; Amiens; Epéhy; Canal du Nord; St Quentin Canal; Beaurevoir; Cambrai 1918; Courtrai; Selle; Sambre; France and Flanders 1914–18; Vittorio Veneto; Italy 1917–18; Doiran 1917; Helles; Krithia; Suvla; Landing at Suvla; Scimitar Hill; Rumani; Egypt 1915–17; Sharon; Palestine 1918; Tigris 1916; Kut al Amara 1917; Mesopotamia 1916–18. **Second World War:** Withdrawal to Escaut; Defence of Escaut; St Omer-La Bassée; Ypres-Comines Canal; Esquay; Falaise; Nederrijn; Walcheren Causeway; Flushing; Venlo Pocket; Ourthe; Rhineland; Goch; Weeze; Rhine; Ibbenburen; Dreirwalde; Aller; Bremen; North-West Europe 1940, 1944–5; Monte Gridolfo; Coriano; San Clemente; Gemmano Ridge; Montilgallo; Capture of Forli; Lamone Crossing; Lamone Bridgehead; Rimini Line; Montescudo; Cesena; Italy 1944; Singapore Island; Malaya 1941–2; North Arakan; Pinwe; Shwebo; Myinmu Bridgehead; Irrawaddy; Burma 1944–5.

Awards

Fourteen members of the regiment have been awarded the Victoria Cross: two in the South African War (1899–1902), eleven in the Great War and one in Mesopotamia (1920). First awards: Private J. Pitts, later Corporal (1877–1955) and Private R. Scott (1874–1961) Caesar's Camp, South Africa, 6 January 1900: gazetted 26 July 1901. Corporal K. Horsfield (*d*1944) was awarded the George Cross, Brindisi, Italy, 18 August

1944: gazetted posthumously 23 March 1945.

Memorials
Sandhurst, Surrey. St Anne's Square, Manchester, by Hamo Thornycroft; All Saints Church, Trimulgherry, India; Caesar's Camp, Ladysmith, South Africa; Whitworth Park, adjacent Whitworth Gallery.

Marches
Quick: *The Manchester*. Slow: *Farewell Manchester*.

Allied Regiment in 1914
8th (Southland) Regiment of New Zealand.

Journal
The Manchester Gazette (four times a year): now *The Kingsman* (once a year – November/December).

Association
The King's and Manchester Regimental Association, RHQ(1), TA Centre, Ardwick Green, Manchester M12 6HO.

Museum
The Museum of the Manchesters, Ashton Town Hall; The Market Place, Ashton-under-Lyne, Lancashire (tel 061 344 3078): open Monday–Saturday 1000–1600.

Regimental Histories
Bell, A. C. *History of the Manchester Regiment, 1922–1948*, John Sherratt & Son, 1954. Wylly, H. C. *History of the Manchester Regiment* (2 vols), Forster Groom, 1923.

THE ROYAL ANGLIAN REGIMENT
(The Queen's Division)
Colonel-in-Chief: HM Queen Elizabeth The Queen Mother

History
Formed in 1964 from the 1st East Anglian Regiment (Royal Norfolk and Suffolk); the 2nd East Anglian Regiment (Duchess of Gloucester's Own Royal Lincolnshire and Northamptonshire); the 3rd East Anglian Regiment (16/44th Foot); and the Royal Leicestershire Regiment. Three regular battalions, three volunteer battalions (5th, 6th and 7th).

MOTTO: *Montis insignia Calpe* (The badge of the Rock of Gibraltar).

HEADQUARTERS: The Keep, Gibraltar Barracks, Bury St Edmonds, Suffolk.

RECRUITMENT AREA: Lincolnshire, Leicestershire, Northamptonshire, Cambridgeshire, Norfolk, Suffolk, Bedfordshire, Hertfordshire and Essex.

REGIMENTAL ANNIVERSARIES: Sobraon Day (10 February); Almanza Day (25 April); Royal Tiger Day (25 June); Salamanca Day (22 July); Talavera Day (27 July); Minden Day (1 August); Blenheim Day (2 August).

Emblazoned Battle Honours
War of the League of Augsburg (1689–97): Namur 1695. **War of Spanish Succession** (1701–15): Blenheim; Ramillies; Oudenarde; Malplaquet. **War of Austrian Succession** (1740–8): Dettingen. **Seven Years War** (1756–63): Louisburg; Quebec 1759; Minden; Martinique 1762; Havana. **French Revolutionary Wars** (1793–1802): Martinique 1794. **Fourth Mysore War** (1799): Seringapatam. **Peninsular War** (1808–14): Corunna; Talavera; Albuhera; Badajos; Salamanca; Vittoria; Peninsula. **War of 1812** (1812–14): Bladensburg. **Hundred Days** (1815): Waterloo. **First Burma War** (1824–6): Ava. **First Afghan War** (1839–42): Ghuznee 1839; Khelat, Cabool 1842. **First Sikh War** (1845–76): Moodkee; Ferozeshah; Sobraon. **Second Sikh War** (1848–49): Goojerat; Punjaub. **First Maori War** (1846–7): New Zealand. **Eighth Kaffir War** (1851–3): South Africa 1851–1852–1853. **Crimean War** (1854–5): Inkerman; Sevastopol. **Indian Mutiny** (1857–8): Lucknow. **Second China War** (1857–60): Taku Forts. **Second Afghan War** (1878–80): Afghanistan 1878–80. **Egyptian Campaign** (1885): Nile 1884–5. **Tirah Campaign** (1897–8): Tirah. **Reconquest of Sudan** (1896–8): Atbara; Khartoum. **South African War** (1899–1902): Paardeburg; Defence of Ladysmith; South Africa 1899–1902. **Great War:** Mons; Le Cateau; Marne 1914; Aisne 1914, 1918; Ypres 1914, 1915, 1917, 1918; Neuve Chapelle; Loos; Somme 1916, 1918; Arras 1917, 1918; Cambrai 1917, 1918; France and Flanders 1914–18; Macedonia 1915–18; Gallipoli 1915–16; Gaza; Palestine 1917–18; Shaiba; Mesopotamia 1914–18. **Second World War:** St Omer-La Bassée; Dunkirk 1940; Normandy Landing; Brieux Bridgehead;

Venraij; North-West Europe 1940, 1944–5; Tobruk 1941; Defence of Alamein Line; North Africa 1940–3; Villa Grande; Salerno; Anzio; Cassino I–II; Gothic Line; Italy 1943–5; Crete; Singapore Island; Malaya 1941–2; Yu; Ngakyedauk Pass; Chindits 1944; Burma 1943–5. **Korean War** (1950–3): Korea 1951–3. The castle and key superscribed 'Gibraltar 1779–1783' and a Royal Tiger superscribed 'Hindoostan' are also borne on the colours.

Accredited Battle Honours

Seven Years War (1756–63): Belleisle; Moro. **India** (1797–1809): India. **Napoleonic Wars** (1803–1815): Surinam; Maida. **Peninsular War** (1808–14): Rolica; Vimiera; Douro; Busaco; Pyrenees; San Sebastian; Nivelle; Nive; Orthes; Toulouse. **First Afghan War** (1839–42): Affghanistan 1839. **Second Sikh War** (1848–9): Mooltan. **Crimean War** (1854–5): Alma. **Zulu and Basuto War** (1877–9): South Africa 1879. **Second Afghan War** (1878–1880): Ali Masjid. **Chitral Campaign** (1895): Chitral. **South African War** (1899–1902): Modder River; Relief of Kimberley. **Great War:** Retreat from Mons; La Bassée 1914; Messines 1914, 1917, 1918; Givenchy 1914; Langemarck 1914, 1917; Gheluvelt; Nonne Bosschen; Festubert 1914, 1915; Hill 60; Gravenstafel; St Julien; Frezenberg; Bellewaarde; Aubers; Hooge 1915; Albert 1916, 1918; Bazentin; Delville Wood; Pozières; Guillemont; Flers-Courcelette; Morval; Thiepval; Le Transloy; Ancre Heights; Ancre 1916; Bapaume 1917, 1918; Vimy 1917; Scarpe 1917, 1918; Arleux; Oppy; Pilckem; Menin Road; Polygon Wood; Broodseinde; Poelcapelle; Passchendaele; St Quentin; Rosières; Avre; Villers Bretonneux; Lys; Estaires; Hazebrouck; Bailleul; Kemmel; Béthune; Scherpenberg; Amiens; Drocourt-Quéant; Hindenburg Line; Havrincourt; Epéhy; Canal du Nord; St Quentin Canal; Beaurevoir; Courtrai; Selle; Valenciennes; Sambre; Italy 1917–18; Helles; Landing at Helles; Struma; Doiran 1918; Krithia; Suvla; Landing at Suvla; Scimitar Hill; Rumani; Egypt 1915–17; El Mughar; Nebi Samwil; Jerusalem; Jaffa; Tell'Asur; Megiddo; Sharon; Damascus; Tigris 1916; Kut al Amara 1915, 1917; Ctesiphon; Defence of Kut al Amara; Baghdad. **Second World War:** Vist; Norway 1940; Defence of Escaut; Defence of Arras; Ypres-Comines Canal; St Valéry-en-Caux; Cambes; Tilly sur Seulles; Fontenay le Pesnil; Odon; Defence of Rauray; Caen; Orne; Bourguébus Ridge; Troarn; Le Perier Ridge; Falaise; Nederrijn; Le Havre; Antwerp-Turnhout Canal; Scheldt; Venlo Pocket; Zetten; Rhineland; Hochwald; Lingen; Brinkum; Bremen; Arnhem 1945; Abyssinia 1940; Falluja; Tobruk Sortie; Belhamed; Baghdad 1941; Iraq 1941; Palmyra; Jebel Mazar; Syria 1941; Sidi Barrani; Tobruk Sortie; Belhamed; Mersa Matruh; Deir El Shein; Ruweisat Ridge; El Alamein; Matmata Hill; Akarit; Enfidaville; Djebel Garci; Djedeida; Djebel Djaffa; Montagne Farm; Sedjenane 1; Mine de Sedjenane; Oued Zarga; Djebel Tanngoucha; Argoub Sellah; Sidi Ahmed; Tunis; Ragoubet Souissi; Landing in Sicily; Adrano; Sicily 1943; Trigno; Sangro; Vietri Pass; Capture of Naples; Cava di Tirreni; Volturno Crossing; Calabritto; Garigliano Crossing; Monte Tyga; Castle Hill; Hangman's Hill; Monte Gaddione; Trasimene Line; Monte Gridolfo; Gemmano Ridge; Lamone Crossing; Monte Colombo; San Marino; Monte La Pieve; Argenta Gap; Athens; Greece 1944–5; Heraklion; Madagascar; Kampar; Johore; Muar; Batu Pahat; Donbaik; Point 201 (Arakan); North

Arakan; Buthidaung; Tamu Road; Bishenpur; Aradura; Monywa 1945; Mandalay; Myinmu Bridgehead; Irrawaddy. **Korean War** (1950–3): Ramree; Maryang-San.

Dress
DIFFERENCES: Blue dress cap, scarlet band and piping; blue side cap, scarlet peak piped gold; khaki beret, black flash. Blue stable belt, central scarlet band, narrow central yellow stripe.
REGIMENTAL TIE: Red emblems on dark blue ground.

Marches
Quick: *Rule Britannia* and *Speed the Plough*. Slow: *The Northamptonshire*.

Alliances
Sherbrook Hussars, of Canada; The Lincoln and Welland Regiment, of Canada; The Essex and Kent Scottish, of Canada; The Lake Superior Scottish Regiment, of Canada; The Royal Tasmanian Regiment, of Australia; 3rd Battalion (Auckland (Countess of Ranfurly's Own) and Northland) Royal New Zealand Infantry Regiment; 5th Battalion The Frontier Force Regiment, of Pakistan; 1st Battalion The Royal Malay Regiment; The Barbados Regiment; The Bermuda Regiment; The Gibraltar Regiment.

Journal
The Castle (twice a year: June and December).

Record Office
Except officers: Higher Barracks, Exeter; officers: MS(AODO), London Rd, Stanmore, Middlesex.

Regimental History
Barthorp, M. *Crater to the Creggan: The History of the Royal Anglian Regiment 1964–1974*, Leo Cooper, 1976.

Predecessors

THE 1st EAST ANGLIAN REGIMENT (ROYAL NORFOLK AND SUFFOLK)

History
Formed in 1959 by the amalgamation of the Royal Norfolk Regiment and the Suffolk Regiment.

Predecessors of the 1st East Anglian Regiment

THE ROYAL NORFOLK REGIMENT

History
Raised in 1785 as Cornwell's Regiment (9th Foot in 1751, Royal 1935).
REGIMENTAL ANNIVERSARY: Almanza Day (25 April).
FORMER MEMBERS: Field Marshal Sir William Gomm (1784–1875), gazetted 1794; Field Marshal Lord Clyde (1792–1863), commissioned 1808.

Emblazoned Battle Honours
Seven Years War (1756–63): Belleisle; Havannah. **French Revolutionary Wars** (1793–1802): Martinique 1794. **Peninsular War** (1808–14): Rolica; Vimiera; Corunna; Busaco; Salamanca; Vittoria; San Sebastian; Nive; Peninsula. **First Afghan War** (1839–42): Cabool 1842. **First Sikh War** (1845–6): Moodkee; Ferozeshah; Sobraon. **Crimean War** (1854–5): Sevastopol. **Second Afghan War** (1878–80): Kabul; Afghanistan 1879–80. **South African War** (1899–1902): Paardeburg; South Africa 1900–02. **Great War:** Mons; Le Cateau; Marne 1914; Ypres 1914, 1915, 1917, 1918; Somme 1916, 1918; Hindenburg Line; Landing at Suvla; Gaza; Shaiba; Kut al Amara 1915, 1917. **Second World War:** St Omer-La Bassée; Normandy Landing; Brieux Bridgehead; Venraij; Rhineland; North-West Europe 1940, 1944–5; Singapore Island; Kohima; Aradura; Burma 1944–5. **Korean War** (1950–3): Korea 1951–2.

Accredited Battle Honours
Great War: Retreat from Mons; Aisne 1914; La Bassée 1914; Gravenstafel; St Julien; Frezenberg; Bellewaarde; Loos; Albert 1916, 1918; Delville Wood; Pozières; Guillemont; Flers-Courcelette; Morval; Thiepval; Le Transloy; Ancre Heights; Ancre 1916, 1918; Arras 1917; Vimy 1917; Scarpe 1917; Arleux; Oppy; Pilckem; Langemarck 1917; Polygon Wood; Broodseinde; Poelcapelle; Passchendaele; Cambrai 1917, 1918; St Quentin; Bapaume 1918; Lys; Bailleul; Kemmel; Scherpenberg; Amiens; Epéhy; Canal du Nord; St Quentin Canal; Beaurevoir; Selle; Sambre; France and Flanders 1914–18; Italy 1917–18; Suvla; Scimitar Hill; Gallipoli 1915; Egypt 1915–17; El Mughar; Nebi Samwil; Jerusalem; Jaffa; Tell'Asur; Megiddo; Sharon; Palestine 1917–18; Ctesiphon; Defence of Kut al Amara; Mesopotamia 1914–18. **Second World War:** Defence of Escaut; St Valéry-en-Caux; Caen; Le Perier Ridge; Hochwald; Lingen; Brinkum; Johore; Muar; Batu Pahat; Malaya.

Awards
Six members of the regiment have been awarded the Victoria Cross: one in the Great War and five in the Second World War. First award: Lieutenant-Colonel J. Sherwood-Kelly CMG DSO (1880–1931), Marcoing, France, 20 November 1917: gazetted 11 January 1918.

Marches
Quick and slow: *Rule Britannia*.

Museum
Cameron House, Britannia Barracks, Norwich, Norfolk (tel 0603 628455): open Monday–Friday 0900–1600.

Regimental Histories
Kemp, P. W. *The History of the Norfolk Regiment, 1919–1951*, Regimental Association, 1953. Petre, F. L. *The History of the Norfolk Regiment, 1685–1914* (2 vols), Jarrold, 1924. Carew, T. *The Royal Norfolk Regiment*, Hamish Hamilton, 1967.

THE SUFFOLK REGIMENT

History
Raised in 1685 as the Duke of Norfolk's Regiment (12th Foot in 1751).
Motto: *Montis insignia Calpe* (The badge of the Rock of Gibraltar).
Regimental Anniversary: Minden Day (1 August).
Former Member: Field Marshal Viscount Wolsley (1833–1913), commissioned 1852 – statue Whitehall, London.

Emblazoned Battle Honours
War of Austrian Succession (1740–8): Dettingen. Seven Years War (1756–63): Minden. War of American Independence (1775–83): Gibraltar 1779–83. Fourth Mysore War (1799): Seringapatam. India (1797–1809): India. Eighth Kaffir War (1851–3): South Africa 1851–1852–1853. Second Maori War (1860–1): New Zealand. Third Maori War (1863–6): New Zealand. Second Afghan War (1878–80): Afghanistan 1878–80. South African War (1899–1902): South Africa 1899–1902. Great War: Le Cateau; Neuve Chapelle; Ypres 1915, 1917, 1918; Somme 1916, 1918; Arras 1917, 1918; Cambrai 1917, 1918; Hindenburg Line; Macedonia 1915–18; Landing at Suvla; Gaza. Second World War: Dunkirk 1940; Normandy Landing; Odon; Falaise; Venraij; Brinkum; Singapore Island; North Arakan; Imphal; Burma 1943–5. A castle and key superscribed 'Gibraltar 1779–1783' with 'Montis insignia Calpe' beneath was also borne on the colours.

Accredited Battle Honours
Great War: Mons; Retreat from Mons; Marne 1914; Aisne 1914; La Bassée 1914; Givenchy 1914; Gravenstafel; St Julien; Frezenberg; Bellewaarde; Aubers; Hooge 1915; Loos; Albert 1916, 1918; Bazentin; Delville Wood; Pozières; Flers-Courcelette; Morval; Thiepval; Le Transloy; Ancre Heights; Ancre 1916, 1918; Scarpe 1917, 1918; Arleux; Pilckem; Langemarck 1917; Menin Road; Polygon Wood; Poelcapelle; Passchendaele; St Quentin; Bapaume 1918; Lys; Estaires; Messines 1918; Hazebrouck; Bailleul; Kemmel; Béthune; Scherpenberg; Amiens; Epéhy; Canal du Nord; Courtrai; Selle; Valenciennes; Sambre; France and Flanders 1914–18; Struma; Doiran 1918; Suvla; Scimitar Hill; Gallipoli 1915; Egypt 1915–17; El Mughar; Nebi Samwil; Jerusalem; Jaffa; Tell'Asur; Megiddo; Sharon; Palestine 1917–18. Second World War: North-West Europe 1940, 1944–5; Malaya 1942.

Awards
Two members of the regiment have been awarded the Victoria Cross: both in the Great War. First award: Sergeant A. F. Saunders (1879–1947), near Loos 26 September 1915: gazetted 30 March 1916.

Marches
Quick: *Speed the Plough*. Slow: *The Slow March of the Suffolk Regiment*.

Museum
The Keep, Gibraltar Barracks, Bury St Edmonds, Suffolk (tel 0284 2394): open Monday–Friday 0900–1200, 1400–1600, weekends by appointment.

Regimental Histories
Godfrey, F. A. *The History of the Suffolk Regiment 1946–1959*, Leo Cooper, 1988. Webb, E. A. H. *History of the 12th (The Suffolk) Regiment 1685–1913*, Spottiswoode, 1914. Murphy, C. C. R. *A History of the Suffolk Regiment, 1914–1927*, Hutchinson, 1928. Nicholson, W. N. *The Suffolk Regiment 1928–1946*, The Anglian Magazine, 1948. Moir, G. *The Suffolk Regiment*, Leo Cooper, 1969.

THE 2nd EAST ANGLIAN REGIMENT (DUCHESS OF GLOUCESTER'S OWN ROYAL LINCOLNSHIRE AND NORTHAMPTONSHIRE)

Predecessors of the 2nd East Anglian Regiment

Badge as 1st East Anglian Regiment.

History
Formed in 1960 by the amalgamation of the Royal Lincolnshire Regiment and the Northamptonshire Regiment.

THE ROYAL LINCOLNSHIRE REGIMENT

History
Raised in 1685 as Greville's Regiment (10th Foot in 1751, Lincolnshire Regiment in 1881, Royal in 1946).
REGIMENTAL ANNIVERSARY: Sobraon Day (10 February).

Emblazoned Battle Honours
War of Spanish Succession (1701–15): Blenheim; Ramillies; Oudenarde; Malplaquet. Peninsular War (1808–14): Peninsula. First Sikh War (1845–6): Sobraon; Mooltan; Punjaub; Goojerat. Indian Mutiny (1857–8): Lucknow. Reconquest of the Sudan (1896–8): Atbara; Khartoum. South African War (1899–1902): Paardeburg; South Africa 1900–1902. Great War: Mons; Marne 1914; Messines 1914, 1917, 1918; Ypres 1914, 1915, 1917; Neuve Chapelle; Loos; Somme 1916, 1918; Lys; Hindenburg Line; Suvla. Second World War: Dunkirk 1940; Normandy Landing; Fontenay le Pesnil; Antwerp–Turnhout Canal; Rhineland; North Africa 1943; Salerno; Gothic Line; Ngadyedauk Pass; Burma 1943–5. The Sphinx superscribed 'Egypt' was also borne on the colours.

Accredited Battle Honours
Great War: Le Cateau; Retreat from Mons; Aisne 1914, 1918; La Bassée 1914; Armentières 1914; Nonne Bosschen; Gravenstafel; St Julien; Frezenberg; Bellewaarde; Aubers; Albert 1916, 1918; Bazentin; Delville Wood; Pozières; Flers-Courcelette; Morval; Thiepval; Ancre 1916, 1918; Arras 1917, 1918; Scarpe 1917, 1918; Arleux; Pilckem; Langemarck 1917; Menin Road; Polygon Wood; Broodseinde; Poelcapelle; Passchendaele; Cambrai 1917, 1918; St Quentin; Bapaume 1918; Estaires; Bailleul; Kemmel; Amiens; Drocourt-Quéant; Epéhy; Canal du Nord; St Quentin Canal; Beaurevoir; Selle; Sambre; France and Flanders 1914–18; Landing at Suvla; Scimitar Hill; Gallipoli 1915; Egypt 1916. Second World War: Vist; Norway 1940; Cambes; Defence of Rauray; Caen; Orne; Bourguébus Ridge; Troarn; Nederrijn; Le Havre; Venraij; Venlo Pocket; Hochwald; Lingen; Bremen; Arnhem 1945; North-West Europe 1940, 1944–5; Sedjenane I; Mine de Sedjenane; Argoub Sellah; Vietri Pass; Capture of Naples; Cava di Tirreni; Volturno Crossing; Garigliano Crossing; Monte Tuga; Monte Gridolfo; Gemmano Ridge; Lamone Crossing; San Marino; Italy 1943–5; Donbaik; Point 201 (Arakan); North Arakan; Buthidaung; Ramree.

Awards
Seven members of the regiment have been awarded the Victoria Cross: three in the Indian Mutiny (1857–8), three in the Great War and one in the Second

World War. First award: Private J. Kirk (1827–65), Benares 4 April 1857: gazetted 20 January 1860.

March
Quick: *The Lincolnshire Poacher.*

Allied Regiment in 1914
19th Lincoln Regiment, Ontario, of Canada.

Journal
The Imps (up to 1960).

Museum
Museum of Lincolnshire Life, Old Barracks, Burton Rd, Lincoln, Lincolnshire (tel 0522 528448): open Monday–Saturday 1000–1730, Sunday 1400–1730.

Regimental Histories
Simpson, C. R. *The History of the Lincolnshire Regiment, 1914–1918*, Medici Society, 1931. Lee, A. *The History of the 10th Foot (Lincolnshire Regiment)* (2 vols.), vol. 1, *1685–1813*; vol. 2, *1813–1910*, Gale & Polden, 1911.

THE NORTHAMPTONSHIRE REGIMENT

History
Raised in 1741 as Cholmondeley's Regiment (48th Foot in 1751) and in 1755 as the 58th foot. These two regiments became the 1st and 2nd Battalions of the Northamptonshire Regiment in 1881.

MOTTO: *Montis insignia Calpe* (The badge of the Rock of Gibraltar).

REGIMENTAL ANNIVERSARY: Talavera Day (27 July).

Emblazoned Battle Honours
(awards before 1881 to 58th★; awards to both 48th and 58th★★)
Seven Years War (1756–63): Louisburg 1758; Quebec 1759; Martinique 1762; Havannah. **War of American Independence** (1775–83): ★Gibraltar 1779–83. **French Revolutionary Wars** (1793–1802): ★Martinique 1794. **Peninsular War** (1808–14): Talavera; Albuhera; Badajos; ★★Salamanca; ★★Vittoria; ★★Pyrenees; ★★Nivelle; ★★Orthes;

Toulouse; ★★Peninsula. **First Maori War** (1846–7): ★New Zealand. **Crimean War** (1854–5): Sevastopol. **Zulu and Basuto War** (1877–9): ★South Africa 1879. **Tirah Campaign** (1897–8): Tirah. **South African War** (1899–1902): Modder River; South Africa 1899–1902. **Great War:** Mons; Marne 1914; Aisne 1914, 1918; Ypres 1914, 1917; Neuve Chapelle; Loos; Somme 1916, 1918; Arras 1917, 1918; Epéhy; Gaza. **Second World War:** North-West Europe 1940, 1945; North Africa 1942–3; Garigliano Crossing; Anzio; Cassino II; Italy 1943–5; Yu; Imphal; Myinmu Bridgehead; Burma 1943–5. A castle and key superscribed 'Gibraltar 1779–1783' with '*Montis insignia Calpe*' beneath and the Sphinx superscribed 'Egypt' were also borne on the colours.

Accredited Battle Honours
Great War: Retreat from Mons; Langemarck 1914, 1917; Gheluvelt; Nonne Bosschen; Givenchy 1914; Aubers; Albert 1916, 1918; Bazentin; Delville Wood; Pozières; Flers-Courcelette; Morval; Thiepval; Le Transloy; Ancre Heights; Ancre 1916, 1918; Bapaume 1917, 1918; Vimy 1917; Scarpe 1917, 1918; Arleux; Messines 1917; Pilckem; Passchendaele; Cambrai 1917, 1918; St Quentin; Rosières; Avre; Villers Bretonneux; Amiens; Drocourt-Quéant;

Hindenburg Line; St Quentin Canal; Selle; Sambre; France and Flanders 1914–18; Suvla; Landing at Suvla; Scimitar Hill; Gallipoli 1915; Egypt 1915–17; El Mughar; Nebi Samwil; Jerusalem; Jaffa; Tell'Asur; Megiddo; Sharon; Palestine 1917–18. **Second World War:** Defence of Escaut; Defence of Arras; Ypres-Comines Canal; Djedeida; Djebel Djaffa; Oued Zarga; Djebel Tanngoucha; Sidi Ahmed; Landing in Sicily; Adrano; Sicily 1943; Sangro; Monte Gabbione; Trasimene Line; Monte La Pieve; Argenta Gap; Madagascar; Tamu Road; Bishenpur; Monywa 1945; Irrawaddy.

Awards
Seven members of the regiment have been awarded the Victoria Cross: two in the Boer War (1881) and five in the Great War. First award: Lieutenant A. R. Hill (1859–1944) Laing's Nek 28

January 1881: gazetted 14 March 1882 (58th).

Marches
Quick: *The Lincolnshire Poacher (Hard Up)*. Slow: *The Duchess.*

Allied Regiment in 1914
15th (North Auckland) Regiment, of New Zealand.

Museum
Abington Park Museum, Abington, Northampton, Northamptonshire (tel 0604 31454): open Monday–Saturday 1000–1230, 1400–1800, April–September Sunday 1430–1700.

Regimental Histories
Barthorp, M. *The Northamptonshire Regiment*, Leo Cooper, 1974. Gurney, R. *History of the Northamptonshire Regiment, 1742–1934*, Gale & Polden, 1935.

THE 3rd EAST ANGLIAN REGIMENT (16/44th)

Badge as 1st East Anglian Regiment.

Predecessors of the 3rd East Anglian Regiment (16/44th)

History
Formed in 1958 by the amalgamation of the Bedfordshire and Hertfordshire Regiment and the Essex Regiment.

THE BEDFORDSHIRE AND HERTFORDSHIRE REGIMENT

History
Raised in 1688 as Douglas's Regiment (16th Foot in 1751, Bedfordshire Regiment in 1881, redesignated Bedfordshire and Hertfordshire Regiment in 1919). REGIMENTAL ANNIVERSARY: Blenheim Day (2 August).

Emblazoned Battle Honours
War of the League of Augsburg (1689–97): Namur 1695. **War of Spanish Succession** (1701–15): Blenheim; Ramillies; Oudernarde; Malplaquet. **Napoleonic Wars** (1803–15): Expedition against Dutch – Surinam. **Chitral Campaign** (1895): Chitral. **South African War** (1899–1902): South Africa 1900–02. **Great War:** Mons; Marne 1914; Ypres 1914, 1915, 1917; Loos; Somme 1916, 1918; Arras 1917, 1918; Cambrai 1917, 1918; Sambre; Suvla; Gaza. **Second World War:** Dunkirk 1940; North-West Europe 1940; Tobruk Sortie 1941; Belhamed; Tunis; North

Africa 1941, 1943; Cassino II; Trasimene Line; Italy 1944–5; Chindits 1944.

Accredited Battle Honours

Great War: Le Cateau; Retreat from Mons; Aisne 1914; La Bassée 1914; Langemarck 1914, 1917; Gheluvelt; Nonne Bosschen; Neuve Chapelle; Hill 60; St Julien; Frezenberg; Bellewaarde; Aubers; Festubert 1915; Albert 1916, 1918; Bazentin; Delville Wood; Pozières; Guillemont; Flers-Courcelette; Morval; Thiepval; Le Transloy; Ancre Heights; Ancre 1916, 1918; Vimy 1917; Scarpe 1917; Arleux; Oppy; Messines 1917; Pilckem; Polygon Wood; Broodseinde; Poelcapelle; Passchendaele; St Quentin; Bapaume 1918; Rosières; Avre; Villers Bretonneux; Lys; Hazebrouck; Scherpenberg; Amiens; Drocourt-Quéant; Hindenburg Line; Epéhy; Canal du Nord; St Quentin Canal; Selle; France and Flanders 1914–18; Italy 1917–18; Landing at Suvla; Scimitar Hill; Gallipoli 1915; Egypt 1915–17; El Mughar; Nebi Samwil; Jerusalem; Jaffa; Tell'Asur; Megiddo; Sharon; Palestine 1917–18. **Second World War:** Tobruk 1941; Athens; Greece 1944–5; Singapore Island; Malaya 1942; Burma 1944.

Awards

Seven members of the regiment have been awarded the Victoria Cross: all in the Great War. First award: Captain C. C. Foss DSO, later Brigadier C. C. Foss DSO (1883–1953), Neuve Chapelle 12 March 1915: gazetted 23 August 1915.

March

Quick: *Mandolinata.*

Journal

The Wasp (1922–58); *The Wasp and the Eagle* (1959–64).

Museum

Luton Museum, Wardown Park, Luton, Bedfordshire (tel 0582 36941 and 36492): open Monday–Saturday 1030–1700, Sunday 1300–1700.

Regimental Histories

Sainsbury, J. D. *A Guide to the History of the Bedfordshire and Hertfordshire Regiment*, Hart Books (Welwyn), 1988. Webster, F. A. M. *The History of the 5th Battalion Bedfordshire and Hertfordshire Regiment*, Waren, 1930. Maurice, Sir Frederick. *A History of the Bedfordshire and Hertfordshire Regiment*, Constable, 1930. Peters, G. W. H. *The Bedfordshire and Hertfordshire Regiment*, Leo Cooper, 1970. Barrow, J. *The Story of the Bedfordshire and Hertfordshire Regiment* (2 vols.), HQ Royal Anglian Regiment, 1987.

THE ESSEX REGIMENT

History

Raised in 1741 as Long's Regiment (44th Foot in 1751) and in 1755 as the 58th Foot (56th Foot in 1757). These two regiments became the 1st and 2nd Battalions of the Essex Regiment in 1881.
MOTTO: *Montis insignia Calpe* (The Badge of the Rock of Gibraltar).
REGIMENTAL ANNIVERSARIES: Arras Day (28 March) 2nd Battalion; Gallipoli Day (25 April) 1st Battalion; Salamanca Day (22 July); Gaza Day (4 November) Territorials.

Emblazoned Battle Honours

(awards before 1881 to 56th★; awards to both 44th and 56th★★)
Seven Years War (1756–63): ★Moro; ★Havannah. **War of American Indepen-**

REGIMENTS OF FOOT 137

dence (1775–9): *Gibraltar 1779–83. Peninsular War (1808–14): Badajos; Salamanca; **Peninsula. War of 1812 (1812–14): Bladensburg. Hundred Days (1815): Waterloo. First Burma War (1824–6): Ava. Crimean War (1854–5): Alma; Inkerman; Sevastopol. Second China War (1857–60): Taku Forts. Egyptian Campaign (1885): Nile 1884–5. South African War (1899–1902): Relief of Kimberley; Paardeburg; South Africa 1899–1902. Great War: Le Cateau; Marne 1914; Ypres 1915, 1917; Loos; Somme 1916, 1918; Arras 1917, 1918; Cambrai 1917, 1918; Selle; Gallipoli 1915–16; Gaza. Second World War: Zetten; North-West Europe 1940, 1944–5; Palmyra; Tobruk 1941; Defence of Alamein Line; Enfidaville; Sangro; Villa Grande; Cassino II; Chindits 1944. A castle and key superscribed 'Gibraltar 1779–1783' with '*Montis insignia Calpe*' beneath and the Sphinx superscribed 'Egypt' were also borne on the colours.

Accredited Battle Honours

Great War: Retreat from Mons; Aisne 1914; Messines 1914; Armentières 1914; St Julien; Frezenberg; Bellewaarde; Albert 1916, 1918; Bazentin; Delville Wood; Pozières; Flers-Courcelette; Morval; Thiepval; Le Transloy; Ancre Heights; Ancre 1916, 1918; Bapaume 1917, 1918; Scarpe 1917, 1918; Arleux; Pilckem; Langemarck 1917; Menin Road; Broodseinde; Poelcapelle; Passchendaele; St Quentin; Avre; Villers Bretonneux; Lys; Hazebrouck; Béthune; Amiens; Drocourt-Quéant; Hindenburg Line; Havrincourt; Epéhy; St Quentin Canal; Sambre; France and Flanders 1914–18; Helles; Landing at Helles; Krithia; Suvla; Landing at Suvla; Scimitar Hill; Rumani; Egypt 1915–17; Jaffa; Megiddo; Sharon; Palestine 1917–18. Second World War: St Omer-La Bassée; Tilly sur Seulles; Le Havre; Antwerp-Turnhout Canal; Scheldt; Arnhem 1945; Abyssinia 1940; Falluja; Baghdad 1941; Iraq 1941; Syria 1941;

Belhamed; Mersa Matruh; Deir el Shein; Ruweisat; Ruweisat Ridge; El Alamein; Matmata Hills; Akarit; Djebel Garci; Tunis; Ragoubet Souissi; North Africa 1941–3; Trigno; Castle Hill; Hangman's Hill; Italy 1943–4; Athens; Greece 1944–5; Kohima; Burma 1943–5.

Awards

Six members of the regiment have been awarded the Victoria Cross: one in the Crimean War (1854–5), two in the Second China War (1860), one in the South African War (1899–1902), one in the Great War and one in the Second World War. First award: Sergeant W. McWheeney (1837–66), siege operations, Crimea, 20 October 1854, 5 December 1854 and 18 June 1855: gazetted 24 February (44th). Private J. Mott (1913–83) was awarded the Empire Gallantry Medal (later exchanged for the George Cross), Haifa 25 December 1937: gazetted 25 February 1938.

Memorials

Regimental Chapel, Eagle Way, Warley, Brentwood, Essex: open by appointment. Bell Meadow, Chelmsford Cathedral, Chelmsford.

Marches

Quick: *We'll gang nae mair to yon toun* (1st Battalion); *The Hampshire* and *The Essex* (2nd Battalion).

Journal

The Eagle.

Museum

Essex Regiment Museum, Oaklands Park, Moulsham St, Chelmsford, Essex (tel 0245 260614): open Monday–Saturday 1000–1700, Sunday 1400–1700.

Regimental Histories

Martin, T. A. *The Essex Regiment, 1929–1950*, Essex Regimental Association,

1952. Burrows, J. W. *Essex Units in the War 1914–1919* (5 vols.): vol. 1, *1st Battalion*; vol. 2, *2nd Battalion*; vol. 3, *Essex Territorial Infantry Brigade, 4th–8th Battalions*; vol. 5, *Service Battalions*; vol.

6, *Essex Militia*, J. M. Burrows (Southend), 1923, 1927 and 2nd eds. in 1937. Title is misleading, as all volumes cover period from formation to publication.

THE ROYAL LEICESTERSHIRE REGIMENT

History
Raised in 1688 as Richard's Regiment (17th Foot in 1751, Royal in 1746). REGIMENTAL ANNIVERSARY: Royal Tiger Day (25 June).

Emblazoned Battle Honours
War of the League of Augsburg (1689–97): Namur 1695. **Seven Years War** (1756–63): Louisburg; Martinique 1762; Havannah. **India** (1804–23): Hindoostan. **Second Afghan War** (1878–80): Afghanistan 1878–9. **South African War** (1899–1902): Defence of Ladysmith; South Africa 1899–1902. **Great War:** Aisne 1914, 1918; Neuve Chapelle; Somme 1916, 1918; Ypres 1917; Cambrai 1917, 1918; Lys; St Quentin Canal; France and Flanders 1914–18; Palestine 1918; Mesopotamia 1915–18. **Second World War:** Scheldt; North-West Europe 1944–5; Sidi Barrani; North Africa 1940–1, 1943; Salerno; Gothic Line; Italy 1943–5; Crete; Malaya 1941–2; Chindits 1944. **Korean War** (1950–3): Korea 1951–2. A Royal Tiger superscribed 'Hindoostan' was also borne on the colours.

Accredited Battle Honours
Great War: La Bassée 1914; Armentières 1914; Festubert 1914, 1915; Aubers; Hooge 1915; Bazentin; Flers-Courcelette; Morval; Le Transloy; Polygon Wood; St Quentin; Bailleul; Kemmel; Scherpenberg; Albert 1918; Bapaume 1918; Hindenburg Line; Epéhy; Beaurevoir; Selle; Sambre; Megiddo; Sharon; Damascus; Tigris 1916; Kut al Amara 1917; Baghdad. **Second World War:** Norway 1940; Antwerp-Turnhout Canal; Zetten; Jebel Mazar; Syria 1941; Tobruk 1941; Montagne Farm; Calabritto; Monte Gridolfo; Monte Colombo; Heraklion; Kampar. **Korean War** (1950–3): Maryang-San.

Awards
Four members of the regiment have been awarded the Victoria Cross: one in the Crimean War (1854–5) and three in the Great War. First award: Lance-Sergeant P. Smith, later Sergeant (1825–1906), Sevastopol 18 June 1855: gazetted 24 February 1857.

Marches
Quick: *A Hunting Call* and *Romaika*. Slow: *General Monckton*.

Journal
The Green Tiger.

Museum
The Magazine, Oxford St, Leicester, Leicestershire (tel 0533 555839): open Monday–Thursday 1000–1730, Sunday 1400–1730.

Regimental History
Underhill, W. E. (ed.) *The Royal Leicestershire Regiment (1928–1956)*, privately printed, 1958.

THE DEVONSHIRE AND DORSET REGIMENT
(The Prince of Wales's Division)
Colonel-in-Chief:
Major-General HRH The Duke of Kent KG GCMG GCVO ADC

History
Formed in 1958 by the amalgamation of the Devonshire Regiment and the Dorset Regiment. One regular battalion, one volunteer battalion (4th).
MOTTOES: *Semper fidelis* (Ever faithful); *Montis insignia Calpe* (The Badge of the Rock of Gibraltar); *Primus in Indis* (First in India).
HEADQUARTERS: Wyvern Barracks, Exeter, Devon.
RECRUITMENT AREA: Devon and Dorset.
REGIMENTAL ANNIVERSARIES: Wagon Hill Day (6 January); Amalgamation Day (17 May); Bois des Buttes Day (27 May); Sarah Sands Day (11 November).

Emblazoned Battle Honours
War of Austrian Succession (1740–8): Dettingen. **Overthrow of Suraj-ud-Dowlah** (1757): Plassey. **French Revolutionary Wars** (1793–1802): Martinique 1794; Marabout. **Peninsular War** (1808–14): Albuhera; Salamanca; Vittoria; Pyrenees; Nivelle; Nive; Orthes; Toulouse; Peninsula. **First Burma War** (1824–6): Ava. **Gwalior Campaign** (1843): Maharajpore. **Crimean War** (1854–5): Sevastopol. **Second Afghan War** (1878–80): Afghanistan 1879–80. **Tirah Campaign** (1897–8): Tirah. **South African War** (1899–1902): Defence of Ladysmith; Relief of Ladysmith; South Africa 1899–1902. **Great War**: Mons; Marne 1914; La Bassée 1914; Ypres 1915, 1917; Loos; Somme 1916, 1918; Bois des Buttes; Hindenburg Line; Sambre; Vittorio Veneto; Doiran 1917, 1918; Suvla; Gaza; Palestine 1917–18; Ctesiphon; Khan Baghdadi; Mesopotamia 1916–18. **Second World War**: St Omer-La Bassée; Normandy Landing; Caen; Arnhem 1944; Aam; Geilenkirchen; Rhine; North-West Europe 1940, 1944–5; Landing in Sicily; Regalbuto; Malta 1940–2; Imphal; Kohima; Mandalay; Myinmu Bridgehead; Burma 1943–5. The castle and key superscribed 'Gibraltar 1779–1783' with the motto '*Montis insignia Calpe*' and the Sphinx superscribed 'Gibraltar 1779–1783' with the motto '*Montis insignia Calpe*' and the Sphinx superscribed '*Semper fidelis Primus in Indis*' are also borne on the colours.

Accredited Battle Honours
Great War: Le Cateau; Retreat from Mons; Aisne 1914, 1918; Armentières 1914; Neuve Chapelle; Hill 60; Gravenstafel; St Julien; Frezenberg; Bellewaarde; Aubers; Albert 1916, 1918; Bazentin; Delville Wood; Guillemont; Flers-

Courcelette; Morval; Thiepval; Ancre 1916, 1918; Arras 1917; Vimy 1917; Scarpe 1917; Bullecourt; Messines 1917; Pilckem; Langemarck 1917; Polygon Wood; Broodseinde; Poelcapelle; Passchendaele; St Quentin; Rosières; Villers Bretonneux; Lys; Hazebrouck; Marne 1918; Tardenois; Amiens; Bapaume 1918; Havrincourt; Epéhy; Canal du Nord; St Quentin Canal; Beaurevoir; Cambrai 1918; France and Flanders 1914–18; Piave; Italy 1917–18; Macedonia 1915–18; Landing at Suvla; Scimitar Hill; Gallipoli 1915; Egypt 1916–17; El Mughar; Nebi Samwil; Jerusalem; Tell'Asur; Megiddo; Sharon; Basra; Kut al Amara 1915, 1917; Defence of Kut al Amara; Tigris 1916; Baghdad. **Second World War:** Port en Bessin; Villers Bocage; Tilly sur Seulles; Mont Pinçon; St Pierre La Vieille; Nederrijn; Roer; Goch; Ibbenburen; Twente Canal; Agira; Sicily 1943; Landing at Porto San Venere; Italy 1943; Tamu Road Shenam Pass; Ukhrul; Kyaukse 1945; Mt Popa.

Dress
DIFFERENCES: Blue dress cap; grass green side cap, blue flags, officers' piped gold. Green stable belt, orange centre stripe. *Croix de Guerre* ribbon as arm badge.
REGIMENTAL TIE: Thin orange stripes on green ground.

Marches
Quick: *Widdicombe Fair, We've Lived and Loved Together* and *The Maid of Glenconnel.*

Alliances
Les Fusiliers de Sherbrooke, of Canada; The Royal New South Wales Regiment, of Australia; 6th Battalion The Royal Malay Regiment; HMS *Exeter;* RAF *Chivenor.*

Journal
Journal of the Devonshire and Dorset Regiment (twice a year).

Predecessors

THE DEVONSHIRE REGIMENT

History
Raised in 1685 as the Duke of Beaufort's Musketeers (11th Foot in 1751, Devonshire Regiment in 1881).

MOTTO: *Semper fidelis* (Always faithful).
REGIMENTAL ANNIVERSARIES: Wagon Hill Day (6 January); Bois des Buttes Day (27 May).

Emblazoned Battle Honours
War of Austrian Succession (1740–8): Dettingen (1743). **Peninsular War** (1808–14): Salamanca (1812); Pyrenees (1813); Nivelle (1813); Nive (1813); Orthes (1814); Toulouse (1814); Peninsula. **Second Afghan War** (1878–80): Afghanistan 1879–80. **Tirah Campaign** (1897–8): Tirah. **South African War**

(1899–1902): Defence of Ladysmith (1899); Relief of Ladysmith (1900); South Africa 1899–1900. **Great War:** La Bassée 1914; Ypres 1915, 1917; Loos (1915); Somme 1916, 1918; Bois des Buttes (1917); Hindenburg Line (1918); Vittorio Veneto (1918); Doiran 1917, 1918; Palestine 1917–18; Mesopotamia 1916–18. **Second World War:** Normandy Landing (1944); Caen (1944); Rhine (1945); North-West Europe 1944–5; Landing in Sicily (1943); Regalbuto (1943); Malta 1940–2; Imphal (1944); Myinmu Bridgehead (1945); Burma 1943–5.

Accredited Battle Honours

Great War: Aisne 1914, 1918; Armentières 1914; Neuve Chapelle; Hill 60; Gravenstafel; St Julien; Frezenberg; Aubers; Albert 1916; Bazentin; Delville Wood; Guillemont; Flers-Courcelette; Morval; Arras 1917; Vimy 1917; Scarpe 1917; Bullecourt; Pilckem; Langemarck 1917; Polygon Wood; Broodseinde; Poelcapelle; Passchendaele; Rosières; Villers Bretonneux; Lys; Hazebrouck; Marne 1918; Tardenois; Bapaume 1918; Havrincourt; Epéhy; Canal du Nord; Beaurevoir; Cambrai 1918; Selle; Sambre; France and Flanders 1914–18; Piave; Italy 1917–18; Macedonia 1915–18; Egypt 1916–17; Gaza; Nebi Samwil; Jerusalem; Tell'Asur; Tigris 1916; Kut al Amara 1917. **Second World War:** Port en Bessin; Tilly sur Seulles; St Pierre le Vielle; Nederrijn; Roer; Ibbenburen; Sicily 1943; Landing at Porto San Veners; Italy 1943; Shenam Pass; Tamu Road; Ukhrul; Kyaukse 1945.

Awards

Three members of the regiment have been awarded the Victoria Cross: one in the South African War (1899–1902) and two in the Great War. First award: Lieutenant J. E. Masterson, later Major (1862–1935), Wagon Hill, South Africa, 6 January 1900: gazetted 4 June 1901.

Marches

Quick: *We've Lived and Loved Together* and *Widdicombe Fair.* Slow: *The Rose of Devon.*

Journal

The Journal of the Devonshire Regiment.

Museum

RHQ Devonshire and Dorset Regiment Wyvern Barracks, Barrack Rd, Exeter, Devonshire (tel 0392 218178 ext 2436): open Monday–Friday 0900–1630.

Regimental Histories

Taylor, J. *The Devons: A History of the Devonshire Regiment 1685–1945*, White Swan, 1951. Atkinson, C. T. *The Devonshire regiment, 1914–18*, Eland, 1926.

DORSET REGIMENT

History

Raised in 1701 as Coote's Regiment (39th Foot in 1751) and in 1755 as the 56th Foot (54th Foot in 1757). These two regiments became the 1st and 2nd Battalions of the Dorsetshire Regiment in 1881 (Dorset in 1951).

MOTTOES: *Primus in Indis* (First in India), *Montis insignia Calpe* (The badge of the Rock of Gibraltar).

REGIMENTAL ANNIVERSARIES: Plassey Day (23 June); Sarah Sands Day (11 November).

FORMER MEMBER: Field Marshal Sir George Nugent (1751–1849), commissioned 1773 (39th).

Emblazoned Battle Honours

(awards before 1881 to 54th★)

Overthrow of Suraj-ud-Dowlah (1751): Plassey. War of American Independence (1775–83): Gibraltar 1779–83. French Revolutionary Wars (1793–1802): Martinique 1794; ★Marabout (1801). Peninsular War (1808–14): Albuhera; Vittoria; Pyrenees; Nivelle; Nive; Orthes; Peninsula. First Burma War (1824–6): Ava. Gwalior Campaign (1843): Maharajpore. Crimean War (1854–5): Sevastopol. Tirah Campaign (1897–8): Tirah. South African War (1899–1902): Relief of Ladysmith; South Africa 1899–1902. Great War: Mons; Marne 1914; Ypres 1915, 1917; Somme 1916, 1918; Hindenburg Line; Sambre; Suvla; Gaza; Shaiba; Ctesiphon; Khan Baghdadi. Second World War: St Omer-La Bassée; Normandy Landing; Caen; Arnhem 1944; Aam; Geilenkirchen; landing in Sicily; Malta 1940–2; Kohima; Mandalay. 'Primus in Indis', a castle and key superscribed 'Gibraltar 1779–1783' with 'Montis insignia Calpe' beneath and the Sphinx superscribed 'Egypt' were also borne on the colours.

Accredited Battle Honours

Great War: Le Cateau; Retreat from Mons; Aisne 1914; La Bassée 1914; Armentières 1914; Gravenstafel; St Julien; Bellewaarde; Albert 1916, 1918; Flers-Courcelette; Thiepval; Ancre 1916, 1918; Arras 1917; Scarpe 1917; Messines 1917; Langemarck 1917; Polygon Wood; Broodseinde; Poelcapelle; Passchendaele; St Quentin; Amiens; Bapaume 1918; Epéhy; Canal du Nord; St Quentin Canal; Beaurevoir; Cambrai 1918; Selle; France and Flanders 1914–18; Landing at Suvla; Scimitar Hill; Gallipoli 1915; Egypt 1916; El Mughar; Nebi Samwil; Jerusalem; Tell'Asur; Megiddo; Sharon; Palestine 1917–18; Basra; Kut al Amara 1915, 1917; Defence of Kut al Amara; Baghdad; Mesopotamia 1914–18. Second World War: Villers Bocage; Tilly sur Seulles; Mont Pinçon; St Pierre La Vielle; Goch; Rhine; Twente Canal; North-West Europe 1940, 1944–5; Agira; Regalbuto; Sicily 1943; Landing at Porto San Venere; Italy 1943; Mt Popa; Burma 1944–5.

Awards

Private S. Vickery, later Sergeant (1873–1952) was awarded the Victoria Cross, Tirah 20 October 1897: gazetted 20 May 1898. Four members of the regiment have been awarded the Empire Gallantry Medal (later exchanged for the George Cross). First awards: Sergeant. W. G. Hand MM (1896–1961) and Private T. F. Miller (1887–1974) Malabar, India, 24 September 1921: gazetted 2 June 1923.

March

Quick: The Maid of Glenconnel.

Journal

The Dorset Regimental Journal (Dorset Regimental Quarterly before 1939).

Museum

The Keep, Bridport Rd, Dorchester, Dorset (tel 03052 64066): open Monday–Friday 0900–1700, Saturday July–September 0900–1700 October–June 0900–1200.

Regimental Histories

Popham, H. The Dorset Regiment, Leo Cooper, 1970. Atkinson, C. T. The Dorset Regiment (2 vols), OUP, 1947.

THE LIGHT INFANTRY
(The Light Division)
Colonel-in-Chief: HM Queen Elizabeth The Queen Mother

History
Formed in 1968 from the Somerset and Cornwall Light Infantry; the King's Own Yorkshire Light Infantry; the King's Shropshire Light Infantry; and the Durham Light Infantry. Three regular battalions, four volunteer battalions (5th, 6th, 7th and 8th).

MOTTOES: *Aucto splendore resurgo* (I rise again with increased splendour); *Cede nullis* (Yield to none); *Faithful*.

HEADQUARTERS: Peninsula Barracks, Andover Rd North, Winchester, Hampshire.

RECRUITMENT AREA: Cleveland, Durham, South Yorkshire, Shropshire, Herefordshire, Somerset, Avon and Cornwall.

REGIMENTAL DAY: Salamanca Day (22 July).

Emblazoned Battle Honours
War of Spanish Succession (1701–15): Gibraltar 1704–5. **War of Austrian Succession** (1740–8): Dettingen. **Seven Years War** (1756–63): Minden. **French Revolutionary Wars** (1793–1802): Nieuport; St Lucia 1796. **Peninsular War** (1808–14): Corunna; Fuentes d'Onor; Salamanca; Vittoria; Pyrenees; Nivelle; Orthes; Peninsula. **War of 1812** (1812–14): Bladensburg. **Hundred Days** (1815): Waterloo. **First Afghan War** (1839–42): Affghanistan 1839. **Crimean War** (1854–5): Inkerman; Sevastopol. **Persian War** (1856–7): Persia. **Indian Mutiny** (1857–8): Lucknow. **First Maori War** (1846–7): New Zealand. **Second Burma War** (1852–3): Pegu. **Zulu and Basuto War** (1877–9): South Africa 1878–9. **Second Afghan War** (1878–80): Ali Masjid; Afghanistan 1878–80. **Third Burma War** (1885–7): Burma 1885–7. **South African War** (1899–1902): Modder River; Paardeburg; Relief of Ladysmith; South Africa 1899–1902. **Great War:** Mons; Le Cateau; Aisne 1914, 1915; Messines 1914, 1917, 1918; Ypres 1914, 1915, 1917, 1918; Hooge 1915; Somme 1916, 1918; Albert 1916, 1918; Arras 1917, 1918; Passchendaele; Cambrai 1917, 1918; Havrincourt; Doiran 1917, 1918; Jerusalem; Palestine 1917, 1918; Tigris 1916. **Third Afghan War** (1919): Afghanistan 1919. **Second World War:** Norway 1940; Dunkirk 1940; Normandy Landing; Fontenay le Pesnil; Hill 112; Gheel; North-West Europe 1940, 1944–5; El Alamein; Mareth; Argoub Sellah; Primosole Bridge; Sicily 1943; Salerno; Anzio; Cassino II; Italy 1943–5; North Arakan; Kohima; Burma 1942, 1943–5. **Korean War** (1950–3): Korea 1951–3. The Sphinx superscribed 'Egypt' and a mural crown superscribed 'Jellalabad' are also borne on the colours.

Accredited Battle Honours

French Revolutionary Wars (1793–1802): Tournay. Napoleonic Wars (1803–15): Dominica: Peninsular War (1808–14): Rolica; Vimiera. Napoleonic Wars (1803–15): Martinique 1809. Peninsular War (1808–14): Talavera; Nive; Toulouse. First Burma War (1824–6): Ava. First Afghan War (1839–42): Ghuznee 1839; Cabool 1842. First Sikh War (1845–6): Aliwal; Sobraon. Second Sikh War (1848–9): Mooltan; Goojerat; Punjaub. Crimean War (1854–5): Alma. Persian War (1856–7): Reshire; Bushire; Koosh-ab. Revolt of Arabi Pasha (1882): Tel-el-Kebir. First Sudan War (1882–4): Egypt 1882; Nile 1884–5. Reconquest of Sudan (1896–8): Suakin 1885. Great War: Retreat from Mons; Marne 1914, 1918; La Bassé 1914; Armentières 1914; Hill 60; Gravenstafel; St Julien; Frezenberg; Bellewaarde; Loos; Mount Sorrel; Bazentin; Delville Wood; Pozières; Guillemont; Flers-Courcelette; Morval; Le Transloy; Ancre Heights; Ancre 1916, 1918; Bapaume 1917, 1918; Vimy 1917; Scarpe 1917, 1918; Arleux; Hill 70; Pilckem; Langemarck 1917; Menin Road; Polygon Wood; Broodseinde; Poelcapelle; St Quentin; Rosières; Avre; Lys; Estaires; Hazebrouck; Bailleul; Kemmel; Béthune; Scherpenberg; Marne 1918; Soissonais-Ourcq; Tardenois; Amiens; Drocourt-Quéant; Bligny; Hindenburg Line; Epéhy; Canal du Nord; St Quentin Canal; Beaurevoir; Courtrai; Selle; Valenciennes; Sambre; France and Flanders 1914–18; Piave; Vittorio Veneto; Italy 1917–18; Struma; Macedonia 1915–18; Suvla; landing at Suvla; Scimitar Hill; Gallipoli 1915; Rumani; Egypt 1915–17; Gaza; El Mughar; Nebi Samwil; Jericho; Tell'Asur; Megiddo; Sharon; Sharqat; Mesopotamia 1916–18; NW Frontier India 1915, 1916–17; Aden; Archangel 1918–19. Second World War: Kvam; Dyle; Defence of Escaut; Arras Counter-attack; St Omer-La Bassée; Villers Bocage; Tilly sur Seulles; Odon; Cheux; Defence of Rauray; Caen; Bourguébus Ridge; Cagny; Troarn; Mont Pinçon; Souleuvre; Le Perier Ridge; St Pierre Le Vieille; Noireau Crossing; Falaise; Seine 1944; Antwerp; Hechel; Nederrijn; Le Havre; Antwerp-Turnhout Canal; Lower Maas; Opheusden; Venraij; Geilenkirchen; Venlo Pocket; Roer; Rhineland; Cleve; Goch; Halfaya 1941; Tobruk 1941; Relief of Tobruk; Gazala; Gabr el Fachri; Zt El Mrasses; Mersa Matruh; Point 174; Sedjenane; Mine de Sedjenane; El Kourzia; Medjez Plain; Gueriat el Atach Ridge; Si Abdallah; Tunis; Djebel Bou Aoukaz 1941; North Africa 1940–3; Landing in Sicily; Solarino; Hochwald; Xanten; Rhine; Ibbenburen; Lingen; Aller; Bremen; Syria 1941; Salerno Hills; Cava di Tirreni; Volturno Crossing; Monte Cassino; Garigliano Crossing; Minturno; Monte Tuga; Campoleone; Carroceto; Trasimene Line; Arezzo; Advance to Florence; Incontro; Gothic Line; Gemmano Ridge; Carpineta; Capture of Forli; Cosina Canal Crossing; Defence of Lamone Bridgehead; Pergola Ridge; Rimini Line; Cesena; Monte Ceco; Monte Grande; Sillaro Crossing; Athens; Greece 1944–5; Cos; Middle East 1942; Sittang 1942; Donbaik; Buthidaung; Ngakyedauk Pass; Mandalay. Korean War (1950–3): Kowang-San; Hill 227.

Dress

DIFFERENCES: Rifle green dress cap; rifle green side cap. Rifle green stable belt; black cross-belt for officers and WOIs; Inkerman chain worn by WOs and SNCOs with scarlet sash.

Marches
Double past: *The Keel Row*. Quick: *The Light Infnatry*.

Alliances and Associations
The Royal Hamilton Light Infantry (Wentworth Regiment), of Canada; Le Régiment du Maisonneuve, of Canada; The North Saskatchewan Regiment, of Canada; The Monash University Regiment, of Australia; 2nd Battalion (Canterbury Nelson Marlborough West Coast) Royal New Zealand Infantry Regiment; 11th and 13th Battalions The Baluch Regiment, of Pakistan; 1st Battalion The Kenya Rifles; The Mauritius Special Mobile Force; HMS *Invincible*; HMS *Cornwall*.

Journal
The Silver Bugle (twice a year – spring and autumn).

Museum
Peninsula Barracks, Romsey Road, Winchester, Hampshire (tel 0962 885222 ext 5130); open Tuesday–Saturday.

Record Office
Except officers: Higher Barracks, Exeter; officers: MS(AODO), London Rd, Stanmore, Middlesex.

Predecessors

THE SOMERSET AND CORNWALL LIGHT INFANTRY

History
Formed in 1959 by the amalgamation of the Somerset Light Infantry (Prince Albert's) and the Duke of Cornwall's Light Infantry.

Marches
Quick: *Prince Albert* and *Trelawney*.

THE SOMERSET LIGHT INFANTRY (PRINCE ALBERT'S)

History
Raised in 1685 as the Earl of Hunting- don's Regiment (13th Light Infantry in 1822).

Emblazoned Battle Honours
War of Spanish Succession (1701–15): Gibraltar 1704–5; War of Austrian Succession (1740–8): Dettingen. Napoleonic Wars (1803–15): Martinique 1809. First Burma War (1824–6): Ava. First Afghan War (1839–42): Ghuznee 1839; Affghanistan 1839; Cabool 1842. First Sikh War (1845–6): Aliwal. Crimean War (1854–5): Sevastopol.

Zulu and Basuto War (1877–9): South Africa 1878–9. Third Burma War (1885–7): Burma 1885–7. South African War (1899–1902): Relief of Ladysmith; South Africa 1899–1902. Great War: Marne 1914, 1918; Aisne 1914; Ypres 1915, 1917, 1918; Somme 1916, 1918; Albert 1916, 1918; Arras 1917, 1918; Cambrai 1917, 1918; Hindenburg Line; Palestine 1917–18; Tigris 1916. Third Afghan War (1919): Afghanistan 1919. Second World War: Hill 112 (1944); Mont Pinçon (1944); Rhineland (1944); Rhine (1945); North-West Europe 1944–5; Cassino II (1944); Cosina Canal Crossing (1944); Italy 1944–5; Italy 1944–5; North Arakan (1944); Ngakyedauk Pass (1944). The Sphinx superscribed 'Egypt' and a mural crown superscribed 'Jellalabad' were also borne on the colours.

Accredited Battle Honours
Great War: Le Cateau; Retreat from Mons; Armentières 1914; St Julien; Frezenberg; Bellewaarde; Hooge 1915; Loos; Mount Sorrel; Delville Wood; Guillemont; Flers-Courcelette; Morval; Le Transloy; Ancre 1916, 1918; Vimy 1917; Scarpe 1917, 1918; Arleux; Langemarck 1917; Menin Road; Polygon Wood; Broodseinde; Poelcapelle; Passchendaele; St Quentin; Bapaume 1918; Rosières; Avre; Lys; Hazebrouck; Béthune; Soissonais-Ourcq; Drocourt-Quéant; Havrincourt; Epéhy; Canal du Nord; Courtrai; Selle; Valenciennes; Sambre; France and Flanders 1914–18; Gaza; El Mughar; Nebi Samwil; Jerusalem; Megiddo; Sharon; Sharqat; Mesopotamia 1916–18; NW Frontier India 1914. Second World War: Odon; Caen; Noireau Crossing; Seine 1944; Nederrijn; Geilenkirchen; Roer; Cleve; Goch; Hochwald; Xanten; Bremen; Trasimene Line; Arezzo; Advance to Florence; Capture of Forli; Athens; Greece 1944–5; Buthidaung; Burma 1943–4.

Awards
Five members of the regiment have been awarded the Victoria Cross: two in the Indian Mutiny (1857–8), one in the Zulu and Basuto War (1878–80), one in the Great War and one in the Second World War. First awards: Sergeant W. Napier, later Sergeant-Major (1828–1908) and Private P. Carlin (1838–95) Azimgurh, India, 6 April 1858: gazetted 24 December 1858 and 26 October 1858. Two members of the regiment have been awarded the George Cross – both in the Second World War. First award: Private J. H. Silk (1916–43) Burma 4 December 1943: gazetted posthumously 13 June 1944.

Marches
Quick: *Prince Albert's March*. Slow: *Palace Guard*.

Museum
Somerset Military Museum, The Castle, Taunton, Somerset (tel 0823 255504): open Monday–Saturday 1000–1700.

Regimental Histories
Popham, H. *The Somerset Light Infantry*, Hamish Hamilton, 1968. Everett, Sir Henry. *The History of the Somerset Light Infantry, 1685–1914*, Methuen, 1924. Wyrall, E. *The History of the Somerset Light Infantry, 1914–1918*, Methuen, 1927. Molesworth, G. *The History of the Somerset Light Infantry, 1919–1945*, Regimental Committee, 1951. Whitehead, K. *The History of the Somerset Light Infantry, 1946–1960*, Regimental Committee, 1961.

THE DUKE OF CORNWALL'S LIGHT INFANTRY

History

Raised in 1702 as Fox's Regiment of Marines (32nd Foot in 1751) and in 1741 as Price's Regiment (46th Foot in 1751). These two regiments became the 1st and 2nd Battalions of the Duke of Cornwall's Light Infantry in 1881.

REGIMENTAL ANNIVERSARIES: Relief of Lucknow (17 November) 1st Battalion; Paardeberg (18 February) 2nd Battalion.

Emblazoned Battle Honours

(awards before 1881 to 46th*)

War of Spanish Succession (1701–15): Gibraltar 1704–5. **War of Austrian Succession (1740–8):** Dettingen. **War of American Independence (1775–83):** *St Lucia 1778. **Peninsular War (1808–14):** Rolica; Vimiera; Corunna; Salamanca; Pyrenees; Nivelle; Nive; Orthes; Peninsula. **Hundred Days (1815):** Waterloo. **Second Sikh War (1848–9):** Mooltan; Goojerat; Punjaub. **Crimean War (1854–5):** Sevastopol. **Indian Mutiny (1857–8):** Lucknow. **Revolt of Arabi Pasha (1882):** Tel-el-Kebir. **First Sudan War (1882–4):** Egypt 1882. **Egyptian Campaign (1885):** Nile 1884–5. **South African War (1899–1902):** South Africa 1899–1902. **Great War:** Mons; Marne 1914; Ypres 1915, 1917; Somme 1916, 1918; Arras 1917; Passchendaele; Cambrai 1917, 1918; Sambre; Doiran 1917, 1918; Gaza. **Second World War:** Hill 112; Mont Pinçon; Nederrijn; Geilenkirchen; Rhineland; North-West Europe 1940, 1944–5; Gazala; Medjez Plain; Cassino II; Incontro.

Accredited Battle Honours

Great War: Le Cateau; Retreat from Mons; Aisne 1914; La Bassée 1914; Armentières 1914; Gravenstafel; St Julien; Frezenberg; Bellewaarde; Hooge 1915; Mount Sorrel; Delville Wood; Guillemont; Flers-Courcelette; Morval; Le Transloy; Ancre 1916; Bapaume 1917, 1918; Vimy 1917; Scarpe 1917; Arleux; Langemarck 1917; Menin Road; Polygon Wood; Broodseinde; Poelcapelle; St Quentin; Rosières; Lys; Estaires; Hazebrouck; Albert 1918; Hindenburg Line; Havrincourt; Canal du Nord; Selle; France and Flanders 1914–18; Italy 1917–18; Struma; Macedonia 1915–18; Nebi Samwil; Jerusalem; Tell'Asur; Megiddo; Sharon; Palestine 1917–18; Aden. **Second World War:** Defence of Escaut; Cheux; Noireau Crossing; Opheusden; Goch; Rhine; Si Abdallah; North Africa 1942–3; Trasimene Line; Advance to Florence; Rimini Line; Italy 1944–5.

Awards

Eight members of the regiment have been awarded the Victoria Cross: four in the Indian Mutiny (1857–8), two in Somaliland (1903–4), one in the Great War and one in the Korean War (1950–3). First award: Corporal W. Oxenham (1824–74) Lucknow 30 June 1857: gazetted 21 November 1859 (32nd).

Marches

Quick: *One and All* and *Trelawny* – combined in 1933 as *One and All*.

Journal

One and All, from 1886 the journal of the 1st Battalion and from 1929 the regimental journal published at various intervals from monthly to twice a year; the journal of the 2nd Battalion 1906–29 was *Cornish Chough*, and in the first two years of the Great War the 6th Battalion published *Red Feather*.

Museum

The Keep, Bodmin, Cornwall (tel 0208 2810): open Monday–Friday 0800–1645.

Regimental Histories

Goldsmith, R. F. K. *The Duke of Cornwall's Light Infantry*, Leo Cooper, 1970.

Wyrall, E. *The History of the Duke of Cornwall's Light Infantry, 1914–1919*, Methuen, 1932.

THE KING'S OWN YORKSHIRE LIGHT INFANTRY

History

Raised in 1755 as the 53rd Foot (51st Foot in 1757) and in 1839 as HEICo's 2nd Madras (European Light Infantry) Regiment (105th (Madras Light Infantry) Regiment in 1861). These two regiments became the 1st and 2nd Battalions of the King's Own Light Infantry (Yorkshire) in 1881.

MOTTO: *Cede nullis* (Yield to none).

REGIMENTAL ANNIVERSARY: Minden Day (1 August).

FORMER MEMBER: Lieutenant-General Sir John Moore (1761–1809), commissioned 1776 (51st).

Emblazoned Battle Honours

Seven Years War (1756–63): Minden. **Peninsular War** (1808–14): Corunna; Fuentes d'Onor; Salamanca; Vittoria; Pyrenees; Nivelle; Orthes; Peninsula. **Hundred Days** (1815); Waterloo. **Second Burma War** (1852–3): Pegu. **Second Afghan War** (1878–80): Ali Masjid; Afghanistan 1878–80. **Third Burma War** (1885–7): Burma 1885–7. **South African War** (1899–1902): Modder River; South Africa 1899–1902. **Great War:** Le Cateau; Marne 1914, 1918; Messines 1914, 1917, 1918; Ypres 1914, 1915, 1917, 1918; Somme 1915, 1918; Cambrai 1917, 1918; Havrincourt; Sambre; Italy 1917–18; Macedonia 1915–17. **Second World War:** Norway 1940; Fontenay le Pesnil; North-West Europe 1944–5; Argoub Sellah; Sicily 1943; Salerno; Minturno; Anzio; Gemmano Ridge; Burma 1942.

Accredited Battle Honours

Great War: Mons; Retreat from Mons; Aisne 1914, 1918; La Bassée 1914; Hill 60; Gravenstafel; St Julien; Frezenberg; Bellewaarde; Hooge 1915; Loos; Albert 1916, 1918; Bazentin; Delville Wood; Pozières; Guillemont; Flers-Courcelette; Morval; Le Transloy; Ancre 1916; Arras 1917, 1918; Scarpe 1917; Langemarck 1917; Menin Road; Polygon Wood; Broodseinde; Poelcapelle; Passchendaele; St Quentin; Bapaume 1918; Lys; Hazebrouck; Bailleul; Kemmel; Scherpenberg; Tardenois; Amiens; Hindenburg Line; Epéhy; Canal du Nord; St Quentin Canal; Beaurevoir; Selle; Valenciennes; France and Flanders 1914–18; Piave; Vittorio Veneto; Struma; Egypt 1915–16. **Second World War:** Kvam; Le Havre; Antwerp-Turnhout Canal; Lower Maas; Mine de Sedjenane; North Africa 1943; Salerno Hills; Cava di Tirreni; Volturno Crossing; Monte Tuga; Carpineta; Lamone Bridgehead; Italy 1943–5; Sittang 1942.

Awards

Eight members of the regiment have been awarded the Victoria Cross: one in the South African War (1899–1902) and seven in the Great War. First award: Private C. Ward (1877–1921) Lindley, South Africa, 26 June 1900: gazetted 28 September 1900.

Memorial

Chapel, York Minster (Great War and Second World War).

Marches

Quick: *With Jocky to the Fair*. Slow: *Minden March*.

Journal

The Bugle (up to 1968).

Association

KOYLI Regimental Association, Light Infantry Office (Yorkshire), Wakefield Road, Pontefract, West Yorkshire WF8 4ES.

Museums

Chequer Rd, Doncaster, South Yorkshire (tel 0302 734287): open Monday–Thursday, Saturday 1000–1700, Sunday 1400–1700.

THE KING'S SHROPSHIRE LIGHT INFANTRY

History

Raised in 1755 as the 55th Foot (53rd Foot in 1757) and in 1794 as the 85th, or Bucks Volunteers, Regiment (two previous 85th regiments 1759–63 and 1779–1783). These two regiments became the 1st and 2nd Battalions of The King's Light Infantry (Shropshire Regiment) in 1881.

MOTTO: *Aucto splendore resurgo* (I rise again with increased splendour).

REGIMENTAL DAYS: Anzio (2nd Friday in May) 1st Battalion; Paardeberg (27 February) 2nd Battalion; Bligny (Sunday nearest 6 June) 4th Battalion.

FORMER MEMBERS: Field Marshal Sir George Nugent (1757–1849), Colonel 1793 (85th); Field Marshal Lord William Paulet (1804–93), commissioned 1821 (85th); Field Marshal Lord Raglan (1788–1855), commissioned 1855 (53rd); Field Marshal Sir John Fitzgerald (1784–1877), gazetted 1793. He held commissioned rank for 84 years (85th).

Emblazoned Battle Honours

(awards before 1881 to 85th★; awards to both 53rd and 85th★★)

Regimental Histories

Cooper, L. *The King's Own Yorkshire Light Infantry*. Leo Cooper, 1970. *A History of the King's Own Yorkshire Light Infantry, 1755–1948* (6 vols.): vols. 1 and 2, H. C. Wylly, Lund Humphries, 1926; vol. 3, R. C. Bond, 1930; vols. 4 and 5, W. Hingston, 1946 and 1950; vol. 6, G. F. Ellenberger, Gale & Polden, 1961.

French Revolutionary Wars (1793–1802): Nieuport; Tournay; St Lucia 1796. **Peninsular War** (1808–14): Talavera; ★Fuentes d'Onor; Salamanca; Vittoria; Pyrenees; Nivelle; ★Nive; Toulouse; ★★Peninsula. **War of 1812** (1812–14): ★Bladensburg. **First Sikh War** (1845–6): Aliwal; Sobraon. **Second Sikh War** (1848–9): Goojerat; Punjaub. **Indian Mutiny** (1857–8): Lucknow. **Second Afghan War** (1878–80): ★Afghanistan 1879–80. **First Sudan War** (1882–4): Egypt 1882. **Egyptian Campaign** (1882): Suakin 1885. **South African War** (1899–1902): Paardeburg; South Africa 1899–1902. **Great War:** Armentières 1914; Ypres 1915, 1917; Frezenberg; Somme 1916, 1918; Arras 1917, 1918; Cambrai 1917, 1918; Bligny; Epéhy; Doiran 1917, 1918; Jerusalem. **Second World War:** Dunkirk 1940; Normandy Landing; Antwerp; Venraij; Hochwald; Bremen; North-West Europe 1940, 1944–5; Tunis; Anzio; Italy 1943–5. **Korean War** (1950–3): Kowang-San; Korea 1951–2. The Croix de Guerre avec Palme awarded to the Fourth Battalion for Bligny was displayed on the Regimental Colour.

Accredited Battle Honours

Great War: Aisne 1914, 1918; Gravenstafel; St Julien; Bellewaarde; Hooge 1915; Mount Sorrel; Albert 1916, 1918; Bazentin; Delville Wood; Guillemont; Flers-Courcelette; Morval; Le Transloy; Ancre 1916; Scarpe 1917; Arleux; Hill

70; Langemarck 1917; Menin Road; Polygon Wood; Passchendaele; St Quentin; Bapaume 1918; Rosières; Lys; Estaires; Messines 1918; Hazebrouck; Bailleul; Kemmel; Béthune; Hindenburg Line; Canal du Nord; Selle; Valenciennes; Sambre; France and Flanders 1914–18; Macedonia 1915–18; Gaza; Jericho; Tell'Asur; Palestine 1917–18. **Second World War:** Defence of Escaut; Odon; Caen; Bourguébus Ridge; Troarn; Mont Pinçon; Souleuvre; Le Perier Ridge; Falaise; Nederrijn; Rhineland; Ibbenburen; Lingen; Aller; Gueriat el Atach Ridge; Djebel Bou Aoukaz 1943 II; North Africa 1943; Campoleone; Carroceto; Gothic Line; Monte Ceco; Monte Grande. **Korean War** (1950–3): Hill 227 I.

Awards

Ten members of the regiment have been awarded the Victoria Cross: five in the Indian Mutiny (1857–8); one in the Zulu and Basuto War (1878–9); one in the Great War; one on NW Frontier India (1935); and two in the Second World War. First award: Sergeant D. Dynon (1822–63) Chota Behar, India, 2 October 1857, gazetted 25 February 1862 (53rd Foot). Captain R. Deedes, later Major (1896–1975) was awarded the Empire Gallantry Medal (later exchanged for the George Cross) Chittagong, India, 7 January 1934; gazetted 7 May 1934.

Memorials

Shrewsbury. St Aidan's Chapel, St Chad's Church: Regimental memorial chapel, colours and carved oak panels; entrance hall: Books of Remembrance – Great War, Second World War, since 1945; marble tablets Aliwal, Sobraon, Sutlej, Indian Mutiny (53rd), Egypt 1882, Suakin 1885, Sudan 1884–6 (1st Battalion KSLI), Capt G. C. Vesey, Hong Kong plague 1894, Lieutenant A. K. Ffrench VC 1872. St Mary's Church: 85 KLI Afghanistan 1879–80. St Chad's

Terrace: South African War 1899–1902, marble statue of soldier by Gaffin (1904). The Quarry Park: County war memorial, Great War and Second World War, bronze statue of St Michael by A. G. Wyon (1922). Pembroke. St Mary's Church: stained glass window Great War, to men of 3rd Battalion KSLI trained at Golden Hill and Green Camps. Pembroke Dock. St John's Church: carved screens Great War, to men of 3rd Battalion KSLI trained at Bush Camp.

Marches

Quick: *Old Towler* (1st Battalion); *Daughter of the Regiment* (2nd Battalion).

Journal

The KSLI and Herefordshire LI Regimental Journal (31 vols. 1926–68).

Associations

The King's Shropshire and Herefordshire Light Infantry Association, the Light Infantry Regimental Association and the Light Infantry Benevolent Association, The Regimental County Secretary, The Light Infantry Office (Shropshire and Herefordshire), Copthorne Barracks, Shrewsbury, Shropshire.

Museum

The Castle, Shrewsbury, Shropshire (tel 0743 58516): open Monday–Saturday 1000–1700, Sunday Easter–October 1000–1700.

Regimental Histories

Moulsdale, J. R. D. *The King's Shropshire Light Infantry*, Leo Cooper, 1972. Rogerson, W. *The Historical Records of 53rd (Shropshire) Regiment 1755–1889*, Simpkin Marshall Hamilton Kent, 1891. Gubbins, R. R. (ed. Barrett, C. R. B.). *The 85th King's Light Infantry*, Spottiswoode, 1913. Wood, W. de B. *The History of the King's Shropshire Light Infantry, 1914–1918*, Medici Society,

1925. Radcliffe, C. L. Y., and Sale, R. *History of 2nd Battalion KSLI 1944–1945*, Blackwell, 1947. Kemp, P. K. *History of 4th Battalion KSLI (TA)*, Wilding and Son, 1955. The History of The Corps of The King's Shropshire Light Infantry (4 vols.), published by regiment, 1970 +

Parfitt, G. Archer. *Historical Records of the Herefordshire Light Infantry* (1 vol.), 1962. Thornburn, U. *First into Antwerp: Liberation of the City September 1944*, 4 KSLI Museum Trust, 1987. Thornburn, U. *The 4th Battalion KSLI in Normandy*, 4 KSLI Museum Trust, 1990.

THE DURHAM LIGHT INFANTRY

History

Raised in 1756 as the 2nd Battalion of the 23rd Foot (68th Foot in 1758) and in 1839 as HEICo's 2nd Bombay European Regiment (106th Bombay Light Infantry in 1861). These two regiments became the 1st and 2nd Battalions of the Durham Light Infantry in 1881.

REGIMENTAL ANNIVERSARY: Inkerman Day (5 November).

Emblazoned Battle Honours

(awards before 1881 to 106th★)
Peninsular War (1808–14): Salamanca; Vittoria; Pyrenees; Nivelle; Orthes; Peninsula. **Crimean War** (1854–5): Alma; Inkerman; Sevastopol. **Persian War** (1856–7): ★Reshire; ★Bushire; ★Koosh-ab; ★Persia 1856–7. **Third Maori War** (1863–6): New Zealand. **South African War** (1899–1902): Relief of Ladysmith; South Africa 1899–1902. **Great War**: Aisne 1914, 1918; Ypres 1915, 1917, 1918; Hooge 1915; Loos; Somme 1916, 1918; Arras 1917, 1918; Messines 1917; Lys; Hindenburg Line; Sambre. **Third Afghan War** (1919): Afghanistan 1919. **Second World War**: Dunkirk 1940; Tilly sur Seulles; Defence of Rauray; Gheel; Tobruk 1941; El

Alamein; Mareth; Primosole Bridge; Salerno; Kohima. **Korean War** (1950–3): Korea 1952–3.

Accredited Battle Honours

Great War: Armentières 1914; Gravenstafel; St Julien; Frezenberg; Bellewaarde; Albert 1916, 1918; Bazentin; Delville Wood; Pozières; Guillemont; Flers-Courcelette; Morval; Le Transloy; Ancre Heights; Scarpe 1917; Arleux; Hill 170; Pilckem; Langemarck 1917; Menin Road; Polygon Wood; Broodseinde; Passchendaele; Cambrai 1917, 1918; St Quentin; Rosières; Estaires, Hazebrouck; Bailleul; Kemmel; Scherpenberg; Marne 1918; Tardenois; Bapaume 1918; Havrincourt; Epéhy; Canal du Nord; St Quentin Canal; Beaurevoir; Courtrai; Selle; France and Flanders 1914–18; Piave; Vittorio Veneto; Italy 1917–18; Macedonia 1916–18; Egypt 1915–16; NW Frontier India 1915, 1916–17; Archangel 1918–19. **Second World War**: Dyle; Arras Counter-attack; St Omer-La Bassée; Villers Bocage; St Pierre La Vieille; Roer; Ibbenburen; North-West Europe 1940, 1944–5; Syria 1941; Halfaya 1941; Relief of Tobruk; Gazala; Gabr el Fachri; Zt el Mrasses; Mersa Matruh; Point 174; Sedjenane I; El Kourzia; North Africa 1940–3; Landing in Sicily; Sicily 1943; Volturno Crossing; Teano; Monte Camino; Monte Tuga; Gothic Line; Gemmano Ridge; Cosino Canal Crossing; Pergola Ridge; Cesena; Sillaro Crossing; Italy 1943–5; Athens; Greece 1944–5; Cos; Middle East 1943; Malta 1942; Donbaik; Mandalay; Burma 1943–5.

Awards

Eleven members of the regiment have been awarded the Victoria Cross: two in the Crimean War (1854–5), one in the Third Maori War (1863–6), six in the Great War and two in the Second World War. First award: Private J. Byrne, later Corporal (1832–79) Inkerman 5 November 1854 and 11 May 1855: gazetted 24 February 1857 (68th Foot).

War Memorial

Durham Light Infantry Chapel, Durham Cathedral.

Marches

Double past: *The Keel Row* and *Monymusk*. Quick: *The Light Barque*; Slow: *Old 68th*.

Journal

Regimental Journal of The Durham Light Infantry.

Museum

Aykley Heads, Durham City, Co Durham (tel 091 384 2214): open Thursday–Saturday, Monday (Bank Holiday) 1000–1700, Sunday 1400–1700.

Regimental Histories

Moore, W. *The Durham Light Infantry*, Leo Cooper, 1975. Miles, W. *The Durham Forces in the Field, 1914–1918*, Cassell, 1920. Lowe, W. D. *War History of the 18th (S) Battalion Durham Light Infantry*, OUP, 1920. Leather, K. J. W. *20th (Service) Battalion The Durham Light Infantry*, published by the Regiment, 1920. Veitch, E. H. *8th Battalion The Durham Light Infantry*, J. H. Veitch (Durham), 1926. Raimes, A. L. *The Fifth Battalion The Durham Light Infantry*, published by the Regiment, 1931. Stringer, L. E. *The History of The Sixteenth Battalion The Durham Light Infantry*, published by the Regiment, 1946. Lewis, P. K., and English, *8th Battalion The Durham Infantry 1939–45*, J. and P. Bealls (Newcastle), 1949: reprinted London Stamp Exchange, 1990. Ward, S. G. P. *The Story of The Durham Light Infantry*, Nelson, 1962.

THE PRINCE OF WALES'S OWN REGIMENT OF YORKSHIRE

(The King's Division)

Colonel-in-Chief: Hon Major-General HRH The Duchess of Kent GCVO

History

Formed in 1958 by the amalgamation of the West Yorkshire Regiment (The Prince of Wales's Own) and the East Yorkshire Regiment (The Duke of York's Own). One regular battalion.

MOTTO: *Nec aspera terrent* (Nor do difficulties deter).

HEADQUARTERS: 3 Tower St, York.

RECRUITMENT AREA: Yorkshire and North Humberside.

REGIMENTAL ANNIVERSARIES: Imphal Day (22 June); Quebec Day (13 September).

Emblazoned Battle Honours

War of the League of Augsburg (1689–97): Namur 1695. **War of Spanish Succession** (1701–15): Blenheim; Ramillies; Oudenarde; Malplaquet. **Seven Years War** (1756–63): Louisburg; Quebec 1759; Martinique 1762; Havannah. **War of American Independence** (1775–83): St Lucia 1778. **French Revolutionary Wars** (1793–1802): Martinique 1794; Tournay. **Napoleonic Wars** (1803–1815): Martinique 1809. **Peninsular War** (1808–14): Corunna. **Napoleonic Wars** (1803–15): Guadaloupe 1810. **Operations against Dutch** (1811): Java. **Hundred Days** (1815): Waterloo. **Revolt of Rajah of Bhurtpore** (1826): Bhurtpore. **Crimean War** (1854–5): Sevastopol. **Second** and **Third Maori Wars** (1860–1, 1863–6): New Zealand. **Second Afghan War** (1878–80): Afghanistan 1879–80. **South African War** (1899–1902): Relief of Ladysmith; South Africa 1899–1902. **Great War:** Aisne 1914, 1918; Armentières 1914; Neuve Chapelle; Ypres 1915, 1917, 1918; Loos; Somme 1916, 1918; Arras 1917, 1918; Cambrai 1917, 1918; Villers Bretonneux; Lys; Tardenois; Selle; Piave; Doiran; Suvla; Gallipoli 1915. **Second World War** Dunkirk 1940; Normandy Landing; Odon; Schaddenhof; North-West Europe 1940, 1944–5; Keren; Gazala; Defence of Alamein Line; El Alamein; Mareth; Sicily 1943; Pegu 1942; Yenangyaung 1942; Maungdaw; Defence of Sinzweya; Imphal; Bishenpur; Defence of Meiktila; Sittang 1945; Burma 1942–5. A Royal Tiger superscribed 'India' is also borne on the colours.

Accredited Battle Honours

Great War: Gravenstafel; St Julien; Frezenberg; Bellewaarde; Aubers; Hooge 1915; Albert 1916, 1918; Bazentin; Delville Wood; Pozières; Flers-Courcelette; Morval; Thiepval; Le Transloy; Ancre Heights; Ancre 1916; Scarpe 1917, 1918; Arleux; Oppy; Bullecourt; Hill 70; Messines 1917, 1918; Pilckem; Langemarck

1917; Menin Road; Polygon Wood; Broodseinde; Poelcapelle; Passchendaele; St Quentin; Bapaume 1918; Rosières; Estaires; Hazebrouck; Bailleul; Kemmel; Scherpenberg; Marne 1918; Amiens; Drocourt-Quéant; Hindenburg Line; Havrincourt; Epéhy; Canal du Nord; St Quentin Canal; Valenciennes; Sambre; France and Flanders 1914–16; Vittorio Veneto; Italy 1917–18; Struma; Macedonia 1915–18; Landing at Suvla; Scimitar Hill; Egypt 1915–18. **Second World War:** Withdrawal to Escaut; Defence of Escaut; Defence of Arras; French Frontier 1940; Ypres–Comines Canal; Tilly sur Seulles; Caen; Bourguébus Ridge; Troarn; Mont Pinçon; St Pierre la Vieille; Gheel; Nederrijn; Aam; Venraij; Rhineland; Brinkum; Bremen; Jebel Dafeis; Ad Teclesan; Abyssinia 1940–1; Cauldron; Mersa Matruh; Wadi Zigzaou; Akarit; North Africa 1940–3; Primosole Bridge; North Arakan; Kanglatongbi; Meiktila; Rangoon Road; Pyawbwe.

Dress
DIFFERENCES: Blue dress cap; maroon side cap piped black, buff insert. Maroon stable belt, central yellow stripe, black edges.
REGIMENTAL TIE: Maroon, black and gold stripes.

Marches
Quick: *Ca Ira* and *The Yorkshire Lass*. Slow: *God Bless the Prince of Wales* and *March of the XV Regiment.*

Alliances
Les Voltigeurs de Quebec, of Canada; 1st Battalion The Royal New Brunswick Regiment (Carleton and York), of Canada; The Royal Montreal Regiment, of Canada; The Falkland Islands Defence Force.

Journal
The White Rose (once a year).

Museum
Museum, Tower St, York (tel 0904 642038): open Monday–Saturday 0930–1630.

Record Office
Except officers: Imphal Barracks, York; officers: MS(AODO), London Rd, Stanmore, Middlesex.

Regimental History
Spencer, H. A. V. *A Short History of the Prince of Wales's Own Regiment of York (XIV and XV Foot) 1685–1966*, 1975.

Predecessors

THE WEST YORKSHIRE REGIMENT (THE PRINCE OF WALES'S OWN)
History
Raised in 1685 as Hales's Regiment (14th Foot in 1751).

MOTTO: *Nec aspera terrent* (Nor do difficulties deter).
REGIMENTAL ANNIVERSARY: Imphal Day (22 June).

Emblazoned Battle Honours

War of the League of Augsburg (1689–97): Namur 1695. French Revolutionary Wars (1793–1802): Tournay. Peninsular War (1808–14): Corunna. Operations against Dutch (1811): Java. Hundred Days (1815): Waterloo. India (1807–31): India. Revolt of Rajah of Bhurtpore (1826): Bhurtpore. Crimean War (1854–5): Sevastopol. Second Maori War (1860–1): New Zealand. Second Afghan War (1878–80): Afghanistan 1879–80. South African War (1899–1902): Relief of Ladysmith; South Africa 1899–1902. Great War: Armentières 1914; Neuve Chapelle; Somme 1916, 1918; Ypres 1917, 1918; Cambrai 1917, 1918; Villers Bretonneux; Lys; Tardenois; Piave; Suvla. Second World War: Keren; Defence of Alamein Line; Pegu 1942; Yenangyaung 1942; Maungdaw; Defence of Sinzweya; Imphal; Bishenpur; Defence of Meiktila; Sittang 1945. A Royal Tiger superscribed 'India' was also borne on the colours.

Accredited Battle Honours

Great War: Aisne 1914, 1918; Aubers; Hooge 1915; Loos; Albert 1916, 1918; Bazentin; Pozières; Flers-Courcelette; Morval; Thiepval; Le Transloy; Ancre Heights; Ancre 1916; Arras 1917, 1918; Scarpe 1917, 1918; Bullecourt; Hill 70; Messines 1917, 1918; Pilckem; Langemarck 1917; Menin Road; Polygon Wood; Poelcapelle; Passchendaele; St Quentin; Rosières; Hazebrouck; Bailleul; Kemmel; Marne 1918; Amiens; Bapaume 1918; Drocourt-Quéant; Hindenburg Line; Havrincourt; Epéhy; Canal du Nord; Selle; Valenciennes; Sambre; France and Flanders 1914–18; Vittorio Veneto; Italy 1917–18; Landing at Suvla; Scimitar Hill; Gallipoli 1915; Egypt 1915–16. Second World War: North-West Europe 1940; Jebel Dafeis; Ad Teclesan; Abyssinia 1940–1; Cauldron; North Africa 1940–2; North Arakan; Kanglatongbi; Capture of Meiktila; Defence of Meiktila; Rangoon Road; Pyawbwe; Burma 1942–5.

Awards

Seven members of the regiment have been awarded the Victoria Cross: two in the South African War (1899–1902), four in the Great War and one in the Second World War. First award: Captain C. Mansel-Jones (1871–1942), Terrace Hill, South Africa, 27 February 1900: gazetted 27 July 1900. Lieutenant T. E. Waters (1929–51) was awarded the George Cross, POW Camp, Korea, 1951: gazetted posthumously 13 April 1954. Private E. M. Elston (1908–82) was awarded the Empire Gallantry Medal (later exchanged for the George Cross), Quetta earthquake 31 May/1 June 1935: gazetted 19 November 1935.

Marches

Quick: *Ca Ira.* Slow: *God Bless the Prince of Wales.*

Allied Regiment in 1914

16th (Waikato) Regiment, of New Zealand.

Journal

Ça Ira (four times a year – up to 1958).

Museum

Museum, Tower St, York (tel 0904 642038): open Monday–Saturday 0930–1630.

Regimental Histories

Barker, A. J. *The West Yorkshire Regiment,* Leo Cooper, 1974. O'Donnell, Captain. *Historical Records 14th Regiment (1685–1892),* Swiss (Devonport). Wyrall, E. *The West Yorkshire Regiment, 1914–1918* (2 vols.), Bodley Head, 1924 and 1927.

THE EAST YORKSHIRE REGIMENT (THE DUKE OF YORK'S)

History
Raised in 1685 as Clifton's Regiment (15th Foot in 1751).
REGIMENTAL ANNIVERSARY: Quebec Day (13 September).

Emblazoned Battle Honours
War of Spanish Succession (1701–15): Blenheim; Ramillies; Oudenarde; Malplaquet. **Seven Years War** (1756–63): Louisburg; Quebec 1759; Martinique 1762; Havannah. **War of American Independence** (1775–83): St Lucia 1778. **French Revolutionary Wars** (1793–1802): Martinique 1794. **Napoleonic Wars** (1803–15): Martinique 1809; Guadaloupe 1810. **Second Afghan War** (1878–80): Afghanistan 1879–80. **South African War** (1899–1902): South Africa 1900–1902. **Great War:** Aisne 1914, 1918; Armentières 1914; Ypres 1915, 1917, 1918; Loos; Somme 1916, 1918; Arras 1917, 1918; Cambrai 1917, 1918; Selle; Doiran 1917; Gallipoli 1915. **Second World War:** Dunkirk 1940; Normandy Landing; Odon; Schaddenhof; North-West Europe 1940, 1944–5; Gazala; El Alamein; Mareth; Sicily 1943; Burma 1945.

Accredited Battle Honours
Great War: Gravenstafel; St Julien; Frezenberg; Bellewaarde; Hooge 1915; Albert 1916, 1918; Bazentin; Delville Wood; Pozières; Flers-Courcelette; Morval; Thiepval; Ancre Heights; Ancre 1916; Scarpe 1917, 1918; Arleux; Oppy; Messines 1917, 1918; Pilckem; Langemarck 1917; Menin Road; Polygon Wood; Broodseinde; Poelcapelle; Passchendaele; St Quentin; Bapaume 1918; Rosières; Lys; Estaires; Hazebrouck; Kemmel; Scherpenberg; Amiens; Hindenburg Line; Epéhy; Canal du Nord; St Quentin Canal; Sambre; France and Flanders 1914–18; Struma; Macedonia 1915–18; Suvla; Landing at Suvla; Scimitar Hill; Egypt 1915–16. **Second World War:** Withdrawal to Escaut; Defence of Escaut; Defence of Arras; French Frontier 1940; Ypres-Comines Canal; Tilly sur Seulles; Caen; Bourguébus Ridge; Troarn; Mont Pinçon; St Pierre la Vieille; Gheel; Nederrijn; Aam; Venraij; Rhineland; Brinkum; Bremen; Mersa Matruh; Defence of Alamein Line; Wadi Zigzaou; Akarit; North Africa 1942–3; Primosole Bridge; Sittang 1945.

Awards
Five members of the regiment have been awarded the Victoria Cross: four in the Great War and one in the Second World War. First award: Private G. W. Chafer (1894–1966), east of Meaulte, France, 3/4 June 1916: gazetted 5 August 1916.

Memorial
Beverley Minster, Yorkshire (Great War).

Marches
Quick: *The Yorkshire Lass.* Slow: *The XV von England.*

Journal
The Snapper (four times a year – up to 1958).

Museum
Museum, Tower St, York (tel 0904 642038): open Monday–Saturday 0930–1630.

Regimental Histories
Barker, A. J. *The East Yorkshire Regiment*, Leo Cooper, 1971. Jones, R. J. *A History of the 15th (East Yorkshire) Regiment 1865–1914*, published privately. Wyrall, E. *The East Yorkshire Regiment, 1914–18*, 1928.

THE GREEN HOWARDS
(ALEXANDRA, PRINCESS OF WALES'S OWN YORKSHIRE REGIMENT)
(The King's Division)

History
Raised in 1688 as Luttrell's Regiment (19th Foot in 1751). One regular battalion.
HEADQUARTERS: Trinity Church Sq, The Market Place, Richmond, North Yorkshire.
REGIMENTAL ANNIVERSARY: Alma Day (20 September).
FORMER MEMBERS: Field Marshal Sir Samuel Hulse (1746–1837), commissioned 1761; Field Marshal Sir William Rowan (1789–1879), commissioned 1803; Field Marshal Sir Nigel Bagnall (b1927), commissioned 1946.

Emblazoned Battle Honours
War of Spanish Succession (1701–15): Malplaquet. Seven Years War (1756–63): Belleisle. Crimean War (1854–5): Alma; Inkerman; Sevastopol. Tirah Campaign (1897–8): Tirah. South African War (1899–1902): Relief of Kimberley; Paardeburg; South Africa 1899–1902. Great War: Ypres 1914, 1915, 1917; Loos; Somme 1916, 1918; Arras 1917, 1918; Messines 1917, 1918; Valenciennes; Sambre; France and Flanders 1914–18; Vittorio Veneto; Suvla. Third Afghan War (1919): Afghanistan 1919. Second World War: Norway 1940; Normandy Landing; North-West Europe 1940, 1944–5; Gazala; El Alamein; Mareth; Akarit; Sicily 1943; Minturno; Anzio.

Accredited Battle Honours
Great War: Langemarck 1914, 1917; Gheluvelt; Neuve Chapelle; St Julien; Frezenberg; Bellewaarde; Aubers; Festubert 1915; Albert 1916; Bazentin; Pozières; Flers-Courcelette; Morval; Thiepval; Le Transloy; Ancre Heights; Ancre 1916; Scarpe 1917, 1918; Pilckem; Menin Road; Polygon Wood; Broodseinde; Poelcapelle; Passchendaele; Cambrai 1917, 1918; St Quentin; Bapaume 1918; Rosières; Lys; Estaires; Hazebrouck; Kemmel; Scherpenberg; Aisne 1918; Drocourt-Quéant; Hindenburg Line; Canal du Nord; Beaurevoir; Selle; Piave; Italy 1917–18; Landing at Suvla; Scimitar Hill; Gallipoli 1915; Egypt 1916; Archangel 1918. Second World War: Otta; Defence of Arras; Dunkirk 1940; Tilly sur Seulles; St Pierre la Vieille; Gheel; Nederrijn; Defence of Alamein Line; North Africa 1942–3; Landing in Sicily; Lentini; Italy 1943–4; Arakan Beaches; Burma 1945.

Awards
Eighteen members of the regiment have been awarded the Victoria Cross: two

in the Crimean War (1854–5), one in the South African War (1899–1902), twelve in the Great War and three in the Second World War. First award: Private J. Lyons, later Corporal (1823–67) Sevastopol 10 June 1855: gazetted 24 February 1857. Three members of the regiment have been awarded the Empire Gallantry Medal (later exchanged for the George Cross) one in 1930 and two in 1939. First award: Lance-Sergeant T. E. Alder (1907–73) Yangtse-Kiang River, China, 14 November 1930: gazetted 4 August 1931.

Memorial
Memorial Chapel, Richmond; Fricourt; York (South Africa 1899–1902).

Dress
DIFFERENCES: Blue dress cap; grass green side cap, blue flaps piped gold; khaki beret. Grass green stable belt, central white stripe. Grass green lanyard.
REGIMENTAL TIE: Thin silver stripes on green ground.

Marches
Quick: *Bonnie English Rose*. Slow: *Maria Theresa*.

Alliances
The Rocky Mountain Rangers, of Canada; The Queen's York Rangers (1st American Rangers), of Canada.

Journal
Green Howards Gazette (four times a year).

Museum
Trinity Church Sq, The Market Place, Richmond, North Yorkshire (tel 0748 2133): open April–October Monday–Saturday 0930–1630, Sunday 1400–1630; November, February Monday–Friday 1000–1600; March Monday–Saturday 1000–1630; closed December, January.

Record Office
Except officers: Imphal Barracks, York; officers: MS(AODO), London Rd, Stanmore, Middlesex.

Regimental Histories
Powell, G. *The Green Howards*, Leo Cooper/Secker & Warburg, 2nd ed., 1983. Ferrar, M. L. *Historical Record of The Green Howards*, Eden Fisher, 1911. Wylly, H. C. *The Green Howards in the Great War*, privately printed, 1926. Synge, W. A. T. *The Story of the Green Howards, 1939–1945*, privately printed, 1952. Oldfield, J. B. *The Green Howards in Malaya*, Gale & Polden, 1953.

THE ROYAL HIGHLAND FUSILIERS
(PRINCESS MARGARET'S OWN GLASGOW AND AYRSHIRE REGIMENT)
(The Scottish Division)
Colonel-in-Chief: HRH The Princess Margaret,
Countess of Snowdon CI GCVO

History
Formed in 1959 by the amalgamation of the Royal Scots Fusiliers and the Highland Light Infantry (City of Glasgow Regiment). One regular battalion.
MOTTO: *Montis insignia Calpe* (The badge of the Rock of Gibraltar).
HEADQUARTERS: 518 Sauchiehall St, Glasgow.
RECRUITMENT AREA: Glasgow and that part of Strathclyde which was Ayrshire.
REGIMENTAL ANNIVERSARY: Assaye Day (23 September).

Emblazoned Battle Honours
War of Spanish Succession (1701–15): Blenheim; Ramillies; Oudenarde; Malplaquet. **War of Austrian Succession** (1740–8): Dettingen. **Seven Years War** (1756–63): Belleisle. **India** (1780–98, 1780–4, 1790–2): Hindustan; Carnatic. **Second Mysore War** (1781–3): Sholinghur. **Third Mysore War** (1789–91): Mysore. **Fourth Mysore War** (1799): Seringapatam. **French Revolutionary Wars** (1793–1802): Martinique 1794. **Expedition against Dutch** (1806): Cape of Good Hope 1806. **Peninsular War** (1808–14): Rolica; Vimiera; Corunna; Busaco; Fuentes d'Onor; Ciudad Rodrigo; Badajos; Almaraz; Salamanca; Vittoria; Pyrenees; Nivelle; Nive; Orthes; Toulouse; Peninsula. **War of 1812** (1812–14): Bladensburg. **Hundred Days** (1815): Waterloo. **Eighth Kaffir War** (1851–3): South Africa 1851–1852–1853. **Crimean War** (1854–5): Alma; Inkerman; Sevastopol. **Indian Mutiny** (1857–8): Central India (1857–8). **Zulu and Basuto War** (1877–9): South Africa 1879. **Revolt of Arabi Pasha** (1882): Tel-el-Kebir. **Egyptian Campaign** (1882–4): Egypt 1882. **Third Burma War** (1885–7): Burma 1885–7. **Tirah Campaign** (1897–8): Tirah. **South African War** (1899–1902): Modder River; Relief of Ladysmith; South Africa 1899–1902. **Great War:** Mons; Marne 1914; Aisne 1914; La Bassée 1914; Ypres 1914, 1915, 1917, 1918; Loos; Somme 1916, 1918; Arras 1917, 1918; Lys; Hindenburg Line; Doiran 1917, 1918; Gallipoli 1915–16; Palestine 1917–18; Mesopotamia 1916–18; Archangel. **Second World War:** Ypres-Comines Canal; Odon; Falaise; Scheldt; Walcheren Causeway; Reichswald; Rhine; Bremen; North-West Europe 1940, 1944–5; Keren; Cauldron; Landing in Sicily 1943; Garigliano Crossing; Greece 1944–5; North Arakan; Pinwe. A castle and key superscribed 'Gibraltar 1780–1783' and '*Montis insignia Calpe*' and an elephant superscribed 'Assaye' are also borne on the colours.

Accredited Battle Honours

Great War: Le Cateau; Retreat from Mons; Langemarck 1914, 1917; Gheluvelt; Nonne Bosschen; Givenchy 1914; Neuve Chapelle; St Julien; Aubers; Festubert 1915; Albert 1916, 1918; Bazentin; Delville Wood; Pozières; Flers-Courcelette; Le Transloy; Ancre Heights; Ancre 1916; Vimy 1917; Scarpe 1917, 1918; Arleux; Messines 1917, 1918; Pilckem; Menin Road; Polygon Wood; Passchendaele; Cambrai 1917, 1918; St Quentin; Bapaume 1918; Rosières; Estaires; Hazebrouck; Bailleul; Kemmel; Béthune; Scherpenberg; Amiens; Drocourt-Quéant; Havrincourt; Canal du Nord; St Quentin Canal; Beaurevoir; Courtrai; Selle; Sambre; France and Flanders 1914–18; Macedonia 1916–18; Helles; Rumani; Egypt 1916–17; Gaza; El Mughar; Nebi Samwil; Jerusalem; Jaffa; Tell'Asur; Tigris 1916; Kut al Amara 1917; Sharqat. **Second World War:** Defence of Arras; Somme 1940; Withdrawal to Seine; Withdrawal to Cherbourg; Fontenay le Pesnil; Cheux; Defence of Rauray; Esquay; Mont Pinçon; Quarry Hill; Estry; La Vie Crossing; La Touques Crossing; Seine 1944; Aaart; Nederrijn; Best; Le Havre; Antwerp-Turnhout Canal; South Beveland; Lower Maas; Meijel; Venlo Pocket; Roer; Ourthe; Rhineland; Cleve; Goch; Moyland Wood; Weeze; Ibbenburen; Dreirwalde; Aller; Uelzen; Artlenberg; Jebel Shiba; Barentu; Massawa; Abyssinia 1941; Gazala; Mersa Matruh; Fuka; North Africa 1940–2; Sangro; Minturno; Anzio; Advance to Tiber; Italy 1943, 1944, 1945; Madagascar; Adriatic; Middle East 1942, 1944; Athens; Razabil; Shweli; Mandalay; Burma 1944–5.

Dress

DIFFERENCES: Blue glengarry, diced band. Mackenzie tartan trews: on the amalgamation of the Royal Scots Fusiliers and the Highland Light Infantry, the Colonels of the two regiments agreed that the kilt should be adopted rather than trews, but the Army Council were determined that the new regiment should be in trews and the two Colonels were forced to resign.

REGIMENTAL TIE: Thin pale gold stripes on thick olive and navy stripes.

Marches

Band, Quick: *British Grenadiers* and *Whistle o'er the Lave o't*. Band, slow: *The Garb of Old Gaul* and *March of the 21st Regiment*. Pipes and drums, quick: *Hielan Laddie* and *Blue Bonnets are over the Border*. Pipes and drums, slow: *My Home*.

Alliances

The Highland Fusiliers of Canada; 1st Battalion Royal New Zealand Infantry Regiment; 11th Battalion The Baluch Regiment, of Pakistan.

Journal

Royal Highland Fusilier (twice a year).

Museum

518 Sauchiehall St, Glasgow (tel 041 3320961): open Monday–Thursday 0900–1630, Friday 0900-1600.

Record Office
Except officers: Imphal Barracks, York; officers: MS(AODO), London Rd, Stanmore, Middlesex.

Predecessors

THE ROYAL SCOTS FUSILIERS

History
Raised in 1678 as the Earl of Mar's Regiment and taken on the English establishment in 1688 (21st Foot in 1751).
MOTTO: *Nemo me impune lacessit* (No one provokes me with impunity).
FORMER MEMBERS: Marshal of the Royal Air Force Viscount Trenchard (1875–1956), commissioned 1893.

Emblazoned Battle Honours
War of Spanish Succession (1701–15): Blenheim; Ramillies; Oudenarde; Malplaquet. **War of Austrian Succession** (1740–8): Dettingen. **Seven Years War** (1756–63): Belleisle. **French Revolutionary Wars** (1793–1802): Martinique 1794. **War of 1812** (1812–14): Bladensburg. **Crimean War** (1854–5): Alma; Inkerman; Sevastopol. **Zulu and Basuto War** (1877–9): South Africa 1879. **Third Burma War** (1885–7): Burma 1885–7. **Tirah Campaign** (1897–8): Tirah. **South African War** (1899–1902): Relief of Ladysmith; South Africa 1899–1902. **Great War**: Mons; Marne 1914; Ypres 1914, 1917, 1918; Somme 1916, 1918; Arras 1917, 1918; Lys; Hindenburg Line; Doiran 1917, 1918; Gallipoli 1915–16; Palestine 1917–18. **Second World War**: Ypres-Comines Canal; Odon; Falaise; Scheldt; Rhine; Bremen; Land-

ing in Sicily; Garigliano Crossing; North Arakan; Pinwe.

Accredited Battle Honours
Great War: Le Cateau; Retreat from Mons; Aisne 1914; La Bassée 1914; Langemarck 1914; Gheluvelt; Nonne Bosschen; Neuve Chapelle; Aubers; Festubert 1915; Loos; Albert 1916, 1918; Bazentin; Delville Wood; Pozières; Flers-Courcelette; Le Transloy; Ancre Heights; Ancre 1916; Scarpe 1917, 1918; Arleux; Messines 1917; Pilckem; Menin Road; Polygon Wood; St Quentin; Bapaume 1918; Rosières; Estaires; Hazebrouck; Bailleul; Béthune; Scherpenberg; Drocourt-Quéant; Canal du Nord; Courtrai; Selle; France and Flanders 1914–18; Macedonia 1916–1918; Helles; Rumani; Egypt 1916–17; Gaza; El Mughar; Nebi Samwil; Jerusalem; Jaffa Tell'Asur. **Second World War:** Defence of Arras; Somme 1940; Withdrawal to Seine; Fontenay le Pesnil; Cheux; Defence of Rauray; Mont Pinçon; Estry; La Vie Crossing; La Touques Crossing; Aart; Nederrijn; Best; Le Havre; Antwerp-Turnhout Canal; South Beveland; Lower Maas; Meijel; Venlo Pocket; Roer; Rhineland; Reichswald; Cleve; Goch; Dreirwald; Uelzen; Artlenberg; North-West Europe 1940, 1944–5; Sicily 1943; Sangro; Minturno; Anzio; Advance to Tiber; Italy 1943–4; Madagascar; Middle East 1942; Razabil; Schweli; Mandalay; Burma 1944–5.

Awards
Six members of the regiment have been awarded the Victoria Cross: one in the South African War (1899–1902), four in the Great War and one in the Second

World War. First award: Private G. Ravenhill (1878–1921), Colenso 15 December 1899: gazetted 4 June 1901. Lance-Corporal W. Barnett, later QMSI (1914–72) was awarded the Empire Gallantry Medal (later exchanged for the George Cross) Palestine April–September 1936: gazetted 27 November 1936.

Marches
Quick: *The British Grenadiers.* Slow: *The Garb of Old Gaul.*

Journal
The Journal of the Royal Scots Fusiliers.

Museum
518 Sauchiehall St, Glasgow (tel 041 3320961): open Monday–Thursday 0900–1630, Friday 0900–1600.

Regimental Histories
Kemp, J. C. *The History of the Royal Scots Fusiliers, 1919–1939,* Maclehose, 1963. Buchan, J. *The History of the Royal Scots Fusiliers (1678–1918),* Nelson, 1925.

THE HIGHLAND LIGHT INFANTRY (CITY OF GLASGOW REGIMENT)

History
Raised in 1777 as the 73rd Foot (71st Foot in 1786) and in 1787 as the 74th Highland Regiment (74th Foot in 1816). These two regiments became the 1st and 2nd Battalions of the Highland Light Infantry in 1881.
Motto: *Montis insignia Calpe* (The badge of the Rock of Gibraltar).
Regimental Anniversary: Assaye Day (23 September).

Emblazoned Battle Honours
(awards before 1881 to 74th*; awards to both 71st and 74th**)
War of American Independence (1775–83): Gibraltar 1780–3. **India (1780–1, 1780–4, 1790–2):** Hindoostan; Carnatic. **Second Mysore War (1781–3):** Sholinghur. **Third Mysore War (1789–91):** Mysore. **Fourth Mysore War (1799):** *Seringapatam. **Expedition against Dutch (1806):** Cape of Good Hope 1806. **Peninsular War (1808–14):** Rolica;

Vimiera; Corunna; *Busaco; *Fuentes d'Onor; *Ciudad Rodrigo; *Badajos; *Almaraz; *Salamanca; **Vittoria; **Pyrenees; *Nivelle; *Nive; **Orthes; *Toulouse; **Peninsula. **Hundred Days (1815):** *Waterloo. **Eighth Kaffir War (1851–3):** *South Africa 1851–1852–1853. **Crimean War (1854–5):** Sevastopol. **Indian Mutiny (1857–8):** Central India. **Revolt of Arabi Pasha (1882):** Tel-el-Kebir. **First Sudan War (1882–4):** Egypt 1882. **South African War (1882–4):** Egypt 1882. **South African War (1899–1902):** Modder River; South Africa 1899–1902. **Great War:** Mons; Ypres 1914, 1915, 1917, 1918; Loos; Somme 1916, 1918; Arras 1917, 1918; Hindenburg Line; Gallipoli 1915–16; Palestine 1917–18; Mesopotamia 1916–18; Archangel. **Second World War:** Odon; Scheldt; Walcheren Causeway; Reichswald; Rhine; North-West Europe 1940, 1944–5; Keren; Cauldron; Landing in Sicily; Greece 1944–5. A castle and key superscribed 'Gibraltar 1779–83' with '*Montis insignia Calpe*' beneath and an elephant superscribed 'Assaye' were also borne on the colours.

Accredited Battle Honours
Great War: Retreat from Mons; Marne 1914; Aisne 1914; Langemarck 1914, 1917; Gheluvelt; Nonne Bosschen; Givenchy 1914; Neuve Chapelle; St

Julien; Aubers; Festubert 1915; Albert 1916, 1918; Bazentin; Delville Wood; Pozières; Flers-Courcelette; Le Transloy; Ancre Heights; Ancre 1916, 1918; Vimy 1917; Scarpe 1917, 1918; Arleux; Pilckem; Menin Road; Polygon Wood; Passchendaele; Cambrai 1917, 1918; St Quentin; Bapaume 1918; Lys; Estaires; Messines 1918; Hazebrouck; Bailleul; Kemmel; Amiens; Drocourt-Quéant; Havrincourt; Canal du Nord; St Quentin Canal; Beaurevoir; Courtrai; Selle; Sambre; France and Flanders 1914–18; Rumani; Egypt 1916; Gaza; El Mughar; Nebi Samwil; Jaffa; Tigris 1916; Kut al Amara 1917; Sharqat; Murman 1919. **Second World War:** Withdrawal to Cherbourg; Cheux; Esquay; Mont Pinçon; Quarry Hill; Estry; Falaise; Seine 1944; Alart; Nederrijn; Best; Lower Maas; South Beveland; Asten; Roer; Ourthe; Rhineland; Goch; Moyland Wood; Weeze; Ibbenburen; Dreirwalde; Aller; Uelzen; Bremen; Artlenberg; Jebel Shiba; Barentu; Massawa; Abyssinia 1941; Gazala; Mersa Matruh; Fuka; North Africa 1940–2; Sicily 1943; Italy 1943, 1945; Athens; Adriatic; Middle East 1944.

Awards

Thirteen members of the regiment have been awarded the Victoria Cross: one in the Indian Mutiny (1857–8), one in the First Sudan War (1882), one during the reconquest of the Sudan (1898), two in the South African War (1899–1902), seven in the Great War and one in the Second World War. First awards: Private G. Rodgers (1829–70), Marar, India, 16 June 1858: gazetted 11 November 1859 (71st); Lieutenant W. M. M. Edwards, later Major (1855–1912) Tel-el-Kebir 13 September 1882: gazetted 13 February 1883 (74th).

Marches

Quick: *Highland Laddie*. Slow: *Scotland the Brave*.

Journal

The HLI Chronicle.

Museum

518 Sauchiehall St, Glasgow (tel 0412 3320961): open Monday–Thursday 0900–1630, Friday 0900–1600.

Regimental Histories

Oatts, L. B. *The Highland Light Infantry*, 1969. Oatts, L. B. *Proud Heritage: The Story of the Highland Light Infantry* (4 vols.); vols. 1 and 2, Nelson, 1953 and 1959; vols. 3 and 4, House of Grant, 1961 and 1963.

THE CHESHIRE REGIMENT
(The Prince of Wales's Division)
Colonel-in-Chief: HRH The Prince of Wales
and Earl of Chester KG KT GCB AK QSO ADC

History
Raised in 1689 as the Duke of Norfolk's Regiment (22nd Foot in 1751). One regular battalion, one volunteer battalion (3rd).
HEADQUARTERS: The Castle, Chester.
RECRUITMENT AREA: Cheshire (less Warrington), Wirral and Stockport.
REGIMENTAL ANNIVERSARY: Meeanee Day (17 February).

Emblazoned Battle Honours
Seven Years War (1756–63): Louisburg; Matrinique 1762; Havannah. **Conquest of Scinde** (1843): Meeanee; Hyderabad; Scinde. **South African War** (1899–1902): South Africa 1900–1902. **Great War:** Mons; Ypres 1914, 1915, 1917, 1918; Somme 1916, 1918; Arras 1917, 1918; Messines 1917, 1918; Bapaume 1918; Doiran 1917, 1918; Suvla; Gaza; Kut al Amara 1917. **Second World War:** St Omer-La Bassée; Normandy Landing; Capture of Tobruk; El Alamein; Mareth; Sicily 1943; Salerno; Rome; Gothic Line; Malta 1941–2.

Accredited Battle Honours
Great War: Le Cateau; Retreat from Mons; Marne 1914, 1918; Aisne 1914, 1918; La Bassée 1914; Armentières 1914; Nonne Bosschen; Gravenstafel; St Julien; Frezenberg; Bellewaarde; Loos; Albert 1916, 1918; Bazentin; Delville Wood; Pozières; Guillemont; Flers-Courcelette; Morval; Thiepval; Le Transloy; Ancre Heights; Ancre 1916; Vimy 1917; Scarpe 1917, 1918; Oppy; Pilckem; Langemarck 1917; Menin Road; Polygon Wood; Broodseinde; Poelcapelle; Passchendaele; Cambrai 1917, 1918; St Quentin; Rosières; Lys; Estaires; Hazebrouck; Bailleul; Kemmel; Scherpenberg; Soissonais-Ourcq; Hindenburg Line; Canal du Nord; Courtrai; Selle; Valenciennes; Sambre; France and Flanders 1914–18; Italy 1917–18; Struma; Macedonia 1915–18; Sari Bair; Landing at Suvla; Scimitar Hill; Gallipoli 1915; Egypt 1915–17; El Mughar; Jerusalem; Jericho; Tell'Asur; Palestine 1917–18; Tigris 1916; Baghdad; Mesopotamia 1916–18. **Second World War:** Dyle; Withdrawal to Escaut; Wormhoudt; Cassel; Dunkirk 1940; Mont Pinçon; St Pierre La Vieille; Gheel; Nederrijn; Aam; Aller; North-West Europe 1940, 1944–5; Sidi Barrani; Gazala; Mersa Matruh; Defence of Alamein Line; Deir el Shein; Wadi Zeuss East; Wadi Zigzaou; Akarit; Wadi Akarit East; Enfidaville; North Africa 1940–3; Landing in Sicily; Primosole Bridge; Simeto Bridgehead; Sangro; Santa Lucia; Battipaglia; Volturno Crossing; Monte Maro; Teano; Monte Camino; Garigliano

Crossing; Minturno; Damiano; Anzio; Coriano; Gemmano Ridge; Savignano; Senio Floodbank; Rimini Line; Ceriano Ridge; Valli di Comacchio; Italy 1943–5.

Awards
Two members of the regiment have been awarded the Victoria Cross: both in the Great War. First award: Private T. A. Jones DCM (1880–1956), Morval, France, 25 September 1916: gazetted 26 October 1916. Private R. Blackburn, later Sergeant (b1912) was awarded the Empire Gallantry Medal (later exchanged for the George Cross) Kasauli, India, 7 June 1935: gazetted 23 June 1936.

Memorial
Chester Cathedral (South African War 1899–1902, Great War, Second World War).

Dress
DIFFERENCES: Blue dress cap; blue side cap piped buff. Cerise and buff stable belt.
REGIMENTAL TIE: Black with narrow stripes of cerise and buff.

Marches
Quick: *Wha' Wadna Fecht for Charlie*. Slow: *The 22nd Regiment Slow March 1772*.

Alliance
2nd Battalion The Nova Scotia Highlanders (Cape Breton), of Canada.

Journal
The Oak Tree (once a year: May)

Association
The Cheshire Regiment Association, The Castle, Chester, CH1 2DN.

Museum
The Castle, Chester, Cheshire (tel 0244 37617): open daily 0900–1700.

Record Office
Except officers: Imphal Barracks, York; Officers: MS(AODO), London Rd, Stanmore, Middlesex.

Regimental Histories
Rigby, B. *Ever Glorious*, vol. 1 (1689–1939), Evans, 1983. Crookenden, A. *The History of the Cheshire Regiment* (2 vols.); vol. 1, 1914–18; vol. 2, 1939–45; Evans, 1948 and 1949. Anderson, W. H. *The History of the Twenty-Second Cheshire Regiment, 1689–1849*, Hugh Rees, 1920. Crookenden, A. *Twenty-Second Footsteps, 1849–1914*, Evans, 1956.

THE ROYAL WELCH FUSILIERS
(The Prince of Wales's Division)
Colonel-in-Chief: HM The Queen

History
Raised in 1689 as Lord Herbert's Regiment (23rd Foot in 1751). One regular battalion, one volunteer battalion (3rd).
MOTTO: *Nec aspera terrent* (Nor do difficulties deter).
HEADQUARTERS: Hightown Barracks, Wrexham, Clwyd.
RECRUITMENT AREA: North Wales.
REGIMENTAL CELEBRATION: St David's Day (1 March).
FORMER MEMBER: Field Marshal Viscount Combermere (1773–1865), commissioned 1790.

Emblazoned Battle Honours
War of the League of Augsburg (1689–97): Namur 1695. **War of Spanish Succession** (1701–15): Blenheim; Ramillies; Oudenarde; Malplaquet. **War of Austrian Succession** (1740–8): Dettingen. **Seven Years War** (1756–63): Minden. **French Revolutionary Wars** (1793–1802): Egypt 1801. **Napoleonic Wars** (1803–15): Martinique 1809. **Peninsular War** (1808–14): Albuhera; Badajos; Corunna; Salamanca; Vittoria; Pyrenees; Nivelle; Orthes; Toulouse; Peninsula. **Hundred Days** (1815): Waterloo. **Crimean War** (1854–5): Alma; Inkerman; Sevastopol. **Indian Mutiny** (1857–8): Lucknow. **Ashantee War** (1873–4): Ashantee 1873–4. **Third Burma War** (1885–7): Burma 1885–7. **South African War** (1899–1902): Relief of Ladysmith; South Africa 1899–1902. **Boxer Rising** (1900): Pekin 1900. **Great War:** Marne 1914; Ypres 1914, 1917, 1918; Somme 1916, 1918; Hindenburg Line; Vittorio Veneto; Doiran 1917, 1918; Gallipoli 1915–16; Egypt 1915–17; Gaza 1917; Baghdad. **Second World War:** St Omer-La Bassée; Caen; Lower Maas; Reichswald; Weeze; Rhine; Madagascar; Donbaik; North Arakan; Kohima. The Sphinx superscribed 'Egypt' is also borne on the colours.

Accredited Battle Honours
Great War: Mons; Le Cateau; Retreat from Mons; Aisne 1914, 1918; La Bassée 1914; Messines 1914, 1917; Armentières 1914; Langemarck 1914, 1917; Gheluvelt; Givenchy 1914; Neuve Chapelle; Aubers; Festubert 1915; Loos; Albert 1916, 1918; Bazentin; Delville Wood; Pozières; Guillemont; Flers-Courcelette; Morval; Le Transloy; Ancre Heights; Ancre 1916, 1918; Arras 1917; Scarpe 1917; Arleux; Bullecourt; Pilckem; Menin Road; Polygon Wood; Broodseinde; Poelcapelle; Passchendaele; Cambrai 1917, 1918; St Quentin; Bapaume 1918; Lys; Bailleul; Kemmel; Scherpenberg; Havrincourt; Epéhy; St

Quentin Canal; Beaurevoir; Selle; Valenciennes; Sambre; France and Flanders 1914–18; Piave; Italy 1917–1918; Macedonia 1915–18; Suvla; Sari Bair; Landing at Suvla; Scimitar Hill; Rumani; El Mughar; Jerusalem; Jericho; Tell'Asur; Megiddo; Nablus; Palestine 1917–18; Tigris 1916; Kut al Amara 1917; Mesopotamia 1916–18. **Second World War:** Dyle; Defence of Escaut; Esquay; Falaise; Nederrijn Venlo Pocket; Ourthe; Rhineland; Goch; Ibbenburen; Aller; North-West Europe 1940, 1944–5; Middle East 1942; Mandalay; Ava; Burma 1943–5.

Awards

Fourteen members of the regiment have been awarded the Victoria Cross: four in the Crimean War (1854–5), two in the Indian Mutiny (1857–8) and eight in the Great War. First awards: Sergeant L. O'Connor, later Major-General Sir Luke O'Connor KCB (1831–1915), Alma 20 September 1854 and Sevastopol 8 September 1855, and Captain E. W. D. Bell, later Major-General (1824–79), Alma 20 September 1854: both gazetted 24 February 1857. It is generally accepted that Sergeant O'Connor was the first soldier to perform an act rewarded with the VC.

Memorial

Wrexham, Clwyd (Great War, Second World War).

Dress

DIFFERENCES: Blue beret, white hackle. Five black swallow-tail ribbons (The Flash) at rear of collar.
REGIMENTAL TIE: Medium blue stripes spaced on maroon ground.

Marches

Quick: *The British Grenadiers.* Slow: *The War March of the Men of Glamorgan* and *Forth to the Battle.*

Regimental Mascot

Goat – first adopted in the 18th century.

Alliances

Royal 22e Régiment, of Canada; 3rd Battalion The Frontier Force Regiment, of Pakistan; 4th Battalion The Royal Malay Regiment; The United States Marine Corps.

Journal

Y Ddraig Goch (once a year).

Museum

The Queen's Tower, Caernarfon Castle, Caernarfon, Gwynedd (tel 0286 673362): open mid-March to mid-October daily 0930–1830; mid-October to mid-March Monday–Saturday 0930–1600, Sunday 1400–1800.

Record Office

Except officers: Imphal Barracks, York; officers: MS(AODO), London Rd, Stanmore, Middlesex.

Regimental Histories

Glover, M. *That Astonishing Infantry*, Leo Cooper, 1989. Broughton, Mainwaring, R. *Historical Record of the Welch Fusiliers*, 1889. Avray Tipping, H. *The Story of the Royal Welsh Fusiliers*, 1915. Thomas, Howell. *A History of the Royal Welsh Fusiliers*, 1916. Sraife, E. O. *A Short History of the Royal Welch Fusiliers*, var. edns., 1913–24. Cary, A. D. L., and McCance, S. *Regimental Records of the Royal Welch Fusiliers (late the 23rd Foot)* (2 vols.); vol. 1, *1689–1815*; vol. 2, *1816–1914*, Forster Groom, 1921 and 1923. Dudley Ward, C. H. *Regimental Records of the Royal Welch Fusiliers, 1914–18* (2 vols), Forster Groom, 1928 and 1929. Kemp, P. K., and Graves, J. *The Red Dragon: Royal Welsh Fusiliers, 1919–1945*, by Gale & Polden, 1960.

THE ROYAL REGIMENT OF WALES
(24th/41st FOOT)
(The Prince of Wales's Division)
Colonel-in-Chief: HRH The Princess of Wales KG KT GCB AK QSO ADC

History

Formed in 1969 by the amalgamation of the South Wales Borderers and the Welch Regiment. One regular battalion, two volunteer battalions (3rd and 4th).
MOTTO: *Gwell angau na Chywilydd* (Death before dishonour).
HEADQUARTERS: Maindy Barracks, Cardiff, South Glamorgan.
RECRUITMENT AREA: South Wales.
REGIMENTAL DAYS: St David's Day (1 March); Geluvelt Day (31 October).

Emblazoned Battle Honours

War of Spanish Succession (1701–15): Blenheim; Ramillies; Oudenarde; Malplaquet. **Seven Years War** (1756–63): Belleisle; Martinique 1762. **French Revolutionary Wars** (1793–1802): St Vincent 1797. **Expedition against Dutch** (1806): Cape of Good Hope 1806. **India** (1805–25): India. **Peninsular War** (1808–14): Talavera; Corunna; Busaco; Fuentes d'Onor; Salamanca; Vittoria; Pyrenees; Nivelle; Orthes; Peninsula. **Operations against French** (1810): Bourbon. **Operations against Dutch** (1811): Java. **War of 1812** (1812–14): Detroit; Queenstown; Miami; Niagara. **Hundred Days** (1815): Waterloo. **First Burma War** (1824–6): Ava. **First Afghan War** (1839–42): Kandahar 1842. Ghuznee 1842; Cabool 1842. **Second Sikh War** (1848–9): Chillianwallah; Goojerat; Punjaub. **Crimean War** (1854–5): Alma; Inkerman; Sevastopol. **Zulu and Basuto War** (1877–9): South Africa 1877–9. **Third Burma War** (1885–7): Burma 1885–7. **South African War** (1899–1902): Relief of Kimberley; Paardeburg; South Africa 1899–1902. **Great War:** Mons; Marne 1914; Aisne 1914, 1918; Ypres 1914, 1915, 1917, 1918; Gheluvelt; Loos; Somme 1916, 1918; Pilckem; Cambrai 1917, 1918; Doiran 1917, 1918; Macedonia 1915–18; Landing at Helles; Gallipoli 1915–16; Gaza; Baghdad; Tsingtao. **Second World War:** Norway 1940; Normandy Landing; Sully; Caen; Falaise; Le Havre; Lower Maas; Reichswald; North-West Europe 1944–5; North Africa 1940–2; Croce; Italy 1943–5; Crete; Canea; Mayu Tunnels; Pinwe; Kyaukmyaung Bridgehead; Sittang; Burma 1944–5. **Korean War** (1950–3): Korea 1951–2. The Sphinx superscribed 'Egypt' and a naval crown superscribed '12th April 1782' are also borne on the colours.

Accredited Battle Honours

Great War: Retreat from Mons; Langemarck 1914, 1917; Nonne Bosschen; Givenchy 1914; Gravenstafel; St Julien; Frezenberg; Bellewaarde; Aubers;

Albert 1916, 1918; Bazentin; Pozières; Flers-Courcelette; Morval; Ancre Heights; Ancre 1916, 1918; Scarpe 1917; Messines 1917, 1918; Menin Road; Polygon Wood; Broodseinde; Poelcapelle; Passchendaele; St Quentin; Bapaume 1918; Lys; Estaires; Hazebrouck; Bailleul; Kemmel; Béthune; Scherpenberg; Drocourt-Quéant; Hindenburg Line; Havrincourt; Epéhy; St Quentin Canal; Beaurevoir; Courtrai; Selle; Valenciennes; Sambre; France and Flanders 1914–18; Struma; Helles; Krithia; Suvla; Sari Bair; Landing at Suvla; Scimitar Hill; Egypt 1915–7; El Mughar; Jerusalem; Jericho; Tell'Asur; Megiddo; Nablus; Palestine 1917–18; Aden; Tigris 1916; Kut al Amara 1917; Mesopotamia 1916–18. **Second World War:** Odon; Bourguébus Ridge; Mont Pinçon; Souleuvre; Le Perier Ridge; Risle Crossing; Antwerp; Nederrijn; Antwerp-Turnhout Canal; Scheldt; Venlo Pocket; Zetten; Ourthe; Rhineland; Weeze; Hochwald; Rhine; Ibbenburen; Aller; Arnhem 1945; Benghazi; Gazala; Sicily 1943; Coriano; Rimini Line; Ceriano Ridge; Argenta Gap; Withdrawal to Sphakia; Middle East 1941; North Arakan; Shweli; Myitson; Maymyo; Rangoon Road.

Dress
DIFFERENCES: Blue dress cap, scarlet band and piping. Grass green stable belt, broad white stripe edged in red. Officers wear distinctive pattern of Eversleigh star and large crown as badges of rank (unofficial from 1890 to 1956).
REGIMENTAL TIE: White and red stripes on green ground.

Marches
Quick: *Men of Harlech*. Slow: *Scipio*.

Regimental Mascot
Goat (first adopted by the Welch Regiment at the time of the Crimean War). Present mascot Taffy (3rd Battalion Dewi, 4th Battalion Sospan).

Alliances
The Ontario Regiment RCAC, of Canada; The Royal New South Wales Regiment, of Australia.

Journal
The Men of Harlech (twice a year: April and December).

Associations
Regimental Association has nineteen branches: details from Assistant Regimental Secretary, RHQ Royal Regiment of Wales, Maindy Barracks, Cardiff CF4 3YE (tel 0222 227611).

Museums
The Barracks, Brecon, Powys (tel 0874 3111 ext 2310); open Monday–Friday 0900–1700; (April–30 September Saturday 1000–1700). Black and Barbican Towers, Cardiff Castle, Cardiff (tel 0222 229367); open daily January, February 1000–1630; March, April 1000–1700; May–September 1000–1700; November, December 1000–1630; closed Christmas, Boxing and New Year's Days.

Record Office
Except officers: Imphal Barracks, York; officers: MS(AODO), London Rd, Stanmore, Middlesex.

Predecessors

THE SOUTH WALES BORDERERS

History
Raised in 1689 as Dering's Regiment (24th Foot in 1751).
REGIMENTAL ANNIVERSARY: Rorke's Drift Day (22 January).

Emblazoned Battle Honours
War of Spanish Succession (1701–15): Blenheim; Ramillies; Oudenarde; Malplaquet. Expedition against Dutch (1806): Cape of Good Hope 1806. Peninsular War (1808–14): Talavera; Busaco; Fuentes d'Onor; Salamanca; Vittoria; Pyrenees; Nivelle; Orthes; Peninsular. Second Sikh War (1848–9): Chillianwallah; Goojerat; Punjab. Zulu and Basuto War (1877–9): South Africa 1877–9. Third Burma War (1885–7): Burma 1885–7. South African War (1899–1902): South Africa 1900–1902. Great War: Mons; Marne 1914; Ypres 1914, 1917, 1918; Gheluvelt; Somme 1916, 1918; Cambrai 1917, 1918; Doiran 1917, 1918; Landing at Helles; Baghdad; Tsingtao. Second World War: Norway 1940; Normandy Landing; Sully; Caen; Le Havre; North-West Europe 1944–5; North Africa 1942; Mayu Tunnels; Pinwe; Burma 1944–5. The Sphinx superscribed 'Egypt' was also borne on the colours.

Accredited Battle Honours
Great War: Retreat from Mons; Aisne 1914, 1918; Langemarck 1914, 1917; Nonne Bosschen; Givenchy 1914; Aubers; Loos; Albert 1916, 1918; Bazentin; Pozières; Flers-Courcelette; Morval; Ancre Heights; Ancre 1916; Arras 1917, 1918; Scarpe 1917; Messines 1917, 1918; Pilckem; Menin Road; Polygon Wood; Broodseinde; Poelcapelle; Passchendaele; St Quentin; Bapaume 1918; Lys; Estaires; Hazebrouck; Bailleul; Kemmel; Béthune; Scherpenberg; Drocourt-Quéant; Hindenburg Line; Havrincourt; Epéhy; St Quentin Canal; Beaurevoir; Courtrai; Selle; Valenciennes; Sambre; France and Flanders 1914–18; Macedonia 1915–18; Helles; Krithia; Suvla; Sari Bair; Scimitar Hill; Gallipoli 1915–16; Egypt 1916; Tigris 1916; Kut al Amara 1917; Mesopotamia 1916–18. Second World War: Falaise; Risle Crossing; Antwerp-Turnhoudt Canal; Scheldt; Zetten; Arnhem 1945; Gazala; North Arakan; Schweli; Myitson.

Awards
Twenty-two members of the regiment have been awarded the Victoria Cross: five in the Andaman Islands (1867), one in the Ashanti War (1873–4), ten in the Zulu and Basuto War (1877–9) and six in the Great War. First awards: Private D. Bell, later Sergeant (1845–1920); Private J. Cooper (1840–89); Assistant-Surgeon C. M. Douglas, later Lieutenant-Colonel (1840–1909); Private W. Griffiths (1841–79) and Private T. Murphy (1839–1900), Little Andaman Island, Indian Ocean, 7 May 1867: gazetted 17 December 1867. Private Griffiths was killed at Isandhlawana.

Memorial
Chelsea Hospital Gardens, London, by Cockerell (Chillianwallah 1849).

Marches
Quick: *Men of Harlech*.

Museum
The Barracks, Brecon, Powys (tel 0874 3111 ext 2310): open daily 0900–1300.

Regimental Histories
Adams, J. *The South Wales Borderers*, Hamish Hamilton, 1968. *History of the South Wales Borderers and the Monmouthshire Regiment* (5 parts); part 1, by G. A. Brett, 1953; part 2, by J. T. Boon, 1955; part 3, by G. A. Brett, 1953; part 4, by J. J. How, 1954; part 5, by G. A. Brett, 1956, Hughes. Atkinson, C. T. *The South Wales Borderers, 24th Foot, 1689–1937*, CUP, 1937.

THE WELCH REGIMENT

History
Raised in 1719 as Colonel Fielding's Regiment of Invalids (41st Invalids in 1751) and in 1756 as the 2nd Battalion of the 24th Foot (69th Foot in 1758). These two regiments became the 1st and 2nd Battalions of the Welsh Regiment in 1881 (Welch in 1920).
MOTTO: *Gwell angau na Chywilydd* (Death before dishonour).
FORMER MEMBER: Field Marshal The Duke of Wellington (1769–1852) Lieutenant 1788.
REGIMENTAL ANNIVERSARY: Gheluvelt Day (31 October).

Emblazoned Battle Honours
(awards before 1881 to 69th★)
Seven Years War (1756–63): ★Belleisle 1761; ★Martinique 1762. **French Revolutionary Wars** (1793–1802): ★St Vincent 1797. **India** (1805–25): ★India. **Operations against French** (1810): ★Bourbon. **Operations against Dutch** (1811): ★Java. **War of 1812** (1812–14): Detroit; Queenstown; Miami; Niagara. **Hundred Days** (1815): ★Waterloo. **First Burma War** (1824–6): Ava. **First**

Afghan War (1839–42): Candahar 1842; Ghuznee 1842; Cabool 1842. **Crimean War** (1854–5): Alma; Inkerman; Sevastopol. **South African War** (1899–1902): Relief of Kimberley; Paardeburg; South Africa 1899–1902. **Great War:** Aisne 1914, 1918; Ypres 1914, 1915, 1917; Gheluvelt; Loos; Somme 1916, 1918; Pilckem; Cambrai 1917, 1918; Macedonia 1915–1918; Gallipoli 1915; Gaza; Mesopotamia 1916–18. **Second World War:** Falaise; Lower Maas; Reichswald; Croce; Italy 1943–5; Crete; Canea; Kyaukmyaung Bridgehead; Sittang 1945; Burma 1944–5. **Korean War** (1950–3): Korea 1951–2. A naval crown superscribed '12th April 1782' and the scroll 'St Vincent 1797' were also borne on the colours: these two emblazoned naval honours are unique to this regiment.

Accredited Battle Honours
Great War: Mons; Retreat from Mons; Marne 1914; Langemarck 1914, 1917; Nonne Bosschen; Givenchy 1914; Gravenstafel; St Julien; Frezenberg; Bellewaarde; Aubers; Albert 1916, 1918; Bazentin; Pozières; Flers-Courcelette; Morval; Ancre Heights; Ancre 1916; Messines 1917, 1918; Menin Road; Polygon Wood; Broodseinde; Poelcapelle; Passchendaele; St Quentin; Bapaume 1918; Lys; Estaires; Hazebrouck; Bailleul; Kemmel; Béthune; Scherpenberg; Arras 1918; Drocourt-Quéant; Hindenburg Line; Epéhy; St

Quentin Canal; Beaurevoir; Selle; Valenciennes; Sambre; France and Flanders 1914–18; Struma; Doiran 1917, 1918; Suvla; Sari Bair; Landing at Suvla; Scimitar Hill; Egypt 1915–17; El Mughar; Jerusalem; Tell'Asur; Megiddo; Nablus; Palestine 1917–18; Tigris 1916; Kut al Amara 1917; Baghdad. **Second World War:** North-West Europe 1944–5; Benghazi; North Africa 1940–2; Sicily 1943; Coriano; Rimini Line; Ceriano Ridge; Argenta Gap; Crete; Withdrawal to Sphakia; Middle East 1941; Maymyo; Rangoon Road.

Awards
Six members of the regiment have been awarded the Victoria Cross: two in the Crimean War (1854–5), three in the Great War and one in the Second World War. First award: Sergeant-Major A. Madden, later Lieutenant (1820–63) siege operations, Crimea 25 October 1854: gazetted 24 February 1857 (41st).

Marches
Quick: *Ap Shenkin.*

Journal
Men of Harlech (up to June 1969).

Museum
The Welch Regiment Museum of the Royal Regiment of Wales, Black and Barbican Towers, Cardiff Castle, Cardiff (tel 0222 229367): open daily January, February 1000–1600; March, April 1000–1700; May–September 1000–1800; October 1000–1700; November, December 1000–1630, closed Christmas, Boxing and New Year's Days.

Regimental Histories
Brereton, J. M. *A History of the Royal Regiment of Wales (24th/41st Foot) 1689–1989*, published by the Royal Regiment of Wales, 1989. Butler, W. F. *Historical Events 69th Regiment*, W. Mitchell, 1870. Lomax, D. A. N. *A History of the Services of the 41st (the Welch) Regiment*, Hiorns & Miller, 1899. Whitehorn, A. C. *The History of the Welch Regiment*, *Western Mail & Echo*, 1932. Lomax, C. E. N., and de Courcy, J. *The History of the Welch Regiment 1919–1951*, *Western Mail & Echo*, 1952.

THE KING'S OWN SCOTTISH BORDERERS
(The Scottish Division)
Colonel-in-Chief:
HRH Princess Alice, Duchess of Gloucester GCB CI GCVO GBE

History
Raised in 1689 as the Earl of Leven's Regiment (25th Foot in 1751). One regular battalion.

MOTTOES: *Nisi Dominus frustra* (Unless the Lord be with us all is in vain); *In veritate religionis confido* (I believe in the truth of my faith); *Nec aspera terrent* (Nor do difficulties deter); In this sign conquer.

HEADQUARTERS: The Barracks, Berwick-on-Tweed, Northumberland.

RECRUITMENT AREA: Borders, and Dumfries and Galloway (Berwickshire, Selkirkshire, Roxburghshire, Wigtownshire and Lanarkshire).

REGIMENTAL ANNIVERSARY: Minden Day (1 August).

Emblazoned Battle Honours
War of the League of Augsburg (1689–97): Namur 1695. **Seven Years War** (1756–63): Minden. **French Revolutionary Wars** (1793–1802): Egmont op Zee. **Napoleonic Wars** (1803–15): Martinique 1809. **Second Afghan War** (1878–80): Afghanistan 1878–80. **Chitral Campaign** (1895): Chitral. **Tirah Campaign** (1897–8): Tirah. **South African War** (1899–1902): Paardeburg; South Africa 1900–1902. **Great War** Mons; Aisne 1914; Ypres 1914, 1915, 1917, 1918; Loos; Somme 1916, 1918; Arras 1917, 1918; Soissonais-Ourcq; Hindenburg Line; Gallipoli 1915–16; Gaza. **Second World War:** Dunkirk 1940; Odon; Caen; Arnhem 1944; Flushing; Rhine; Bremen; Ngakyedauk Pass; Imphal; Irrawaddy. **Korean War** (1950–3): Kowang-San; Korea 1951–2. The Sphinx superscribed 'Egypt' is also borne on the colours.

Accredited Battle Honours
Great War: Le Cateau; Retreat from Mons; Marne 1914, 1918; La Bassée 1914; Messines 1914; Nonne Bosschen; Hill 60; Gravenstafel; St Julien; Frezenberg; Bellewaarde; Albert 1916, 1918; Bazentin; Delville Wood; Pozières; Guillemont; Flers-Courcelette; Morval; Le Transloy; Ancre Heights; Vimy 1917; Scarpe 1917, 1918; Arleux; Pilckem; Langemarck 1917; Menin Road; Polygon Wood; Broodseinde; Poelcapelle; Passchendaele; Cambrai 1917, 1918; St Quentin; Lys; Estaires; Hazebrouck; Kemmel; Bapaume 1918; Drocourt-Quéant; Epéhy; Canal du Nord; Courtrai; Selle; Sambre; France and Flanders 1914–18; Italy 1917–18; Helles; Landing at Helles; Krithia; Suvla; Scimitar Hill; Rumani; Egypt 1916; El Mughar; Nebi Samwil; Jaffa; Palestine 1917–18. **Second World War:** Cambes; Cheux; Defence of Rauray; Esquay; Troarn;

Mont Pinçon; Estry; Aart; Nederrijn; Best; Scheldt; Venraij; Meijel; Venlo
Pocket; Roer; Rhineland; Reichswald; Cleve; Goch; Ibbenburen; Lingen;
Dreirwalde; Uelzen; Artlenberg; North-West Europe 1940, 1944–5; North
Arakan; Buthidaung; Kanglatongbi; Ukhrul; Meiktila; Kama; Burma 1943,
1945. **Korean War** (1950–3): Maryang-San.

Awards
Six members of the regiment have been awarded the Victoria Cross: one in the
South African War (1899–1902), four in the Great War and one in the Korean
War (1950–3). First award: Lieutenant G. H. B. Coulson DSO (1879–1901)
Lambrechtfontein 18 May 1901: gazetted posthumously 8 August 1902.

Dress
DIFFERENCES: Blue glengarry, diced border. Leslie tartan trews.
REGIMENTAL TIE: Chequered thin red and white stripes with green centres on
navy ground.

Marches
Band, quick: *Blue Bonnets are over the Border.* Band, slow: *The Garb of Old Gaul.*
Pipes and drums, quick: *Blue Bonnets are over the Border.* Pipes and drums, slow:
The Borderers.

Alliances
1st Battalion The Royal New Brunswick Regiment (Carleton and York), of
Canada; 25th Battalion, The Royal Queensland Regiment, of Australia; 5th
Battalion The Royal Malay Regiment.

Journal
The Borderers Chronicle (once a year).

Museum
The Barracks, Berwick-on-Tweed, Northumberland (tel 0289 307426): open
Monday–Friday 0900–1600, Saturday 0900–1200.

Record Office
Except officers: Imphal Barracks, York; officers: MS(AODO), London Rd,
Stanmore, Middlesex.

Regimental Histories
Woollcombe, R. *All the Blue Bonnets,* Arms & Armour Press, 1980. Gillon, S.
The King's Own Scottish Borderers, 1914–1918, Nelson, 1930. Cunning, H.
Borderers in Battle, Martin's Printing, 1948.

THE ROYAL IRISH RANGERS
(27th (INNISKILLING) 83rd and 87th)
(The King's Division)
Colonel-in-Chief: HRH The Duchess of Gloucester

History

Formed in 1968 by the amalgamation of the Royal Inniskilling Fusiliers; the Royal Ulster Rifles; and the Royal Irish Fusiliers (Princess Victoria's). Two regular battalions, two volunteer battalions (4th (The North Irish Militia) and 5th).

HEADQUARTERS: 5 Waring St, Belfast.

RECRUITMENT AREA: Ireland.

REGIMENTAL ANNIVERSARIES: Barrosa Day (5 March); Vesting Day (1 July) known as Rangers' Day.

Emblazoned Battle Honours

Seven Years War (1756–6): Martinique 1762; Havannah. **War of American Independence** (1775–83): St Lucia 1778. **French Revolutionary Wars** (1793–1802): St Lucia 1796. **India** (1799–1819): India. **Operations against Dutch** (1806): Cape of Good Hope 1806. **Napoleonic Wars** (1803–15): Maida. **Operations against Spanish** (1807): Monte Video. **Operations against French** (1810): Bourbon. **Operations against Dutch** (1811): Java. **Peninsular War** (1808–14): Talavera; Busaco; Barrosa; Fuentes d'Onor; Tarifa; Ciudad Rodrigo; Badajos; Salamanca; Vittoria; Pyrenees; Nivelle; Orthes; Toulouse; Peninsula. **War of 1812** (1812–14): Niagara. **Hundred Days** (1815): Waterloo. **First Burma War** (1824–6): Ava. **Sixth Kaffir War** (1835): South Africa 1835. **Seventh Kaffir War** (1846–7): South Africa 1846–7. **Crimean War** (1854–5): Sevastopol. **Indian Mutiny** (1857–8): Central India. **Revolt of Arabi Pasha** (1882): Tel-el-Kebir. **First Sudan War** (1882–4): Egypt 1882, 1884. **South African War** (1899–1902): Relief of Ladysmith; South Africa 1899–1902: **Great War:** Mons; Le Cateau; Marne 1914; Messines 1914, 1917, 1918; Ypres 1914, 1915, 1917, 1918; Neuve Chapelle; Loos; Somme 1916, 1918; Albert 1916; Arras 1917; Cambrai 1917, 1918; St Quentin; Hindenburg Line; France and Flanders 1914–18; Macedonia 1915–17; Suvla; Gallipoli 1915–16; Gaza; Jerusalem; Palestine 1917–18. **Second World War:** Dyle; St Omer-La Bassée; Dunkirk 1940; Normandy Landing; Caen; Rhine; Bremen; Bou Arada; Djebel Tanngoucha; North Africa 1942–3; Centuripe; Sicily 1943; Sangro; Garigliano Crossing; Anzio; Cassino II; Argenta Gap; Italy 1943–5; Malta 1940; Yenangyaung Pass 1942; Burma 1942–3. **Korean War** (1950–3): Imjin; Korea 1950–1.

Accredited Battle Honours

Great War: Retreat from Mons; Aisne 1914; La Bassée 1914; Armentières 1914; Nonne Bosschen; Frezenberg; Aubers; Festubert 1915; Gravenstafel; St Julien; Bellewaarde; Bazentin; Pozières; Guillemont; Ginchy; Le Transloy; Ancre Heights; Ancre 1916; Scarpe 1917; Pilckem; Langemarck 1917; Polygon Wood; Broodseinde; Poelcapelle; Rosières; Lys; Bailleul; Beaurevoir; Kemmel; Courtrai; Selle; Sambre; Kosturino; Struma; Helles; Landing at Helles; Krithia; Sari Bair; Landing at Suvla; Scimitar Hill; Egypt 1916; Tell'Asur; Megiddo; Nablus. **Second World War:** Withdrawal to Escaut; Defence of Arras; Ypres-Comines Canal; Cambes; Troarn; Venlo Pocket; North-West Europe 1940, 1944–5; Two Tree Hill; Stuka Farm; Oued Zarga; Djebel Bel Mahdi; Djebel Ang; Landing in Sicily; Solarino; Simeto Bridgehead; Adrano; Salso Crossing; Simeto Crossing; Malleto; Pursuit to Messina; Termoli; Trigno; San Salvo; Fossacesia; Minturno; Massa Tambourini; Liri Valley; Rome; Advance to Tiber; Trasimene Line; Monte Spaduro; Monte Grande; San Nicolo Canal; Leros; Middle East 1942; Donbaik.

Dress

DIFFERENCES: Piper green caubeen bonnet, piper green cut-feather hackle. Piper green stable belt, brown leather pouch belt for officers. Piper green trousers.

Marches

Quick: *Killaloe*. Slow: *Eileen Alannah*.

Alliances

The Princess Louise Fusiliers, of Canada; 2nd Battalion The Irish Regiment of Canada (Sudbury); The Irish Fusiliers of Canada (The Vancouver Regiment); Adelaide University Regiment, of Australia; 2nd Battalion (Canterbury Nelson Marlborough West Coast) Royal New Zealand Infantry Regiment; 1st Battalion The Punjab Regiment, of Pakistan; 9th Battalion (Wilde's) The Frontier Force Regiment, of Pakistan.

Journal

The Blackthorn (once a year).

Museum

5 Waring St, Belfast (tel 0232 232086): open Monday–Friday 1000–1600 by appointment.

Record Office

Except officers: Imphal Barracks, York; officers: MS(AODO), London Rd, Stanmore, Middlesex.

Regimental History

Corbally, M. J. P. M. *An Outline History of the Royal Irish Rangers 1689–1969*, Trimble, 1970.

Predecessors

THE ROYAL INNISKILLING FUSILIERS

History
Raised in 1690 as Tiffin's Regiment (27th Foot in 1751) and in 1854 as the 3rd Madras European Infantry (HEICo) (108th (Madras Infantry) Regiment in 1861). These two regiments became the 1st and 2nd Battalions of the Royal Inniskilling Fusiliers in 1881.
MOTTO: *Nec aspera terrent* (Nor do difficulties deter).
FORMER MEMBERS: Field Marshal Sir George White (1835–1912), commissioned 1853; Field Marshal Sir Claude Auchinlech (1884–1982).

Emblazoned Battle Honours
(awards before 1881 to 3rd MEI*)
Seven Years War (1756–63): Martinique 1762; Havannah. **War of American Independence** (1775–83): St Lucia 1778. **French Revolutionary Wars** (1793–1802): St Lucia 1796. **Napoleonic Wars** (1803–15): Maida. **Peninsular War** (1808–14): Badajos; Salamanca; Vittoria; Pyrenees; Nivelle; Orthes; Toulouse; Peninsula. **Hundred Days** (1815): Waterloo. **Sixth Kaffir War** (1835): South Africa 1835. **Seventh Kaffir War** (1846–7): South Africa 1846–7. **Indian Mutiny** (1857–8): *Central India. **South African War** (1899–1902): Relief of Ladysmith; South Africa 1899–1902. **Great War:** Le Cateau; Somme 1916, 1918; Ypres 1917, 1918; Hindenburg Line; France and Flanders 1914–18; Macedonia 1915–18; Landing at Helles; Gallipoli 1915–16; Palestine 1917–18. **Second World War:** North-West Europe 1940; Djebel Tanngoucha;

North Africa 1942–3; Centuripe; Sicily 1943; Garigliano Crossing; Cassino II; Italy 1943–5; Yenangyaung 1942; Burma 1942–3. The Sphinx superscribed 'Egypt' was also borne on the colours.

Accredited Battle Honours
Great War: Retreat from Mons; Marne 1914, 1918; Aisne 1914; Messines 1914, 1918; Armentières 1914; Aubers; Festubert 1915; Albert 1916; Bazentin; Guillemont; Ginchy; Ancre 1916; Arras 1917; Scarpe 1917; Pilckem; Langemarck 1917; Polygon Wood; Broodseinde; Poelcapelle; Cambrai 1917, 1918; Rosières; Beaurevoir; Courtrai; Selle; Sambre; Kosturino; Struma; Helles; Krithia; Suvla; Landing at Suvla; Scimitar Hill; Egypt 1916; Gaza; Jerusalem; Tell'Asur. **Second World War:** Defence of Arras; Ypres-Comines Canal; Two Tree Hill; Bou Arada; Oued Zarga; Djebel Bel Mahdi; Landing in Sicily; Solarino; Simeto Bridgehead; Adrano; Simeto Crossing; Pursuit to Messina; Termoli; Trigno; San Salvo; Sangro; Minturno; Anzio; Massa Tambourini; Liri Valley; Rome; Advance to Tiber; Trasimene Line; Monte Spadura; Argenta Gap; Middle East 1942; Donbaik.

Awards
Eight members of the regiment have been awarded the Victoria Cross: all in the Great War. First awards: Captain G. R. O'Sullivan (1888–1915) and Sergeant J. Somers (1884–1918), Gallipoli 1–2 July 1915: gazetted (the first award posthumously) 1 September 1915.

Marches
Quick: 1st Battalion: *Rory O'More; The Sprig of Shillelagh* 2nd Battalion.

Museum
The Castle, Enniskillen, Co Fermanagh, Northern Ireland (tel 0365 323142): open Monday–Friday 0930–1230, 1400–1630.

Regimental Histories

Filmer-Bennet, J. *The Royal Inniskilling Fusiliers: A Record of the Regiment's Activities 1945–1968*, Instance Printers, 1978. *Royal Inniskilling Fusiliers 1688–1914*, Regimental History Committee, Constable, 1928. Fox, Sir Frank. *The Royal Inniskilling Fusiliers in the World War*, Gale & Polden, 1951.

THE ROYAL ULSTER RIFLES

History

Raised in 1793 as the 83rd Foot and as General Cuyler's Shropshire Volunteers (86th, or Shropshire Volunteers in 1794). These two regiments became the 1st and 2nd Battalions of the Royal Irish Rifles in 1881 (Royal Ulster Rifles in 1922).

MOTTO: *Quis separabit* (Who shall separate us?)

Emblazoned Battle Honours

(awards before 1881 to 86th★; awards to both 83rd and 86th★★)
India (1799–1819): ★India. **Expedition against Dutch** (1806): Cape of Good Hope 1806. **Expedition against French** (1810): ★Bourbon. Peninsular War (1808–14): Talavera; Busaco; Fuentes d'Onor; Ciudad Rodrigo; Badajos; Salamanca; Vittoria; Nivelle; Orthes; Toulouse; Peninsula. **Indian Mutiny** (1857–8): ★★Central India. **South African War** (1899–1902): South Africa 1899–1902. **Great War**: Mons; Marne 1914; Ypres 1914, 1915, 1917, 1918; Neuve Chapelle; Somme 1916, 1918; Albert 1916; Courtrai; Struma; Suvla; Jerusalem. **Second World War**: Dyle; Dunkirk 1940; Normandy Landing; Caen; Rhine; Bremen. **Korean War** (1950–3): Imjin; Korea 1950–1. The Sphinx superscribed 'Egypt' was also borne on the colours.

Accredited Battle Honours

Great War: Le Cateau; Retreat from Mons; Aisne 1914; La Bassée 1914; Messines 1914, 1917, 1918; Armentières 1914; Nonne Bosschen; Frezenberg; Aubers; Bazentin; Pozières; Guillemont; Ginchy; Ancre Heights; Pilckem; Langemarck 1917; Cambrai 1917; St Quentin; Rosières; Lys; Bailleul; Kemmel; France and Flanders 1914–18; Kosturino; Macedonia 1915–17; Sari Bair; Gallipoli 1915; Gaza; Tell'Asur; Palestine 1917–18. **Second World War**: Cambes; Troarn; Venlo Pocket; North-West Europe 1940, 1944–5. **Korean War** (1950–3): Seoul.

Awards

Seven members of the regiment have been awarded the Victoria Cross: four in the Indian Mutiny (1857–8) and three in the Great War. First award: Lieutenant H. S. Cochrane, later Colonel (1829–64), Jhansi 1 April 1858: gazetted 24 December 1858 (86th).

Marches

Quick: *Off, Off, said the Stranger*. Slow: *The South Down Militia*.

Journal

Quis Separabit (four times a year up to autumn 1968).

Museum

5 Waring St, Belfast (tel 0232 232086): open Monday–Friday 1000–1600 by appointment – also small display in HMS *Belfast*, London.

Regimental Histories

Corbally, Lieutenant-Colonel M. J. P. M. *The Royal Ulster Rifles*, 1960. *The Royal Ulster Rifles in Korea*, Mullan, 1953. Laurie, G. B., Falls, C., and

Graves, C. *History of the Royal Irish Rifles, 1793–1948* (3 vols.), vols. 1 and 2, Gale & Polden, 1914 and 1925; vol. 3, *Times*, 1950.

THE ROYAL IRISH FUSILIERS (PRINCESS VICTORIA'S)

History

Raised in 1793 as the 87th Foot and in 1794 as the 89th Foot. These two regiments became the 1st and 2nd Battalions of Princess Victoria's (Royal Irish Fusiliers) in 1881.

MOTTO: *Faugh-a-Ballagh* (Clear the way).

FORMER MEMBER: Field Marshal Sir Gerald Templer (1895–1979), commissioned 1916.

Emblazoned Battle Honours

(awards before 1881 to 89th★; awards to both 87th and 89th★★)

French Revolutionary Wars (1793–1802): ★Egypt 1801. **Expedition against Spanish** (1807): Monte Video. **Peninsular War** (1808–14): Talavera; Barrosa; Tarifa; Vittoria; Nivelle; Orthes; Toulouse; Peninsula. **Expedition against Dutch** (1811): ★Java. **War of 1812** (1812–14): ★Niagara. **First Burma War** (1824–6): ★★Ava. **Crimean War** (1854–5): ★Sevastopol. **Revolt of Arabi Pasha** (1882): Tel-el-Kebir. **First Sudan War**)1882–4): Egypt 1882, 1884. **South African War** (1899–1902): Relief of Ladysmith; South Africa 1899–1902. **Great War:** Le Cateau; Marne 1914; Ypres 1915, 1917, 1918; Somme 1916, 1918; Arras 1917; Messines 1917, 1918; Lys; Macedonia 1915–17; Suvla; Palestine 1917–18. **Second World War:** St Omer-La Bassée; Bou Arada; Oued Zarga; Djebel Tanngoucha; Centuripe;

Termoli; Sangro; Cassino II; Argenta Gap; Malta 1940. The Sphinx superscribed 'Egypt' was also borne on the colours.

Accredited Battle Honours

Great War: Retreat from Mons; Aisne 1914; Armentières 1914; Gravenstafel; St Julien; Frezenberg; Bellewaarde; Albert 1916; Guillemont; Ginchy; Le Transloy; Scarpe 1917; Langemarck 1917; Cambria 1917; St Quentin; Rosières; Bailleul; Kemmel; Courtrai; France and Flanders 1914–18. **Second World War:** Withdrawal to Escaut; Stuka Farm; Djebel Bel Mahdi; Dejebel Ang; Adrano; Salso Crossing; Simeto Crossing; Malleto; Trigno; Fossacesia; Liri Valley; Trasimene Line; Monte Spadura; Monte Grande; San Nicolo Canal; Leros.

Awards

Two members of the regiment have been awarded the Victoria Cross: both in the Great War. First award: Private R. Morrow (1891–1915) near Messines 12 April 1915: gazetted posthumously 22 May 1915.

Journal

Faugh-a-Ballagh.

Marches

Quick: *Barrosa* and *St Patrick's Day.* Slow: *Garry Owen.*

Museum

Sovereign's House, The Mall, Armagh, Co Armagh, Northern Ireland (tel 0861 522911): open Monday–Friday 1000–1230, 1400–1630.

Regimental Histories

Harris, H. *The Royal Irish Fusiliers*, Leo Cooper, 1972. Cunliffe, M. *The Royal Irish Fusiliers, 1793–1950.* OUP, 1952.

THE GLOUCESTERSHIRE REGIMENT
(The Prince of Wales's Division)
Colonel-in-Chief: HRH The Duke of Gloucester GCVO

History
Raised in 1694 as Gibson's Regiment (28th Foot in 1751) and as the 2nd Battalion of the 3rd Foot in 1756 (61st Foot in 1758). These two regiments became the 1st and 2nd Battalions of the Gloucestershire Regiment in 1881. One regular battalion.
HEADQUARTERS: Custom House, Commercial Rd, Gloucester, Gloucestershire.
RECRUITMENT AREA: Gloucestershire and Avon.
REGIMENTAL ANNIVERSARY: Back Badge Day (21 March).

Emblazoned Battle Honours
(awards before 1881 to 61st*; awards to both 28th and 61st**)
War of Spanish Succession (1701–15): Ramillies. **Seven Years War** (1756–6): Louisburg; Guadaloupe 1759; Quebec 1759; Martinique 1762; Havannah. **War of American Independence** (1775–83): St Lucia 1778. **Napoleonic Wars** (1803–15): **Egypt 1801; *Maida. **Peninsular War** (1808–14): Corunna; *Talavera; *Busaco; Barrosa; Albuhera; *Salamanca; Vittoria; **Pyrenees; **Nivelle; **Nive; **Orthes; **Toulouse; **Peninsula. **Hundred Days** (1815): Waterloo. **Second Sikh War** (1848–9): *Chillianwallah; *Goojerat; *Punjaub. **Crimean War** (1854–5): Alma; Inkerman; Sevastopol. **Indian Mutiny** (1857–8): *Delhi 1857. **South African War** (1899–1902): Relief of Kimberley; Defence of Ladysmith; Paardeburg; South Africa 1899–1902. **Great War:** Mons; Ypres 1914, 1915, 1917; Loos; Somme 1916, 1918; Lys; Selle; Vittorio Veneto; Doiran 1917; Sari Bair; Baghdad. **Second World War:** Defence of Escaut; Cassel; Mont Pinçon; Falaise; North-West Europe 1940, 1944–5; Taukyan; Paungde; Pinwe; Myitson; Burma 1942, 1944–5. **Korean War** (1950–3): Imjin; Korea 1950–1. The Sphinx superscribed 'Egypt' is also borne on the colours.

Accredited Battle Honours
Great War: Retreat from Mons; Marne 1914, 1918; Aisne 1914, 1918; Langemarck 1914, 1917; Gheluvelt; Nonne Bosschen; Givenchy 1914; Gravenstafel; St Julien; Frezenberg; Bellewaarde; Aubers; Albert 1916, 1918; Bazentin; Delville Wood; Pozières; Guillemont; Flers-Courcelette; Morval; Ancre Heights; Ancre 1916; Arras 1917, 1918; Vimy 1917; Scarpe 1917; Messines 1917, 1918; Pilckem; Menin Road; Polygon Wood; Broodseinde; Poelcapelle; Passchendaele; Cambrai 1917, 1918; St Quentin; Bapaume 1918; Rosières; Avre; Estaires; Hazebrouck; Bailleul; Kemmel; Béthune; Drocourt-Quéant; Hindenburg Line; Epéhy; Canal du Nord; St Quentin Canal; Beaurevoir;

Valenciennes; Sambre; France and Flanders 1914–18; Piave; Italy 1917–18; Struma; Macedonia 1915–18; Suvla; Scimitar Hill; Gallipoli 1915–16; Egypt 1916; Tigris 1916; Kut al Amara 1917; Mesopotamia 1916–18; Persia 1918. **Second World War:** St Omer-La Bassée; Wormhoudt; Villers Bocage; Risle Crossing; Le Havre; Zetten; Monywa 1942; North Arakan; Mayu Tunnels; Shweli. **Korean War** (1950–3): Hill 327.

Awards
Six members of the regiment have been awarded the Victoria Cross: one in the Indian Mutiny (1857–8), four in the Great War and one in the Korean War (1950–3). First award: Surgeon H. T. Reade, later Surgeon-General H. T. Reade CB (1828–97), Delhi 14 and 16 September 1857: gazetted 5 February 1861 (61st).

Dress
DIFFERENCES: Blue dress cap with back badge; blue side cap piped scarlet, primrose yellow tip. US presidential citation at top of sleeve.
REGIMENTAL TIE: Thin yellow and red stripes on navy ground.

Marches
Quick: *The Kinnegad Slashers*. Slow: *28th/61st*.

Alliances
The Royal Canadian Regiment; The Royal Western Australia Regiment; 3rd Battalion The Kenya Regiment.

Journal
The Back Badge (twice a year – June, December).

Museum
Custom House, Commercial Rd, Gloucester, Gloucestershire (tel 0452 22682): open Monday–Saturday 1000–1700, Sunday by appointment.

Record Office
Except officers: Imphal Barracks, York; officers: MS(AODO), London Rd, Stanmore, Middlesex.

Regimental Histories
Carew, T. *The Glorious Glosters*, Lee Cooper, 1970. Wyrall, E. *The Gloucestershire Regiment in War, 1914–1918*, Methuen, 1931. Daniell, D. S. *Cap of Honour: The Story of the Glosters, 1694–1950*, Harrap, 1953.

THE WORCESTERSHIRE AND SHERWOOD FORESTERS REGIMENT
(29th/45th FOOT)
(The Prince of Wales's Division)
Colonel-in-Chief: HRH The Princess Royal GCVO

History
Formed in 1970 by the amalgamation of the Worcestershire Regiment and the Sherwood Foresters (Nottinghamshire and Derbyshire Regiment). One regular battalion, two territorial battalions (3rd and 4th).
HEADQUARTERS: Norton Barracks, Worcester: Outstation Headquarters, TA Centre, Triumph Rd, Lenton, Nottingham.
RECRUITMENT AREA: Worcestershire, Derbyshire and Nottinghamshire.
REGIMENTAL ANNIVERSARIES: Badajoz Day (6 April); Glorious First of June (1 June); Alma Day (20 September); Gheluvelt Day (31 October).

Emblazoned Battle Honours
War of Spanish Succession (1701–15): Ramillies. **Seven Years War** (1756–63): Belleisle; Louisburg. **Third Mysore War** (1789–91): Mysore. **India** (1790–3): Hindoostan. **Peninsular War** (1808–14): Rolica; Vimiera; Corunna; Talavera; Busaco; Fuentes d'Onor; Albuhera; Ciudad Rodrigo; Badajos; Salamanca; Vittoria; Pyrenees; Nivelle; Nive; Orthes; Toulouse; Peninsula. **First Burma War** (1824–6): Ava. **First Sikh War** (1845–6): Ferozeshah; Sobraon. **Seventh Kaffir War** (1846–7): South Africa. **Second Sikh War** (1848–9): Chillianwallah; Goojerat; Punjaub. **Crimean War** (1854–5): Alma; Inkerman; Sevastopol. **Indian Mutiny** (1857–8): Central India. **Abyssinian War** (1867–8): Abyssinia. **First Sudan War** (1882–4): Egypt 1882. **Tirah Campaign** (1897–8): Tirah. **South African War** (1899–1902): South Africa 1899–1902. **Great War** (1914–18): Mons; Aisne 1914, 1918; Ypres 1914, 1915, 1917, 1918; Gheluvelt; Neuve Chapelle; Loos; Somme 1916, 1918; Cambrai 1917, 1918; Lys; St Quentin Canal; France and Flanders 1914–18; Italy 1917–18; Gallipoli 1915–16; Baghdad. **Second World War**: Norway 1940; Mont Pinçon; Seine 1944; Geilenkirchen; Goch; North-West Europe 1940, 1944–5; Keren; Gazala; El Alamein; Tunis; Salerno; Anzio; Campoleone; Gothic Line; Coriano; Singapore Island; Kohima; Mandalay; Burma 1944–5. A naval crown superscribed '1st June 1794' is also borne on the colours.

Accredited Battle Honours
Great War: Le Cateau; Retreat from Mons; Marne 1914; La Bassée 1914; Armentières 1914; Langemarck 1914, 1917; Nonne Bosschen; Aubers; Festubert

1915; Hooge 1915; Albert 1916, 1918; Bazentin; Delville Wood; Pozières; Ginchy; Flers-Courcelette; Morval; Thiepval; Le Transloy; Ancre Heights; Ancre 1916; Arras 1917, 1918; Vimy 1917; Scarpe 1917; Arleux; Messines 1917, 1918; Pilckem; Langemarck 1917; Menin Road; Polygon Wood; Broodseinde; Poelcappelle; Passchendaele; St Quentin; Bapaume 1918; Rosières; Villers Bretonneux; Estaires; Hazebrouck; Bailleul; Kemmel; Scherpenberg; Amiens; Drocourt-Quéant; Hindenburg Line; Epéhy; Canal du Nord; Beaurevoir; Courtrai; Selle; Valenciennes; Sambre; Piave; Vittorio Veneto; Doiran 1917, 1918; Macedonia 1915–18; Helles; Landing at Helles; Krithia; Suvla; Sari Bair; Landing at Suvla; Scimitar Hill; Egypt 1916; Tigris 1916; Kut al Amara 1917; Mesopotamia 1916–18; Baku; Persia 1918. **Second World War:** Defence of Escaut; St Omer-La Bassée; Ypres-Comines Canal; Wormhoudt; Dunkirk 1940; Odon; Bourguébus Ridge; Maltot; Jurques, La Varinière; Noireau Crossing; Nederrijn; Rhineland; Rhine; Gogni; Barentu; Amba Alagi; Abyssinia 1940, 1941; Via Balbia; Djebel Guerba; Tamera; Medjez Plain; North Africa 1941–3; Volturno Crossing; Monte Camino; Advance to Tiber; Cosina Canal Crossing; Monte Ceco; Italy 1943–5; Malaya 1942; Relief of Kohima; Naga Village; Mao Songsang; Shwebo; Irrawaddy; Mt Popa.

Dress
DIFFERENCES: Lincoln green stable belt, maroon central stripe. Two buttons on cuffs of officers' service dress. Sword frog always worn with Sam Browne, even without sword (29th custom).
REGIMENTAL TIE: Broad Lincoln green, narrow maize, broad maroon stripes.

Marches
Quick: arrangement of *Young May Moon* and *Royal Windsor*.

Mascot
Ram, traditionally named Derby (originated with 95th).

Alliances
The Grey and Simcoe Foresters, of Canada; 13th Battalion The Punjab Regiment, of Pakistan.

Journal
Firm and Forester (twice a year).

Museums
WORC R Regiment: co-located with City Museum and Art Gallery, Worcester (tel 0905 25371): open Monday-Wednesday, Friday 0930–1730, Saturday 0930–1630, closed Bank Holidays. FORESTERS: The Castle, Nottingham (tel 0602 483504): open 1 April–30 September Sunday–Friday 1000–1745, 1 October–31 March Sunday–Friday 1000–1645, closed Christmas Day. Co-located with Derby Museum and Art Gallery, The Strand, Derby (tel 0332 255586): open Monday 1100–1700, Tuesday–Friday 1000–1800, Saturday 1000–1700, Sunday 1400–1700.

Record Office
Except officers: Imphal Barracks, York; officers: MS(AODO), London Rd, Stanmore, Middlesex.

Predecessors

THE WORCESTERSHIRE REGIMENT

History
Raised in 1694 as Farrington's Regiment (29th Foot in 1751) and in 1701 as Charlemont's Regiment (36th Foot in 1751). These two regiments became the 1st and 2nd Battalions of the Worcestershire Regiment in 1881.
MOTTO: Firm (36th).
REGIMENTAL ANNIVERSARIES: Glorious First of June (1 June); Gheluvelt Day (31 October).
FORMER MEMBER: Field Marshal Sir Claud Jacob (1863–1948), commissioned 1882.

Emblazoned Battle Honours
(awards before 1881 to 36th*; awards to both 29th and 36th**)
War of Spanish Succession (1701–15): Ramillies. Seven Years War (1756–63): *Belleisle. Third Mysore War (1789–91): *Mysore. India (1790–3): *Hindoostan. Peninsular War (1808–14): **Rolica; **Vimiera; *Corunna; Talavera; Albuhera; *Salamanca; *Pyrenees; *Nivelle; *Nive; *Orthes; *Toulouse; **Peninsula. First Sikh War (1845–6): Ferozeshah; Sobraon. Second Sikh War (1848–9): Chillianwallah; Goojerat; Punjaub. South African War (1899–1902): South Africa 1900–02. Great War: Mons; Ypres 1914, 1915, 1917,

1918; Gheluvelt; Neuve Chapelle; Somme 1916, 1918; Cambrai 1917, 1918; Lys; Italy 1917–18; Gallipoli 1915–16; Baghdad. Second World War: Mont Pinçon; Seine 1944; Geilenkirchen; Goch; North-West Europe 1940, 1944–5; Keren; Gazala; Kohima; Mandalay; Burma 1944–5. A naval crown superscribed '1st June 1794' was also borne on the colours.

Accredited Battle Honours
Great War: Le Cateau; Retreat from Mons; Marne 1914; Aisne 1914, 1918; La Bassée 1914; Armentières 1914; Langemarck 1914, 1917; Nonne Bosschen; Aubers; Festubert 1915; Loos; Albert 1916; Bazentin; Delville Wood; Pozières; Le Transloy; Ancre Heights; Ancre 1916; Arras 1917; Scarpe 1917; Arleux; Messines 1917, 1918; Pilckem; Menin Road; Polygon Wood; Broodseinde; Poelcapelle; Passchendaele; St Quentin; Bapaume 1918; Rosières; Villers Bretonneux; Estaires; Hazebrouck; Bailleul; Kemmel; Scherpenberg; Hindenburg Line; Canal du Nord; St Quentin Canal; Beaurevoir; Courtrai; Selle; Valenciennes; Sambre; France and Flanders 1914–18; Piave; Vittorio Veneto; Doiran 1917, 1918; Macedonia 1915–18; Helles; Landing at Helles; Krithia; Suvla; Sari Bair; Scimitar Hill; Egypt 1916; Tigris 1916; Kut al Amara 1917; Mesopotamia 1916–18; Baku; Persia 1918. Second World War: Defence of Escaut; St Omer-La Bassée; Wormhoudt; Odon; Bourguébus Ridge; Maltot; Jurques; La Varinière; Noireau Crossing; Nederrijn; Rhineland; Rhine; Gogni; Barentu; Amba Alagi; Abyssinia 1941–2; Via Balbia; North Africa 1941–

2; Naga Village; Mao Songsang; Shwebo; Irrawaddy; Mt Popa.

Awards

Nine members of the regiment have been awarded the Victoria Cross: all in the Great War. First award: Second Lieutenant H. James, later Major (1888–1958), Gallipoli 28 June and 3 July 1915: gazetted 1 September 1915.

Marches

Quick: *Royal Windsor*. Slow: *Duchess of Kent*.

Memorial

To 2nd Battalion: originally erected privately on Menin Road outside Gheluvelt – recently removed, refurbished and replaced in Gheluvelt beside that of South Wales Borderers.

Journal

Firm (four times a year). Superseded *The Green 'Un*, journal of the 2nd Battalion (also including items from 7th and 8th (TA) Battalions and the Depot) published from November 1922 to March 1927.

Associations

Worcestershire and Sherwood Foresters Regimental Association, Norton Barracks, Worcester WR5 2PA.

Museum

Worcester City Museum and Art Gallery, Foregate St, Worcester (tel 0905 25371): open Monday–Wednesday, Friday 0930–1730, Saturday 0930–1630, closed Bank Holidays.

Regimental Histories

Gate, R. *The Worcestershire Regiment*, Leo Cooper, 1970. Cannon, R. *Historical Record of the Thirty-Sixth or Herefordshire Regiment*, Parker, Furnivall & Parker, 1853: reissued in 1883 with additional material covering 1852–81. Mitchell. Everard, H. *The 29th (Worcestershire) Regiment*, Littlebury, 1891. Stacke, H. Fitz-M. *The Worcestershire Regiment in the Great War*, Cheshire, 1929. Watson, D. W. *The First Battalion The Worcestershire Regiment in North-West Europe*, Ebenezer Baylis, 1949. Birdwood, Lord. *The Worcestershire Regiment, 1922–1950*, Gale & Polden, 1952.

THE SHERWOOD FORESTERS (NOTTINGHAMSHIRE AND DERBYSHIRE REGIMENT)

History

Raised in 1741 as the 45th Foot and in 1823 as the 95th Foot. These two regiments became the 1st and 2nd Battalions of the Sherwood Foresters (Derbyshire Regiment) in 1881 (Sherwood Foresters (Nottinghamshire and Derbyshire Regiment) in 1902).

REGIMENTAL ANNIVERSARIES: Badajoz Day (6 April), Alma Day (20 September).

Emblazoned Battle Honours

(awards before 1881 to 95th★)
Seven Years War (1756–63): Louisburg. **Peninsular War** (1808–14): Rolica; Vimiera; Talavera; Busaco; Fuentes d'Onor; Ciudad Rodrigo; Badajos; Salamanca; Vittoria; Pyrenees; Nivelle; Orthes; Toulouse; Peninsula. **First Burma War** (1824–6): Ava. **Seventh Kaffir War** (1846–7): South Africa 1846–7. **Crimean War** (1854–5): ★Alma; ★Inkerman; ★Sevastopol. **Indian Mutiny** (1857–8): ★Central India. **Abyssinian War** (1867–8): Abyssinia. **First Sudan War** (1882–4): Egypt 1882. **Tirah Campaign** (1897–8): Tirah. **South African**

War (1899–1902): South Africa 1899–1902. **Great War:** Aisne 1914, 1918; Neuve Chapelle; Loos; Somme 1916, 1918; Ypres 1917, 1918; Cambrai 1917, 1918; St Quentin Canal; France and Flanders 1914–18; Italy 1917–18; Gallipoli 1915. **Second World War:** Norway 1940; Gazala; El Alamein; Tunis; Salerno; Anzio; Campoleone; Gothic Line; Coriano; Singapore Island.

Accredited Battle Honours

Great War: Armentières 1914; Aubers; Hooge 1915; Albert 1916, 1918; Bazentin; Delville Wood; Pozières; Ginchy; Flers-Courcelette; Morval; Thiepval; Le Transloy; Ancre Heights; Ancre 1916; Arras 1917, 1918; Vimy 1917; Scarpe 1917, 1918; Messines 1917; Pilckem; Langemarck 1917; Menin Road; Polygon Wood; Broodseinde; Poelcapelle; Passchendaele; St Quentin; Bapaume 1918; Rosières; Villers Bretonneux; Lys; Bailleul; Kemmel; Scherpenberg; Amiens; Drocourt-Quéant; Hindenburg Line; Epéhy; Canal du Nord; Beaurevoir; Courtrai; Selle; Sambre; Piave; Suvla; Landing at Suvla; Scimitar Hill; Egypt 1916. **Second World War:** St Omer-La Bassée; Ypres-Comines Canal; Dunkirk 1940; North-West Europe 1940; Djebel Guerba; Tamera; Medjez Plain; North Africa 1942–3; Volturno Crossing; Monte Camino; Advance to Tiber; Cosina Canal Crossing; Monte Ceco; Italy 1943–5; Malaya 1942.

Awards

Fourteen members of the regiment have been awarded the Victoria Cross: one in the Indian Mutiny (1857–8), one in the Tirah Campaign (1897–8), two in the South African War (1899–1902), nine in the Great War and one in the Second

World War. First award: Private B. McQuirt (1829–88) Rowa, India, 6 January 1858: gazetted 24 December 1858 (95th).

Memorial

Crich, Derbyshire.

Marches

Quick: *Young May Moon* and *I'm ninety-five*.

Mascot

Ram, traditionally named Derby – first acquired during the Indian Mutiny (95th).

Journal

The Forester (no longer published).

Associations

Worcestershire and Sherwood Foresters Regimental Association, Norton Barracks, Worcester.

Museums

The Castle, Nottingham (tel 0602 483504): open 1 April–30 September daily 1000–1745; October–March closing each day at 1645. Derby Museum and Art Gallery, The Strand, Derby, Derbyshire (tel 0332 255586): open Monday 1100–1700, Tuesday–Friday 1000–1800, Saturday 1000–1700, Sunday 1400–1700.

Regimental Histories

Barclay, G. N. *The History of the Sherwood Foresters, 1919–1957*, Clowes, 1959. Wylly, H. C. *The Sherwood Foresters in the Great War*, Gale & Polden, 1924. Wylly, H. C. (comp.). *History of the 1st and 2nd Battalions, The Sherwood Foresters, 1740–1914* (2 vols.), privately printed, 1929.

THE QUEEN'S LANCASHIRE REGIMENT
(The King's Division)
Colonel-in-Chief: HM The Queen

History
Formed in 1970 by the amalgamation of the Lancashire Regiment (Prince of Wales's Volunteers) and the Loyal Regiment (North Lancashire). One regular battalion, one volunteer battalion (4th).

Motto: Loyally I serve.

Headquarters: Fulwood Barracks, Preston, Lancashire.

Recruitment Area: Central Lancashire.

Regimental Anniversaries: Waterloo Day (18 June); Quebec Day (13 September).

Emblazoned Battle Honours
War of Spanish Succession (1701–15): Gibraltar 1704–5. **Seven Years War** (1756–63): Louisburg; Quebec 1759; Belleisle; Havannah. **Expedition against Dutch** (1806): Cape of Good Hope 1806. **Expedition against Spanish** (1807): Monte Video. **Napoleonic Wars** (1803–15): Maida. **Peninsular War** (1808–14): Vimiera; Corunna; Talavera; Tarifa; Badajos; Salamanca; Vittoria; Pyrenees; San Sebastian; Nivelle; Nive; Orthes; Toulouse. **Operations against Dutch** (1811): Java. **War of 1812** (1812–14): Niagara. **Hundred Days** (1815): Waterloo. **Revolt of Rajah of Bhurtpore** (1826): Bhurtpore. **First Burma War** (1824–6): Ava. **First Afghan War** (1839–42): Candahar 1842; Ghuznee 1842; Cabool 1842. **Gwalior Campaign** (1843): Maharajpore. **Crimean War** (1854–5): Alma; Inkerman; Sevastopol. **Indian Mutiny** (1857–8): Lucknow. **Second China War** (1857–60): Canton. **Second Maori War** (1860–1): New Zealand. **Second Afghan War** (1878–80): Ali Masjid; Ahmed Khel. **Chitral Campaign** (1895): Chitral. **South African War** (1899–1902): Defence of Kimberley; Relief of Ladysmith. **Great War:** Mons; Retreat from Mons; Marne 1914, 1918; Aisne 1914, 1918; Messines 1914, 1917, 1918; Ypres 1914, 1915, 1917, 1918; Neuve Chapelle; Somme 1916, 1918; Arras 1917, 1918; Lys; Hindenburg Line; Doiran 1917, 1918; Helles; Suvla; Sari Bair; Gaza; Kut al Amara 1917; Baghdad; Kilimanjaro; Baluchistan 1918. **Third Afghan War** (1919): Afghanistan 1919. **Second World War:** Dunkirk 1940; Normandy Landing; Bourguébus Ridge; Falaise; Lower Maas; Ourthe; Rhineland; Reichswald; Weeze; Aller; Djebel Kess Kiss; Gueriat al Atach Ridge; Anzio; Fiesole; Monte Grande; Madagascar; Johore; Singapore Island; North Arakan; Kohima; Pinwe; Nyaungu Bridgehead. The Sphinx superscribed 'Egypt' is also borne on the colours.

Accredited Battle Honours
Seven Years War (1756–63): Martinique 1762. **War of American Independence** (1775–83): St Lucia 1778. **Peninsular War** (1808–14): Rolica; Peninsula. **Second Afghan War** (1878–80): Afghanistan 1878–1880. **South African War**

(1899–1902): South Africa 1899–1902. **Great War:** Le Cateau; La Bassée 1914; Armentières 1914; Langemarck 1914, 1917; Gheluvelt; Nonne Bosschen; Givenchy 1914; St Julien; Frezenberg; Bellewaarde; Aubers; Festubert 1915; Loos; Albert 1916, 1918; Bazentin; Pozières; Guillemont; Ginchy; Flers-Courcelette; Morval; Le Transloy; Ancre Heights; Ancre 1916, 1918; Vimy 1917; Scarpe 1917, 1918; Arleux; Oppy; Pilckem; Menin Road; Polygon Wood; Broodseinde; Poelcapelle; Passchendaele; Cambrai 1917, 1918; St Quentin; Bapaume 1918; Rosières; Villers-Bretonneux; Estaires; Hazebrouck; Bailleul; Kemmel; Béthune; Scherpenberg; Soissonais-Ourcq; Drocourt-Quéant; Epéhy; Canal du Nord; St Quentin Canal; Courtrai; Selle; Valenciennes; Sambre; France and Flanders 1914–18; Kosturino; Macedonia 1915–18; Krithia; Gallipoli 1915; Rumani; Egypt 1915–17; Nebi Samwil; Jerusalem; Jaffa; Tell'Asur; Palestine 1917–18; Tigris 1916; Mesopotamia 1916–18; East Africa 1914–16. **Second World War:** Defence of Escaut; Odon; Caen; Troarn; Nederrijn; Venraij; Hochwald; Rhine; Ibbenburen; Bremen; North-West Europe 1940, 1944–5; Banana Ridge; Medjez Plain; Gab Gab Gap; Djebel Bou Aoukaz 1943; North Africa 1943; Rome; Gothic Line; Monte Gamberaldi; Monte Ceco; Italy 1944–5; Middle East 1942; Batu Pahat; Malaya 1941–2; Mayu Tunnels; Meiktila; Letse; Irrawaddy; Burma 1943–5.

Dress
DIFFERENCES: Blue dress cap, red-backed badge; blue side cap, piped scarlet. Maroon lanyard.
REGIMENTAL TIES: Maroon, bearing the regimental badge. Maroon, black and Brunswick green stripes ('Town and Country').

Marches
Quick; *L'Attaque* and *The Red Rose*. Slow: *Long Live Elizabeth*.

Alliances
The Princess of Wales's Own Regiment, of Canada; The West Nova Scotia Regiment, of Canada; The Loyal Edmonton Regiment (4th Battalion Princess Patricia's Light Infantry), of Canada; The Royal Tasmania Regiment, of Australia; 7th Battalion (Wellington (City of Wellington's Own) and Hawkes Bay) Royal New Zealand Infantry Regiment; 8th Battalion The Punjab Regiment, of Pakistan; 2nd Battalion The Royal Malay Regiment.

Journal
The Lancashire Lad (twice a year – May, October).

Association
The Regimental Association, The Queen's Lancashire Regiment, incorporating The Lancashire Regiment (PWV), The East Lancashire Regiment and the South Lancashire Regiment (PWV), Fulwood Barracks, Preston, Lancashire.

Museums
County and Regimental Museum, Stanley St, Preston, Lancashire (tel 0772 264075): open Monday, Wednesday–Saturday 1300–1700. Fulwood Barracks, Preston, Lancashire (tel 0772 264075): open Monday–Wednesday, Friday, Saturday 1000–1700.

Record Office
Except officers: Imphal Barracks, York; officers: MS(AODO), London Rd, Stanmore, Middlesex.

Predecessors

THE LANCASHIRE REGIMENT (PRINCE OF WALES'S VOLUNTEERS)

History
Formed in 1958 by the amalgamation of the East Lancashire Regiment and the South Lancashire Regiment (Prince of Wales's Volunteers).

Marches
Quick: *L'Attaque*. Slow: *God Bless the Prince of Wales*.

Association
The Regimental Association, The Queen's Lancashire Regiment, incorporating the Lancashire Regiment (PWV), the East Lancashire Regiment and the South Lancashire Regiment (PWS), Fulwood Barracks, Preston, Lancashire.

Museum
Peninsula Barracks, Orford, Warrington, Lancashire (tel 0925 33563): open Monday–Friday 0900–1400.

Predecessors of the Lancashire Regiment

(Prince of Wales's Volunteers) THE EAST LANCASHIRE REGIMENT

History
Raised in 1689 as Lord Castleton's Regiment (30th Foot in 1751) and in 1755 as the 59th Foot. These regiments became the 1st and 2nd Battalions of the East Lancashire Regiment in 1881.

MOTTO: *Spectemur agendo* (Let us be judged by our deeds).

REGIMENTAL ANNIVERSARY: Somme Day (18 June).

Emblazoned Battle Honours
(awards before 1881 to 59th★; awards to both 30th and 59th★★)
War of Spanish Succession (1701–15): Gibraltar 1704–5. Seven Years War (1756–63): Belleisle. Expedition against Dutch (1811): ★Java. Peninsular War (1808–14): Badajos; Salamanca; ★Vittoria; ★San Sebastian; ★Nive; ★★Peninsula. Hundred Days (1815): Waterloo. Revolt of Rajah of Bhurtpore (1826): ★Bhurtpore. Crimean War (1854–5): Alma; Inkerman; Sevastopol. Second China War (1857–60): ★Canton. Second Afghan War (1878–80): ★Ahmed Khel; ★Afghanistan 1878–1880. Chitral Campaign (1895): Chitral. South African War (1899–1902): South Africa 1900–02. Great War: Retreat from Mons; Marne 1914; Aisne 1914, 1918; Neuve Chapelle; Ypres 1915, 1917, 1918; Somme 1916, 1918; Arras 1917, 1918; Doiran 1917, 1918; Helles; Kut al Amara 1917. Second World War: Dunkirk 1940; Falaise; Lower Maas; Ourthe; Reichswald; Weeze; Aller; Madagascar; Pinwe; Burma 1944–5. The Sphinx superscribed 'Egypt' was also borne on the colours.

Accredited Battle Honours
Seven Years War (1756–63): Belleisle. Great War: Le Cateau; Armentières 1914; St Julien; Frezenberg; Belle-

waarde; Aubers; Albert 1916, 1918; Bazentin; Pozières; Le Transloy; Ancre Heights; Ancre 1916, 1918; Vimy 1917; Scarpe 1917, 1918; Arleux; Oppy; Messines 1917; Pilckem; Langemarck 1917; Menin Road; Polygon Wood; Broodseinde; Poelcapelle; Passchendaele; St Quentin; Bapaume 1918; Rosières; Villers Bretonneux; Lys; Estaires; Hazebrouck; Bailleul; Kemmel; Hindenburg Line; Canal du Nord; Cambrai 1918; Selle; Valenciennes; Sambre; France and Flanders 1914–18; Kosturino; Macedonia 1915–18; Krithia; Suvla; Sari Bair; Gallipoli 1915; Rumani; Egypt 1915–17; Tigris 1916; Baghdad; Mesopotamia 1916–17. **Second World War:** Defence of Escaut; Caen; Nederrijn; Rhineland; Rhine; Ibbenburen; North-West Europe 1940, 1944–5; North Arakan.

Awards

Six members of the regiment have been awarded the Victoria Cross: one in the Second Afghan War (1878–80), four in the Great War and one in the Second World War. First award: Captain E. H. Sartorius (1844–1925), Shahjui, Afghanistan, 23 October 1879: gazetted 16 May 1881 (59th Foot). His brother was awarded the Victoria Cross in the Indian Army.

Association

The Regimental Association, The Queen's Lancashire Regiment, incorporating The Lancashire Regiment (PWV), The East Lancashire Regiment and the South Lancashire Regiment (PWV), Fulwood Barracks, Preston, Lancashire.

Museum

Blackburn Museum and Art Gallery, Museum St, Blackburn, Lancashire (tel 0254 667130): open Tuesday–Saturday 1000–1700.

Regimental Histories

Lewis, A. S. *The Lilywhite 59th*, Blackburn Borough Council, 1985. *Historical Records of the Thirtieth Regiment*, (London), 1887. Ballantyne, N. *History of the Thirtieth Regiment 1689–1881*, Littlebury, 1923. Nicholson, Sir C. L., and MacMullen, H. T. *History of the East Lancashire Regiment 1914–1918*, Littlebury, 1939. Burden, G. W. P. N. *History of the East Lancashire Regiment, 1939–1945*, Rawson, 1953. Aytoun, J. *Redcoats in the Caribbean*, Blackburn Borough Council, 1984. Turner, W. *The Accrington Pals*, Lancashire County Council, 1986.

THE SOUTH LANCASHIRE REGIMENT (THE PRINCE OF WALES'S VOLUNTEERS)

History

Raised in 1717 as Philip's Regiment (40th Foot in 1751) and in 1793 as the 82nd, or Prince of Wales's Volunteers, Regiment. These two regiments became the 1st and 2nd Battalions of the Prince of Wales's Volunteers (South Lancashire Regiment) in 1881.

Emblazoned Battle Honours

(awards before 1881 to 82nd*; awards to both 40th and 82nd**)
Seven Years War (1756–62): Louisburg; Martinique 1762; Havannah. **War of American Independence** (1775–83): St Lucia 1778. **Expedition against Spanish** (1807): Monte Video. **Peninsular War** (1808–14): **Rolica; **Vimiera; *Corunna; Talavera; Badajos; Salamanca; **Vittoria; **Pyrenees; **Nivelle; **Orthes; Toulouse; **Peninsula. **War of 1812** (1812–14):

*Niagara. **Hundred Days** (1815): Waterloo. **First Afghan War** (1839–42): Candahar 1842; Ghuznee 1842; Cabool 1842. **Gwalior Campaign** (1843): Maharajpore. **Crimean War** (1854–5): *Sevastopol. **Indian Mutiny** (1857–8): *Lucknow. **Second Maori War** (1860–1): New Zealand. **South African War** (1899–1902): Relief of Ladysmith; South Africa 1899–1902. **Great War:** Mons; Aisne 1914, 1918; Messines 1914, 1917, 1918; Ypres 1914, 1915, 1917, 1918; Somme 1916, 1918; Lys; Doiran 1917, 1918; Sari Bair; Baghdad; Baluchistan 1918. **Third Afghan War** (1919): Afghanistan 1919. **Second World War:** Dunkirk 1940; Normandy Landing; Bourguébus Ridge; Falaise; Rhineland; North-West Europe 1940, 1944–5; Madagascar; North Arakan; Kohima; Nyaungu Bridgehead. The Sphinx superscribed 'Egypt' was also borne on the colours.

Accredited Battle Honours
Great War: Le Cateau; Retreat from Mons; Marne 1914; La Bassée 1914; Armentières 1914; Nonne Bosschen; St Julien; Frezenberg; Bellewaarde; Albert 1916; Bazentin; Pozières; Guillemont; Ginchy; Flers-Courcelette; Morval; Le Transloy; Ancre Heights; Ancre 1916; Arras 1917, 1918; Scarpe 1917, 1918; Pilckem; Langemarck 1917; Menin Road; Polygon Wood; Passchendaele; Cambria 1917, 1918; St Quentin; Bapaume 1918; Rosières; Estaires; Hazebrouck; Bailleul; Kemmel; Scherpenberg; Drocourt-Quéant; Hindenburg Line; Canal du Nord; Courtrai; Selle; Sambre; France and Flanders 1914–18; Macedonia 1915–18; Suvla; Gallipoli 1915; Egypt 1916; Tigris 1916; Kut al Amara 1917; Mesopotamia 1916–18. **Second World War:** Odon; Troarn; Venraij; Hochwald; Bremen; Middle East 1942; Mayu Tunnels; Meiktila; Letse; Irrawaddy; Burma 1943–5.

Awards
Five members of the regiment have been awarded the Victoria Cross: one in the Second Maori War (1860–1) and four in the Great War. First award: Colour-Sergeant J. Lucas, later Sergeant-Major (1827–92), New Zealand 18 March 1861: gazetted 17 July 1861 (40th).

Marches
Quick: *God Bless the Prince of Wales.* Slow; *The Lancashire Witches.*

Allied Regiment in 1914
9th (Wellington East Coast) Regiment, of New Zealand.

Journal
Newsletter.

Association
The Regimental Association, The Queen's Lancashire Regiment, incorporating The Lancashire Regiment (PWV), The East Lancashire Regiment and the South Lancashire Regiment (PWV), Fulwood Barracks, Preston, Lancashire.

Museum
Peninsula Barracks, Orford, Warrington, Lancashire (tel 0925 33563): open Monday–Friday 0900–1400.

Regimental History
Mullaly, B. R. *The South Lancs Regiment (The Prince of Wales's Volunteers)*, White Swan, 1905.

THE LOYAL REGIMENT (NORTH LANCASHIRE)

History
Raised in 1741 as Mordaunt's Regiment (47th Foot in 1748) and in 1793 as The 81st, or Loyal Lincoln Volunteers, Regi-

ment. These two regiments became the 1st and 2nd Battalions of the Loyal North Lancashire Regiment in 1881 (Loyal Regiment (North Lancashire) in 1921).

REGIMENTAL ANNIVERSARIES: Kimberley Day (15 February); Quebec Day (13 September).

MOTTO: Loyanté m'oblige (Loyalty binds me).

Emblazoned Battle Honours

(awards before 1881 to 81st*; awards to both 47th and 81st**)

Seven Years War (1756–62): Louisburg; Quebec 1759. **Napoleonic Wars** (1803–15): *Maida. **Peninsular War** (1808–14): *Corunna; Tarifa; Vittoria; San Sebastian; Nive; **Peninsula. **First Burma War** (1824–6): Ava. **Crimean War** (1854–5): Alma; Inkerman; Sevastopol. **Second Afghan War** (1878–80): *Ali Masjid; *Afghanistan 1878–9. **South African War** (1899–1902): Defence of Kimberley; South Africa 1899–1902. **Great War**: Mons; Aisne 1914, 1918; Ypres 1914, 1917, 1918; Somme 1916, 1918; Lys; Hindenburg Line; Suvla; Gaza; Baghdad; Kilimanjaro. **Second World War**: Dunkirk 1940; Djebel Kess Kiss; Gueriat el Atach Ridge; North Africa 1943; Anzio; Fiesole; Monte Grande; Italy 1944–5; Johore; Singapore Island.

Accredited Battle Honours

Great War: Retreat from Mons; Marne 1914, 1918; Langemarck 1914; Gheluvelt; Nonne Bosschen; Givenchy 1914; Aubers; Festubert 1915; Loos; Albert 1916; Bazentin; Pozières; Guillemont; Ginchy; Flers-Courcelette; Morval; Ancre Heights; Ancre 1916; Arras 1917, 1918; Scarpe 1917; Arleux; Messines 1917; Pilckem; Menin Road; Polygon Wood; Poelcapelle; Passchendaele; Cambrai 1917, 1918; St Quentin; Bapaume 1918; Estaires; Bailleul; Kemmel; Béthune; Scherpenberg; Soissonnais-Ourcq; Drocourt-Quéant; Epéhy; Canal du Nord; St Quentin Canal; Courtrai; Selle; Sambre; France and Flanders 1914–18; Doiran 1917; Macedonia 1917; Sari Bair; Gallipoli 1915; Egypt 1916; Nebi Samwil; Jerusalem; Jaffa; Tell'Asur; Palestine 1917–18; Tigris 1916; Kut al Amara 1917; Mesopotamia 1916–18; East Africa 1914–16. **Second World War**: North-West Europe 1940; Banana Ridge; Medjez Plain; Djebel Bou Aoukaz 1943 I; Gab Gab Gap; Rome; Gothic Line; Monte Gamberaldi; Monte Ceco; Batu Pahar; Malaya 1941–2.

Awards

Five members of the regiment have been awarded the Victoria Cross: one in the Crimean War (1854–5), three in the Great War and one in the Second World War. First award: Private J. Mc-Dermond (1832–68), Inkerman 5 November 1854: gazetted 24 February 1857 (47th).

Marches

Quick: *The Red, Red Rose*. Slow: *No Name* (similar to *Mountain Rose*).

Journal

The Lancashire Lad.

Museum

Fulwood Barracks, Preston, Lancashire (tel 0772 716543 ext 2362): open Monday, Wednesday, Friday, Saturday 1000–1700.

Regimental Histories

Langley, M. *The Loyal Regiment*, Leo Cooper, 1976. Wylly, CB, Colonel H. C. *The Loyal North Lancashire Regiment* (2 vols.), RUSI, 1933. Dean Preston, C. G. T. *The Loyal North Lancashire Regiment 1919–1953*, Regimental Headquarters, 1955.

THE DUKE OF WELLINGTON'S REGIMENT (WEST RIDING)
(The King's Division)
Colonel-in-Chief: The Duke of Wellington KG

History
Raised in 1702 as Huntingdon's Regiment (33rd Foot in 1751) and in 1787 as the 76th Foot. These two regiments became the 1st and 2nd Battalions of the Duke of Wellington's West Riding Regiment in 1881. One regular battalion.
MOTTO: *Virtutis fortuna comes* (Fortune favours the brave).
HEADQUARTERS: Wellesley Park, Halifax, West Yorkshire.
RECRUITMENT AREA: West Yorkshire.
REGIMENTAL ANNIVERSARY: St George's Day (23 April).
FORMER MEMBERS: Field Marshal The Duke of Wellington (1769–1852), joined 76th Foot from the 73rd Foot in 1787 and was gazetted as a major to the 33rd Foot in 1793 – statues Hyde Park Corner, London, and Royal Exchange, London; Field Marshal HRH The Duke of Cambridge (1819–1904), attached to 33rd Foot for drill in 1838 – statue Whitehall, London.

Emblazoned Battle Honours
(awards before 1881 to 76th★)
War of Austrian Succession (1740–8): Dettingen. **Third Mysore War** (1789–91): ★Mysore. **Fourth Mysore War** (1799): Seringapatam. **First Maratha War** (1803–5): ★Ally Ghur; ★Delhi 1803; ★Leswarree; ★Deig. **Peninsular War** (1808–14): ★Corunna; ★Nive; Peninsula. **Hundred Days** (1815): Waterloo. **Crimean War** (1854–5): Alma; Inkerman; Sevastopol. **Abyssinian War** (1867–8): Abyssinia. **South African War** (1899–1902): Relief of Kimberley; Paardeburg; South Africa 1900–1902. **Great War**: Mons; Marne 1914, 1918; Ypres 1914, 1915, 1917; Hill 60; Somme 1916, 1918; Arras 1917, 1918; Cambrai 1917, 1918; Lys; Piave; Landing at Suvla. **Third Afghan War** (1919): Afghanistan 1919. **Second World War**: Dunkirk 1940; St Valéry-en-Caux; Fontenay le Pesnil; North-West Europe 1940, 1944–5; Djebel Bou Aoukaz; Anzio; Monte Ceco; Sittang 1942; Chindits 1944; Burma 1942–4. **Korean War** (1950–3): The Hook 1953; Korea 1952–3. An elephant with howdah and mahout circumscribed 'Hindoostan' is also borne on the colours.

Accredited Battle Honours
Great War: Le Cateau; Retreat from Mons; Aisne 1914; La Bassée 1914; Nonne Bosschen; Gravenstafel; St Julien; Aubers; Albert 1916, 1918; Bazentin; Delville Wood; Pozières; Flers-Courcelette; Morval; Thiepval; Le Transloy; Ancre Heights; Scarpe 1917, 1918; Arleux; Bullecourt; Messines 1917, 1918; Lange-

marck 1917; Menin Road; Polygon Wood; Broodseinde; Poelcapelle; Passchen-daele; St Quentin; Ancre 1918; Estaires; Hazebrouck; Bailleul; Kemmel; Béthune; Scherpenberg; Tardenois; Amiens; Bapaume 1918; Drocourt-Quéant; Hindenburg Line; Havrincourt; Epéhy; Canal du Nord; Selle; Valenciennes; Sambre; France and Flanders 1914–18; Vittorio Veneto; Italy 1917–18; Suvla; Scimitar Hill; Gallipoli 1915; Egypt 1916. **Second World War:** Tilly sur Seulles; Banana Ridge; Medjez Plain; Gueriat el Atach Ridge; Tunis; North Africa 1943; Campoleone; Rome; Italy 1943–5; Paungde; Kohima.

Awards
Seven members of the regiment have been awarded the Victoria Cross: two in the Abyssinian War (1867–8), one in the South African War (1899–1902), two in the Great War and one in the Second World War. First awards: Drummer M. Magner, later Corporal (1840–95) and Private F. Bergin, later Sergeant (1845–80) Magdala, Abyssinia, 13 April 1868: gazetted 8 July 1868 (33rd Foot).

Dress
DIFFERENCES: Blue dress cap, red-backed badge; blue side cap piped gold. Scarlet lanyard.
REGIMENTAL TIE: Thin silver stripes on chestnut ground.

Marches
Quick: *The Wellesley*.

Alliances
Les Voltigeurs de Quebec, of Canada; 10th Battalion The Baluch Regiment, of Pakistan.

Journal
The Iron Duke (three times a year – April, August, December).

Associations
Friends of the Regiment Fund, Wellesley Barracks, High Rd Well, Halifax, West Yorkshire.

Museum
Bankfield Museum, Akroyd Park, Halifax, West Yorkshire (tel 0422 54823): open Monday–Saturday 1000–1230, 1400–1630.

Record Office
Except officers: Imphal Barracks, York; officers: MS(AODO), London Rd, Stanmore, Middlesex.

Regimental Histories
Lunt, J. *The Duke of Wellington's Regiment*, Leo Cooper, 1971. Bruce, C. D. *History of the Duke of Wellington's Regiment, 1881–1923*, Medici Society, 1927. Barclay, C. N. *History of the Duke of Wellington's Regiment, 1919–1952*, Clowes, 1953.

THE ROYAL HAMPSHIRE REGIMENT
(The Prince of Wales's Division)
Colonel-in-Chief: HRH The Prince of Wales

History
Raised in 1702 as Meredith's Regiment (37th Foot in 1751) and in 1786 as the
67th Foot. These two regiments became the 1st and 2nd Battalions of The
Hampshire Regiment in 1881 (Royal in 1946). One regular battalion.
HEADQUARTERS: Serle's House, Southgate St, Winchester, Hampshire.
RECRUITMENT AREA: Hampshire, Isle of Wight, Jersey and Guernsey.
REGIMENTAL ANNIVERSARIES: Gallipoli Day (25 April); Minden Day (1 August).
FORMER MEMBER: Field Marshal Prince Edward of Saxe-Weimar (1828–1902),
commissioned 1841, originally attached to 67th Foot.

Emblazoned Battle Honours
(awards before 1881 to 67th★; awards to both 37th and 67th★★)
War of Spanish Succession (1701–15): Blenheim; Ramillies; Oudenarde;
Malplaquet. **War of Austrian Succession** (1740–8): Dettingen. **Seven Years
War** (1756–63): Minden; ★Belleisle. **French Revolutionary Wars** (1793–1802):
Tournay. **Peninsular War** (1808–14): ★Barrosa; ★★Peninsula. **Second China
War** (1857–60): ★Taku Forts; ★Pekin 1860. **Second Afghan War** (1878–80):
★Charasiah; ★Kabul 1879; ★Afghanistan 1878–80. **Third Burma War** (1885–7):
Burma 1885–7. **South African War** (1899–1902): Paardeburg; South Africa
1900–1902. **Great War:** Retreat from Mons; Ypres 1915, 1917, 1918; Somme
1916, 1918; Arras 1917, 1918; Cambrai 1917, 1918; Doiran 1917, 1918; Landing
at Helles; Suvla; Gaza; Kut al Amara 1915, 1917. **Second World War:** Dunkirk
1940; Normandy Landing; Caen; Rhine; Tebourba Gap; Hunt's Gap; Salerno;
Cassino II; Gothic Line; Malta 1941–2. A Royal Tiger superscribed 'India' is
also borne on the colours.

Accredited Battle Honours
Great War: Le Cateau; Marne 1914, 1918; Aisne 1914; Armentières 1914; St
Julien; Frezenberg; Bellewaarde; Albert 1916; Guillemont; Ginchy; Flers-
Courcelette; Thiepval; Le Transloy; Ancre Heights; Ancre 1916; Vimy 1917;
Scarpe 1917, 1918; Messines 1917; Pilckem 1917; Langemarck 1917; Menin
Road; Polygon Wood; Broodseinde; Poelcapelle; Passchendaele; St Quentin;
Bapaume 1918; Rosières; Lys; Estaires; Hazebrouck; Bailleul; Kemmel;
Béthune; Tardenois; Drocourt-Quéant; Hindenburg Line; Havrincourt; Canal
du Nord; Courtrai; Selle; Valenciennes; Sambre; France and Flanders 1914–18;
Italy 1917–18; Kosturino; Struma; Macedonia 1915–18; Helles; Krithia; Sari
Bair; Landing at Suvla; Scimitar Hill; Gallipoli 1915–16; Egypt 1915–17; El

Mughar; Nebi Samwil; Jerusalem; Jaffa; Tell'Asur; Megiddo, Sharon; Palestine 1917–18; Aden; Shaiba; Tigris 1916; Baghdad; Sharqat; Mesopotamia 1915–18; Persia 1918–19; Archangel 1919; Siberia 1918–19. **Second World War:** Tilly sur Seulles; Hill 112; Mont Pinçon; Jurques; St Pierre La Vieille; Nederrijn; Roer; Rhineland; Goch; North-West Europe 1940, 1944–5; Sidi Nsir; Montagne Farm; Fondouk; Pichon; El Kourzia; Ber Rabai; North Africa 1940–3; Landing in Sicily; Regalbuto; Sicily 1943; Landing at Porto San Venere; Salerno Hills; Battipaglia; Cava di Tirreni; Volturno Crossing; Garigliano Crossing; Damiano; Monte Ornito; Cerasola; Massa Vertecchi; Trasimene Line; Advance to Florence; Monte Gridolfo; Montegaudio; Coriano; Montilgallo; Capture of Forli; Cosina Canal Crossing; Lamone Crossing; Pideura; Rimini Line; Montescudo; Frisoni; Italy 1943–5; Athens; Greece 1944–5.

Awards
Ten members of the regiment have been awarded the Victoria Cross: four in the Second China War (1860), three in the Great War and three in the Second World War. First awards: Lieutenant N. Burslem, later Captain (1830–65), Ensign J. W. Chaplin, later Colonel (1840–1920), Private L. Lane (1836–89) and Lieutenant E. H. Lenon, later Lieutenant-Colonel (1830–93), Taku Forts, China, 21 August 1860: gazetted 13 August 1861 (67th Foot).

Memorial
Garden at regimental museum, Winchester.

Dress
DIFFERENCES: Blue dress cap, scarlet band and piping; blue side cap, yellow tip and piping. Regimental colours on black stable belt, yellow/red/green/mauve stripes; whistle on brace to officers' Sam Brownes.
REGIMENTAL TIE: Thin yellow/red/green/mauve stripes on black ground.

Marches
Quick: *The Hampshire.*

Alliances
49th (Sault Ste Marie) Field Artillery Regiment RCA(M), of Canada; 5th Battalion (Wellington West Coast and Taranaki) The Royal New Zealand Regiment.

Journal
Royal Hampshire Regimental Magazine (twice a year).

Museum
Serle's House, Southgate St, Winchester (tel 0962 863658): open Monday–Friday 1000–1230, 1400–1600; Easter–October Saturday, Sunday 1200–1600.

Regimental Histories
Wykes, A. *The Royal Hampshire Regiment*, Hamish Hamilton, 1968. *Regimental History of the Royal Hampshire Regiment, 1702–1953* (3 vols.); vols. 1 and 2 by C. T. Atkinson; vol. 3 by D. S. Daniell; Gale & Polden, 1955.

THE STAFFORDSHIRE REGIMENT
(THE PRINCE OF WALES'S)
(The Prince of Wales's Division)
Colonel-in-Chief: HRH The Duke of York CVO ADC

History
Formed in 1959 by the amalgamation of the South Staffordshire Regiment and the North Staffordshire Regiment (The Prince of Wales's). One regular battalion, one volunteer battalion (3rd).

HEADQUARTERS: Whittington Barracks, Lichfield, Staffordshire.

RECRUITMENT AREA: Staffordshire and part of West Midlands.

REGIMENTAL ANNIVERSARIES: Anzio Day (22 January); Ypres Day (31 July); Arnhem Day (17 September); Ferozeshah Day (21 December).

Emblazoned Battle Honours
Seven Years War (1756–63): Guadaloupe 1759; Martinique 1762. **French Revolutionary Wars** (1793–1802): Martinique 1794. **Napoleonic Wars** (1803–15): St Lucia 1803. **Expedition against Dutch** (1804): Surinam. **Expedition against Spanish** (1807): Monte Video. **Peninsular War** (1808–14): Rolica; Vimiera; Corunna; Busaco; Badajos; Salamanca; Vittoria; San Sebastian; Nive; Peninsula. **First Burma War** (1824–6): Ava. **First Sikh War (1845–6): Moodkee; Ferozeshah; Sobraon. Second Sikh War** (1848–9): Punjaub. **Second Burma War** (1852–3): Pegu. **Crimean War** (1854–5): Alma; Inkerman; Sevastopol. **Persian War** (1856–7): Reshire; Bushire; Koosh-ab; Persia. **Indian Mutiny** (1857–8): Lucknow; Central India. **Zulu and Basuto War** (1878–9): South Africa 1878–9. **First Sudan War** (1882–4): Egypt 1882. **Egyptian Campaign** (1885): Kirbekan; Nile 1884–5. **Reconquest of the Sudan** (1896–8): Hafir. **South African War** (1899–1902): South Africa 1900–02. **Great War:** Mons; Marne 1914; Aisne 1914, 1918; Armentières 1914; Ypres 1914, 1917, 1918; Langemarck 1914, 1917; Gheluvelt; Nonne Bosschen; Neuve Chapelle; Aubers; Festubert 1915; Loos; Somme 1916, 1918; Arras 1917, 1918; Messines 1917, 1918; Cambrai 1917, 1918; St Quentin Canal; Selle; Vittorio Veneto; Suvla; Sari Bair; Kut al Amara 1917; NW Frontier India 1915. **Third Afghan War** (1919): Afghanistan 1919. **Second World War:** Dyle; Ypres-Comines Canal; Caen; Noyers; Brieux Bridgehead; Falaise; Arnhem 1944; North-West Europe 1940, 1944–5; Medjez Plain; North Africa 1940, 1943; Landing in Sicily; Sicily 1943; Anzio; Carroceto; Rome; Marradi; Chindits 1944; Burma 1943, 1945. The Sphinx superscribed 'Egypt' and a dragon superscribed 'China' are also borne on the colours.

Accredited Battle Honours
Great War: Retreat from Mons; Langemarck 1914, 1917; Gheluvelt; Nonne

Bosschen; Neuve Chapelle; Aubers; Festubert 1915; Loos; Somme 1916, 1918; Albert 1916, 1918; Bazentin; Delville Wood; Pozières; Guillemont; Flers-Courcelette; Morval; Thiepval; Ancre Heights; Ancre 1916; Bapaume 1917, 1918; Scarpe 1917, 1918; Arleux; Bullecourt; Hill 70; Pilckem; Menin Road; Polygon Wood; Broodseinde; Poelcapelle; Passchendaele; St Quentin; Rosières; Avre; Lys; Bailleul; Kemmel; Scherpenberg; Drocourt-Quéant; Hindenburg Line; Havrincourt; Canal du Nord; Beaurevoir; Courtrai; Valenciennes; Sambre; France and Flanders 1914–18; Piave; Italy 1917–18; Landing at Suvla; Scimitar Hill; Gallipoli 1915–16; Egypt 1916; Tigris 1916; Baghdad; Mesopotamia 1916–18; Baku; Persia 1918. **Second World War:** Defence of Escaut; Orne; Mont Pinçon; Sidi Barrani; Djebel Kess Kiss; Gueriat el Atach Ridge; Gab Gab Gap; Carroceto; Advance to Tiber; Gothic Line; Italy 1943–5.

Dress
DIFFERENCES: Blue dress cap, buff Holland backed badge; blue side cap piped gold. Black stable belt. Black lanyard. Gold glider badge on upper arm.
REGIMENTAL TIE: Thin red and thin silver stripes on green ground.

Marches
Quick: *The Staffordshire Regiment*, a combination of *Come Lasses and Lads* and *The Days We Went A'Gypsying*. Slow: *God Bless the Prince of Wales*.

Alliances and Associations
4e Bataillon, Royal 22e Regiment (Chateaugay), of Canada; 2nd Battalion The Royal Victorian Regiment, of Australia; The Antigua and Barbuda Defence Force, of the Leeward Islands; 7th Battalion The Baluch Regiment, of Pakistan; The Jamaica Regiment; HMS *Ocelot*.

Journal
The Staffordshire Knot (once a year).

Museum
Whittington Barracks, Lichfield, Staffordshire (tel 0543 433333): open Monday–Friday 0900–1630; Saturday, Sunday by appointment; closed two weeks over Christmas and on Bank Holidays.

Association
Regimental Association, RHQ The Staffordshire Regiment, Whittington Barracks, Lichfield, Staffordshire (tel 021-311 3263). The Association has sixteen branches.

Record Office
Except officers: Imphal Barracks, York; officers: MS(AODO), London Rd, Stanmore, Middlesex.

Predecessors

THE SOUTH STAFFORDSHIRE REGIMENT

History
Raised in 1702 as Lillingstone's Regiment (38th Foot in 1751) and as the 80th,

or Staffordshire Volunteers, Regiment in 1793. These two regiments became the 1st and 2nd Battalions of the South Staffordshire Regiment in 1881.
REGIMENTAL ANNIVERSARIES: Arnhem Day (17 September); Ferozeshah Day (21 December).

Emblazoned Battle Honours
(awards before 1881 to 80th*)
Seven Years War (1756–63): Guadaloupe 1759; Martinique 1762. **Expedition against Spanish** (1807): Monte Video. **Peninsular War** (1808–14): Rolica; Vimiera; Corunna; Busaco; Badajos; Salamanca; Vittoria; San Sebastian; Nive; Peninsula. **First Burma War** (1824–6): Ava. **First Sikh War** (1845–6): *Moodkee; *Ferozeshah; *Sobraon. **Second Burma War** (1852–3): *Pegu. **Crimean War** (1854–5): Alma; Inkerman; Sevastopol. **Indian Mutiny** (1857–8). Lucknow; *Central India. **Zulu and Basuto War** (1878–9): *South Africa 1878–9. **First Sudan War** (1882–4): Egypt 1882. **Egyptian Campaign** (1885): Kirbekan; Nile 1884–5. **South African War** (1899–1902): South Africa 1900–02. **Great War:** Mons; Marne 1914; Aisne 1914, 1918; Ypres 1914, 1917; Loos; Somme 1916, 1918; Cambrai 1917, 1918; St Quentin Canal; Vittorio Veneto; Suvla. **Second World War:** Caen; Noyers; Falaise; Arnhem 1944; North-West Europe 1940, 1944; North Africa 1940; Landing in Sicily; Sicily 1943; Chindits 1944; Burma 1944. The Sphinx superscribed 'Egypt' was also borne on the colours.

Accredited Honours
Great War: Retreat from Mons; Langemarck 1914, 1917; Gheluvelt; Nonne Bosschen; Neuve Chapelle; Aubers; Festubert 1915; Albert 1916, 1918; Bazentin; Delville Wood; Pozières; Flers-Courcelette; Morval; Thiepval;

Ancre 1918; Bapaume 1917, 1918; Arras 1917, 1918; Scarpe 1917, 1918; Arleux; Bullecourt; Hill 70; Messines 1917, 1918; Menin Road; Polygon Wood; Broodseinde; Poelcapelle; Passchendaele; St Quentin; Lys; Bailleul; Kemmel; Scherpenberg; Drocourt-Quéant; Hindenburg Line; Havrincourt; Canal du Nord; Beaurevoir; Selle; Sambre; France and Flanders 1914–18; Piave; Italy 1917–18; Landing at Suvla; Scimitar Hill; Gallipoli 1915; Egypt 1916. **Second World War:** Sidi Barrani; Italy 1943.

Awards
Six members of the regiment have been awarded the Victoria Cross: two in the Zulu and Basuto War (1878–9), two in the Great War and two in the Second World War. First award: Private S. Wassall (1856–1927). Isandhlwana, 22 January 1879: gazetted 17 June 1879 (80th Foot).

Marches
Quick: *Come Lasses and Lads.* Slow: *The 80th.*

Journal
The Knot.

Museum
Whittington Barracks, Lichfield, Staffordshire (tel 0543 433333): open Monday–Friday 0930–1630, Saturday, Sunday by appointment, closed two weeks over Christmas, and on Bank Holidays.

Regimental Histories
Vale, W. L. *History of the South Staffordshire Regiment,* Gale & Polden, 1969. Jones, J. P. *A History of the South Staffordshire Regiment, 1705–1923,* Whitehead, 1923.

THE NORTH STAFFORDSHIRE REGIMENT (THE PRINCE OF WALES'S)

History
Raised in 1756 as the 2nd Battalion of the 11th Foot (64th Foot in 1758) and as the 98th Foot in 1824. These two regiments became the 1st and 2nd Battalions of the (Prince of Wales's) North Staffordshire Regiment in 1881.
REGIMENTAL ANNIVERSARIES: Anzio Day (22 January); Ypres Day (31 July).

Emblazoned Battle Honours
(awards before 1881 to 98th★)
Seven Years War (1756–63): Guadaloupe 1759. French Revolutionary Wars (1793–1802): Martinique 1794. Napoleonic Wars (1803–15): St Lucia 1803. Expedition against Dutch (1804): Surinam. Second Sikh War (1848–9): ★Punjaub. Persian War (1856–7): Reshire; Bushire; Koosh-ab; Persia. Indian Mutiny (1857–8): Lucknow. Reconquest of the Sudan (1896–8): Hafir. South African War (1899–1902): South Africa 1900–02. Great War: Armentières 1914; Somme 1916, 1918; Arras 1917; Messines 1917, 1918; Ypres 1917, 1918; St Quentin Canal; Selle; Sari Bair; Kut al Amara 1917; NW Frontier India 1915. Third Afghan War (1919): Afghanistan 1919. Second World War: Dyle; Ypres-Comines Canal; Caen; Brieux Bridgehead; Medjez Plain; North Africa 1943; Anzio; Rome; Marradi; Burma 1943. A dragon superscribed 'China' was also borne on the colours.

Accredited Battle Honours
Great War: Aisne 1914, 1918; Loos; Albert 1916, 1918; Bazentin; Delville Wood; Pozières; Guillemont; Ancre Heights; Ancre 1916; Scarpe 1917; Arleux; Pilckem; Langemarck 1917; Menin Road; Polygon Wood; Broodseinde; Poelcapelle; Passchendaele; Cambrai 1917, 1918; St Quentin; Bapaume 1918; Rosières; Avre; Lys; Bailleul; Kemmel; Hindenburg Line; Havrincourt; Canal du Nord; Beaurevoir; Courtrai; Valenciennes; Sambre; France and Flanders 1914–18; Suvla; Gallipoli 1915–16; Egypt 1916; Tigris 1916; Baghdad; Mesopotamia 1916–18; Baku; Persia 1918. Second World War: Defence of Escaut; Orne; Noyers; Mont Pinçon; North-West Europe 1940, 1944; Djebel Kess Kiss; Gueriat al Atach Ridge; Gab Gab Gap; Carroceto; Advance to Tiber; Gothic Line; Italy 1944–5.

Awards
Five members of the regiment have been awarded the Victoria Cross: one in the Indian Mutiny (1857–8) and four in the Great War. First award: Drummer T. Flinn (1842–92), India 28 November 1857: gazetted 12 April 1859 (64th Foot). At the age of 15¼, he is one of the two youngest recipients of the Victoria Cross.

Marches
Quick: *The Days We Went A'Gypsying*. Slow: *God Bless the Prince of Wales*.

Journal
The China Dragon.

Museum
Whittington Barracks, Lichfield, Staffordshire (tel 0543 433333): open Monday–Friday 0930–1630, Saturday, Sunday by appointment, closed two weeks over Christmas and on Bank Holidays.

Regimental History
Cook, H. C. B. *The North Staffordshire Regiment*, Leo Cooper, 1970.

THE BLACK WATCH
(ROYAL HIGHLAND REGIMENT)
(The Scottish Division)
Colonel-in-Chief: HM Queen Elizabeth The Queen Mother

History
Raised in 1739 as the Highland Regiment (43rd) (42nd Foot in 1751) and in 1758 as the 2nd Battalion of the 42nd Regiment (73rd Highland Regiment in 1780). These two regiments became the 1st and 2nd Battalions of the Black Watch (Royal Highlanders) in 1881. One regular battalion.
MOTTO: *Nemo me impune lacessit* (No one provokes me with impunity).
HEADQUARTERS: Balhousie Castle, Perth.
RECRUITMENT AREA: Tayside (Perthshire and Angus) and Fife.
REGIMENTAL ANNIVERSARY: Red Hackle Day (5 January).
FORMER MEMBERS: Field Marshal The Duke of Wellington (1769–1852), commissioned 1787 (73rd Foot) – statues Hyde Park Corner, London, and Royal Exchange, London; Field Marshal Earl Wavell (1883–1950), commissioned 1901.

Emblazoned Battle Honours
(awards before 1881 to 73rd★; awards to both 42nd and 73rd★★)
Seven Years War (1756–63): Guadaloupe 1759; Martinique 1762; Havannah. **Pontiac's Conspiracy** (1763–4): North America 1763–4. **Second Mysore War** (1781–3): ★Mangalore 1783. **Third Mysore War** (1789–91): ★Mysore. **Fourth Mysore War** (1799): ★Seringapatam. **Peninsular War** (1808–14): Corunna; Busaco; Fuentes d'Onor; Salamanca; Pyrenees; Nivelle; Nive; Orthes; Toulouse; Peninsula. **Hundred Days** (1815): ★★Waterloo. **Seventh Kaffir War** (1846–7): ★South Africa 1846–7. **Eighth Kaffir War** (1851–3): ★South Africa 1851–1852–1853. **Crimean War** (1854–5): Alma; Sevastopol. **Indian Mutiny** (1857–8): Lucknow. **Ashantee War** (1873–4): Ashantee 1873–4. **Revolt of Arabi Pasha** (1882): Tel-el-Kebir. **First Sudan War** (1882–4): Egypt 1882, 1884. **Egyptian Campaign** (1885): Kirbekan; Nile 1884–5. **Great War:** Marne 1914, 1918; Ypres 1914, 1917, 1918; Loos; Somme 1916, 1918; Arras 1917, 1918; Lys; Hindenburg Line; Doiran 1917; Megiddo; Kut al Amara 1917. **Second World War:** Falaise Road; Rhine; Tobruk 1941; El Alamein; Akarit; Tunis; Sicily 1943; Cassino II; Crete; Burma 1944. **Korean War** (1950–3): The Hook 1952; Korea 1952–3. The Sphinx superscribed 'Egypt' is also borne on the colours.

Accredited Battle Honours
Great War: Retreat from Mons; Aisne 1914; La Bassée 1914; Langemarck 1914; Gheluvelt; Nonne Bosschen; Givenchy 1914; Neuve Chapelle; Aubers; Fes-

tubert 1915; Albert 1916; Bazentin; Delville Wood; Pozières; Flers-Courcelette; Morval; Thiepval; Le Transloy; Ancre Heights; Ancre 1916; Vimy 1917; Scarpe 1917, 1918; Arleux; Pilckem; Menin Road; Polygon Wood; Poelcapelle; Passchendaele; Cambrai 1917, 1918; St Quentin; Bapaume 1918; Rosières; Estaires; Messines 1918; Hazebrouck; Kemmel; Béthune; Scherpenberg; Soissonais-Ourcq; Tardenois; Drocourt-Quéant; Epéhy; St Quentin Canal; Beaurevoir; Courtrai; Selle; Sambre; France and Flanders 1914–18; Macedonia 1915–18; Egypt 1916; Gaza; Jerusalem; Tell'Asur; Sharon; Damascus; Palestine 1917–18; Tigris 1916; Baghdad; Mesopotamia 1915–17. **Second World War:** Defence of Arras; Ypres-Comines Canal; Dunkirk 1940; St Valéry-en-Caux; Saar; Breville; Odon; Fontenay le Pesnil; Defence of Rauray; Caen; Falaise; La Vie Crossing; Le Havre; Lower Maas; Venlo Pocket; Ourthe; Rhineland; Reichswald; Goch; North-West Europe 1940, 1944–5; Barkasan; British Somaliland 1940; Tobruk Sortie; Advance on Tripoli; Medenine; Zemlet el Lebene; Mareth; Wadi Akarit East; Djebel Roumana; Medjez Plain; Si Mediene; North Africa 1941–3; Landing in Sicily; Vizzini; Sferro; Gerbini; Adrano; Sferro Hills; Liri Valley; Advance to Florence; Monte Scalari; Casa Fortis; Rimini Line; Casa Fabbri Ridge; Savio Bridgehead; Italy 1944–5; Athens; Greece 1944–5; Heraklion; Middle East 1941; Chindits 1944.

Awards

Fifteen members of the regiment have been awarded the Victoria Cross: eight in the Indian Mutiny (1857–8), one in the Ashanti War (1873–4), one in the First Sudan War (1882–4), four in the Great War and one in the Korean War (1950–3). First award: Lieutenant F. E. H. Farquharson, later Major (1837–75) Lucknow 9 March 1858: gazetted 18 June 1859 (42nd Foot).

Dress

DIFFERENCES: Blue tam o'shanter. Black Watch tartan kilt, white hair sporran, five short black tassels.
REGIMENTAL TIE: Medium red and green stripes on dark blue ground.

Marches

Band, quick: *All the Blue Bonnets are over the Border*. Band, slow: *The Garb of Old Gaul*. Pipes and drums, quick: *Highland Laddie*. Pipes and drums, slow: *My Home* and *Highland Cradle Song*.

Alliances

The Prince Edward Island Regiment, of Canada; The Black Watch (Royal Highland Regiment), of Canada; The Lanark and Renfrew Scottish Regiment, of Canada; The Royal Queensland Regiment, of Australia; The Royal New South Wales Regiment, of Australia; 1st and 2nd Squadrons New Zealand Scottish, RNZAC.

Allied Regiments in 1914

5th Royal Highlanders, of Canada; 1st Battalion New South Wales Scottish Rifles, of Australia.

THE DUKE OF EDINBURGH'S ROYAL REGIMENT (BERKSHIRE AND WILTSHIRE)

(Prince of Wales's Division)
Colonel-in-Chief: Field Marshal HRH The Prince Philip
Duke of Edinburgh KG KT OM GBE QSO

History
Formed in 1959 by the amalgamation of the Royal Berkshire Regiment (Princess Charlotte of Wales's) and the Wiltshire Regiment (Duke of Edinburgh's). One regular battalion.

HEADQUARTERS: The Wardrobe, 58 The Close, Salisbury, Wiltshire.

RECRUITMENT AREA: Berkshire and Wiltshire.

REGIMENTAL ANNIVERSARIES: Maiwand Day (27 July); Ferozeshah Day (21 December).

Emblazoned Battle Honours
Seven Years War (1756–63): Louisburg. **War of American Independence** (1775–83): St Lucia 1778. **French Revolutionary Wars** (1793–1802): Egmont op Zee; Copenhagen. **Peninsular War** (1808–14): Douro; Talavera; Albuhera; Vittoria; Pyrenees; Nivelle; Nive; Orthes; Peninsula. **War of 1812** (1812–14): Queenstown. **First Maori War** (1846–7): New Zealand. **First Sikh War** (1845–6): Ferozeshah; Sobraon. **Crimean War** (1854–5): Alma; Inkerman; Sevastopol. **Second China War** (1857–60): Pekin 1860. **Zulu and Basuto War** (1877–9): South Africa 1879. **Second Afghan War** (1878–80): Kandahar 1880; Afghanistan 1879–80. **First Sudan War** (1882–4): Egypt 1882. **Egyptian Campaign** (1885): Tofrek; Suakin. **South African War** (1899–1902): South Africa 1899–1902. **Great War**: Retreat from Mons; Messines 1914, 1917, 1918; Ypres 1914, 1917; Neuve Chapelle; Loos; Somme 1916, 1918; Arras 1917, 1918; Cambrai 1917, 1918; Bapaume 1918; Selle; Vittorio Veneto; Doiran 1917, 1918; Macedonia 1915–18; Gallipoli 1915–16; Palestine 1917–18; Baghdad. **Second World War**: Dyle; Dunkirk 1940; Normandy Landing; Hill 112; Maltot; Mont Pinçon; Seine 1944; Sicily 1943; Garigliano Crossing; Damiano; Anzio; Rome; North Arakan; Kohima; Mandalay; Burma 1942–5. A dragon superscribed 'China' and a naval crown superscribed '2nd April 1801' are also borne on the colours.

Accredited Battle Honours
Great War: Mons; Le Cateau; Marne 1914; Aisne 1914, 1918; La Bassée 1914; Armentières 1914; Langemarck 1914, 1917; Gheluvelt; Nonne Bosschen; Aubers; Festubert 1915; Albert 1916, 1918; Bazentin; Delville Wood; Pozières;

Flers-Courcelette; Morval; Thiepval; Le Transloy; Ancre Heights; Ancre 1916, 1918; Scarpe 1917, 1918; Arleux; Pilckem; Menin Road; Polygon Wood; Broodseinde; Poelcapelle; Passchendaele; St Quentin; Rosières; Avre; Villers Bretonneux; Lys; Hazebrouck; Bailleul; Kemmel; Béthune; Scherpenberg; Amiens; Hindenburg Line; Havrincourt; Epéhy; Canal du Nord; St Quentin Canal; Beaurevoir; Valenciennes; Sambre; France and Flanders 1914–18; Piave; Italy 1917–18; Suvla; Sari Bair; Gaza; Nebi Samwil; Jerusalem; Megiddo; Sharon; Tigris 1916; Kut al Amara 1917; Mesopotamia 1916–18. **Second World War:** Defence of Arras; St Omer-La Bassée; Ypres-Comines Canal; Odon; Caen; Bourguébus Ridge; Le Varinière; Nederrijn; Roer; Rhineland; Goch; Xanten; Bremen; North-West Europe 1940, 1944–5; Solarino; Simeto Bridgehead; Pursuit to Messina; Monte Camino; Calabritto; Minturno; Carroceto; Advance to Tiber; Italy 1943–5; Middle East 1942; Donbaik; Point 551; Mayu Tunnels; Ngakyedauk Pass; Mao Songsang; Shwebo; Kyaukmyaung Bridgehead; Fort Dufferin; Rangoon Road; Toungoo.

Dress
DIFFERENCES: Blue dress cap, scarlet band and piping, red-backed badge; blue side cap, piped scarlet. Blue stable belt, two narrow scarlet bands.
REGIMENTAL TIE: Thin red/navy/red stripes on navy ground.

Marches
Quick: *The Farmer's Boy*. Slow: *Auld Robin Grey*.

Alliances
The Lincoln and Welland Regiment, of Canada; The Algonquin Regiment, of Canada; 7th Battalion (Wellington (City of Wellington's Own) and Hawke's Bay) Royal New Zealand Infantry Regiment; 13th Battalion The Frontier Force Regiment, of Pakistan.

Journal
The Journal of the Duke of Edinburgh's Royal Regiment (once a year – February).

Museum
The Wardrobe, 58 The Close, Salisbury, Wiltshire (tel 0722 336222): open February–November Monday–Friday 1000–1630, April Sunday, November–February Monday–Thursday 1000–17000, Friday 1000–1630.

Record Office
Except officers: Imphal Barracks, York; officers: MS(AODO), London Rd, Stanmore, Middlesex.

Predecessors

THE ROYAL BERKSHIRE REGIMENT (PRINCESS CHARLOTTE OF WALES'S)

History
Raised in 1744 as Trelawney's Regiment (49th Foot in 1748) and in 1755 as the 2nd Battalion of the 19th Foot (66th Foot in 1758). These two regiments became the 1st and 2nd Battalions of Princess Charlotte's (Berkshire Regiment) in 1881 (Royal in 1885).
REGIMENTAL ANNIVERSARY: Maiwand Day (27 July).

Emblazoned Battle Honours
(awards before 1881 to 66th★)
War of American Independence (1775–83): St Lucia 1778. **French Revolutionary Wars** (1793–1802): Egmont op Zee; Copenhagen. **War of 1812** (1812–14): Queenstown. **Peninsular War** (1808–14): ★Douro; ★Talavera; ★Vittoria; ★Pyrenees; ★Nivelle; ★Nive; ★Orthes; ★Peninsula. **Crimean War** (1854–5): Alma; Inkerman; Sevastopol. **Second Afghan War** (1878–80): ★Kandahar 1880; ★Afghanistan 1879–80. **First Sudan War** (1882–4): Egypt 1882. **Egyptian Campaign** (1885): Tofrek; Suakin 1885. **South African War** (1899–1902): South Africa 1899–1902. **Great War**: Mons; Ypres 1914, 1918; Neuve Chapelle; Loos; Somme 1916, 1918; Arras 1917, 1918; Cambrai 1917, 1918; Selle; Vittorio Veneto; Doiran 1917, 1918. **Second World War**: Dyle; Dunkirk 1940; Normandy Landing; Rhine; Sicily 1943; Damiano; Anzio; Kohima; Mandalay; Burma 1942–5. A dragon superscribed 'China' was also borne on the colours.

Accredited Battle Honours
Great War: Retreat from Mons; Marne 1914; Aisne 1914, 1918; Langemarck 1914, 1917; Gheluvelt; Nonne Bosschen; Aubers; Festubert 1915; Albert 1916, 1918; Bazentin; Delville Wood; Pozières; Flers-Courcelette; Morval; Thiepval; Le Transloy; Ancre Heights; Ancre 1916; Scarpe 1917, 1918; Arleux; Pilckem; Polygon Wood; Broodseinde; Poelcapelle; Passchendaele; St Quentin; Bapaume 1918; Rosières; Avre; Villers Bretonneux; Lys; Hazebrouck; Béthune; Amiens; Hindenburg Line; Havrincourt; Epéhy; Canal du Nord; St Quentin Canal; Valenciennes; Sambre; France and Flanders 1914–18; Piave; Italy 1917–18; Macedonia 1915–18. **Second World War:** St Omer-La Bassée; North-West Europe 1940, 1944–5; Pursuit to Messina; Monte Camino; Calabritto; Garigliano Crossing; Carroceto; Italy 1943–5; Donbaik; Mao Sonsang; Shwebo; Kyaukmyaung Bridgehead; Fort Dufferin; Rangoon Road; Toungoo.

Awards
Six members of the regiment have been awarded the Victoria Cross: three in the Crimean War (1854–5), one in the South African War (1899–1902) and two in the Great War. First award: Lieutenant J. A. Conolly, later, Colonel, CB (1829–88) Shell Hill, Crimea, 26 October 1854: gazetted 5 May 1857 (49th Foot).

Marches
Quick: *The Dashing White Serjeant* and *The Farmer's Boy.*

Journal
The China Dragon.

Museum

The Wardrobe, 58 The Close, Salisbury, Wiltshire (tel 0722 336222 ext 2683): open April–October Sunday–Thursday 1000–1700, Friday 1000–1630; July, August Sunday–Thursday, Saturday 1000–1700, Friday 1000–1630; November–March Monday–Thursday 1000–1700, Friday 1000–1630.

Regimental Histories

Myatt, F. *The Royal Berkshire Regiment*, Hamish Hamilton, 1968. Petre, F. L. *The Royal Berkshire Regiment* (2 vols.), The Barracks, 1925. Blight, G. *The History of the Royal Berkshire Regiment, 1920–1947*, Staples, 1953.

THE WILTSHIRE REGIMENT (DUKE OF EDINBURGH'S)

History

Raised in 1756 as the 2nd Battalion of the 4th Foot (62nd Foot in 1758) and in 1824 as the 99th, or Lanarkshire, Regiment (99th (The Duke of Edinburgh's) Regiment in 1874). These two regiments became the 1st and 2nd Battalions of The Duke of Edinburgh's (Wiltshire Regiment) in 1881.

REGIMENTAL ANNIVERSARY: Ferozeshah Day (21 December).

Emblazoned Battle Honours

(awards before 1881 to 99th★)
Seven Years War (1756–63): Louisburg. **Peninsular War** (1808–14): Nive; Peninsula. **First Maori War** (1846–7): ★New Zealand. **First Sikh War** (1845–6): Ferozeshah; Sobraon. **Crimean War** (1954–5): Sevastopol. **Second China War** (1857–60): ★Pekin 1860. **Zulu and Basuto War** (1877–9): ★South Africa 1879. **South African War** (1899–1902): South Africa 1900–02. **Great War:** Mons; Messines 1914, 1917, 1918; Ypres 1914, 1917; Somme 1916, 1918; Arras 1917; Bapaume 1918; Macedonia 1915–18; Gallipoli 1915–16; Palestine 1917–18;

Baghdad. **Second World War:** Defence of Arras; Hill 112; Maltot; Mont Pinçon; Seine 1944; Cleve; Garigliano Crossing; Anzio; Rome; North Arakan.

Accredited Battle Honours

Great War: Le Cateau; Retreat from Mons; Marne 1914; Aisne 1914, 1918; La Bassée 1914; Armentières 1914; Langemarck 1914; Nonne Bosschen; Neuve Chapelle; Aubers; Festubert 1915; Loos; Albert 1916, 1918; Pozières; Le Transloy; Ancre Heights; Ancre 1916; Scarpe 1917; Pilckem; Menin Road; Polygon Wood; Broodseinde; Poelcapelle; Passchendaele; St Quentin; Lys; Bailleul; Kemmel; Scherpenberg; Hindenburg Line; Epéhy; Canal du Nord; St Quentin Canal; Beaurevoir; Cambrai 1918; Selle; Sambre; France and Flanders 1914–18; Doiran 1917; Suvla; Sari Bair; Gaza; Nebi Samwil; Jerusalem; Megiddo; Sharon; Tigris 1916; Kut al Amara 1917; Mesopotamia 1916–18. **Second World War:** Ypres-Comines Canal; Odon; Caen; Bourguébus Ridge; La Varinière; Nederrijn; Roer; Rhineland; Goch; Xanten; Rhine; Bremen; North-West Europe 1940, 1944–5; Solarino; Simeto Bridgehead; Sicily 1943; Minturno; Advance to Tiber; Italy 1943–4; Middle East 1942; Point 551; Mayu Tunnels; Ngakyedauk Pass; Burma 1943–4.

Awards

Two members of the regiment have been awarded the Victoria Cross: one in the Great War and one in the Second World War. First award: Captain R. F.

J. Hayward, later Lieutenant-Colonel MC (1891–1970) near Fremicourt, France, 21–22 March 1918: gazetted 24 April 1918.

Marches
Quick: *The Wiltshire.* Slow: *Auld Robin Grey.*

Journal
The Journal of the Wiltshire Regiment.

Museum
The Wardrobe, 58 The Close, Salisbury, Wiltshire (tel 0722 6222 ext 2683): open April–October Sunday–Thursday 1000–1700, Friday 1000–1630; July, August Sunday–Thursday, Saturday 1000–1600, Friday 1000–1630; November–March Monday–Thursday 1000–1600, Friday 1000–1600.

Regimental Histories
Gibston, T. *The Wiltshire Regiment,* Leo Cooper, 1969. Kenrick, N. C. E. *The Story of the Wiltshire Regiment (1756–1959),* Gale & Polden, 1963.

QUEEN'S OWN HIGHLANDERS
(SEAFORTH AND CAMERONS)
(The Scottish Division)
Colonel-in-Chief: Field Marshal HRH The Prince Philip
Duke of Edinburgh KG KT OM GBE QSO

History
Formed in 1961 by the amalgamation of the Seaforth Highlanders (Ross-shire Buffs, the Duke of Albany's) and The Queen's Own Cameron Highlanders. One regular battalion, elements of one volunteer battalion (2nd Battalion 51st Highland Volunteers).
MOTTO: *Cuidich'n Righ* (Save the King).
HEADQUARTERS: Cameron Barracks, Inverness.
RECRUITMENT AREA: Highland (Sutherland, Caithness, Ross and Cromarty, Inverness-shire, Nairn), Morayshire, the Western Isles and the Orkney Islands.

Emblazoned Battle Honours
India (1780–4, 1790–2): Carnatic; Hindustan. **Third Mysore War** (1789–91): Mysore. **French Revolutionary Wars** (1793–1802): Egmont op Zee. **Expedition against Dutch** (1806): Cape of Good Hope 1806. **Napoleonic Wars** (1802–15): Maida. **Operations against Dutch** (1811): Java. **Peninsular War** (1808–14): Corunna; Busaco; Fuentes d'Onor; Salamanca; Pyrenees; Nivelle; Nive; Toulouse; Peninsula. **Hundred Days** (1815): Waterloo. **Sixth Kaffir War** (1835): South Africa 1835. **Crimean War** (1854–5): Alma; Sevastopol. **Persian War** (1856–7): Koosh-ab; Persia. **Indian Mutiny** (1857–8): Lucknow; Central India. **Second Afghan War** (1878–80): Peiwar Kotal; Charasiah; Kabul 1879; Kandahar 1880; Afghanistan 1878–80. **Revolt of Arabi Pasha** (1882): Tel-el-Kebir 1882. **First Sudan War** (1882–4): Egypt; Nile 1884–5. **Chitral Campaign** (1895): Chitral. **Reconquest of Sudan** (1896–8): Atbara; Khartoum. **South African War** (1899–1902): Paardeburg; South Africa 1899–1902. **Great War:** Marne 1914, 1918; Aisne 1914; Ypres 1914, 1915, 1917, 1918; Neuve Chapelle; Somme 1916, 1918; Delville Wood; Arras 1917, 1918; Vimy 1917; Cambrai 1917, 1918; Valenciennes; Sambre; Macedonia 1915–18; Palestine 1918; Baghdad. **Second World War:** St Omer-La Bassée; St Valéry-en-Caux; Caen; Rhineland; Reichswald; Rhine; Keren; Sidi Barrani; El Alamein; Akarit; Sicily 1943; Anzio; Gothic Line; Madagascar; Imphal; Kohima; Mandalay; Burma 1942–5. The Sphinx superscribed 'Egypt' and the Elephant superscribed 'Assaye' are also borne on the colours.

Accredited Battle Honours
Great War: Le Cateau; Retreat from Mons; La Bassée 1914; Armentières 1914;

Langemarck 1914; Gheluvelt; Nonne Bosschen; Festubert 1914, 1915; Givenchy 1914; Hill 60; Gravanstafel; St Julien; Frezenberg; Bellewaarde; Aubers; Albert 1916; Bazentin; Pozières; Flers–Courcelette; Morval; Le Transloy; Ancre Heights; Ancre 1916; Scarpe 1917, 1918; Arleux; Pilckem; Menin Road; Polygon Wood; Broodseinde; Poelcapelle; Passchendaele; St Quentin; Bapaume 1918; Lys; Estaires; Messines 1918; Hazebrouck; Bailleul; Kemmel; Béthune; Soissonais–Ourcq; Tardenois; Drocourt–Quéant; Hindenburg Line; Epéhy; St Quentin Canal; Courtrai; Selle; France and Flanders 1914–18; Struma; Megiddo; Sharon; Tigris 1916; Kut al Amara 1917; Mesopotamia 1915–18. **Second World War:** Defence of Escaut; Ypres–Comines Canal; Somme 1940; Withdrawal to Seine; Odon; Cheux; Troarn; Mont Pinçon; Quarry Hill; Falaise; Falaise Road; Dives Crossing; La Vie Crossing; Lisieux; Nederrijn; Best; Le Havre; Lower Maas; Meijel; Venlo Pocket; Ourthe; Goch; Moyland; Uelzen; Artlenberg; North-West Europe 1940, 1944–5; Agordat; Abyssina 1941; Tobruk 1941, 1942; Gubi II; Carmusa; Gazala; Advance on Tripoli; Mareth; Wadi Zigzaou; Djebel Roumana; North Africa 1940–3; Landing in Sicily; Augusta; Francofonte; Adrano; Sferro Hills; Garigliano Crossing; Cassino I; Poggio del Grillo; Tavoleto; Coriano; Pian di Castello; Monte Reggiano; Rimini Line; San Marino; Italy 1943–4; Middle East 1942; Shenam Pass; Litan; Relief of Kohima; Naga Village; Aradura; Tengnoupal; Shwebo; Ava; Irrawaddy; Mt Popa.

Dress
DIFFERENCES: Blue glengarry, blue hackle. 79th (Cameron of Erracht) tartan trews, or Mackenzie tartan kilt, black hair sporran, two long white tassels. Pipers, drummers and bandsmen 79th (Cameron of Erracht) kilt or Mackenzie trews.
REGIMENTAL TIE: Buff and blue stripes on piper green ground.

Marches
Band, quick: *Regimental March of the Queen's Own Highlanders.* Band, slow: *The Garb of Old Gaul.* Pipes and drums, quick: *Pibroch of Donuil Dubh.* Pipes and drums, slow: *The Garb of Old Gaul.*

Alliances
The Cameron Highlanders of Ottawa, of Canada; The Queen's Own Cameron Highlanders of Canada; The Seaforth Highlanders of Canada; The Royal South Australia Regiment; The Royal Western Australia Regiment; 4th Battalion (Otago and Southland) Royal New Zealand Infantry Regiment; 7th Battalion (Wellington (City of Wellington's Own) and Hawke's Bay) Royal New Zealand Infantry Regiment.

Allied Regiment
7th Duke of Edinburgh's Own Gurkha Rifles.

Association
Queen's Own Highlanders Regimental Association, Cameron Barracks, Inverness.

Journal

The Queen's Own Highlander (twice a year).

Museum

Fort George, Ardersier, By Inverness, Highland (tel 0463 224380): open April–September Monday–Saturday 1000–1800, Sunday 1400–1800; October–March Monday–Friday 1000–1600.

Record Office

Except officers: Imphal Barracks, York; officers: MS(AODO), London Rd, Stanmore, Middlesex.

Regimental History

Fairrie, Lieutenant-Colonel A. A. *'Cuidich'n Righ': A History of the Queen's Own Highlanders (Seaforth and Camerons)*, RHQ, 1983.

Predecessors

SEAFORTH HIGHLANDERS (ROSS-SHIRE BUFFS, THE DUKE OF ALBANY'S)

History

Raised in 1778 as the 78th Highland Regiment (72nd Highland Regiment in 1786) and in 1793 as the 78th Highland Regiment. These two regiments became the 1st and 2nd Battalions of the Seaforth Highlanders (Ross-shire Buffs, The Duke of Albany's) in 1881.

MOTTO: *Cuidich'n righ* (Save the King).

FORMER MEMBERS: Field Marshal Sir Patrick Grant (1804–95), commissioned 1820; Field Marshal Sir James Cassels (*b*.1907), commissioned 1926.

Emblazoned Battle Honours

(awards before 1881 to 78th★; awards to 72nd and 78th★★)

India (1780–4, 1790–2): Carnatic; Hindoostan. Third Mysore War (1789–91): Mysore. Expedition against Dutch (1806): Cape of Good Hope 1806. Napoleonic Wars (1803–15): ★Maida. Operations against Dutch (1811): ★Java. Sixth Kaffir War (1835): South Africa 1835. Crimean War (1854–5): Sevastopol. Persian War (1856–7): ★Kooshab; ★Persia. Indian Mutiny (1857–8): ★Lucknow; Central India. Second Afghan War (1878–80): Peiwar Kotal; Charasiah; Kabul; Kandahar 1880; ★★Afghanistan 1878–80. Revolt of Arabi Pasha (1882): Tel-el-Kebir. First Sudan War (1882–4): Egypt 1882. Chitral Campaign (1895): Chitral. Reconquest of the Sudan (1896–8): Atbara; Khartoum. South African War (1899–1902): Paardeburg; South Africa 1899–1902. Great War: Marne 1914, 1918; Ypres 1915, 1917, 1918; Loos; Somme 1916, 1918; Arras 1917–18; Vimy 1917; Cambrai 1917, 1918; Valenciennes; Palestine 1918; Baghdad. Second World War: St Valéry-en-Caux; Caen; Rhineland; El Alamein; Akarit; Sicily 1943; Anzio; Madagascar; Imphal; Burma 1942–4. The Elephant superscribed '*Assaye*' was also borne on the colours.

Accredited Battle Honours

Great War: Le Cateau; Retreat from Mons; Aisne 1914; La Bassée 1914; Armentières 1914; Festubert 1914, 1915; Givenchy 1914; Neuve Chapelle; St Julien; Frezenberg; Bellewaarde; Aubers; Albert 1916; Bazentin; Delville Wood; Pozières; Flers-Courcelette; Le Transloy; Ancre Heights; Ancre 1916; Scarpe 1917, 1918; Arleux; Pilckem; Menin Road; Polygon Wood; Broodsein Poelcapelle; Passchendaele; St Quentin; Bapaume 1918; Lys; Estaires; Messines 1918; Hazebrouck; Bailleul; Kemmel; Béthune; Soissonais-Ourcq; Tardenois; Drocourt-Quéant; Hindenburg Line; Courtrai; Selle; France and Flanders 1914–18; Macedonia 1917–18; Megiddo; Sharon; Tigris 1916; Kut al Amara 1917; Mesopotamia 1915–18. **Second World War:** Ypres-Comines Canal; Somme 1940; Withdrawal to Seine; Odon; Cheux; Troarn; Mont Pinçon; Quarry Hill; Falaise; Falaise Road; Dives Crossing; La Vie Crossing; Lisieux; Nederrijn; Best; Le Havre; Lower Maas; Meijel; Venlo Pocket; Ourthe; Reichswald; Goch; Moyland; Rhine; Uelzen; Artlenberg; North-West Europe 1940, 1944–5; Advance on Tripoli; Mareth; Wadi Zigzaou; Djebel Roumana; North Africa 1942–3; Landing in Sicily; Augusta; Francofonte; Adrano; Sferro Hills; Garigliano Crossing; Italy 1943–4; Middle East 1942; Shenam Pass; Litan; Tengnoupal.

Awards

Eighteen members of the regiment have been awarded the Victoria Cross: nine in the Indian Mutiny (1857–8), one in the Second Afghan War (1878–80), one in the Ashanti Campaign (1900) and seven in the Great War. First awards: Lieutenant A. S. Cameron later Colonel CB (1833–1909) Kotch, Indian, 30 March 1858: gazetted 11 November 1859 (72nd Foot). Lieutenant A. C. Bogle, later Major (1829–90) Onao, India, 29 July 1857: gazetted 2 September 1859 (78th Foot).

Marches

Band, quick: *Scotland for ever*. Pipes and drums, quick: *Pibroch of Donuil Dubh*.

Allied Regiments in 1914

72nd Regiment (The Seaforth Highlanders of Canada); 75th Pictou Regiment (Highlanders), of Canada.

Journal

Cabar Feidh.

Museum

Fort George, Ardersier, By Inverness, Highland (tel 0463 224380): open April–September Monday–Saturday 1000–1800, Sunday 1400–1830; October–March Monday–Friday 1000–1600.

Regimental Association

Seaforth Highlanders Regimental Association, Cameron Barracks, Inverness.

THE QUEEN'S OWN CAMERON HIGHLANDERS

History

Raised in 1793 as the 79th Foot or Cameronian Volunteers (79th Foot or Cameron Highlanders in 1806; 2nd Battalion in 1897).

Emblazoned Battle Honours

French Revolutionary Wars (1793–1802): Egmont op Zee. **Peninsular War** (1808–14): Corunna; Busaco; Fuentes d'Onor; Salamanca; Pyrenees; Nivelle; Nive; Toulouse; Peninsula. **Hundred Days** (1815): Waterloo. **Crimean War** (1854–5): Alma; Sevastopol. **Indian**

Mutiny (1857–8): Lucknow. **Revolt of Arabi Pasha** (1882): Tel-el-Kebir; Egypt 1882. **First Sudan War** (1882–4): Egypt 1882. **Egyptian Campaign** (1885): Nile 1884–5. **Reconquest of the Sudan** (1896–8): Atbara; Khartoum. **South African War** (1899–1902): South Africa 1900–02. **Great War:** Marne 1914, 1918; Aisne 1914; Ypres 1914, 1915, 1917, 1918; Neuve Chapelle; Loos; Somme 1916, 1918; Delville Wood; Arras 1917, 1918; Sambre; Macedonia 1915–18. **Second World War:** St Omer-La Bassée; Reichswald; Rhine; Keren; Sidi Barrani; El Alamein; Akarit; Gothic Line; Kohima; Mandalay. The Sphinx superscribed 'Egypt' was also borne on the colours.

Accredited Battle Honours

Great War: Retreat from Mons; Langemarck 1914; Gheluvelt; Nonne Bosschen; Givenchy 1914; Hill 60; Gravenstafel; St Julien; Frezenberg; Bellewaarde; Aubers; Festubert 1915; Albert 1916; Bazentin; Pozières; Flers-Courcelette; Morval; Le Transloy; Ancre Heights; Scarpe 1917; Arleux; Pilckem; Menin Road; Polygon Wood; Poelcapelle; Passchendaele; St Quentin; Bapaume 1918; Lys; Estaires; Messines 1918; Kemmel; Béthune, Soissonais-Ourcq; Drocourt-Quéant; Hindenburg Line; Epéhy; St Quentin Canal; Courtrai; Selle; France and Flanders 1914–18; Struma. **Second World War:** Defence of Escaut; Somme 1940; St Valéry-en-Caux; Falaise; Falaise Road; La Vie Crossing; Le Havre; Lower Maas; Venlo Pocket; Rhineland; Goch; North-West Europe 1940, 1944–5; Agordat; Abyssinia 1941; Tobruk 1941, 1942; Gubi II; Carmusa; Mareth; Wadi Zigzaou; Djebel Roumana; North Africa 1940–3; Francofonte; Adrano; Sferro Hills; Sicily 1943; Cassino I; Poggio del Grillo; Tavoleto; Coriano; Pian di Castello; Monte Reggiano; Rimini Line; San Marino; Italy 1944; Relief of Kohima; Naga Village; Aradura; Shwebo; Ava; Irrawaddy; Mt Popa; Burma 1944–5.

Awards

Four members of the regiment have been awarded the Victoria Cross: one in the South African War (1899–1902) and three in the Great War. First award: Sergeant D. D. Farmer, later Lieutenant-Colonel D. D. Farmer MSM (1877–1956), Nooitgedacht, South Africa, 13 December 1900: gazetted 12 April 1901.

Marches

Pipes and drums, quick: *Pibroch of Donuil Dubh*. Band, slow: *Logie o'Buchan*.

Allied Regiment in 1914

79th Cameron Highlanders, of Canada.

Journal

The 79th News.

Association

The Queen's Own Cameron Highlanders Regimental Association, Cameron Barracks, Inverness.

Museums

Fort George, Ardersier, By Inverness, Highland (tel 0463 224380): open April–September Monday–Friday 1000–1830, Sunday 1400–1830; October–March Monday–Friday 1000–1600.

Regimental History

Historical Records of the Queen's Own Cameron Highlanders (7 vols.), Blackwood, 1909, 1931, 1952, 1962.

THE GORDON HIGHLANDERS
(The Scottish Division)
Colonel-in-Chief: HRH The Prince of Wales KG KT GCB AK QSO ADC

History
Raised in 1787 as the 75th Highland Regiment (75th Foot in 1809) and in 1794 as the 100th Foot (92nd Foot in 1798). These two regiments became the 1st and 2nd Battalions of The Gordon Highlanders in 1881. One regular battalion.
MOTTO: *Bydand* (Firm).
HEADQUARTERS: Viewfield Rd, Aberdeen.
RECRUITMENT AREA: Grampian (Aberdeenshire, Banffshire and Kincardineshire) and the Shetland Islands.
FORMER MEMBER: Field Marshal Sir George White VC (1835–1912), commissioned 1853.

Emblazoned Battle Honours
(awards before 1881 to 92nd★)
Third Mysore War (1789–91): Mysore. **Fourth Mysore War** (1799): Seringapatam. **French Revolutionary Wars** (1793–1802): ★Egmont op Zee; ★Mandora. **Peninsular War** (1808–14): ★Corunna; ★Fuentes d'Onor; ★Almaraz; ★Vittoria; ★Pyrenees; Nive; ★Orthes; ★Peninsula. **Hundred Days** (1815): ★Waterloo. **Sixth Kaffir War** (1835): South Africa 1835. **Indian Mutiny** (1857–8): Delhi; Lucknow. **Second Afghan War** (1878–80): ★Charasiah; ★Kabul; ★Kandahar 1880; ★Afghanistan 1878–80. **Revolt of Arabi Pasha** (1882): Tel-el-Kebir. **First Sudan War** (1882–4): Egypt 1882, 1884. **Egyptian Campaign** (1885): Nile 1884–5. **Chitral Campaign** (1895): Chitral. **Tirah Campaign** (1897–8): Tirah. **South African War** (1899–1902): Defence of Ladysmith; Paardeburg; South Africa 1899–1902. **Great War:** Mons; Le Cateau; Marne 1914, 1918; Ypres 1914, 1915, 1917; Loos; Somme 1916, 1918; Ancre 1916; Arras 1917, 1918; Cambrai 1917, 1918; Vittorio Veneto. **Second World War:** Odon; Reichswald; Goch; Rhine; North-West Europe 1940, 1944–5; El Alamein; Mareth; Sferro; Anzio. A Royal Tiger superscribed 'India' and the Sphinx superscribed 'Egypt' are also borne on the colours.

Accredited Battle Honours
Great War: Retreat from Mons; Aisne 1914; La Bassée 1914; Messines 1914; Armentières 1914; Langemarck 1914; Gheluvelt; Nonne Bosschen; Neuve Chapelle; Frezenberg; Bellewaarde; Aubers; Festubert 1915; Hooge 1915; Albert 1916, 1918; Bazentin; Delville Wood; Pozières; Guillemont; Flers-Courcelette; Le Transloy; Vimy 1917; Scarpe 1917, 1918; Arleux; Bullecourt; Pilckem; Menin Road; Polygon Wood; Broodseinde; Poelcapelle; Passchen-

daele; St Quentin; Bapaume 1918; Rosières; Lys; Estaires; Hazebrouck; Bethune; Soissonais-Ourcq; Tardenois; Hindenburg Line; Canal du Nord; Selle; Sambre; Piave; Italy 1917–18. **Second World War:** Withdrawal to Escaut; Ypres-Comines Canal; Dunkirk 1940; Somme 1940; St Valéry-en-Caux; La Vie Crossing; Lower Maas; Venlo Pocket; Rhineland; Cleve; Advance on Tripoli; Medjez Plain; North Africa 1942–3; Landing in Sicily; Sicily 1943; Rome; Italy 1944–5.

Awards
Nineteen members of the regiment have been awarded the Victoria Cross: one in the Crimean War, three in the Indian Mutiny (1857–8), two in the Second Afghan War (1878–80), two in the Tirah campaign (1897–8), six in the South African War (1899–1902), four in the Great War and one in the Second World War. First award: Colour-Sergeant C. Coghlan (1828–1915) Badle-ke-Serai 8 June 1857 and Subzee Mundi 18 July 1857: gazetted 11 November 1862 (75th Foot); Major G. S. White CB (1835–1912) Charasiah 6 October 1879: gazetted 2 June 1881 (92nd Foot).

Memorial
Outside Ladysmith, South Africa (Lieutenant-Colonel W. H. Dick-Cunynham VC)

Dress
DIFFERENCES: Blue glengarry, diced band. Gordon tartan kilt or trews, white hair sporran, two long black tassels.
REGIMENTAL TIE: Medium pale/gold/green/black/blue stripes.

Marches
Band, quick: *Cock o'the North*. Band, slow: *The Garb of Old Gaul*. Drums and pipes, quick: *Cock o'the North*. Drums and pipes, slow: *St Andrew's Cross*.

Alliances
48th Highlanders of Canada; The Toronto Scottish Regiment, of Canada; 5th/7th Battalion Royal Australian Regiment; 5th/6th Battalion The Royal Victoria Regiment, of Australia.

Allied Regiments in 1914
48th Highlanders of Canada; The Cape Town Highlanders, of South Africa.

Journal
The Tiger and Sphinx (once a year).

Associations
1/2 Bns Association; 5/7 Association; FEPOW Association.

Museum
St Luke's, Viewfield Rd, Aberdeen (tel 0224 318174): open Wednesday and Sunday 1400–1700; other times by appointment (closed at present).

Record Office
Except officers: Imphal Barracks, York; officers: MS(AODO), London Rd, Stanmore, Middlesex.

Regimental Histories
Sinclair-Stevenson, C. *The Gordon Highlanders*, Hamish Hamilton, 1968. *The Life of a Regiment* (7 vols.); vol 1, *1794–1816*, C. C. Gardyne, Douglas; vol. 2, *1816–98*, Medici Society; vol. 3, *1898–1914*, A. D. G. Gardyne, Medici Society; vol. 4, *1914–19*; C. Falls, Aberdeen UP; vol. 5, *1919–45*, W. Miles, Aberdeen UP; vol. 6, *1945–70*; vol. 70, *1970–94* (to be published in 1994).

THE ARGYLL AND SUTHERLAND HIGHLANDERS
(PRINCESS LOUISE'S)
(The Scottish Division)
Colonel-in-Chief: HM The Queen

History
Raised in 1794 as the 98th Argyllshire Highlanders (91st Foot in 1809) and in 1799 as the 93rd Highlanders. These two regiments became the 1st and 2nd Battalions of Princess Louise's (Argyll and Sutherland Highlanders) in 1881. One regular battalion, one volunteer battalion (3rd 51st Highland Volunteers (Argyll and Sutherland Highlanders)).

MOTTOES: *Sans peur* (Without fear); *Ne obliviscaris* (Do not forget).
HEADQUARTERS: The Castle, Stirling.
RECRUITMENT AREA: Central Scotland (Stirlingshire, and Clackmannan) and that part of Strathclyde which was Argyll, Bute, Renfrewshire and Dunbartonshire.
REGIMENTAL ANNIVERSARY: Balaklava Day (25 October).

Emblazoned Battle Honours
(awards before 1881 to 93rd★; awards to both 91st and 93rd★★)
Expedition against Dutch (1806): ★Cape of Good Hope 1806. **Peninsular War** (1808–14): Rolica; Vimiera; Corunna; Pyrenees; Nivelle; Nive; Orthes; Toulouse; ★★Peninsula. **Seventh Kaffir War** (1846–7): South Africa 1846–7: **Eighth Kaffir War** (1851–3): South Africa 1851–1852–1853. **Crimean War** (1854–5): ★Alma; ★Balaklava; ★Sevastopol. **Indian Mutiny** (1857–8): ★Lucknow. **Zulu and Basuto War** (1877–9): South Africa. **South African War** (1899–1902): Modder River; Paardeburg; South Africa 1899–1902. **Great War:** Mons; Le Cateau; Marne 1914, 1918; Ypres 1915, 1917, 1918; Loos; Somme 1916, 1918; Arras 1917, 1918; Cambrai 1917, 1918; Doiran 1917, 1918; Gaza. **Second World War:** Odon; Rhine; Sidi Barrani; El Alamein; Akarit; Longstop Hill 1943; Italy 1943–5; Crete; Grik Road; Malaya 1941–2. **Korean War** (1950–3): Pakchon; Korea 1950–1.

Accredited Battle Honours
Great War: Retreat from Mons; Aisne 1914; La Bassée 1914; Messines 1914, 1918; Armentières 1914; Gravenstafel; St Julien; Frezenberg; Bellewaarde; Festubert 1915; Albert 1916, 1918; Bazentin; Delville Wood; Pozières; Flers-Courcelette; Morval; Le Transloy; Ancre Heights; Ancre 1916; Scarpe 1917, 1918; Arleux; Pilckem; Menin Road; Polygon Wood; Broodseinde; Poelcapelle; Passchendaele; St Quentin; Bapaume 1918; Rosières; Lys; Estaires; Hazebrouck

Bailleul; Kemmel; Béthune; Soissonais-Ourcq; Tardenois; Amiens; Hindenburg Line; Epéhy; Canal du Nord; St Quentin Canal; Beaurevoir; Courtrai; Selle; Sambre; France and Flanders 1914–18; Italy 1917–18; Struma; Macedonia 1915–18; Gallipoli 1915–16; Rumani; Egypt 1916; El Mughar; Nebi Samwil; Jaffa; Palestine 1917–18. **Second World War:** Somme 1940; Tourmauville Bridge; Caen; Esquay; Mont Pinçon; Quarry Hill; Estry; Falaise; Dives Crossing; Aart; Lower Maas; Meijel; Venlo Pocket; Ourthe; Rhineland; Reichswald; Uelzen; Artlenberg; North-West Europe 1940, 1944–5; Abyssinia 1941; Medenine; Djebel Azzag 1942; Kef Ouiba Pass; Mine de Sedjenane; Medjez Plain; North Africa 1940–3; Landing in Sicily; Gerbini; Adrano; Centuripe; Sicily 1943; Termoli; Sangro; Cassino II; Liri Valley; Aquino; Monte Casalino; Monte Spadura; Monte Grande; Senio; Santerno Crossing; Argenta Gap; Heraklion; Middle East 1941; North Malaya; Central Malaya; Ipoh; Slim River; Singapore Island.

Awards
Sixteen members of the regiment have been awarded the Victoria Cross: seven in the Indian Mutiny (1857–8), six in the Great War, two in the Second World War and one in the Korean War (1950–3). First awards: Private D. Mackay (1830–80), Colour-Sergeant J. Munro (1827–71), Lance-Corporal J. Dunley (1831–68), Sergeant J. Paton (1833–1914), Captain W. G. D. Stewart (1831–68) and Private P. Grant (1824–68) Lucknow 16 November 1857: gazetted 24 December 1858 – five of these awards were by regimental election (93rd Foot).

Dress
DIFFERENCES: Blue glengarry, diced band. Government tartan kilt or trews, black hair sporran, six short white tassels.
REGIMENTAL TIE: Thin gold stripes on purple and green ground.

Regimental Mascot
Shetland pony.

Marches
Band, quick: *The Thin Red Line*. Band, slow: *The Garb of Old Gaul*. Pipes and drums, quick: *The Campbells are Coming* and *Hielan' Laddie*. Pipes and drums, slow: *Skye Boat Song*.

Alliances
The Argyll and Sutherland Highlanders of Canada (Princess Louise's); The Calgary Highlanders, of Canada; The Royal New South Wales Regiment, of Australia; 9th Battalion (Wilde's), The Frontier Force Regiment, of Pakistan.

Allied Regiment in 1914
91st Regiment (Canadian Highlanders).

Journal
The Thin Red Line (twice a year).

Museum

The Castle, Stirling (tel 0786 75165): open Easter–September Monday–Saturday 1000–1700, Sunday 1200–1730.

Record Office

Except officers: Imphal Barracks, York; officers: MS(AODO), London Rd, Stanmore, Middlesex.

Regimental Histories

Anderson, R. C. B. *History of the Argyll and Sutherland Highlanders, 1939–1954*, Constable, 1956. Malcolm G. I. *The Argylls in Korea*, Nelson, 1952. Anderson, R. C. B. *History of the Argyll and Sutherland Highlanders, 1st Battalion, 1909–1939*, privately published, 1954. History of all the Battalions (1st, 2nd, 5th, 6th, 7th, 8th, 9th) in the Second World War.

THE PARACHUTE REGIMENT
Colonel-in-Chief: HRH The Prince of Wales KG KT GCB AK QSO ADC

History
Raised in 1942. Three regular battalions, three volunteer battalions (4th, 10th County of London) and 15th (Scottish)).
MOTTO: *Utrinque paratus* (Ready for anything).
HEADQUARTERS: Browning Barracks, Aldershot, Hampshire.
RECRUITMENT AREA: Nationwide.

Emblazoned Battle Honours
Second World War: Bruneval; Normandy Landing; Breville; Arnhem 1944; Southern France; Oudna; Tamera; Primosole Bridge; Athens 1944–5. **Falklands War** (1982): Falkland Islands 1982.

Accredited Battle Honours
Second World War: Pegasus Bridge; Merville Battery; Dives Crossing; La Touques Crossing; Ourthe; Rhine; North-West Europe 1942, 1944–5; Soudia; Djebel Azzag 1943; Djebel Alliliga; El Hadjeba; Djebel Dahra; Kef el Debna; North Africa 1942–3; Sicily 1943; Taranto; Orsogna; Italy 1943–4; Greece 1944–5. **Falklands War** (1982): Goose Green; Mount Longdon; Wireless Ridge.

Awards
Four members of the regiment have been awarded the Victoria Cross: two in the Second World War and two in the Falklands War (1982). First award: Lieutenant J. H. Grayburn (1918–44), Arnhem 17–20 September 1944: gazetted posthumously 25 January 1945. Two members of the regiment have been awarded the George Cross: one in the Second World War and one in 1971. First award: Private C. A. Duncan (1908–43) M'Saken, North Africa, 10 July 1943: gazetted posthumously 9 November 1943.

Dress
DIFFERENCES: Maroon beret. Different pattern lanyard for each battalion.
REGIMENTAL TIE: Pale blue-winged parachutes on maroon ground.

Regimental Mascot
Shetland pony.

Marches
Quick: *The Ride of the Valkyries.* Slow: *Pomp and Circumstance No 4.*

Alliances
The Canadian Airborne Regiment; 8th/9th Battalion The Royal Australian Regiment.

Journal
Pegasus (three times a year – April, August, September).

Museum
Airborne Forces Museum, Browning Barracks, Aldershot, Hampshire (tel 0252 24431 ext 4619): open Tuesday–Saturday 1000–1630, Monday by appointment.

Record Office
Except officers: Higher Barracks, Exeter; officers: MS(AODO), London Rd, Stanmore, Middlesex.

Regimental Histories
Norton, G. G. *The Red Devils*, Leo Cooper, 1971. Saunders, H. St G. *The Story of the Parachute Regiment at War, 1940–1945*, Michael Joseph, 1950.

THE BRIGADE OF GURKHAS
Staff Band Cap Badge

History
CONSTITUTED: 1948.
HEADQUARTERS: HONG KONG.
RECRUITMENT AREA: Nepal.
MOTTO: *Kaphar hunnu bhanda marnu ramro* (It is better to die than live a coward).

Alliances
Queen's Own Rifles of Canada; The Royal Australian Regiment.

Journal
The Kukri

Museum
Peninsular Barracks, Romsey Rd, Winchester, Hampshire (tel 0962 842832).

Record Office
Gun Club Barracks, Hong Kong.

Brigade History
Smith, E. D. *Britain's Brigade of Gurkhas*, Leo Cooper, 1973.

2nd KING EDWARD VII's OWN GURKHA RIFLES (THE SIRMOOR RIFLES)
Colonel-in-Chief: HRH The Prince of Wales KG KT GCB AK QSO ADC

History
Raised in 1815 as the Sirmoor Battalion (2nd Goorkha Regiment in 1861, brought on to British establishment in 1948). Two battalions.
REGIMENTAL ANNIVERSARY: Delhi Day (14 September).

Emblazoned Battle Honours

Revolt of Rajah of Bhurtpore (1826): Bhurtpore. **First Sikh War** (1845–6): Aliwal; Sobraon. **Indian Mutiny** (1857–8): Delhi 1857. **Second Afghan War** (1878–80): Kabul 1879; Kandahar 1880; Afghanistan 1878–80. **Tirah Campaign** (1897–8): Tirah; Punjab Frontier (1897–8). **Great War:** La Bassée 1914; Festubert 1914–15; Givenchy 1914; Neuve Chapelle; Aubers; Loos; Tigris 1916; Kut el Amara 1917; Baghdad 1915; Persia 1918. **Third Afghan War** (1919): Afghanistan 1919. **Second World War:** El Alameain; Akarit; Tunis; Cassino I; Gothic Line; Jitra; Slim River; North Arakan; Irrawaddy; Tamandu. The regiment was granted a Truncheon for distinguished service at Delhi in 1857.

Accredited Battle Honours

Great War: France and Flanders 1914–15; Egypt 1915; Mesopotamia 1916–18; Baluchistan 1918. **Second World War:** Mareth; Djebel el Meida; Enfidaville; North Africa 1942–3; Monastery Hill; Pian di Maggio; Coriano; Poggio San Giovanni; Monte Reggiano; Italy 1944–5; Greece 1944–5; North Malaya; Central Malaya; Kampar; Johore; Singapore Island; Malaya 1941–2; Magwe; Sittang 1945; Point 1433; Arakan Beaches; Myebon; Chindits 1943; Burma 1943–5.

Awards

Two members of the regiment have been awarded the Victoria Cross: one in the Looshai Campaign (1872) and one in the Second World War. First award: Major D. Macintyre, later Major-General (1831–1903), Looshai, India, 4 January 1872: gazetted 27 September 1872.

Dress

DIFFERENCES: Black pillbox kilmarnock, diced band, black toorie, red-backed badge. Green centred stable belt, scarlet bands, black outer edges. Black patent leather shoulder-belt for officers, with silver ram's head mask, silver chain and whistle.

Marches

Quick: *Lutzow's Wild Hunt* and *Wha's a'the Steer, Kimmer.* Slow: *God Bless the Prince of Wales.*

Affiliated Regiment

The Royal Green Jackets.

Allied Regiment of Commonwealth Forces

Royal Brunei Armed Forces.

Regimental Histories

James, H., and Sheil-Small, D. *A Pride of Gurkhas: The 2nd King Edward VII's Own Goorkhas (The Sirmoor Rifles) 1948–1971*, Leo Cooper, 1975. Shakespear, L. W. *History of the 2nd King Edward VII's Own Gurkha Rifles (The Sirmoor Rifles)* (2 vols.), Gale & Polden, 1912 and 1924.

6th QUEEN ELIZABETH'S OWN GURKHA RIFLES

History
Raised in 1817 as the Cuttach Legion (42nd Goorkha Light Infantry in 1866, 6th Gurkha Rifles in 1903, brought on to British establishment in 1948). One battalion.

Emblazoned Battle Honours
Third Burma War (1885–7): Burma 1885–7. **Great War:** Helles; Krithia; Suvla; Sari Bair; Gallipoli 1915; Suez Canal; Khan Baghdadi; Mesopotamia 1916–18; Persia 1918; NW Frontier India 1915. **Third Afghan War** (1919): Afghanistan 1919. **Second World War:** Monte Chicco; Medecina; Italy 1944–5; Kyauk-myaung Bridgehead; Mandalay; Fort Dufferin; Rangoon Road; Sittang 1945; Chindits 1944; Burma 1944–5.

Accredited Battle Honours
Great War: Egypt 1915–16. **Second World War:** Coriano; Santarcangelo; Lamone Crossing; Senio Floodbank; Gaiana Crossing; Shwebo; Maymyo; Toungoo.

Dress
DIFFERENCES: Black kilmarnock, scarlet toorie. Black patent leather shoulder-belt for officers, with silver lion's head mask, chain and whistle. Green and black lanyard. Badge of 14th/20th King's Hussars on upper sleeve.

Marches
Band, quick: *Young May Moon.* Pipes, quick: *Queen Elizabeth's Own.*

Affiliated Regiments
14th/20th King's Hussars; The Royal Green Jackets.

Alliance
2nd/1st Battalion The Royal New Zealand Infantry Regiment.

Regimental History
Gibbs, H. R. K. *Historical Record of the 6th Gurkha Rifles* (2 vols.), Gale & Polden, 1955.

7th DUKE OF EDINBURGH'S OWN GURKHA RIFLES

History
Raised in 1902 as the 8th Gurkha Rifles (7th Gurkha Rifles in 1907, brought on to British establishment in 1948). One battalion.

Emblazoned Battle Honours
Great War: Egypt 1915; Megiddo; Sharon; Palestine 1918; Kut al Amara 1915, 1917; Baghdad; Sharqat. **Third Afghan War** (1919): Afghanistan 1918. **Second World War:** Cassino I; Poggio del Grillo; Tavoleto; Sittang 1942, 1945; Kyaukse 1942; Imphal; Bishenpur; Meiktila; Rangoon Road.

Accredited Battle Honours
Great War: Suez Canal; Shaiba; Mesopotamia 1915–18. **Second World War:** Tobruk 1942; North Africa 1942; Campriano; Montebello-Scorticata Ridge; Italy 1944; Pegu 1942; Shwegyin; Capture of Meiktila; Defence of Meiktila; Pyawbwe; Burma 1942–5.

Awards
Rifleman Ganju Lama, later Jemadar (*b*1922) was awarded the Victoria Cross, Imphal 12 June 1944: gazetted 7 September 1944.

Dress
DIFFERENCES: Kilmarnock, black toorie. Black patent leather shoulder-belt for officers, with silver Maltese cross, lion's head mask, chain and whistle.

Marches
Band, quick: *Old Monmouthshire*. Pipes and drums, quick: *All the Blue Bonnets are over the Border*.

Affiliated Regiment
Queen's Own Highlanders (Seaforth and Camerons).

Affiliated Regiment of Commonwealth Forces
The Pacific Islands Regiment Papua New Guinea.

Regimental History
Mackay, J. N. *History of 7th Duke of Edinburgh's Own Gurkha Rifles*, Blackwood, 1962.

10th PRINCESS MARY'S OWN GURKHA RIFLES

History
Raised in 1867 as the Kubo Valley Police Battalion (10th (Burma) Regiment Madras Infantry in 1890, 10th Gurkha Rifles in 1901, brought on to British establishment in 1948). One battalion.

Emblazoned Battle Honours
Great War: Helles; Krithia; Suvla; Sari Bair; Gallipoli 1915; Suez Canal; Egypt 1915; Sharqat; Mesopotamia 1916–18. **Third Afghan War** (1919): Afghanistan 1919. **Second World War:** Coriano; Santarcangelo; Bologna; Imphal; Tuitum; Mandalay; Myinmu Bridgehead; Meiktila; Rangoon Road.

Accredited Battle Honours
Second World War: Iraq 1941; Deir ez Zor; Syria 1941; Senio Floodbank; Sillaro Crossing; Italy 1944–5; Monywa 1942; Tamu Road; Shenam Pass; Litan; Bishenpur; Tengnoupal; Kyaukse 1945; Capture of Meiktila; Irrawaddy; Pegu 1945; Sittang; Burma 1942–5.

Dress
DIFFERENCES: Black kilmarnock. Black patent leather shoulder-belt for officers, with silver badge, lion's mask, chain and whistle.

Marches
Quick: *Hundred Pipers.*

Affiliated Regiment
The Royal Scots (The Royal Regiment).

Regimental History
Mullary, B. R. *Bugle and Kukri: The Story of the 10th Princess Mary's Own Gurkha Rifles*, Blackwood, 1957.

228

THE QUEEN'S GURKHA ENGINEERS

History
Raised in 1948 as 67 Gurkha Squadron RE (Gurkha Engineers in 1955, Queen's in 1977).

Dress
DIFFERENCES:

Marches
Band, quick: *Wings*. Pipes, quick: *Far o'er the Sea*.

Affiliated Corps
Corps of Royal Engineers.

QUEEN'S GURKHA SIGNALS

History
Formed in 1950 as the Gurkha Signal Training and Holding Wing (Gurkha Signals in 1955, Queen's in 1977).
MOTTO: *Certa cito* (Swift and sure).

Marches
Quick: *Scotland the Brave*.

Affiliated Corps
Royal Corps of Signals.

GURKHA TRANSPORT REGIMENT

History
Formed in 1958 as the Gurkha Army Service Corps (Gurkha Transport Regiment in 1965).

Marches
Quick: *Wait for the Wagon.*

Affiliated Corps
Royal Corps of Transport.

THE ROYAL GREEN JACKETS
(The Light Division)
Colonel-in-Chief: HM The Queen

History
Formed in 1966 from the 1st Green Jackets (43rd and 52nd) (formed in 1958 from the Oxfordshire and Buckinghamshire Regiment (43rd and 52nd)); the 2nd Green Jackets (The King's Royal Rifle Corps); and the 3rd Green Jackets (The Rifle Brigade). Three regular battalions, two volunteer battalions (4th and 5th).
HEADQUARTERS: Sir John Moore Barracks, Andover Rd North, Winchester, Hampshire.
RECRUITMENT AREA: Greater London, Buckinghamshire and Oxfordshire.
REGIMENTAL ANNIVERSARY: Waterloo Day (18 June).

Battle Honours
Seven Years War (1756–63): Quebec 1759. **French Revolutionary Wars** (1793–1802): Copenhagen. **Peninsular War** (1808–14): Corunna; Badajos; Salamanca; Vittoria; Peninsula. **Hundred Days** (1815): Waterloo. **Crimean War** (1854–5): Inkerman. **Indian Mutiny** (1857–8): Delhi 1857. **Second Afghan War** (1878–80): Afghanistan 1878–80. **South African War** (1899–1902): Defence of Ladysmith. **Great War:** Ypres 1914, 1915, 1917, 1918; Nonne Bosschen; Somme 1916, 1918. **Second World War** (1939–45): Calais 1940; Pegasus Bridge; El Alamein.

Accredited Battle Honours
Seven Years War (1756–63): Louisburg; Martinique 1762; Havannah. **Pontiac's Conspiracy** (1763–4): North America 1763–4. **Third Mysore War** (1789–91): Mysore. **India** (1790–3): Hindoostan. **French Revolutionary Wars** (1793–1802): Martinique 1794. **Expedition against Spanish** (1807): Monte Video. **Napoleonic Wars** (1803–15): Martinique 1809. **Peninsular War** (1808–14): Rolica; Vimiera; Talavera; Busaco; Barrosa; Fuentes d'Onor; Albuhera; Ciudad Rodrigo; Pyrenees; Nivelle; Nive; Orthes; Toulouse. **Seventh Kaffir War** (1846–7): South Africa 1846–7. **Second Sikh War** (1848–9): Mooltan; Goojerat; Punjaub. **Eighth Kaffir War** (1851–3): South Africa 1851–1852–1853. **Crimean War** (1854–5): Alma; Sevastopol. **Indian Mutiny** (1857–8): Lucknow. **Second China War** (1857–60): Taku Forts; Pekin 1860. **Third Maori War** (1863–6): New Zealand. **Ashantee War** (1873–4): Ashantee 1873–4. **Second Afghan War** (1878–80): Ali Masjid. **Zulu and Basuto War** (1877–9): South Africa 1879. **Second Afghan War** (1878–80): Ahmed Khel; Kandahar 1880. **Revolt of Arabi Pasha** (1882): Tel-el-Kebir. **First Sudan War** (1882–4): Egypt 1882, 1884. **Third Burma War** (1885–7): Burma 1885–7. **Chitral Campaign** (1895): Chitral.

Reconquest of the Sudan (1896–8): Khartoum. South African War (1899–1902): Relief of Kimberley; Paardeburg; Relief of Ladysmith; South Africa 1899–1902. Great War: Mons; Le Cateau; Retreat from Mons; Marne 1914; Aisne 1914, 1918; Armentières 1914; Langemarck 1914, 1917; Gheluvelt; Givenchy 1914; Neuve Chapelle; Gravenstafel; St Julien; Frezenberg; Bellewaarde; Aubers; Festubert 1915; Hooge 1915; Loos; Mount Sorrel; Albert 1916, 1918; Bazentin; Delville Wood; Pozières; Guillemont; Flers-Courcelette; Morval; Le Transloy; Ancre Heights; Ancre 1916, 1918; Vimy 1917; Scarpe 1917, 1918; Arleux; Messines 1917, 1918; Pilckem; Menin Road; Polygon Wood; Broodseinde; Poelcapelle; Passchendaele; Cambrai 1917, 1918; St Quentin; Rosières; Avre; Villers-Bretonneux; Lys; Hazebrouck; Bailleul; Kemmel; Béthune; Drocourt-Quéant; Hindenburg Line; Havrincourt; Epéhy; Canal du Nord; St Quentin Canal; Beaurevoir; Courtrai; Selle; Valenciennes; Sambre; France and Flanders 1914–18; Piave; Vittorio Veneto; Italy 1917–18; Doiran 1917, 1918; Macedonia 1915–18; Kut al Amara 1915; Ctesiphon; Defence of Kut al Amara; Tigris 1916; Khan Baghdadi; Mesopotamia 1914–18. Second World War: Defence of Escaut; Cassel; Ypres-Comines Canal; Normandy Landing; Villers Bocage; Odon; Caen; Esquay; Bourguébus Ridge; Mont Pinçon; Le Perier Ridge; Falaise; Antwerp; Hechtel; Nederrijn; Lower Maas; Roer; Ourthe; Rhineland; Reichswald; Cleve; Goch; Hochwald; Rhine; Ibbenburen; Dreirwalde; Leese; Aller; North-West Europe 1940, 1944–5; Egyptian Frontier 1940; Sidi Barrani; Beda Fomm; Mersa el Brega; Agedabia; Derna Aerodrome; Tobruk 1941; Sidi Rezegh 1941; Chor es Sufan; Saunnu; Gazala; Bir Hacheim; Knightsbridge; Defence of Alamein Line; Ruweisat; Fuka Airfield; Alam el Halfa; Capture of Halfaya Pass; Nofilia; Tebaga Gap; Enfidaville; Medjez el Bab; Kasserine; Thala; Fondouk; Fondouk Pass; El Kourzia; Djebel Kournine; Argoub el Megas; Tunis; Hamman Lif; North Africa 1940–3; Sangro; Salerno; Santa Lucia; Salerno Hills; Cardito; Teano; Monte Camino; Garigliano Crossing; Damiano; Anzio; Cassino II; Liri Valley; Melfa Crossing; Monte Rotondo; Capture of Perugia; Monte Malbe; Arezzo; Advance to Florence; Gothic Line; Coriano; Gemmano Ridge; Lamone Crossing; Orsara; Tossignano; Argenta Gap; Fossa Cembalina; Italy 1943–5; Veve; Greece 1941, 1944, 1945; Middle East 1941; Arakan Beaches; Tamandu; Burma 1943–4.

Dress
DIFFERENCES: Rifle green dress cap. Rifle green stable belt, black patent leather shoulder-belt for officers. Black and green lanyard.

Marches
Double past: *The Road to the Isles*. Quick: *Royal Green Jackets*, a combination of *Huntsman's Chorus* and *The Italian Song*.

Alliances
The British Columbia Regiment (Duke of Connaught's Own), of Canada; Princess Patricia's Canadian Light Infantry; The Queen's Own Rifles of Canada; The Brockville Rifles, of Canada; The Royal Regina Rifle Regiment, of

Canada; The Royal Winnipeg Rifles, of Canada; Western Australia University Regiment; Sydney University Regiment, of Australia; Melbourne University Regiment, of Australia; 1st Battalion Royal New Zealand Infantry Regiment; 6th Battalion (Hanraki) Royal New Zealand Infantry Regiment; The Fiji Infantry Regiment.

Affiliations
2nd King Edward VII's Own Gurkha Rifles (The Sirmoor Rifles); 6th Queen Elizabeth's Own Gurkha Rifles.

Journal
The Royal Green Jackets Chronicle.

Museum
Peninsular Barracks, Romsey Rd, Winchester, Hampshire, open April–September Monday–Friday 1000–1230, 1400–1630, Saturday 1430–1630; October–March Monday–Friday 1030–1230, 1400–1600.

Record Office
Except officers: Higher Barracks, Exeter; officers: MS(AODO), London Rd, Stanmore, Middlesex.

Regimental History
Wilkinson-Latham, C. *The Royal Green Jackets*, Osprey, 1975.

Predecessors

THE OXFORDSHIRE AND BUCKINGHAMSHIRE LIGHT INFANTRY (43rd AND 52nd)

History
Raised in 1741 as the 54th Foot (43rd Foot in 1748) and in 1755 as the 54th Foot (52nd Foot in 1757). These two regiments became the 1st and 2nd Battalions of the Oxfordshire Light Infantry in 1881 (Oxfordshire and Buckinghamshire Light Infantry in 1908).

REGIMENTAL ANNIVERSARY: Waterloo Day (18 June).

Emblazoned Battle Honours
(awards before 1881 to 52nd★; awards to both 43rd and 52nd★★)
Seven Years War (1756–63): Quebec 1759; Martinique 1762; Havannah. **Third Mysore War** (1789–1791): ★Mysore. **India** (1790–3): Hindoostan. **French Revolutionary Wars** (1793–1802): Martinique 1794. **Peninsular War** (1808–14): ★★Vimiera; ★★Corunna; ★★Busaco; ★★Fuentes d'Onor; ★★Ciudad Rodrigo; ★★Badajos; ★★Salamanca; ★★Vittoria; ★★Pyrenees; ★★Nivelle; ★★Nive; Orthes; ★★Toulouse; ★★Peninsula. **Hundred Days** (1815): ★Waterloo. **Eighth Kaffir War** (1851–3): South Africa 1851–1852–1853. **Indian Mutiny**

(1857–8): *Delhi 1857. **Third Maori War** (1863–5): New Zealand. **South African War** (1899–1902): Relief of Kimberley; Paardeburg; South Africa 1900–02. **Great War:** Mons; Ypres 1914, 1917; Langemarck 1914, 1917; Nonne Bosschen; Somme 1916, 1918; Cambrai 1917, 1918; Piave; Doiran 1917, 1918; Ctesiphon; Defence of Kut al Amara. **Second World War** Cassel; Ypres-Comines Canal; Normandy Landing; Pegasus Bridge; Reichswald; Rhine; Enfidaville; Salerno; Anzio; Gemmano Ridge.

Accredited Battle Honours

Great War: Retreat from Mons; Marne 1914; Gheluvelt; Aubers; Festubert 1915; Hooge 1915; Loos; Mount Sorrel; Albert 1916, 1918; Bazentin; Delville Wood; Pozières; Guillemont; Flers-Courcelette; Morval; Le Transloy; Ancre Heights; Ancre 1916; Bapaume 1917, 1918; Arras 1917; Vimy 1917; Scarpe 1917; Arleux; Menin Road; Polygon Wood; Broodseinde; Poelcapelle; Passchendaele; St Quentin; Rosières; Avre; Lys; Hazebrouck; Béthune; Hindenburg Line; Havrincourt; Canal du Nord; Selle; Valenciennes; France and Flanders 1914–18; Vittorio Veneto; Italy 1917–18; Macedonia 1915–18; Kut al Amara 1915; Khan Baghdadi; Mesopotamia 1914–18; Archangel 1919. **Second World War:** Defence of Escaut; Caen; Esquay; Lower Maas; Ourthe; Rhineland; Ibbenburen; North-West Europe 1940, 1944–5; North Africa 1943; St Lucia; Salerno Hills; Teano; Monte Camino; Garigliano Crossing; Damiano; Coriano; Italy 1943–5; Arakan Beaches; Tamandu; Burma 1943–5.

Awards

Six members of the regiment have been awarded the Victoria Cross: three in the Indian Mutiny (1857–8), one in the Third Maori War (1863–6) and two in

the Great War. First awards: Bugler R. Hawthorne (1872–79) Kashmir Gate, Delhi, 14 September 1857; Lance-Corporal H. Smith, later Colour-Sergeant (1825–62), Chandni Chowk, India, 14 September 1857: both gazetted 24 April 1858 (52nd Foot). Private H. Addison (1821–87) Kurrereah, New Zealand, 2 January 1859: gazetted 2 September 1859 (43rd Foot).

Memorials

Obelisk, Rose Hill, Oxford, by Lutyens. Slade Park, Headington, Oxford (South African War 1900–1902).

Marches

Quick: *Ein Schütze bin ich* 1st Battalions; *The Lower Castle Yard* 2nd Battalion.

Allied Regiments in 1914

52nd Regiment (Prince Albert Volunteers), of Canada; 6th (Hanraki) Regiment, of New Zealand.

Journal

The Chronicle of the Oxfordshire and Buckinghamshire Light Infantry (1892–1966).

Museums

TAVR Centre, Slade Park, Headington, Oxford (tel 0865 716060): open Monday–Friday 1400–1600 closed for refurbishment until late 1991. The Royal Green Jackets Museum, Peninsula Barracks, Winchester (tel 0962 63846): open Monday–Saturday 1000–1700, Sunday 1200–1600, closed two weeks over Christmas.

Regimental Histories

Booth, P. *The Oxfordshire and Buckinghamshire Light Infantry*, Leo Cooper, 1971. Levinge, Sir Richard. *History of the 43rd, 1741–1867*, RHQ, 1868. Morson, W. S. *History of the 52nd, 1755–1858*, RHQ, 1860. Newbolt, H. *The Story of the Oxfordshire and Buckinghamshire Light Infantry*, Country Life, 1915. *History of the 43rd, 1867–1892*, Regimental Chronicle, 1952. *History of the 52nd, 1859–1892*, Regimental Chronicle,

1952. Mockler-Ferryman, A. F., and Crosse, R. B. *Regimental War Tales, 1741–1919*, RHQ, 1915 and 1942.

THE KING'S ROYAL RIFLE CORPS

History
Raised in 1755 as the 62nd, or Royal American, Regiment (60th Foot in 1757).
MOTTO: *Celer et audax* (Swift and bold).
FORMER MEMBERS: Field Marshal Lord Bramall (*b.*1924), commissioned 1943.

Battle Honours
Seven Years War (1756–63): Louisburg; Quebec 1759; Martinique 1762; Havannah. **Pontiac's Conspiracy** (1763–4): North America 1763–4. **Napoleonic Wars** (1803–15): Martinique 1809. **Peninsular War** (1808–14): Rolica; Vimiera; Talavera; Busaco; Fuentes d'Onor; Albuhera; Ciudad Rodrigo; Badajos; Salamanca; Vittoria; Pyrenees; Nivelle; Nive; Orthes; Toulouse; Peninsula. **Second Sikh War** (1848–9): Mooltan; Goojerat; Punjaub. **Eighth Kaffir War** (1851–3): South Africa 1851–1852–1853. **Indian Mutiny** (1857–8): Delhi 1857. **Second China War** (1857–60): Taku Forts; Pekin 1860. **Zulu and Basuto War** (1877–9): South Africa 1879. **Second Afghan War** (1878–80): Ali Masjid; Ahmed Khel; Kandahar 1880; Afghanistan 1878–80. **Revolt of Arabi Pasha** (1882): Tel-el-Kebir (1882). **First Sudan War** (1882–4): Egypt 1882, 1884. **Chitral Campaign** (1895): Chitral. **South African War** (1899–1902): Defence of Ladysmith; Relief of Ladysmith; South Africa 1899–1902. **Great War:** Mons; Marne 1914; Ypres 1914, 1915, 1917, 1918; Somme 1916, 1918; Arras 1917, 1918; Messines 1917, 1918; Epéhy; Canal du Nord; Selle; Sambre. **Second World War:** Calais 1940; Rhineland; North-West Europe 1940, 1944–5; Egyptian Frontier 1940; Sidi Rezegh 1941; Alem el Halfa; El Alamein; North Africa 1940–3; Italy 1943–5; Greece 1941, 1944–5.

Accredited Battle Honours
Great War: Retreat from Mons; Aisne 1914; Langemarck 1914, 1917; Gheluvelt; Nonne Bosschen; Givenchy 1914; Gravenstafel; St Julien; Frezenberg; Bellewaarde; Aubers; Festubert 1915; Hooge 1915; Loos; Albert 1916, 1918; Bazentin; Delville Wood; Pozières; Guillemont; Flers-Courcelette; Morval; Le Transloy; Ancre Heights; Ancre 1916; Scarpe 1917; Arleux; Pilckem; Menin Road; Polygon Wood; Broodseinde; Poelcapelle; Passchendaele; Cambrai 1917, 1918; St Quentin; Rosières; Avre; Lys; Bailleul; Kemmel; Béthune; Bapaume 1918; Drocourt-Quéant; Hindenburg Line; Havrincourt; St Quentin Canal; Beaurevoir; Courtrai; France and Flanders 1914–18; Italy 1917–18; Macedonia 1916–18. **Second World War:** Mont Pinçon; Falaise; Roer; Cleve; Goch; Hochwald; Rhine; Dreirwalde; Aller; Sidi Barrani; Derna Aerodrome; Tobruk 1941; Gazala; Bir Hacheim; Knightsbridge; Defence of Alamein Line; Ruweisat; Fuka Airfield; Capture of Halfaya Pass; Nofilia; Tebaga Gap; Argoub el Megas; Tunis; Sangro; Arezzo; Coriano; Lamone Crossing; Argenta Gap; Veve; Crete, Middle East 1941.

Awards
Twenty members of the regiment have been awarded the Victoria Cross: eight

in the Indian Mutiny (1857–8), one in the Zulu and Basuto War (1878–9), one in Egypt (1882), one in the First Sudan War (1882–4), one in the South African War (1899–1902), ten in the Great War and one in the Second World War. First award: Private S. Turner (1826–68) siege of Delhi 19 June 1857: gazetted 20 January 1860.

War Memorial
Winchester Cathedral.

Marches
Quick: *Lutzow's Wild Hunt.*

Allied Regiments in 1914
60th Rifles of Canada; 63rd Regiment Halifax Rifles, of Canada.

Museum
Peninsula Barracks, Romsey Rd, Winchester (tel 0962 63846): open April–September Monday–Friday 1000–1230, 1400–1630, Saturday 1430–1630; October–March Monday–Friday 1030–1230, 1400–1600.

Regimental Histories
Wood, H. F., *The King's Royal Rifle Corps*, Hamish Hamilton, 1967. *The Annals of the King's Royal Rifle Corps* (5 vols.); vols. 1–3, L. B. Butler, Smith Elder, 1913–19; vols. 4 and 5, W. George, John Murray, 1932.

THE RIFLE BRIGADE (THE PRINCE CONSORT'S OWN)

History
Raised in 1800 as the Rifle Corps (95th Foot 1802–15).
FORMER MEMBERS: Field Marshal Lord Grenfell (1841–1925), commissioned 1859; Field Marshal Sir Henry Wilson (1864–1922), commissioned 1884; Field Marshal Lord Wilson (1881–1964), commissioned 1900; Field Marshal Sir Francis Festing (1902–76), commissioned 1921.

Battle Honours
French Revolutionary Wars (1793–1802): Copenhagen. Expedition against Spanish (1807): Monte Video. Peninsular War (1808–14): Rolica; Vimiera; Corunna; Busaco; Barrosa; Fuentes d'Onor; Ciudad Rodrigo; Badajos; Salamanca; Vittoria; Pyrenees; Nivelle; Nive; Orthes; Toulouse; Peninsula. Hundred Days (1815): Waterloo. Seventh Kaffir War (1846–7): South Africa 1846–7. Eighth Kaffir War (1851–3): South Africa 1851–1852–1853. Crimean War (1854–5): Alma; Inkerman; Sevastopol. Indian Mutiny (1857–8): Lucknow. Ashantee War (1873–4): Ashantee 1873–4. Second Afghan War (1878–80): Ali Masjid; Afghanistan 1878–9. Third Burma War (1885–7): Burma 1885–7. Reconquest of the Sudan (1896–8): Khartoum. South African War (1899–1902): Defence of Ladysmith; Relief of Ladysmith; South Africa 1899–1902. Great War: Le Cateau; Marne 1914; Neuve Chapelle; Ypres 1915, 1917; Somme 1916, 1918; Arras 1917, 1918; Messines 1917; Cambrai 1917, 1918; Hindenburg Line; Macedonia 1915–18. Second World War: Calais 1940; North-West Europe 1940, 1944–5; Beda Fomm; Sidi Rezegh 1941; Alem el Halfa; El Alamein; North Africa 1940–3; Cassino II; Capture of Perugia; Italy 1943–5.

Accredited Battle Honours
Great War: Retreat from Mons; Aisne 1914, 1918; Armentières 1914; Graven-

stafel; St Julien; Frezenberg; Belle-
waarde; Aubers; Hooge 1915; Albert
1916, 1918; Bazentin; Delville Wood;
Guillemont; Flers-Courcelette; Morval;
Le Transloy; Ancre Heights; Ancre
1916; Vimy 1917; Scarpe 1917, 1918;
Arleux; Pilckem; Langemarck 1917;
Menin Road; Polygon Wood; Brood-
seinde; Poelcapelle; Passchendaele; St
Quentin; Rosières; Avre; Villers-
Bretonneux; Lys; Hazebrouck; Béthune;
Drocourt-Quéant; Havrincourt; Canal
du Nord; Selle; Valenciennes; Sambre;
France and Flanders 1914–18. **Second
World War:** Villers Bocage; Odon;
Bourguébus Ridge; Mont Pinçon; Le
Perier Ridge; Falaise; Antwerp; Hechtel;
Nederrijn; Lower Maas; Roer; Leese;
Aller; Egyptian Frontier 1940; Mersa el
Brega; Agedabia; Derna Aerodrome;
Tobruk 1941; Chor es Sufan; Saunnu;
Gazala; Knightsbridge; Defence of
Alamein Line; Ruweisat; Tebaga Gap;
Medjez el Bab; Kasserine; Thala; Fon-
douk; Fondouk Pass; El Kourzia; Djebel
Kournine; Tunis; Hammam Lif;
Cardito; Liri Valley; Melfa Crossing;
Monte Rotondo; Monte Malbe; Arezzo;
Advance to Florance; Gothic Line;
Orsara; Tossignano; Argenta Gap; Fossa
Cembalina.

Awards

Twenty-four members of the regiment
have been awarded the Victoria Cross:
eight in the Crimean War (1854–5), four
in the Indian Mutiny (1857–8), one in
Canada (1866), two in the South African
War (1899–1902), one in Somaliland
(1903), seven in the Great War and one

in the Second World War. First award:
Lieutenant J. Knox, later Brevet Major
(1827–97) Alma 20 September 1854 and
Sevastopol 18 July 1855: gazetted 24
February 1857.

Memorials

Grosvenor Place, London, by John
Tweed (Great War); Winchester Cathedral.

Marches

Quick: *I'm Ninety-Five.*

Allied Regiment in 1914

6th Regiment 'The Duke of Connaught's Own Rifles', of Canada.

Journal

The Rifle Brigade Chronicle.

Museum

Peninsula Barracks, Romsey Rd,
Winchester (tel 0962 63846): open April–
September Monday–Friday 1000–1230,
1400–1630, Saturday 1430–1630;
October–March Monday–Friday 1030–
1230, 1400–1630.

Regimental Histories

Harvey, B. *The Rifle Brigade,* Leo
Cooper, 1975. Bale, W. Verner *History
and Campaigns of the Rifle Brigade* (2
vols.), 1912 and 1919. Berkeley, R., and
Seymour, W. W. *The History of the Rifle
Brigade, 1914–1919* (2 vols.), Rifle
Brigade Club, 1927 and 1936. Hastings,
R. H. W. S. *The Rifle Brigade, 1939–
1945,* Gale & Polden, 1950. Bryant, Sir
Arthur. *Jackets of Green,* Collins, 1972.

SPECIAL AIR SERVICE REGIMENT

History
Raised in 1940, disbanded in 1946, reconstituted in 1947; separate regiment in 1950. One regular battalion, two volunteer battalions (21st Artists and 23rd).
MOTTO: *Who dares wins.*
HEADQUARTERS: Centre Block, Duke of York's Headquarters, Chelsea, London.

Emblazoned Battle Honours
Second World War: North-West Europe 1944–5; Tobruk 1941; Benghazi Raid; North Africa 1940–3; Landing in Sicily; Termoli; Valli di Comacchio; Italy 1943–5; Adriatic. **Falklands War** (1982): Falkland Islands 1982.

Accredited Battle Honours
Sicily 1943; Greece 1944–5; Middle East 1943–5.

Dress
DIFFERENCES: Beige beret, blue-backed badge.
REGIMENTAL TIE: Pale blue Pegasus on dull red ground.

Marches
Quick: *Marche du Régiment Parachutiste Belge.*

Alliances
The Special Air Service Regiment, of Australia; New Zealand Special Air Service Squadron.

Journal
Mars and Minerva (twice a year – March, September).

Museum
21st SAS Regiment (Artists') Museum, B Block, Duke of York's Headquarters, Chelsea, London: closed at present.

Regimental Histories
Dadd, D. J. *SAS Operations*, Robert Hale, 1989. James, M. *Born of the Desert*, Collins, 1945. Geraghty, T. *Who Dares Wins* and *This is the SAS*, Arms & Armour Press, 1982.

ARMY AIR CORPS

History
Formed in 1942, disbanded in 1950, re-formed in 1957.
HEADQUARTERS: Army Air Corps Centre, Middle Wallop, Hampshire.

Awards
Lieutenant J. H. Grayburn (1918–44), Parachute Regiment (then part of the corps) was awarded the Victoria Cross Arnhem 17-20 September 1944: gazetted posthumously 28 December 1944. Private C. A. Duncan (1908–43), also Parachute Regiment, was awarded the George Cross M'Saken, North Africa, 10 July 1943: gazetted posthumously 9 November 1943.

Dress
CORPS TIE: Pale blue winged emblem on navy ground.

Marches
Quick: *Recce Flight.* Slow: *Thievish Magpie* and *Doge's March.*

Alliance
Australian Army Aviation Corps.

Museum
Museum of Army Flying, Army Air Corps Centre, Middle Wallop, Hampshire (tel 0264 62121 ext 421 and 428): open daily 1000–1630.

Record Office
Except officers: Higher Barracks, Exeter; officers: MS(AODO), London Rd, Stanmore, Middlesex.

ROYAL ARMY CHAPLAINS' DEPARTMENT

History
Formed in 1796 as the Army Chaplains' Department (Royal in 1919).
MOTTO: *In hoc signo vinces* (In this sign conquer).

Awards
Four members have been awarded the Victoria Cross: one in the Second Afghan
War (1878–80) and three in the Great War. First award: The Revd. J. W. Adams
(1839–1903) Killa Kazi, India, 11 December 1879: gazetted 26 August 1881.

Dress
Black and purple uniform colours.

Marches
Quick and slow: *The Trumpet Voluntary*.

Alliances
Chaplain Branch, of Canada; The Royal Australian Chaplains' Department;
Royal New Zealand Chaplains' Department.

Journal
Journal of the Royal Army Chaplains' Department (twice a year).

Associations
The Royal Army Chaplains' Department Association Fund.

Museum
Bagshot Park, Bagshot, Surrey (tel 0276 71717 ext 2845): open by appointment
Monday–Thursday 1000–1200, 1400–1600.

Department History
Smyth VC, Sir John. *In this Sign Conquer*, Mowbray, 1968.

ROYAL CORPS OF TRANSPORT

Colonel-in-Chief: HRH Princess Alice,
Duchess of Gloucester GCB CI GCVO GBE

History
Formed in 1965 from the Royal Army Service Corps.
HEADQUARTERS: Buller Barracks, Aldershot, Hampshire.

Battle Honours
Peninsular War (1808–14): Peninsula. **Hundred Days** (1815): Waterloo. **India** **Mutiny** (1857–8): Lucknow. **Second Chinese War** (1857–60): Taku Forts 1860 Pekin 1860.

Dress
DIFFERENCES: Dark blue dress cap, two white piping (RASC had three); dark blue side cap, white inside top, gold piping; blue stable belt, two white and two red stripes (corps colours). Dark blue lanyard on left shoulder (RASC had blue/yellow, mounted men white).
CORPS TIE: Diagonal blue, white, blue, white, blue, red stripes.

March
Quick: *Wait for the Wagon.*

Alliances
The Royal Australian Corps of Transport; Royal New Zealand Corps of Transport; Army Service Corps of India; Army Service Corps of Pakistan; The Sri Lanka Army Service Corps; The Malaysian Service Corps.

Affiliated Regiment
Gurkha Transport Regiment.

Journals
The Waggoner (six times a year, including two *Sporting Waggoners*); *Royal Corps of Transport Review* (once a year).

Associations
RASC/RCT Association, Buller Barracks, Aldershot, Hampshire. Benevolent Fund: RASC/RCT Association No 2 Fund.

Museums
Buller Barracks, Aldershot, Hampshire (tel 0252 24431 ext 3834 and 3857)

open Monday–Friday 0900–1200, 1400–1600. Museum of Army Transport, Beverley, North Humberside (tel 0482 860445): open daily 1000–1700.

Record Office
Except officers: Kentigern House, 65 Brown St, Glasgow; officers: MOD(A) (PB8), Government Buildings, London Rd, Stanmore, Middlesex.

Predecessor

ROYAL ARMY SERVICE CORPS

History
Raised in 1794 as the Royal Waggoners (Land Transport Corps in 1855, Military Train in 1856, Army Service Corps in 1869, Royal in 1918).

MOTTO: *Nil sine labore* (Nothing without labour).

Awards
Five members of the corps have been awarded the Victoria Cross: two in the Indian Mutiny (1857–8), one in the Zulu and Basuto War (1879) and two in the Great War. First awards: Farrier M. Murphy, later Farrier-Major (1831–93) and Private S. Morley (1839–88), Azimghur, India, 15 April 1858: gazetted 27 May 1859 and 7 August 1860. Driver J. Hughes (1916–46) was awarded the George Cross, Hong Kong 23 March 1946: gazetted posthumously 24 June 1947.

Memorials
Official Corps Memorial, Buller Barracks, Aldershot. Corps memorials going back to the Zulu and Basuto War, Church of St Michael and St George, Aldershot. Chapel windows, All Souls' Oratory, Burghclere, Hampshire, by Stanley Spencer (Great War).

March
Quick: *Wait for the Wagon*.

Museums
Buller Barracks, Aldershot, Hampshire (tel 0252 24431 ext 3834 and 3857): open Monday–Friday 0900–1200, 1400–1600. Museum of Army Transport, Beverley, North Humberside (tel 0482 860445): open daily 1000–1700.

Corps Histories
Turpin, Major-General P. *The Turn of the Wheel: The History of the RASC 1919–1939*, Barracuda, 1988. Fortescue, Sir John, and Beadon, R. H. *The Royal Army Service Corps: A History of Transport and Supply in the British Army* (2 vols.), OUP, 1930 and 1931. Massé, C. H. *The Predecessors of the Royal Army Service Corps*, Gale & Polden, 1948. *The Story of the Royal Army Service Corps 1939–1945*, Bell & Sons, 1955. Crew, G. *The Royal Army Service Corps*, Leo Cooper, 1970. Sutton, D. J. (Ed.) *The Story of the Royal Army Service Corps and Royal Corps of Transport 1945–1982*, Leo Cooper/Secker & Warburg, 1983.

ROYAL ARMY MEDICAL CORPS
Colonel-in-Chief: HM Queen Elizabeth The Queen Mother

History
Formed in 1898 from the Medical Staff and the Medical Staff Corps.
MOTTO: *In arduis fidelis* (Faithful in adversity).
HEADQUARTERS: Royal Army Medical College, Millbank, London.

Awards
Seventeen members of the corps have been awarded the Victoria Cross: one at
Rorke's Drift (1879), one at Majuba (1881), two in Burma (1889 and 1894),
four in the South African War (1899–1902), eight in the Great War and one in
the Second World War – two of these awards were to previous holders. First
award: Surgeon-Major J. H. Reynolds, later Lieutenant-Colonel (1844–1932),
Rorke's Drift 22 and 23 January 1879: gazetted 17 June 1879. Captain J. R. O.
Thompson (1911–44) was awarded the George Cross Anzio, Italy, 24 January
1944: gazetted 2 February 1945.

Memorials
Chapel windows, All Souls' Oratory, Burghclere, Hampshire, by Stanley
Spencer (Great War); RAMC Headquarters, Millbank, London.

Dress
DIFFERENCES:
CORPS TIE: Broad gold, navy and red stripes.

Marches
Quick: *Here's a Health unto His Majesty*. Slow: *Her Bright Smile Haunts me Still*.

Alliances
Medical Branch, of Canada; The Royalk Australian Army Medical Corps;
Royal New Zealand Army Medical Corps; Army Medical Corps, of Pakistan;
The Sri Lankan Army Medical Corps; Zambia Army Medical Service.

Journals
Journal of the Royal Army Medical Corps (four times a year); Army Medical
Services Magazine.

Museum
Keogh Barracks, Ash Vale, Aldershot, Hampshire (tel 0252 24431 ext Keogh
5212): open Monday–Friday 0830–1600, weekends by appointment.

Corps Histories
MacLaughlin, R. *The Royal Army Medical Corps*, Leo Cooper, 1972. Cantlie,
Sir Neil. *A History of the Army Medical Department*, Churchill Livingstone, 1974.

ROYAL ARMY ORDNANCE CORPS
Colonel-in-Chief: HM The Queen

History

Formed in 1875 from the Ordnance Department (Royal in 1918).
Motto: *Sua tela tonanti* (Thundering forth his weapons).
Headquarters: RAOC Secretariat, Blackdown Barracks, Deepcut, Camberley, Surrey.

Awards

Six members of the corps have been awarded the George Cross: two in the Second World War, two in 1946, one in 1971 and one in 1989. First awards: Lieutenant W. M. Eastman, later Brigadier (1911–80) and Captain R. L. ephson-Jones, later Brigadier (*b*1905), Malta June–November 1940: gazetted 24 December 1940.

Memorial

Junction of Frances Street and Artillery Place, Woolwich, London, by C. M. ordan and Floomans (South Africa 1899–1902).

Dress

Corps Tie: Thin red stripes on black ground.

Marches

Quick: *The Village Blacksmith.*

Alliances

The Royal Australian Army Ordnance Corps; The Royal New Zealand Ordnance Corps; Indian Army Ordnance Corps; Army Ordnance Corps, of Pakistan; The Sri Lanka Ordnance Corps; Malaysian Ordnance Corps.

Journal

The Royal Army Ordnance Corps Gazette.

Museum

Blackdown Barracks, Deepcut, Camberley, Surrey (tel 0252 24431 ext 515 and 16): open Monday–Friday 0830–1230, 1330–1630.

Corps Histories

Fernyhough, A. H. and Harris, H. E. D. *History of the Royal Army Ordnance Corps, 1920–1945,* RAOC, 1967. Forbes, A. *A History of the Army Ordnance Services* (3 vols.), Medici Society, 1929. Harris, H. E. *The First Five Hundred Years: An Outline History of the Predecessors of the Royal Army Ordnance Corps from the beginnings to 1914,* Gale & Polden, 1962.

CORPS OF ROYAL ELECTRICAL AND MECHANICAL ENGINEERS

Colonel-in-Chief: Field Marshal HRH The Prince Philip
Duke of Edinburgh KG KT OM GBE QSO

History

Formed in 1942 as the Royal Electrical and Mechanical Engineers from the Engineering Branch of the Royal Army Ordnance Corps and elements from the Corps of Royal Engineers and the Royal Army Service Corps (Corps of Royal Electrical and Mechanical Engineers in 1949).

MOTTO: *Arte et marte* (By skill and by fighting).

HEADQUARTERS: Corps Secretariat REME, Isaac Newton Rd, Arborfield, Reading, Berkshire.

Dress

DIFFERENCES: Scarlet side cap piped worsted yellow, dark blue flaps and crown piped worsted yellow, metal badge; body piped yellow, dark blue flaps and crown piped gold, embroidered gold badge for officers. Hammer and tongs badge for Staff-Sergeant to WOI – between stripes and crown for Staff-Sergeant, and above rank badge for WO. Dark blue stable belt with two pairs of adjacent gold and scarlet stripes.

CORPS TIE: Thin yellow and red diagonal stripes on dark blue ground.

Marches

Quick: *Lilliburlero* and *Auprès de ma Blonde*. Slow: *Duchess of Kent*.

Alliances

Land Electrical and Mechanical Branch, of Canada; The Royal Corps of Australian Electrical and Mechanical Engineers; The Corps of Royal New Zealand Electrical and Mechanical Engineers; The Corps of Electrical and Mechanical Engineers, of India; Pakistan Electrical and Mechanical Engineers; The Sri Lanka Electrical and Mechanical Engineers; The Malaysian Electrical and Mechanical Engineers.

Journals

The Craftsmen (monthly); *Journal of the Royal Electrical and Mechanical Engineer* (once a year).

Museum

Isaac Newton Rd, Arborfield Cross, Reading, Berkshire (tel 0734 760421 ex

2567): open Monday–Thursday 0900–1230, 1400–1630, Friday 0900–1230, 1400–1600.

Record Office
Except officers: Saffron Rd, Wigston, Leicester; officers: MS(AODO), London Rd, Stanmore, Middlesex.

Patron Saint
St Eligius – the Patron Saint of smiths and metal workers.

Corps History
Kennett, B. B., and Tatman, J. A. *Craftsmen of the Army: The Story of the Royal Electrical and Mechanical Engineers*, Leo Cooper, 1970.

CORPS OF ROYAL MILITARY POLICE
Colonel-in-Chief: HM The Queen

History
Formed in 1926 as the Corps of Military Police from the Military Mounted Police and the Military Foot Police (Royal in 1946).
MOTTO: *Exemplo ducens* (Leading by example).
HEADQUARTERS: Roussillon Barracks, Chichester, West Sussex.
CORPS TIE: Thin red with red stripes, thin navy and red stripes on navy ground.

Marches
Quick: *The Watchtower.*

Alliances
Security Branch, of Canada; The Royal Australian Corps of Military Police; Corps of Royal New Zealand Military Police; Corps of Military Police (Pakistan); The Sri Lanka Corps of Military Police; Malaysian Military Police.

Journal
Royal Military Police Journal (four times a year).

Museum
Red Cap Museum, Roussillon Barracks, Broyle Rd, Chichester, West Sussex (tel 0243 786311 ext 237): open 1 April–30 September Tuesday–Friday 1030–1230, 1330–1630, Saturday, Sunday, public holidays 1400–1800; 1 October–31 March Tuesday–Friday 1030–1230, 1330–1630; closed January.

Corps Histories
Lovell-Knight, A. V. *The Story of the Royal Military Police*, Leo Cooper, 1977. Lovell-Knight, A. V. *The History of the Office of Provost-Marshall and the Corps of Military Police*, Gale & Polden, 1943. Crozier, S. F. *The History of the Corps of Military Police*, Gale & Polden, 1951.

ROYAL ARMY PAY CORPS

History
Formed in 1920 from the Army Pay Department and the Army Pay Corps.
MOTTO: *Fide et fiducia* (Trust and be trusted).
HEADQUARTERS: Worthy Down, Winchester, Hampshire.

Dress
DIFFERENCES: Broad blue stripe, two narrow stripes of primrose yellow and white, broad maroon stripe for stable belt.
CORPS TIE: Broad navy stripe with thin primrose yellow, white and maroon stripes.

Marches
Quick: *Imperial Echoes.*

Alliances
Pay Section, Hong Kong Military Service Corps; Army Pay Corps, of Fiji.

Journal
The Royal Army Pay Corps Journal (twice a year).

Museum
Worthy Down, Winchester, Hampshire (tel 0962 880880 ext 2435): open Monday–Friday 1000–1200, 1400–1600. This museum is chiefly for recruits.

Record Office
Except officers: Higher Barracks, Exeter; officers: MS(AODO), London Rd, Stanmore, Middlesex.

ROYAL ARMY VETERINARY CORPS

History
Formed in 1906 as the Army Veterinary Corps from the Army Veterinary Department and the Army Veterinary Corps (Royal in 1918).
HEADQUARTERS: Minitary of Defence (AVR), Gallway Rd, Aldershot, Hampshire.

Dress
DIFFERENCES: Maroon side cap piped yellow, dark blue peak, maroon tip, dark blue flaps piped yellow – gold piping for officers. Dark blue stable belt, yellow maroon/yellow stripes; leather cross-belt with pouch for officers.
CORPS TIE: Maroon stripes edged both sides yellow/gold on dark blue ground

Marches
Quick: arrangement of *Drink Puppy Drink* and *A'Hunting We Will Go*. Slow *Golden Spurs*.

Alliances
Pakistan Remounts, Veterinary and Farm Corps.

Journal
Chiron Calling.

Museum
Closed for relocation.

Corps History
A History of the Royal Army Veterinary Corps (2 vols.); vol. 1 1796–1919, Sir Frederick Smith, Bailière, Tindall and Cox, 1927; vol. 2 1919–1961, J. Clabby, Allen, 1963.

SMALL ARMS SCHOOL CORPS

History
Formed in 1929 from the Small Arms School, Hythe (established in 1854) and the Machine Gun School, Netheravon (established in 1926).
HEADQUARTERS: The School of Infantry Tactics and Small Arms Wing, Warminster, Wiltshire.

Corps Day
9 September – marking formation of School of Musketry in 1854.

Dress Colours
Green and yellow (from SAS, Hythe); scarlet and dark blue (from SAS, Netheravon); Cambridge blue (no 1 dress piping).

Marches
Quick: *March of the Bowmen.*

Journal
The SASC Journal (once a year – June).

Museum
The Weapons Museum, The School of Infantry, Warminster, Wiltshire (tel 0985 214000 mil ext 2487): open by appointment.

Association
Comrades Association, School of Infantry Tactics and Small Arms Wing, Warminster, Wiltshire (tel 0985 214000 ext 2487).

Record Office
Infantry Manning and Record Office (South).

MILITARY PROVOST STAFF CORPS

History
Formed in 1901 as the Military Prison Staff Corps (Military Provost Staff Corp
in 1906).
HEADQUARTERS PM (A): Empress State Building, Lillie Rd, London.

Marches
Quick: *The Metropolitan.*

Journal
The Journal of the Military Provost Staff Corps.

Record Office
Except officers: Higher Barracks, Exeter; officers: MS(AODO), London Rd
Stanmore, Middlesex.

ROYAL ARMY EDUCATIONAL CORPS
Colonel-in-Chief: HRH The Duchess of Gloucester

History
Formed in 1920 as the Army Education Corps from the Corps of Army Schoolmasters (Royal in 1946).
HEADQUARTERS: Eltham Palace, Eltham, London.

Dress
CORPS TIE: Broad navy and dark purple stripes with thin pale sea green stripes.

Marches
Quick: *Gaudeamus Igitur* and *The Good Comrade*.

Alliances
The Royal Australian Army Educational Corps; The Royal New Zealand Army Education Corps.

Journal
The Torch (twice a year: June, December).

Museum
RAEC Centre, Wilton Park, Beaconsfield, Buckinghamshire (tel 0494 676121 ext 273): closed at present.

Record Office
Officers: MS(AODO), London Rd, Stanmore, Middlesex.

Corps History
White VC, Colonel A. C. T. *The Story of Army Education, 1643–1963*, Harrap, 1963.

ROYAL ARMY DENTAL CORPS

History
Formed in 1921 as The Army Dental Corps (Royal in 1946).
MOTTO: *Ex dentibus ensis* (From the teeth a sword).
HEADQUARTERS: Evelyn Wood's Rd, Aldershot, Hampshire.

Dress
CORPS TIE: Medium navy and olive stripes with thin red stripes.

Marches
Quick: *Green Facings*.

Alliances
The Royal Australian Army Dental Corps; The Royal New Zealand Dental
Corps.

Museum
HQ and Central Group, Evelyn Wood's Rd, Aldershot, Hampshire (tel 0252
24431 ext 2782): open Monday–Friday 1000–1200, 1400–1600.

Record Office
Officers: MS(AODO), London Rd, Stanmore, Middlesex.

ROYAL PIONEER CORPS
Colonel-in-Chief: HRH The Duke of Gloucester GCVO

History
Raised in 1939 as the Auxiliary Military Pioneer Corps (Pioneer Corps in 1940, Royal in 1946).
MOTTO: *Labor omnia vincit* (Work conquers all).
HEADQUARTERS: Simpson Barracks, Northampton, Northamptonshire.

Awards
Corporal J. P. Scully (1909–74) was awarded the George Cross, Liverpool 8 March 1941: gazetted 8 July 1941.

Dress
DIFFERENCES: Navy blue dress cap, red band and piping. Navy blue stable belt, red and green bands, badge buckle.

Marches
Quick: *Pioneer Corps.*

Journal
The Royal Pioneer (three times a year).

Museum
Simpson Barracks, Northampton, Northamptonshire (tel 0604 762742 ext 705): open Monday–Friday 0900–1230, 1400–1600.

Record Office
Except officers: Higher Barracks, Exeter; officers: MS(AODO), London Rd, Stanmore, Middlesex.

Corps History
Rhodes-Wood, E. H. *A War History of the Royal Pioneer Corps*, Gale & Polden, 1960.

INTELLIGENCE CORPS
Colonel-in-Chief: Field Marshal The Prince Philip
Duke of Edinburgh KG KT OM GBE QSO

History
Formed in 1940.
HEADQUARTERS: Templer Barracks, Ashford, Kent.

Dress
CORPS TIE: Thin red and silver stripes on green ground.

Marches
Quick: *The Rose and the Laurel*. Slow: *Trumpet Tune (and Ayre)*.

Alliances
Intelligence Branch, of Canada; The Australian Intelligence Corps.

Journal
The Rose and the Laurel (once a year – January).

Museum
Templer Barracks, Ashford, Kent (tel 0233 25251 ext 208): open Monday–
Friday 1000–1200, 1400–1600.

Record Office
Officers: MS(AODO), London Rd, Stanmore, Middlesex.

ARMY PHYSICAL TRAINING CORPS

History
Formed in 1940 from the Army Physical Training Staff (Army Gymnastic Staff 1860–1918).
HEADQUARTERS: Army School of Physical Training, Queen's Ave, Aldershot, Hampshire.

Dress
DIFFERENCES: Infantry pattern dress cap; black side cap, red piping. Red and black striped stable belt.

Marches
Quick: *Be Fit* (also known as *Even Hearts*).

Journal
Mind, Body and Spirit (once a year).

Museum
Army School of Physical Training, Queen's Ave, Aldershot, Hampshire (tel 0252 24431 ext 2131): open Monday–Friday 0900–1230, 1400–1600; weekends by appointment.

Record Office
Except officers: Higher Barracks, Exeter; officers: MS(AODO), London Rd, Stanmore, Middlesex.

Corps History
Oldfield, E. A. L. *History of the Army Physical Training Corps*, Gale & Polden, 1955.

ARMY CATERING CORPS
Colonel-in-Chief: Hon Major-General HRH The Duchess of Kent GCVO

History
Formed in 1941.
HEADQUARTERS: St Omer Barracks, Aldershot, Hampshire.

Dress
CORPS TIE: Thin silver, yellow and white stripes on black ground.

Marches
Quick: *Sugar and Spice.*

Alliance
The Australian Army Catering Corps.

Journals
Sustainer (once a year: October); *The House Journal of the Army Catering Corps.*

Record Office
Except officers: Higher Barracks, Exeter; officers: MS(AODO), London Rd, Stanmore, Middlesex.

ARMY LEGAL CORPS

History
Formed in 1978 from the Army Legal Services Staff.
MOTTO: *Justitia in armis* (Justice in arms).
HEADQUARTERS: Empress State Building, Lillie Rd, London.

Alliances
Legal Branch of Canada; The Australian Army Legal Corps.

Marches
Quick: *Scales of Justice.*

Record Office
Officers: MS(AODO), Stanmore, Middlesex.

QUEEN ALEXANDRA'S
ROYAL ARMY NURSING CORPS
Colonel-in-Chief: HRH The Princess Margaret
Countess of Snowdon CI GCVO

History
Formed in 1902 from the Army Nursing Service as Queen Alexandra's Imperial Military Nursing Service (Queen Alexandra's Royal Army Nursing Corps in 1949).
MOTTO: *Sub cruce candide* (Under the white cross).
HEADQUARTERS: The Royal Pavilion, Farnborough Rd, Aldershot, Hampshire.

Dress
DIFFERENCES: Ward dress – white cap, scarlet cape, scarlet cuffs, grey dress; No 2 dress – grey forage cap, grey jacket and skirt; Barrack dress – grey forage cap, grey skirt, white blouse, QARANC stable belt; grey beret with combat dress.

Marches
Quick: *Grey and Scarlet.*

Alliances
The Royal Australian Army Nursing Corps; The Royal New Zealand Nursing Corps.

Museum
The Royal Pavilion, Farnborough Rd, Aldershot, Hampshire (tel 0252 349301 and 349315): open Tuesday, Wednesday 0900–1230, 1400–1630, Thursday 0930–1230 and by appointment.

Association
QARANC Association and Benevolent Fund, RHQ Royal Pavilion, Farnborough Rd, Aldershot, Hampshire.

Record Office
Except officers: Queen's Park, Chester; officers: MS(AODO), London Rd, Stanmore, Middlesex.

Corps Histories
Piggott, J. *Queen Alexandra's Royal Army Nursing Corps* (2nd ed.), Leo Cooper, 1990. Hay, I. *One Hundred Years of Army Nursing*, Cassell, 1953.

WOMEN'S ROYAL ARMY CORPS
Commandant-in-Chief: HM Queen Elizabeth The Queen Mother
Controller Commandant: HRH The Duchess of Kent GCVO

History
Raised in 1938 as the Auxiliary Territorial Service (Women's Royal Army Corps in 1949).
HEADQUARTERS: Queen Elizabeth Park, Guildford, Surrey.
MOTTO: *Suaviter in modo, fortiter in re* (Gentle in manner, resolute in deed).
CORPS ANNIVERSARY: 1 February (formation of WRAC).

Dress
DIFFERENCES: Bottle green forage cap; bottle green beret. Bottle green and beech brown stable belt.

Alliances
Women's Royal Australian Corps; New Zealand Women's Royal Army Corps.

Marches
Quick: *Early One Morning* and *Lass of Richmond Hill*. Slow: *Greensleeves*. Pipe air: *The Nut Brown Maiden*.

Journal
The Lioness (twice a year).

Association
ATS and WRAC Benevolent Funds, Corps Headquarters, Queen Elizabeth Park, Guildford, Surrey.

Museum
Queen Elizabeth Park, Guildford, Surrey (tel 0252 24431 ext Guildford 8565): open Monday–Friday 0900–1600, Saturday for parties by prior arrangement only, public holidays closed.

Record Office
Except officers: Queen's Park, Chester; officers: MS(AODO), London Rd, Stanmore, Middlesex.

Corps History
Bidwell, S. *The Women's Royal Army Corps*, Leo Cooper, 1977.

THE RAISING OF THE REGIMENTS AND CORPS OF THE BRITISH A

Date	Cavalry	Infantry	Other
1660	1660 LG 1661 BLUES, ROYALS	1660 GREN GDS (1656); COLDM GDS (1650) 1661 SG (1642); QUEENS; 1662 RS (1633) 1655 BUFFS	
1670	1678 GREYS		
1680	1685 KDG; BAYS; 3DG; 4DG; 5DG; 6DG; 3H: 4H 1688 7DG;	1680 KING'S OWN. 1685 NF; KINGS; WARWICK; RF; NO SUFFOLK; LINCOLNS; DEVON; SOM LI; W YORKS; E Y 1688 LF; BEDFS HERTS; LEICESTERS; GREEN HOWARD 1689 CHESHIRE; B LAN R; RWF; SWB; KOSB	
1690	1693 8H	1690 R INN FUS 1694 GLOSTERS; WORC R.	
1700		1701 R SUSSEX; DORSET 1702 SURREYS; BORDER; DCLI; DWR; R HAMPS; S STA	
1710	1715 9L; 10H; 11H; 12L; 13H; 14H	1717 S LAN R 1719 WELCH	1716 RA;
1720			
1730		1739 BW	
1740		1740 LOYALS 1741 NORTHAMPTONS; ESSEX; FORESTERS; OXF BUC 1744 R BERKS	
1750	1759 15H; 16L; 17L; 18H; 19H; 20H; 21L	1755 KOYLI; MX; KSLI; KRRC 1756 RWK; DLI; N STAFFS; WILTS 1757 MANCH	
1760			
1770		1777 HLI 1778 SEAFORTH	
1780		1787 GORDONS	
1790		1793 RUR; R IR F; CAMERONS 1794 A and SH	1793 RH/ 1794 RAS 1796 RAC
1800		1800 RB	
1810		1815 2GR 1817 6GR.	
1820			

THE WARS AND CAMPAIGNS OF THE BRITISH ARMY

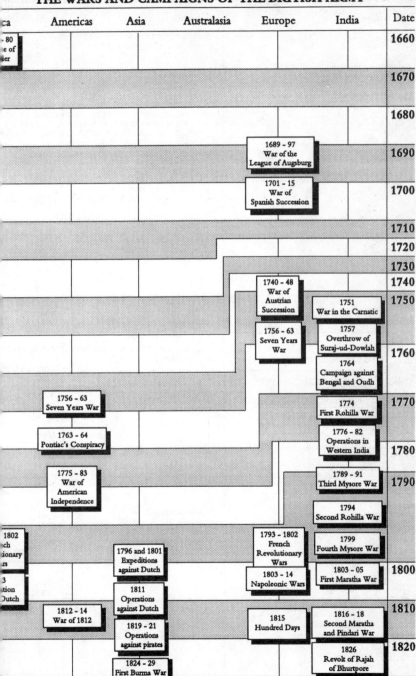

...ca	Americas	Asia	Australasia	Europe	India	Date
- 80 e of ier						1660
						1670
						1680
				1689 – 97 War of the League of Augsburg		1690
				1701 – 15 War of Spanish Succession		1700
						1710
						1720
						1730
				1740 – 48 War of Austrian Succession		1740
					1751 War in the Carnatic	1750
				1756 – 63 Seven Years War	1757 Overthrow of Suraj-ud-Dowlah	
					1764 Campaign against Bengal and Oudh	1760
	1756 – 63 Seven Years War				1774 First Rohilla War	1770
	1763 – 64 Pontiac's Conspiracy				1776 – 82 Operations in Western India	1780
	1775 – 83 War of American Independence				1789 – 91 Third Mysore War	1790
					1794 Second Rohilla War	
1802 ch ionary rs		1796 and 1801 Expeditions against Dutch		1793 – 1802 French Revolutionary Wars	1799 Fourth Mysore War	
3 tion Dutch		1811 Operations against Dutch		1803 – 14 Napoleonic Wars	1803 – 05 First Maratha War	1800
	1812 – 14 War of 1812	1819 – 21 Operations against pirates		1815 Hundred Days	1816 – 18 Second Maratha and Pindari War	1810
		1824 – 29 First Burma War			1826 Revolt of Rajah of Bhurtpore	1820

THE RAISING OF THE REGIMENTS AND CORPS OF THE BRITISH A

Date	Cavalry	Infantry	Other units
1830			
1840			
1850			
1860		1867 10GR	
1870			1875 RAOC
1880		1881 INFANTRY AMALGAMATIONS	
1890			1898 RAMC
1900		1901 IG 1902 7GR	1901 MPSC 1902 QARANC 1906 RAVC
1910	1917 RTR	1915 WG	
1920	1922 CAVALRY AMALGAMATIONS		1920 R SIGNALS RAPC; RABC 1921 RADC 1926 RMP
1930			1929 SASC 1938 WRAC 1939 RPC
1940		1942 PARA; AAC 1947 SAS	1940 INT CORP 1942 REME 1948 QGE
1950			1950 QG SIGNA 1958 GTR
1960	1958 – 1971 CAVALRY AMALGAMATIONS	1958 – 1971 INFANTRY AMALGAMATIONS	
1970			1978 ALC
1980			
1990			

THE WARS AND CAMPAIGNS OF THE BRITISH ARMY

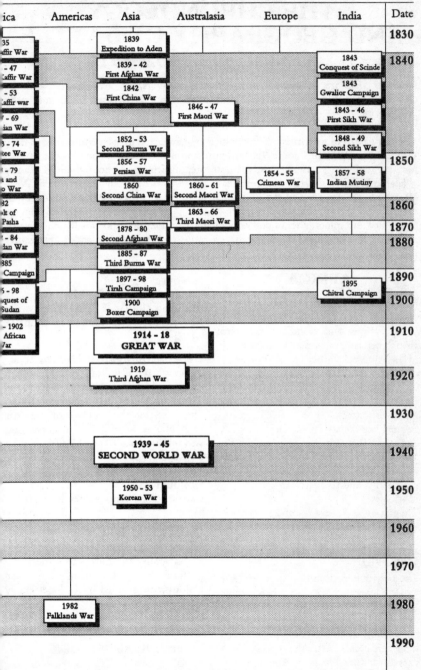

...ica	Americas	Asia	Australasia	Europe	India	Date
...35 ...affir War						1830
...- 47 ...affir War		1839 Expedition to Aden				
...- 53 ...affir war		1839 – 42 First Afghan War			1843 Conquest of Scinde	1840
...7 – 69 ...ian War		1842 First China War			1843 Gwalior Campaign	
...3 – 74 ...tee War			1846 – 47 First Maori War		1843 – 46 First Sikh War	
...t – 79 ...a and ...o War		1852 – 53 Second Burma War			1848 – 49 Second Sikh War	
...32 ...lt of ...Pasha		1856 – 57 Persian War		1854 – 55 Crimean War	1857 – 58 Indian Mutiny	1850
... – 84 ...lan War		1860 Second China War	1860 – 61 Second Maori War			1860
...885 ...Campaign		1878 – 80 Second Afghan War	1863 – 66 Third Maori War			1870 1880
...5 – 98 ...quest of ...Sudan		1885 – 87 Third Burma War				
... – 1902 ...African ...ar		1897 – 98 Tirah Campaign			1895 Chitral Campaign	1890 1900
		1900 Boxer Campaign				
		1914 – 18 GREAT WAR				1910
		1919 Third Afghan War				1920
						1930
		1939 – 45 SECOND WORLD WAR				1940
		1950 – 53 Korean War				1950
						1960
						1970
	1982 Falklands War					1980
						1990

THE CHRONOLOGY AND GEOGRAPHY OF BATTLE HONOURS, 1662–1914

Honours that are celebrated as regimental anniversaries are starred* and are described in more detail on pp 285, though some anniversaries are not battle honours.

The campaigns of the British Army before 1914 are listed here by continents. (Those earned from 1914 on, some 750 or more, would require a book to themselves because they are so numerous; furthermore, information about them is readily available in other sources, whereas those pre-1914 are not so well covered. Post-1914 honours are listed in the individual regimental entries.) After a summary of each campaign, the title of each battle honour is given, together with the number of cavalry and infantry regiments to which it was awarded and, finally, the date of award. A few honours no longer emblazoned (through disbandment or amalgamation) are in *italics*.

AFRICA

Defence of Tangier, 1662–80

After the restoration of Charles II in 1660, Tangier and Bombay came into British possession as part of the dowry of his queen, Catherine of Braganza. Although the harbour and fortifications of Tangier were much improved, the British garrison was under constant Moorish attack. For fifteen years, Samuel Pepys was Treasurer of Tangier, and was then chiefly responsible for arranging the demolition of the fortifications and the evacuation of the inhabitants and the garrison.

Honours
Tangier 1662–80 cav 1, inf 1 [1909]
Tangier 1680 inf 3 [1909]

French Revolutionary Wars, 1793–1802

The British expedition to Egypt in 1801 under General Sir Ralph Abercrombie was intended to expel the French from that country so as to safeguard British possessions in India that were believed to be threatened. After the success of the expedition, the Treaty of Amiens led to a year of peace.

Honours
Mandora (1801) inf 2 [1813, 1817]
Marabout (1801) inf 1 [1841]
Egypt 1801* (with Sphinx) cav 2, inf 31 [1802]

Expedition against Dutch, 1806

Although the Cape of Good Hope had been taken by British forces in 1795, the Treaty of Amiens had restored it to the Dutch. After the renewal of the war with Napoleon in 1803, an expedition was sent under Sir David Baird, and the Dutch surrendered two days after the British landing.

Honours
Cape of Good Hope (1806) inf 6 [1824–6]

Sixth Kaffir War, 1835

A general rising of the Kaffirs in South Africa against the European settlers was quelled by a detachment from Cape Colony commanded by Colonel Harry Smith.

Honours
South Africa 1835 inf 3 [1882]

Seventh Kaffir War, 1846–7

A rising of the Gaikwa tribe on the Natal frontier met with a sharp defeat by

a small force from Cape Colony.
HONOURS
South Africa 1846–7 cav 1, inf 7 [1882]

Eighth Kaffir War, 1851–3
A further rising of the Gaikwas was finally defeated in 1853.
HONOURS
South Africa 1851–1852–1853 cav 1, inf 9 [1882]

Abyssinian War, 1867–8
To obtain the release of a number of Englishmen and Germans held prisoners by King Theodore, an expedition was sent to Abyssinia by Sir Robert Napier, C-in-C of Bombay. Through excellent organization, the British/Indian force was able to cross 300 miles of roadless and largely unmapped country, storm the king's fortress and release the prisoners without the loss of a single man in action.
HONOURS
Abyssinia (1867–8) cav 1, inf 4 [1868]

Ashantee War, 1873–4
After an invasion of British territory on the West coast of Africa, an expeditionary force under Sir Garnet Wolseley successfully penetrated to Coomassie, the Ashantee capital, returned to the coast and re-embarked (further operations took place in 1890 and 1900).
HONOURS
Ashantee (1873–4) inf 3 [1876]

Zulu and Basuto War, 1877–9
As the Zulus bordering Natal Colony had been continually invading that territory, a campaign was embarked upon, aiming at their punishment. After the major disaster to the British force at Isandhlwana, the Zulus were defeated at Ulundi and their king later captured.
HONOURS
South Africa 1877–78–79 inf 4 [1882]
South Africa 1878–9 inf 2 [1882]
South Africa 1879 cav 2, inf 8 [1882]

Revolt of Arabi Pasha, 1882
After the Khedive Ismail, ruler of Egypt, had been deposed in favour of his son by the Sultan of Turkey, discontent in the Egyptian army led to Colonel Arabi Pasha carrying out a *coup d'état* in January 1882 and making himself minister of war. After nationalist riots in Alexandria and the bombardment of the city's forts by a British naval force, Sir Garnet Wolseley's troops destroyed Arabi's army at Tel-el-Kebir after a successful night march.
HONOURS
Tel-el-Kebir (1882) cav 6, inf 13 [1883]

First Sudan War, 1882–4
After Sudanese rebels had totally defeated the Egyptian armies commanded by Hicks Pasha and Baker Pasha, a force under General Sir Gerald Graham fought two general actions at El Teb and Tamai.
HONOURS
Egypt 1882 cav 5, inf 16 [1883]
Egypt 1882, 1884 cav 1, inf 5 [1883, 1885]
Egypt 1884 cav 1 [1885]

Egyptian Campaign, 1885
This campaign was an unsuccessful attempt to restore the authority of the Khedive of Egypt in the Sudan where the Mahdi had led a revolt and to save General Gordon who was besieged in Khartoum.
HONOURS
Abu Klea (1885) cav 1, inf 1 [1886]
Kirbekan (1885) inf 2 [1886]
Nile 1884–5 cav 1, inf 9 [1886]
Suakin 1885 cav 2, inf 1 [1886]

Reconquest of the Sudan, 1896–8
For eleven years after Tofrek, the reorganization of the Egyptian army had been carried out by British officers under the direction of Generals Sir Evelyn Wood, Grenfell and Kitchener,

and the first decisive success was achieved at Hafir in 1896. With Kitchener commanding the British/Egyptian armies, the Mahdi's forces were defeated at Atbara and then totally destroyed at Khartoum.

HONOURS

Hafir (1896) inf 1 [1899]

Atbara (1898) inf 4 [1899]

Khartoum★ (1898) cav 1, inf 8 [1899]

South African War, 1899–1902

The outbreak of war in October 1899 quickly resulted in Boer sieges of Ladysmith, Kimberley and Mafeking. After some disastrous British actions, Kimberley and Ladysmith were relieved in February and Mafeking in May 1900. There followed a long period of guerrilla warfare until conditions of Boer surrender were signed in May 1902. This was the first overseas campaign in which yeomanry and militia units took part.

HONOURS

Modder River (1899) cav 1, inf 8 [1905]

Defence of Kimberley (1900) inf 1 [1905]

Relief of Kimberley (1900) cav 9, inf 7 [1905]

Paardeburg (1900) cav 9, inf 17 [1905]

Defence of Ladysmith★ (1899–1900) cav 4, inf 8 [1905]

Relief of Ladysmith (1900) cav 3, inf 23 [1905]

South Africa 1899–1900 cav 3 [1905]

South Africa 1899–1902 cav 12, inf 51 [1905]

South Africa 1900–2 cav 5, inf 22 [1905]

South Africa 1901–2 cav 5 [1905]

South Africa 1902 cav 1 [1905]

AMERICAS
(including West Indies)

Seven Years War, 1756–63

Three seaborne brigades of the British army, commanded by General Lord Amherst, threatened landings on Cape Breton Island, but the main attack was at Freshwater Cove, about three miles from Louisburg. After a stubborn defence by the French, the landing succeeded, and next day the second brigade, commanded by Wolfe, moved round the city and seized a commanding position on the north side of the harbour: after a heavy bombardment, the French surrendered on 27 July 1758. The capture of the city then encouraged the British prime minister, William Pitt the elder, to attack Quebec: Wolfe was placed in command of a force of three brigades, which landed on an island just below Quebec on 27 June 1759. Wolfe at first made a tactical error in dividing his force, and a determined assault on the city was beaten back with heavy loss. In September, the main force was transferred to a position above Quebec and by scaling the Heights of Abraham made inevitable the fall of a city that had been considered impregnable: the French commander capitulated on 18 September after the loss of Wolfe and Montcalm. Other French colonial possessions also came under attack, and Guadaloupe was captured – for the second time – by an expeditionary force commanded until his death by Lieutenant-General Hopson and then by Major-General Barrington: the campaign had begun with desultory action, with the British troops greatly suffering from the climate, but the change in leadership led finally to the surrender of the island on 1 May. Then the island of Martinique was taken on 12 February 1762, the storming of the Moro having resulted in the capitulation of the French forces shortly afterwards. The expedition against Havannah, which ended successfully on 13 August 1762, suffered three times as many deaths from disease as from French action.

HONOURS

Louisburg (1758) inf 12 [1882]

Quebec 1759★ inf 7 [1882]

Guadaloupe 1759★ inf 8 [1909]

Martinique 1762 inf 13 [1909]

Moro 1762 inf 1 [1827]

Havannah 1762 inf 15 [1909]

Pontiac's Conspiracy, 1763–4

After the surrender of the French in Canada on 8 September 1760, the scattered forts in that country were garrisoned by British troops, but the governor-general's inept policy towards the Indians led to a revolt in 1763 under the leadership of Pontiac, an Ottawa chief. Most of the forts west of Niagara fell to Indian attacks except for Detroit and Pitt, while Ligonier and Bedford, east of Pitt, were able to repulse the attackers. Although Pontiac gained a victory at Bloody Run near Detroit, he lacked material for siege operations and was unable to keep the support of other Indian tribes. A fierce engagement was fought near Fort Pitt, but the campaign was ended by an expedition against the Delawares and Shawnees. Pontiac was murdered by another Indian in 1769.

HONOURS
North America 1763–4 inf 2 [1914]

War of American Independence, 1775–83

After the surrender of General Burgoyne's forces to the American colonists in October 1777, the French seized the opportunity of recapturing their former possessions. The small garrison on Dominica surrendered to a much larger French force on 8 September 1778, but a British and naval expedition succeeded in capturing St Lucia on 28 December 1778.

HONOURS
St Lucia 1778 inf 10 [1909]

Battle of the Saints, 1782

An army detachment acted as marines in Rodney's fleet which defeated the French under de Grasse off the island of Martinique. The detachment suffered 34 casualties.

HONOURS
Naval Crown superscribed '12th April 1782' inf 1 [1909]

French Revolutionary Wars, 1793–1802

Martinique, which had been returned to the French in 1763, was invaded in February 1794 by five British brigades commanded by General Sir Charles Grey and, after the reduction of the fortifications of Fort Royal and the seizure of Fort Louis, the French commander surrendered and the island became British for the second time – but was later restored to France by the Treaty of Amiens. On 26 March 1796, a force commanded by Sir John Moore landed on St Lucia, but the whole island did not fall into British hands until 17 May – for the third time.

HONOURS
Martinique 1794 inf 10 [1909]
St Lucia 1796 inf 2 [1825, 1836]

Napoleonic Wars, 1803–15

The capture of the island of Dominica in 1762 had been confirmed by the Treaty of Paris in 1763, retaken by the French in 1778 and restored to Britain in 1783. The Treaty of Amiens in 1802 had restored Martinique to the French but, on the resumption of the war by Napoleon, the island, which had become a port of call and refit for the privateers in the west Atlantic, was invaded by a force commanded by General Sir George Beckwith. One division landed on the west coast and the other division on the south coast: after their junction, the French governor surrendered on 4 February 1809. Guadaloupe was reduced in the following year for the fourth time: later, after Napoleon's escape from Elba in 1814, the island, which had been restored to France, declared for him and an expedition under Major-General Leith then succeeded in retaking it in 1815 with light casualties. St Lucia had been recaptured in 1803 for the fourth time.

HONOURS
St Lucia 1803 inf 2 [1818, 1821]
Dominica 1805 inf 2 [1808]
Martinique 1809 inf 9 [1816–19]
Guadaloupe 1810 inf 4 [1817–67]

Expedition against Dutch, 1804

On the resumption of hostilities with Holland after the Treaty of Amiens, a British naval and military expedition from Barbados arrived off the mouth of the River Surinam on 25 April 1804. After the refusal of the Dutch commander to surrender, three regiments and a naval brigade were landed and the colony was captured after three days with only light casualties.

HONOURS
Surinam (1804) inf 2 [1818, 1898]

Expedition against Spanish, 1807

The British expedition to South America in 1807 ended in a disastrous capitulation. Buenos Aires was captured at the start of the campaign, but Spanish reinforcements soon forced General Beresford to surrender. After the arrival of reinforcements from South Africa, Monte Video was captured, but a further advance on Buenos Aires led to the capitulation of the British forces under General Whitelock and his subsequent court-martial.

HONOURS
Monte Video (1807) inf 4 [1814–24]

War of 1812

Detroit, Queenstown and Miami were engagements in North America in which few casualties were suffered. Casualties at Niagara were heavier, however. After the successful British action at Bladensburg, north of Washington, the Capitol was burnt as a result of a house having been set on fire when shots had been fired from it after the capital had surrendered: the fire then got out of control.

HONOURS
Detroit (1812) inf 1 [1816]
Queenstown (1812) inf 2 [1816]
Miami (1813) inf 1 [1816]
Niagara (1813) cav 1, inf 7 [1815–24]
Bladensburg (1814) inf 4 [1826–1854]

ASIA
(excluding India)

Expeditions against Dutch, 1796, 1801, 1810

The alliance of the Dutch with the French at the outbreak of the revolutionary wars in 1793 gave them open ports in the Moluccas. A British naval expedition was sent to Amboyna in February 1796 and the Dutch were quickly forced to surrender. However, the Treaty of Amiens in 1802 restored Amboyna and the nearby islands to the Dutch, but they were reoccupied by the British in 1810. The island of Ternate, captured from the Dutch in 1801, was also restored in 1802 but was reoccupied in 1810. The island of Banda was occupied by the British in 1796 and 1810.

HONOURS
Amboyna (1796, 1810) inf 1 [1841]
Ternate (1801) inf 1 [1841]
Banda (1796) and 1810 inf 1 [1841]

Operations in the Persian Gulf, 1809, 1819, 1820

Small forces from India successfully attacked pirate strongholds on the Arabian coast on three occasions.

HONOURS
Arabia inf 1 [1823]

Operations against French, 1810

During the Napoleonic Wars, Bourbon (now Réunion) was a refuge for French privateers and a base for the French fleet in Eastern waters. A small British force landed on the island in 1809 and caused some destruction, but was unable to retain possession. In the following year, a stronger force captured the island.

HONOURS
Bourbon (1810) inf 2 [1823 and 1826]

Operations against Dutch, 1811

A combined force of British and Indian troops landed unopposed near the capital of Java on 4 August 1811. After a sharp encounter with French troops a week later, Fort Cornelis was captured by assault and the island was unconditionally surrendered shortly afterwards.

HONOURS
Java (1811) inf 5 [1818]

Operations against pirates, 1819–21

Strongholds of Arab pirates in the Persian Gulf were destroyed by a British and Indian expeditionary force in December 1819 after an attack by Joassma tribesmen had caused severe casualties.

HONOURS
Beni Boo Ali (1821) inf 1 [1831]

First Burma War, 1824–6

Threats from the Burmese to invade Bengal led to the invasion of Burma by four columns of British and Indian troops in 1824 and the capture of Rangoon. The subsequent campaign chiefly involved expeditions to capture stockaded positions but ended in a victory near Prome in April 1825.

HONOURS
Ava (1824–6) inf 11 [1826–41]

Expedition to Aden, 1839

The future importance of Aden as a coaling station caused the town to be occupied by a small Indian force in 1839. Two later attempts by Arabs to recapture the town were unsuccessful.

HONOURS
Aden (1839) inf 1 [1841]

First Afghan War, 1839–42

A campaign to replace the *de facto* ruler of Afghanistan with a puppet successor began with the storming of the fortress of Ghuznee on 23 July 1839 by a British and Indian force and the installation of Shah Sujah at Kabul a few days later. On the return march to India of part of the British and Indians, a strong force of Baluchis was pursued into the city of Khelat, which was stormed on 13 November 1839. Continuing Afghan hostility then led to a decision to evacuate the country: one brigade reached Jellalabad and withstood a six months' siege there, but there was only one survivor of the army that left Kabul. The honours of Ghuznee 1839, Candahar 1842 and Cabool 1842 were awarded to the forces that had advanced to Kabul to punish the Afghans and release their prisoners.

HONOURS
Affghanistan 1839 cav 2, inf 4 [1840, 1842]
Ghuznee (1839) cav 2, inf 4 [1840]
Khelat (1839) inf 2 [1840]
Jellalabad (1842) inf 1 [1842]
Candahar 1842 inf 2 [1843, 1844]
Ghuznee 1842 inf 2 [1844]
Cabool 1842 cav 1, inf 5 [1844]

First Chinese War (Opium War), 1842

After the refusal of the Chinese government to allow any further imports of opium and their destruction of stocks held in warehouses, a British and Indian force was sent from India in 1840, which occupied Chusan. Although terms were arranged with the Chinese, which included an indemnity and the cession of Hong Kong, the occupying troops suffered many deaths from the lack of suitable food and clothing. Reinforcements were sent in 1841 and, after a year's campaigning, peace was signed.

HONOURS
China (with Dragon) (1842) inf 5 [1843]

Second Burma War, 1852–3

Continued infringements by the King of Burma of the treaty that had ended the

First Burma War resulted in a second British invasion in 1852. Rangoon was captured in April 1853 and Pegu in October.

HONOURS

Pegu (1852–3) inf 5 [1853, 1855]

Persian War, 1856–7

The restoration of the Afghan city of Herat that had been taken by the Persians had been demanded by the Indian government. As this had not taken place, a British and Indian force was sent to Persia and landed without casualties at Bushire in December 1856, capturing the fortifications of the city of Reshire two days later. The battle of Koosh-ab ended the campaign in February 1857.

HONOURS

Reshire (1856) inf 2 [1859, 1861]
Bushire (1856) inf 2 [1859, 1861]
Koosh-ab (1857) inf 3 [1859, 1861]
Persia (1856–7) cav 1, inf 3 [1859, 1861]

Second China War, 1857–60

The treaty which the Chinese government had entered into after the war of 1842 had not been fully observed, so a British expeditionary force was sent to seize Canton in 1858. After the end of the Indian Mutiny, reinforcements captured the Taku Forts on the River Peiho and later entered Pekin.

HONOURS

Canton (1860) inf 1 [1861]
Taku Forts (1860) cav 1, inf 7 [1861]
Pekin 1860 cav 1, inf 5 [1861]

Second Afghan War, 1878–80

After the Russo-Turkish war of 1877, both nations sent missions to Kabul to encourage the Amir of Afghanistan to break his treaty with the Indian government. After an ultimatum from the English Cabinet, the British and Indian armies crossed the Afghan frontier on 21 November 1878. Three columns took part in the invasion – the Peshawar Valley and the Kuram Valley Field Forces and two divisions of the Kanda-

har and Kabul Field Forces. The Peshawar troops advanced on Ali Masjid, a hill fortress at the Afghan entrance of the Khyber Pass, but during the night the Afghans evacuated the fort which was taken with few casualties. The Kuram Valley troops captured the Peiwar Kotal on 2 December 1879 after stubborn resistance. The Kandahar troops occupied strategic positions in the country but, on the death of the Amir Shere Ali in the spring of 1879, his successor concluded a fresh treaty with the Indian government establishing a British envoy at Kabul: however, the members of the mission were attacked and killed on 3 September. Major-General Sir Frederick Roberts then moved on Kabul and dispersed the Afghan army at Charasiah on 6 October. After the entry into Kabul, the army was practically besieged in Sherpur, but successfully repelled an assault by a large Afghan force. Then a column under Sir Donald Stuart which had left Kandahar was attacked by a strong Afghan body near Ghuznee. After the disaster of Maiwand and an unsuccessful sortie by the besieged troops in Kandahar, Roberts' Kabul-Kandahar force, marching 313 miles in 20 days, totally defeated the Afghan army at Kandahar on 1 September 1880.

HONOURS

Ali Masjid (1878) cav 1, inf 4 [1884]
Peiwar Kotal (1878) inf 2 [1881]
Charasiah (1879) cav 1, inf 3 [1881]
Kabul 1879 cav 1, inf 4 [1881]
Ahmed Khel (1880) inf 2 [1881]
Kandahar 1880 cav 1, inf 5 [1881]
Afghanistan 1878–9 cav 1, inf 4 [1881]
Afghanistan 1878–80 cav 2, inf 10 [1881]
Afghanistan 1879–80 cav 2, inf 10 [1881]

Third Burma War, 1885–7

The high-handed treatment of British interests by the King of Burma finally resulted in a declaration of war in October 1885. A combined British and Indian naval and military force advanced rapidly towards Mandalay, and the king

then surrendered unconditionally. However, for the next two years a much larger force had to be maintained in suppressing dacoitry.
HONOURS
Burma 1885–7 inf 10 [1890]

Tirah Campaign, 1897–8

This hard-fought campaign against the Afridis in the mountains west of Peshawar on the Indian NW frontier began with the storming of the Dargai heights in October 1897, followed by a ceaseless war by the Afridi tribesmen against convoys and survey parties. The country was occupied until the middle of December 1897, but peace was not signed until April 1898.
HONOURS
Tirah (1897–8) inf 9 [1899]

Boxer Rising, 1900

An eight-weeks' siege of the European embassies in Pekin by Chinese opposed to Christians and to the ruling dynasty in China was raised by a force of 2,000 seamen and marines from European fleets. This force had to make a stand at Tientsin, but further reinforcements relieved the embassies.
HONOURS
Pekin 1900 inf 1 [1902]

AUSTRALASIA

Maori Wars, 1846–7, 1860–1, 1863–6

The treaty of Waitangi in 1840 had guaranteed the Maoris possession of their lands, forestries and fisheries. Subsequent dissatisfaction with the New Zealand government over the sale of Maori lands had the sympathy of a strong party in the colony, but it was decided that peace had to be restored before any negotiations could take place. The Maori stockades were found to be almost impossible to capture without artillery bombardment, and three sep-

arate campaigns had to be fought between 1846 and 1866. Opposition to the interpretation of the treaty remains to this day.
HONOURS
New Zealand (1846–7) inf 3 [1870]
New Zealand (1860–1) inf 5 [1870]
New Zealand (1863–6) inf 7 [1870]

EUROPE

War of the League of Augsburg, 1689–97

After a three-days' siege of the French fortress of Namur in Flanders, William III ordered an attack on 3 July 1689, followed later by an assault on the walls and finally the capture of the citadel. British casualties were nearly 4,000.
HONOURS
Namur 1695 inf 14 [1910]

War of Spanish Succession, 1701–15

A British fleet carrying infantry as marines silenced the Spanish batteries on Gibraltar on 23 July 1704. The troops were then landed, and were reinforced in December. The besieging French and Spanish forces from the land side made a determined assault on 7 February 1705, but were repulsed with heavy casualties and finally abandoned the siege. The British/Dutch/German armies in this war against the French were commanded by the Duke of Marlborough, four of whose victories were granted as battle honours. The first was Blenheim, on 2 August 1704, where more than 11,000 prisoners were taken. Two years later, on 12 May 1706 at Ramillies the cavalry turned the victory into a rout, the six British regiments taking 50 guns, 80 stand of colours and 2,000 prisoners. Two years later again, on 30 June 1708, a third victory was won at Oudenarde, against a larger French force. Finally, on 1 September 1709, the formidable French entrenchments at Malplaquet were overcome.

HONOURS

Gibraltar 1704–5 (Capture-Defence) inf 8 [1909]

Blenheim (1704)★ cav 7, inf 13 [1882]

Ramillies (1706) cav 7, inf 15 [1882]

Oudenarde (1708) cav 7, inf 14 [1882]

Malplaquet (1709) cav 7, inf 15 [1882]

War of Austrian Succession, 1740–8

The allies of the British at Dettingen were Austrian and Hanoverian troops, but the brunt of the fighting on 27 June 1743 fell on the British, who suffered more than 800 casualties.

HONOURS

Dettingen (1743)★ cav 11, inf 15 (1882)

Seven Years War, 1756–63

Although the British were still the opponents of the French, their allies in the Seven Years War were the armies of Frederick the Great of Prussia. The Allied victory at Minden on 1 August 1759 resulted from the steadiness of the British infantry, the cavalry present not taking part. Nearly a year later, at Emsdorff, a French division was defeated by the gallantry of a British cavalry regiment. Another engagement where the role of cavalry was of importance was at Warburg, on 31 July 1760: although the British infantry suffered more than twice the casualties of the cavalry and bore the brunt of the battle, only the cavalry regiments that took part received the honour. The next year, a combined British naval and military expedition landed on the French island of Belleisle where, after a sharp reverse, additional troops caused the Governor to surrender in June 1761. The last battle in the war to be granted as an honour was fought at Wilhelmstahl on 24 June 1762.

HONOURS

Minden (1759)★ inf 6 [1801]

Emsdorff (1760) cav 1 [1768]

Warburg (1760) cav 12 [1909]

Belleisle (1761) inf 8 [1951]

Wilhelmstahl (1762) inf 1 [1836]

War of American Independence, 1775–83

France and Spain declared war on Britain in 1778 and 1779 in an attempt to recapture their losses of Minorca and Gibraltar. The garrison of Gibraltar had been much strengthened by General Eliott, however. Although a close blockade was maintained by the Spanish, Rodney was able to reinforce the garrison and supply a year's stores. In April 1781, the blockade became a siege from the land side with a heavy bombardment lasting until November. On 27 November, an attack on the Spanish destroyed their batteries, but in May 1782 French reinforcements continued the siege vigorously. Floating batteries convoyed by a large fleet entered the bay in September and opened a fresh bombardment. The garrison still resisted strongly until peace was signed in February 1783.

HONOURS

Gibraltar 1779–83 inf 4 [1784]

Gibraltar 1780–3 inf 1 [1908]

French Revolutionary Wars, 1793–1802

In an early action, three Guards regiments stormed French redoubts at Lincelles on 18 August 1793. Nieuport was defended in October for ten days by 1,300 British and Hessian troops against 12,000 French. At Villers en Cauchie on 24 April 1794, two British squadrons in company with Austrian hussars overthrew a much superior body of French. Two days later, eight cavalry regiments, again with Austrian hussars, attacked 20,000 French infantry, taking 41 guns and 750 prisoners. A fortnight later at Willems, ten cavalry regiments again broke the French infantry formations. Three infantry regiments turned the balance at Tournay on 22 May. In 1799, a division was sent to the Low Countries to co-operate with the Russians, and a severe defeat was inflicted on the French at Egmont op Zee on 2 October. Naval actions in which British troops took part included the Glorious First of June in 1794, St Vincent on 14 February 1797 and Copenhagen on 2 April 1801.

HONOURS

Lincelles (1793) inf 3 [1811]
Nieuport (1793) inf 1 [1825]
Villers en Cauchies (1794) cav 1 [1817]
Beaumont (1794) cav 8 [1909]
Willems (1794) cav 11 [1909]
Tournay (1794) inf 3 [1825–36]
Naval Crown superscribed '1st June 1794' inf 2 [1909]
St Vincent (1797) inf 1 [1891]
Egmont op Zee (1799) cav 1, inf 8 [1814–1913]
Copenhagen (1801) inf 2 [1819, 1821]
Naval Crown superscribed '2nd April 1801' inf 2 [1951]

Napoleonic Wars, 1803–15

The battle of Maida in Italy on 4 July 1806 was a gallant action of seven infantry regiments commanded by General Stuart against a superior French force, after which Spain and Portugal became the chief British theatre of war.

Peninsular War, 1808–14

In the opening battle of Rolica, about 13,000 British troops commanded by Lieutenant-General Sir Arthur Wellesley opposed about half that number of French on 17 August 1808. Four days later, a second defeat was inflicted on the French at Vimiera. The Convention of Cintra, which allowed the French to evacuate Portugal, caused the recall of Wellesley and two other generals to England, so that Sir John Moore took over the command in Spain: a British cavalry regiment routed a much larger body of French at Sahagun on 21 December 1808, and most of the British army were evacuated by sea after the

battle of Corunna on 16 January 1809. After Moore's death, Wellesley was appointed to command the troops in Portugal and, between 10 and 12 May, after crossing the River Douro, drove Marshal Soult's forces out of Oporto. A few weeks later, 20,000 British and Spanish troops crossed the frontier and inflicted heavy casualties on Marshal Victor's forces at Talavera, but had to retire the next day. Wellesley (now Lord Wellington) realized his forces could not face the French reinforcements that were being sent to Spain and retired again to Portugal to construct the defensive lines of Torres Vedras. On 27 September 1810, Wellesley stopped Massena's advance at Busaco, and then retired to Torres Vedras for the winter. The Spanish garrison at Cadiz were supported by a division of British troops under Graham that attacked Marshal Victor's forces at Barrosa on 4 March 1811 in the same month, Massena retired into Spain.

HONOURS

Maida (1806) inf 7 [1807, 1808]
Rolica (1808) inf 14 [1812–33]
Vimiera (1808) cav 1, inf 19 [1812–90]
Sahagun (1808)★ cav 1 [1832]
Corunna (1809)★ inf 29 [1812–1908]
Douro (1809) cav 1, inf 3 [1813–57]
Talavera (1809)★ cav 4, inf 17 [1812–24]
Busaco (1810) inf 17 [1817–1910]
Barrosa (1811)★ inf 7 [1811–17]

After a hard winter blockading the lines of Torres Vedras in Portugal, Massena's army withdrew into Spain, closely followed by Wellington's troops. To relieve the besieged garrison of Ciudad Rodrigo, Wellington fought the action of Fuentes d'Onor 3–5 May 1811, which is particularly remembered for the gallantry of Captain Ramsay's RHA troop. Ten days after Massena's defeat, General Beresford repelled a determined attack by Soult's forces at Albuhera. British casualties were 3,500 from 8,000 engaged and the French lost about 8,000.

There followed a sharp engagement at Almaraz with General Hill commanding British/Portuguese forces, resulting in the capture of 18 guns and a standard. Then two brigades of infantry and one brigade of cavalry drove the French out of the town of Arroyo dos Molinos on 28 November 1811, taking more than 1,000 prisoners at the cost of 65 casualties. The fortress of Tarifa was then gallantly defended by three infantry regiments in December 1811, and a month later heavy casualties were suffered by British troops during the siege and capture of the fortress of Ciudad Rodrigo. In 1811, an attempt to seize the fortress of Badajos had failed with heavy losses, and the siege and assault in March and April 1812 resulted in even greater losses, chiefly through the lack of British heavy guns and howitzers. Then the defeat of the French forces at Salamanca on 22 July 1812 opened the road to Madrid: though the seventy British casualties were little more than half of those of the French. The victory of Vittoria on 21 June 1813 marked the beginning of the end of French occupation of the Spanish peninsula. Almost all the French artillery was taken and very large quantities of booty, a good proportion of which remained in the hands of the British troops. Next, there was hard fighting over three days in the Pyrenees from 28 July to 2 August with heavy casualties on both sides. After Vittoria, the fortress of San Sebastian was besieged by two infantry divisions, but two months passed before it fell with heavy casualties, since the British forces were ill-equipped with material for a siege, and their losses were very severe. The delay in the capture of the fortresses of San Sebastian and Pampeluna had given Soult time to build three strongly entrenched positions. Nivelle was taken on 13 November 1813: the entrenched position at Nive was Soult's last stand before he was driven across the Spanish frontier, after a gallant defence lasting four days in December 1813. Orthes was the first battle fought by Wellington on French soil, resulting in heavy British casualties. The last action of the Peninsular War was fought at Toulouse before news of Napoleon's abdication had been received: the heaviest British casualties were suffered by the Black Watch and by the Cameron Highlanders.

HONOURS

Fuentes d'Onor (1811) cav 3, inf 17 [1817–1910]

Albuhera (1811)* cav 3, inf 12 [1816–90]

Arroyo dos Molinos (1811)* inf 1 [1845

Tarifa (1811) inf 2 [1812, 1816]

Ciudad Rodrigo (1812) inf 11 [1817–21]

Badajos (1812) inf 20 [1817–31]

Almaraz (1812) inf 3 [1815–30]

Salamanca (1812)* cav 7, inf 35 [1816–1951]

Vittoria (1813) cav 8, inf 41 [1817–90]

Pyrenees (1813) cav 1, inf 38 [1817–1910]

San Sebastian (1813) inf 6 [1817–23]

Nivelle (1813) inf 27 [1817–24]

Nive (1813) cav 1, inf 34 [1817–1910]

Orthes (1814) cav 3, inf 37 [1817–93]

Toulouse (1814) cav 4, inf 27 [1816–90]

Peninsula (1808–14) cav 20, inf 66 [1815]

Hundred Days

The victory at Waterloo on 18 June 1815 is generally considered as one of the three most glorious victories won by British troops. It is described in some detail as a regimental anniversary on pp 298.

HONOURS

Waterloo (1815)* cav 15, inf 23 [1815]

Crimean War, 1854–5

The Crimean War, unnecessary as it was, was chiefly remarkable for the general mismanagement of the campaign and for the complete breakdown of the supply of necessaries such as food, shelter and clothing. Florence Nightingale stated that 16,000 of the 25,000

British dead were lost by bad adminis-
ration: she brought the Scutari hos-
pitals' death rate down from 42 per cent
to 2.2 per cent. At the Alma, the strong
natural positions of the Russians had not
been strengthened and, after three
hours' fighting in which the British
troops had many casualties from artil-
ery fire, the Russians were forced to
retreat. Then at Balaclava, the aim of the
Russian forces was to cut the British
ines of communications from the port
of Balaclava. The 93rd Foot, later the
2nd Battalion of the Argyll and Suther-
and Highlanders, withstood the Russian
attack: the Heavy Brigade of cavalry
also beat off a Russian attack, but the
Light Brigade, through mistaken
orders, carried out a disastrous attack
immortalized in Tennyson's poem.
nkerman is called the 'soldiers' battle':
he bravery of the Russian troops is still
remembered. Then all regiments that
had landed in the Crimea before 8
September 1855 were awarded the battle
honour of Sevastopol.

HONOURS
Alma (1854)★ cav 5, inf 29 [1855]
Balaklava (1854)★ cav 10, inf 1 [1855]
nkerman (1854)★ cav 5, inf 27 [1855]
Sevastapol (1854–5)★ cav 14, inf 49
1855]

INDIA

War in the Carnatic, 1751
While the French were besieging East
ndia Company forces in Trichinopoly,
Robert Clive persuaded the Governor of
Madras, which was one of the company's three chief centres in India, to
march on Arcot, the political capital of
he Carnatic. Clive's force of 200 British
nd 300 Indian troops entered a half-
uined fort that dominated the city,
epaired the defences, withstood a siege
or fifty days and then beat off the
ttackers.
HONOURS
Arcot (1751) inf 1 [1841]

Overthrow of Suraj-ud-Dowlah, 1757
After Calcutta had fallen to Suraj-ud-
Dowlah, the ruler of Bengal, Bihar and
Orissa, in 1757, a force of 1,000 British
and 1,500 Indian troops, under Admiral
Watson and Robert Clive, was sent to
relieve Calcutta and, after capturing the
French fortress of Chandernagore, with
some reinforcements joined battle with
Suraj-ud-Dowlah's army of some
50,000 at Plassey on 23 June. Although
the company's forces were outnumbered nearly 30 to 1, the result was
an overwhelming victory at the cost of
72 company casualties.
HONOURS
Plassey (1757) inf 4 [1835]

Expedition to Northern Circars, 1758
After the British forts of Cuddalore and
St David in Madras had been captured
by the French, a small British and Indian
force led by Major Forde defeated the
French troops near the mouth of the
River Godavery.
HONOURS
Condore (1758) inf 2 [1841, 1894]

War in the Carnatic, 1759
Following the victory at Condore, the
fortress of Masulipatam was stormed by
a force led by Forde.
HONOURS
Masulipatam (1759) inf 1 [1894]

Defeat of the Dutch, 1759
Dutch trrops that had landed from a fleet
in the Hoogly river were totally defeated
by Forde's troops. This ended Dutch
ambitions in India.
HONOURS
Badara (1759) inf 1 [1894]

Seven Years War, 1756–63
The army of Hyder Ali with its French
allies led by Lally was engaged and
vanquished by a combined force of

British and Indian troops commanded by Eyre Coote. Pondicherry then surrendered after four months' siege. The restitution of the city on the conclusion of peace in 1763 led to its reduction in 1778 on the renewal of war with France and again in 1793.

HONOURS

Wandiwash (1760) inf 1 [1841]

Pondicherry (1761) inf 1 [1841]

Campaigns against Nawabs of Bengal and Oudh, 1764

A British and Indian force of about 11,000 commanded by Sir Hector Munro defeated the army of Mir Kasim, the deposed Nawab of Begal, numbering more than 45,000.

HONOURS

Buxar (1764) inf 2 [1829, 1844]

First Rohilla War, 1774

The campaign of 1774 by a Bengal army force commanded by Colonel Champion was against the Mahrattas and in defence of the King of Oudh, a British ally. The principal battle took place near Bareilly on 23 April and resulted in the capture of immense booty.

HONOURS

Rohilcund 1774 inf 1 [1894]

Operations in Western India, 1776–82

In 1778, a Bengal army force was sent to the help of the Bombay presidency, crossing India from east to west. Under the command of General Goddard, the army was constantly engaged, but with reinforcements from Madras the provinces of Guzerat and the Concan were finally reduced. In the Carnatic, the renewal of the war with France in 1788 led to three years of operations against Hyder Ali, the ruler of Mysore.

HONOURS

Guzerat (1778, 1782) inf 2 [1829, 1845]

Carnatic (1780–84, 1790–2) inf 3 [1889]

Second Mysore War, 1781–3

On 27 September 1781, Sir Eyre Coote' forces heavily defeated Hyder Ali' army at Sholinghur, although out numbered nearly 7 to 1. Then, after disaster to a column led by General Matthews, the Commander-in-Chief i Bombay, a force of about 1,800 me was besieged in the port of Mangalor by nearly 69,000 troops of Tippo Sultan, the son of Hyder Ali, from May 1783. Although news of the peac between France and England had arrive on 27 July, the siege continued until 3 January 1784, when the garrison had t surrender.

HONOURS

Sholinghur (1781) inf 3 [1841, 1889]

Mangalore (1783) inf 1 [1796]

Third Mysore War, 1789–91

The siege of Nundy Droog, a fortress north of Bangalore that had been considered impregnable, began in September 1791 and was carried by the assaul of Cornwallis's troops. The fall o Tippo Sultan's stronghold of Seringapatam on 7 February ended the war tha had begun with Tippoo's invasion o Travancore.

HONOURS

Nundy Droog (1791) inf 1 [1841]

Mysore (1789–91) cav 1, inf 9 [1889]

Second Rohilla War, 1794

A rising in the independent state o Rampur was suppressed by a force lec by Lord Cornwallis.

HONOURS

Rohilcund 1794 inf 1 [1894]

Fourth Mysore War, 1799

A further campaign against Tippo Sultan in 1799 began with a success a Seedaseer for a Bombay column of thre brigades commanded by Major-Genera Stuart. Then, after three weeks' siege the fortress of Seringapatam was captured on 4 May.

HONOURS

Seringapatam (1799) cav 1, inf 8 [1818, 1822]

India, 1796–1825

The wars and campaigns of British troops over a thirty-year period involved many battles and sieges. Some of these are now forgotten, but they include Kalunga, Hattrass, Chumar, Kamounah, Sattimungulum, Cannanore, Dindigul, Porto Novo, Quilon, Rygur and Kariah. Although no honours were awarded for any of these, these general honours may be taken as commemorating many hard-fought actions.

HONOURS

India (1797–1809) inf 1 [1836]

India (1796–1819) inf 1 [1826]

India (1799–1819) inf 1 [1823]

India (1805–25) inf 1 [1826]

India (with Royal Tiger) (1791–1831) inf 3 [1807–38]

Hindoostan (1780–1822) cav 1, inf 4 [1821–37]

Hindoostan (with Royal Tiger) (1804–23) inf 1 [1825]

Hindoostan (with Elephant and Howdah) (various dates) inf 1 [1806]

First Maratha War, 1803–5

The campaign against the forces of Maharajah Scindia was led by Lord Lake, the Commander-in-Chief in India. His main army took the fortress of Ally Ghur by storm on 3 September 1803 and then fought the action of Delhi on 11 September. Twelve days later, the division commanded by Sir Arthur Wellesley took part in the stubbornly contested battle of Assaye, followed by Lord Lake's army's complete victory at Leswarree on 1 November. Finally, Holkar's city of Deig was stormed on 23 December.

HONOURS

Ally Ghur (1803) inf 1 [1886]

Delhi 1803 inf 1 [1886]

Assaye (1803)★ cav 1, inf 2 [1807]

Leswarree (1803) cav 1, inf 1 [1825, 1886]

Deig (1804) inf 2 [1829, 1886]

Second Maratha and Pindari War, 1816–18

The first battle in this campaign involved a detachment of British and Indian troops commanded by Colonel Burr which was attacked at Kirkee on 5 November 1817 by the army of the Peishwa, chief of the Maratha Confederacy, the result being a serious check to the Peishwa. After actions at Poona and Seetabuldee, the Maratha forces were defeated at Nagpore on 16 December. The only general action of the Marquess of Hastings' main army was at Maheidpoor, where Holkar's forces were totally defeated on 22 December.

HONOURS

Kirkee (1817) inf 1 [1823]

Nagpore (1817) inf 1 [1823]

Maheidpoor (1817) inf 2 [1819, 1823]

Revolt of Rajah of Bhurtpore, 1826

The siege and unsuccessful assaults on the fortress of Bhurtpore in 1804 by a force commanded by Lord Lake had resulted in nearly 3,000 casualties. In 1826, Lord Combermere's army besieged the fortress for two weeks and then succeeded in an assault against a stubborn defence.

HONOURS

Bhurtpore (1826) cav 2, inf 3 [1826]

Conquest of Scinde, 1843

The reverses of the British army during the First Afghan War had encouraged the Amirs of Scinde to violate their treaty. After they had attacked the residency in Hyderabad, a small force led by Sir Charles Napier defeated the Baluchis at Meeanee, a few miles from the city. A second successful action resulted in the annexation of Scinde.

HONOURS
Meeanee (1843)★ inf 1 [1844]
Hyderabad (1843) inf 1 [1844]
Scinde (1843) inf 1 [1843]

Gwalior Campaign, 1843

Two general actions were fought on 29 December in this campaign. General Sir Hugh Gough's army defeated the Marathas after very determined resistance, and General Sir George Grey's forces were successful against another division of the Gwalior army.
HONOURS
Maharajpore (1843) cav 1, inf 2 [1844]
Punniar (1843) cav 1, inf 2 [1844]

First Sikh War, 1845-6

British frontiers in north-west India had been extended to those of the Sikh monarchy, but after the death of Ranjit Singh the Sikh army crossed the boundary River Sutlej, considered an act of war. The first action was at Moodkee on 18 December 1845, where the Ludhiana and Umballa divisions under Sir Hugh Gough succeeded against the resolute Sikhs. Three days later, at Ferozeshah, severe casualties were suffered by both sides, after which the Sikhs withdrew over the frontier. In January 1846, the Sikhs again crossed the Sutlej but were routed at Aliwal. The final action of the campaign was at Sobraon, a very costly victory for the British.
HONOURS
Moodkee (1845) cav 1, inf 4 [1847]
Ferozeshah (1845)★ cav 1, inf 7 [1847]
Aliwal (1846)★ cav 1, inf 3 [1847]
Sobraon (1846)★ cav 3, inf 9 [1847]

Second Sikh War, 1848-9

Although the administration of the Sikh kingdom had been entrusted to a council of regency by the peace treaty after Sobraon, unrest continued and the British prepared to conquer the Punjab. Under orders from the Governor-General, Lord Gough attacked the strongly entrenched position of Chillianwallah on 13 January 1849. The Sikhs fell back during the night, but Gough's army had suffered nearly 2,400 casualties. The siege of Mooltan had begun in September 1848, but the Sikh commander surrendered on 22 January 1849 before the final assault. The final action of the campaign was at Goojerat on 21 February, a total victory being won by Gough's army.
HONOURS
Mooltan (1848) inf 4 [1852, 1853]
Chillianwallah (1849) cav 3, inf 4 [1852, 1853]
Goojerat (1849) cav 3, inf 9 [1852, 1853]
Punjaub (1848-9) cav 3, inf 10 [1852, 1853]

Indian Mutiny, 1857-8

News of an outbreak of mutiny at Meerut reached the Commander-in-Chief at Simla on 12 May 1857. After some delay, the available troops moved on Delhi, which was in mutineers' hands, and after three months' siege the city was taken by storm with heavy casualties on 14 September. The operations at the siege of Lucknow from May 1857 to March 1858 involved, in succession, the defence of the residency, the reinforcement of the garrison, the relief and the withdrawal of women and children, and the siege and capture of the city. The final stage of putting down the mutiny involved a number of independent columns in Central India.
HONOURS
Delhi 1857★ cav 2, inf 7 [1863]
Lucknow (For Defence) (1857) inf 7 [1863]
Lucknow (For Relief) (1857) cav 1, inf 8 [1863]
Lucknow (For Capture) (1858) cav 3, inf 17 [1863]
Central India (1857-8) cav 4, inf 9 [1863, 1879]

Chitral Campaign, 1895

The siege of a small British and Indian force at Chitral, which had lasted for seven weeks, was raised by an Indian ioneer regiment commanded by Colonel Kelly, after a forced march of 00 miles. Tribes which had tried to bar he advance of the main force of three brigades under General Sir Robert Low were then easily dispersed.

HONOURS

Chitral (1895) inf 7 [1897]

THE COUNTY REGIMENTS, 1751–1958

COUNTY AFFILIATIONS 1751–1881

The 3rd (East Kent – The Buffs) Regiment of Foot	1772
5th, or Northumberland, Regiment of Foot	1782
6th (1st Warwickshire) Regiment	1782
9th (East Norfolk) Regiment of Foot	1782
10th, or North Lincolnshire, Regiment	1782
11th, or North Devonshire, Regiment	1782
12th, or East Suffolk, Regiment	1782
13th, or First Somersetshire, Regiment	1782
14th, or Bedfordshire, Regiment	1782
15th, or York, East Riding, Regiment	1782
16th, or Bedfordshire, Regiment	1809
17th, or Leicestershire, Regiment	1782
19th, or 1st Yorkshire, North Riding, Regiment	1782
20th, or East Devonshire, Regiment	1782
22nd, or the Cheshire, Regiment	1782
23rd Regiment of Foot or the Royal Welch Fusiliers	1751
24th, or 2nd Warwickshire, Regiment	1782
25th, or Sussex, Regiment	1782
27th, or Enniskillen, Regiment	1751
28th, or North Gloucestershire, Regiment	1782
29th, or Worcestershire, Regiment	1782
30th, or Cambridgeshire, Regiment	178
31st. or Huntingdonshire, Regiment	178
32nd, or Cornwall, Regiment	178
33rd, or 1st Yorkshire, West Riding, Regiment	178
34th, or Cumberland, Regiment	178
35th, or Sussex, Regiment	180
36th, or Herefordshire, Regiment	178
37th, or North Hampshire, Regiment	178
38th, or 1st Staffordshire, Regiment	178
39th, or Dorsetshire, Regiment	180
40th, or 2nd Somersetshire, Regiment	178
41st, or Welsh, Regiment	182
43rd, or Monmouthshire, Regiment	182
44th, or East Essex, Regiment	178
45th, or 1st Nottinghamshire, Regiment	178
46th, or South Devonshire, Regiment	178
47th, or Lancashire, Regiment	178
48th, or Northamptonshire, Regiment	178
49th, or Hertfordshire, Regiment	178
50th, or West Kent, Regiment	178
51st, or 2nd Yorkshire, West Riding, Regiment	178
52nd, or Oxfordshire, Regiment	178
53rd, or Shropshire, Regiment	178
54th, or West Norfolk, Regiment	178
55th, or Westmorland, Regiment	178
56th, or West Essex, Regiment	178
57th, or West Middlesex,	

Regiment	1782
58th, or Rutlandshire, Regiment	1782
59th, or 2nd Nottinghamshire, Regiment	1782
61st, or South Gloucestershire, Regiment	1782
62nd, or Wiltshire, Regiment	1782
63rd, or West Suffolk, Regiment	1782
64th, or 2nd Staffordshire, Regiment	1782
65th, or 2nd Yorkshire, North Riding, Regiment	1782
66th, or Berkshire, Regiment	1782
67th, or South Hampshire, Regiment	1782
68th, or Durham, Regiment	1782
69th, or South Lincolnshire, Regiment	1782
70th, or Surrey, Regiment	1782
71st, or Glasgow Highland, Regiment	1808
73rd, or Perthshire, Regiment	1862
75th, or Stirlingshire, Regiment	1862
77th, or East Middlesex, Regiment	1807
78th, or Ross-shire Buffs, Regiment	1793
80th, or Staffordshire Volunteers, Regiment	1793
81st, or Loyal Lincoln Volunteers, Regiment	1793
83rd, or County of Dublin, Regiment	1859
84th, or York and Lancaster, Regiment	1809
85th, or Bucks Volunteers, Regiment	1794
86th, or Leinster, Regiment	1869
88th, or Connaught Rangers	1793
90th, or Perthshire Volunteers, Regiment	1794
91st, or Argyllshire, Regiment	1821
93rd, or Sutherland Highlanders, Regiment	1861
95th, or Derbyshire, Regiment	1825
97th, or the Earl of Ulster's, Regiment	1824

99th, or Lanarkshire, Regiment	1824

THE FIRST TWENTY-FIVE REGIMENTS OF FOOT IN 1881
(Two regular battalions to each regiment)

1 The Royal Scots (The Lothian Regiment)
2 The Queen's (Royal West Surrey Regiment)
3 The Buffs (East Kent Regiment)
4 The King's Own (Royal Lancaster Regiment)
5 The Northumberland Fusiliers
6 The Royal Warwickshire Regiment
7 The Royal Fusiliers (City of London Regiment)
8 The King's (Liverpool Regiment)
9 The Norfolk Regiment
10 The Lincolnshire Regiment
11 The Devonshire Regiment
12 The Suffolk Regiment
13 Prince Albert's (Somerset Light Infantry)
14 The Prince of Wales's Own (West Yorkshire Regiment)
15 The East Yorkshire Regiment
16 The Bedfordshire Regiment
17 The Leicestershire Regiment
18 The Royal Irish Regiment*
19 Alexandra, Princess of Wales's Own (Yorkshire Regiment)
20 The Lancashire Fusiliers
21 The Royal Scots Fusiliers
22 The Cheshire Regiment
23 The Royal Welsh Fusiliers
24 The South Wales Borderers
25 The King's Own Borderers

REGIMENTAL AMALGAMATIONS IN 1881
(Two regular battalions to each amalgamated regiment)

Amalgamated Title	Previous Title
The Cameronians (Scottish Rifles)★★	26th, or the Cameronians
	90th, or Perthshire Volunteers Light Infantry
The Royal Inniskilling Fusiliers	27th, or Inniskilling, Regiment
	108th (Madras Infantry) Regiment
The Gloucestershire Regiment	28th, or North Gloucestershire, Regiment
	61st, or South Gloucestershire, Regiment
The Worcestershire Regiment	29th, or Worcestershire, Regiment
	36th, or Herefordshire, Regiment
The East Lancashire Regiment	30th, or Cambridgeshire, Regiment
	59th, or 2nd Nottinghamshire, Regiment
The East Surrey Regiment	31st, or Huntingdonshire, Regiment
	70th, or Surrey, Regiment
The Duke of Cornwall's Light Infantry	32nd, or Cornwall Regiment, Light Infantry
	46th, or South Devonshire, Regiment
The Duke of Wellington's (West Riding Regiment)	33rd (Duke of Wellington's) Regiment
	76th Foot
The Border Regiment	34th, or Cumberland, Regiment
	55th, or Westmorland, Regiment
The Royal Sussex Regiment	35th (Royal Sussex) Regiment
	107th Bengal Infantry
The Hampshire Regiment	37th, or North Hampshire, Regiment
	67th, or South Hampshire, Regiment
The South Staffordshire Regiment	38th, or 1st Staffordshire, Regiment
	80th, or Staffordshire Volunteers, Regiment
The Dorsetshire Regiment	39th, or Dorsetshire, Regiment
	54th, or West Norfolk, Regiment
The Prince of Wales's Volunteers (South Lancashire Regiment)	40th, or 2nd Somersetshire, Regiment
	82nd, or Prince of Wales's Volunteer Regiment
The Welsh Regiment	41st, or the Welsh, Regiment
	69th, or South Lincolnshire, Regiment
The Black Watch (Royal Highlanders)	42nd, or Royal Highland, Regiment (The Black Watch)
	73rd, or Perthshire, Regiment
The Oxfordshire Light Infantry	43rd, or Monmouthshire Light Infantry
	52nd, or Oxfordshire Regiment, Light Infantry
The Essex Regiment	44th, or East Essex, Regiment
	56th, or West Essex, Regiment

Amalgamated Title	Previous Title
The Sherwood Foresters (Derbyshire Regiment)	45th, or Nottinghamshire Sherwood Foresters, Regiment
	95th, or Derbyshire, Regiment
The Loyal North Lancashire Regiment	47th, or Lancashire, Regiment
	81st, or Loyal Lincolnshire Volunteers, Regiment
The Northamptonshire Regiment	48th, or Northampton, Regiment
	58th, or Rutlandshire, Regiment
Princess Charlotte of Wales's (Berkshire) Regiment	49th, or Hertfordshire – Princess Charlotte of Wales's, Regiment
	66th, or Berkshire, Regiment
The Queen's Own (Royal West Kent Regiment)	50th, or the Queen's Own, Regiment
	97th, or Earl of Ulster's, Regiment
The King's Own (Yorkshire Light Infantry)	51st, or 2nd Yorkshire, West Riding, King's Own Light Infantry
	105th (Madras Light Infantry) Regiment
The King's (Shropshire Light Infantry)	53rd, or Shropshire, Regiment
	85th Bucks Volunteers – The King's Light Infantry
The Duke of Cambridge's Own (Middlesex Regiment)	57th, or West Middlesex, Regiment
	77th, or East Middlesex, Regiment
The King's Royal Rifle Corps***	60th, or The King's Royal Rifle Corps
The Duke of Edinburgh's (Wiltshire Regiment)	62nd, or Wiltshire, Duke of Cambridge's Own Regiment
	99th (The Duke of Edinburgh's) Regiment
The Manchester Regiment	63rd, or West Suffolk, Regiment
	96th Foot
The Prince of Wales's (North Staffordshire Regiment)	64th, or 2nd Staffordshire, Regiment
	98th (The Prince of Wales's) Regiment
The York and Lancaster Regiment**	65th, or 2nd Yorkshire, North Riding Regiment
	84th, or York and Lancaster, Regiment
The Durham Light Infantry	68th, or Durham Regiment, Light Infantry
	106th Bombay Light Infantry
The Highland Light Infantry	71st Highland Regiment, Light Infantry
	74th Highlanders
The Seaforth Highlanders (Ross-shire Buffs, The Duke of Albany's)	72nd, or the Duke of Albany's Own Highlanders
	78th Ross-shire Buffs
The Gordon Highlanders	75th, Stirlingshire, Regiment
	92nd Foot, Gordon Highlanders
The Queen's Own Cameron Highlanders****	79th Foot, The Queen's Own Cameron Highlanders
The Royal Irish Rifles	83rd (County of Dublin) Regiment
	86th, or Royal County Down, Regiment

Amalgamated Title	Previous Title
Princess Victoria's (The Royal Irish Fusiliers)	87th, or Royal Irish Fusiliers
	89th (The Princess Victoria's) Regiment
The Connaught Rangers★	88th Foot, or the Connaught Rangers
	94th Foot
Princess Louise's (Argyll and Sutherland Highlanders)	91st (Princess Louise's Argyllshire) Highlanders
	93rd (Sutherland Highlanders)
The Prince of Wales's Leinster Regiment (Royal Canadians)★	100th, Prince of Wales's Royal Canadian Regiment
	109th (Bombay Infantry)
The Royal Munster Fusiliers★	101st Royal Bengal Fusiliers
	104th Bengal Fusiliers
The Royal Dublin Fusiliers★	102nd (Royal Madras) Fusiliers
	103rd (Royal Bombay) Fusiliers
The Rifle Brigade (Prince Consort's Own)★★★	The Prince Consort's Own, Rifle Brigade

★Disbanded in 1922.   ★★Disbanded in 1968.   ★★★Four battalions. ★★★★One battalion until 1897.

CHANGES SINCE 1881

Some minor changes in regimental titles were made in 1881 after the amalgamations, and in the previous list above the later name is used. After 1881, there were other minor changes before the 1958–71 amalgamations.

1885   Princess Charlotte of Wales's (Royal Berkshire Regiment)

1887   The King's Own Scottish Borderers

1908   The Oxfordshire and Buckinghamshire Light Infantry

1919   The Bedfordshire and Hertfordshire Regiment

1920   The West Yorkshire Regiment (The Prince of Wales's Own)
The Royal Welch Fusiliers
The Duke of Wellington's Regiment (West Riding)
The Welch Regiment
The Royal Irish Fusiliers (Princess Victoria's)
The Argyll and Sutherland Highlanders (Princess Louise's)
The Rifle Brigade (Prince Consort's Own)

1921   The Queen's Royal Regiment (West Surrey)
The King's Regiment (Liverpool)
The Green Howards (Alexandra, Princess of Wales's Own Yorkshire Regiment)
The Loyal Regiment (North Lancashire)
The Royal Berkshire Regiment (Princess Charlotte of Wales's)
The Royal Ulster Rifles

1934   The Black Watch (Royal Highland Regiment)

1935   The Buffs (Royal East Kent Regiment)
The Royal Northumberland Fusiliers
The Royal Norfolk Regiment
The East Yorkshire Regiment (The Duke of York's Own)

1946   The Royal Lincolnshire Regiment

Amalgamated Title	Previous Title	
The Royal Leicestershire Regiment	1951	The Dorset Regiment
The Royal Hampshire Regiment	1963	The Royal Warwickshire Fusiliers

REGIMENTAL ANNIVERSARIES

Albuhera – Ypres

These battle anniversary descriptions emphasize the involvement of the regiments concerned.

ALBUHERA 16 May 1811, Peninsular War, near Badajos and Portuguese frontier in south-west Spain. A most bloody battle between a French army of about 24,000 under Marshal Soult and a British/Spanish army of 36,000 (12,000 British) under General Beresford. In his despatch after the battle, Beresford stated that: 'It is impossible by any description to do justice to the distinguished gallantry of the troops; but every individual nobly did his duty; and it was observed that our dead, particularly of the 57th regiment [Middlesex], were lying, as they had fought in the ranks, and every wound was in the front.' (*Wellington's Despatches*, VII, 41n, John Murray, 1838). 'The next cause (of our great loss) [after the defection of the Spanish troops] was the Polish lancers. They had a new form of warfare, to which the British soldiers in Spain were total strangers; for when the 57th formed square with the two front ranks kneeling, their muskets and bayonets forming a chevaux de frize, the lancers rode up to the squares, and with their long lances, not only struck down the kneeling ranks, but reached over the third and fourth ranks and cut them up in all directions.' (*Autobiography of Andrew Pearson*, ed. A. H. Haley, Bullfinch, 1987). The wounded commanding officer of the 57th Foot, Colonel Inglis, called upon his regiment to 'Die Hard!' and the regiment was always afterwards known by this nickname. The 3rd Foot (Buffs) and the 57th both suffered more than 400 casualties. MX.

ALIWAL 28 January 1846, First Sikh War, 50 miles south-east of Lahore in India. The village of Aliwal on the River Sutlej had been captured by two brigades of British and Indian infantry and the nearby Sikh entrenchment was being attacked by two other brigades. While the Sikhs were forming into squares, the 16th Lancers charged through an opening in the entrenchment and, reforming on the far side, charged again: the Sikhs were driven into the river with heavy losses. 'A squadron of 16th Lancers (a corps which . . . first came to India in 1822 . . . and were now clad in scarlet) advanced under Major Smith. [He] received a wound but led his squadron gallantly to the right of the village, bearing and spearing every thing before them . . . using the lance with the most deadly effect.' (N. W. Bancroft, *From Recruit to Staff Serjeant*, 1885, reprinted Ian Henry, 1979). 'At this time I looked to our left and saw the 16th Lancers coming on at a trot, then a gallop. I took off my cap and hollered out: "The first charge of British Lancers!"' (*Serjeant Pearson's Memoirs*, ed. Marquess of Anglesey, Jonathan Cape, 1968). As a result of the battle, the Sikh provinces on the eastern side of the Sutlej made peace with the Indian government. The 16th Lancers suffered 141 casualties. 16/5L (16L).

ALMA 20 September 1854, Crimean War, fifteen miles north of Sevastopol. In the first major action of the Crimean War, the Allied generals decided that the French and Turkish troops should attack the Russian left and the British should assault the Russian front. After clearing the village of Burlink, the British came under a heavy fire before the 95th Foot (Sherwood Foresters) reached the Great Battery. Here, murderous close-quarter fighting took place, and the regiment's

Queen's colour, placed on the walls as a rallying point, was passed from officer to sergeant to private as each was killed or wounded. Then the attack of the Guards and Highland Brigades and pressure from the French caused the withdrawal of the Russian forces to the south. The British suffered nearly 2,000 casualties and the Russians more than 4,500: the 19th Foot (Green Howards) lost 226 and the 95th Foot 175. The battle is commemorated annually by the Worcestershire and Sherwood Foresters Regiment (29th/41st Foot) on 20 September by flying the regimental flag from the flagstaffs at the regimental headquarters, Nottingham Castle and Derby Council House. GREEN HOWARDS, WFR (FORESTERS).

ALMANZA 25 April 1707, War of Spanish Succession, 50 miles north-west of Alicante in Spain. This was probably the greatest battle in Spain during the Duke of Marlborough's campaign in the War of Spanish Succession. The combined British/Dutch/Portuguese army, under the Earl of Galway, was disastrously defeated by the forces of the Duke of Berwick – Marlborough's nephew. The 9th Foot (Royal Norfolk Regiment) are believed to have gained Britannia as a badge through their gallantry in this battle. The 39th Foot (Dorset Regiment) are supposed to have been mounted on mules for a time and nicknamed 'Sankey's Horse'. R ANGLIAN (NORFOLK), GREEN HOWARDS, WFR (WORC R).

ANZIO 22 January 1944, Second World War, 30 miles south of Rome on west coast of Italy. The initial landing by an American and a British division at Anzio, intending to break the Cassino deadlock and open the road to Rome, met with no opposition and an immediate advance on Rome might well have succeeded. However, undue caution by the American commander of the two divisions gave time for German reinforcements to be sent in great strength from the north. The strong counter-attack that was then mounted to drive the bridgehead into the sea was repulsed with very heavy casualties: these were perhaps the most concentrated of the war, the Allies and the Germans each suffering about 30,000. After the counter-attack had been called off, the battle became largely a holding operation until the fall of Cassino allowed the reinforced VI Corps to breakout. STAFFORDS (S STAFFORDS).

ARNHEM 17 September 1944. To secure river and canal crossings ahead of the Allied ground forces, the 1st British Airborne Division and part of the Polish Parachute Regiment were to be dropped to capture and hold the bridge at Arnhem. The division landed short of the bridge but were able to take it. Bad weather and communications added to their difficulties but strong German counter-attacks were withstood. The supporting ground forces were unable to reach the bridgehead, however, and an evacuation of about 2,400 of the airborne troops was finally carried out. Lieutenant J. H. Grayburn (Parachute Regiment) was awarded the Victoria Cross posthumously. STAFFORDS (S STAFFORDS).

ARROYO DOS MOLINOS 28 October 1811, Peninsular War, 50 miles north-east of Badajos in south-west Spain. The town of Arroyo dos Molinos, occupied by the French, was cleared by a charge of Howard's brigade, and the 34th Foot (Border Regiment) with the 28th Foot (Gloucestershire Regiment) and the 39th Foot (Dorset Regiment) attacked the retreating French in the rear. One French general, 35 other officers and more than 1,000 soldiers were captured, including part of the 34e Regiment with the drums: the British casualties were 65. 'There was a terrifying cheer . . . while the driving storm carried with it the enemy up the sierra, the 28th and 34th Regiments at their heels.' (Major-General Sir George Bell, *Soldier's Glory*, ed. by B. Stuart, G Bell, 1956.) KINGS OWN BORDER (BORDER).

ASSAYE 23 September 1803, First Mahratta War, 150 miles north-east of Ahmednagar in India. This was the first battle won by the Duke of Wellington (then Sir Arthur Wellesley) as an independent commander. The First Mahratta War had resulted from the aggression of the Mahrattas under the rule of Scindia, and Assaye was the third battle in the campaign. Wellington's division of 4,500 men included 1,300 British and was opposed by some 30,000, including two brigades commanded by French officers. During the battle, the 74th and 78th Highlanders (Highland Light Infantry and Seaforth Highlanders) crossed the River Kaitna by a ford discovered by Wellington and played a major part in the victory. The battle was one of the most stubbornly contested of any in India, the 74th suffering more than 350 casualties, with every officer but the quartermaster being killed or wounded. 'The general was in the thick of action the whole time . . . though till our troops got the order to advance, the fate of the day seemed doubtful.' (Lieutenant Colin Campbell, in Wellington's *Supplementary Despatches*, IV, 186n, 1858–72). RHF (HLI).

BACK BADGE 21 March 1801, French Revolutionary Wars, Egypt. After the landing of British troops at Aboukir, the French were driven back to Alexandria after the battle of Mandora. A week later, the French counter-attacked the British, who had dug themselves in among the sand dunes. During a confused and desperate struggle, the 28th Foot (Gloucestershire Regiment) turned their rear rank about and, back to back, drove off repeated attacks by the French cavalry. GLOSTER.

BADAJOZ 6 April 1812, Peninsular War, north-west Spain, on River Guadiana. The siege of the fortress of Badajoz began on 17 March and the Picurina redoubt was captured on the 25th. However, it was not until the night of 6 April that days of artillery bombardment had made such breaches in the walls as to make an assault possible. After terrible British casualties of more than 4,800, Lieutenant MacPherson of the 45th Foot (Sherwood Foresters) was the first on to the tower from which the French flag flew. As he had no British flag, he hoisted his own red jacket to show that the fortress had been taken. His gallant deed is commemorated annually by the hoisting of a red jacket on the flagstaffs at the regimental headquarters, Nottingham Castle and Derby Council House. WFR (FORESTERS).

BALAKLAVA 25 October 1854, Crimean War. In an attempt to cut the British lines of communication, a Russian cavalry division attacked a battalion of the 93rd Foot (Argyll and Sutherland Highlanders) under Sir Colin Campbell, but were forced to retreat by two volleys at close range without loss to the Scots. The Heavy Brigade, of some 750 men, then successfully charged the Russian cavalry. However, through mistaken orders, the Light Brigade, of some 636 men, attacked a Russian force of a cavalry division, six infantry battalions and thirty-six guns, suffering 288 casualties. 'The fatal order to advance was . . . given, and, to the horror of all of us on the heights above, we saw our handful of light cavalry advance down towards the Russian batteries. We all saw at once that a lamentable mistake had been made.' (Lieutenant-Colonel S. J. G. Calthorpe, *Letters from Headquarters* *by a Staff Officer,* 1856, reprinted in *Cadogan's Crimea,* Hamish Hamilton, 1978.) 'Our cavalry dashed on to the charge, led by Lord Cardigan, got amongst the Cossacks, and cut them down left and right. But we had gone too far, for now the Russian artillery opened a destructive fire of roundshot and shell upon our people just as they swept round the elbow of the hill. Still our men galloped on and cut down the Russian gunners under a shower of musketry that emptied many of our saddles. It was a terrible slaughter of man and horse without any result other than to prove the metal of British cavalry.' (Major-General Sir George Bell, *Soldier's Glory,* ed. B. Stuart, G. Bell, 1956.) Members of the Light Brigade were awarded six Victoria Crosses: Troop Sergeant-Major J. Berryman, Quartermaster-Sergeant J. Farrell and Sergeant-Major C. Wooden (17L); Private S. Parkes (4H); Lieutenant A. R. Dunn (11H); Sergeant Malone (13H). Members of the Heavy Brigade were awarded two: Sergeant-Major J. Grieve (Greys) and Surgeon J. Mouat CB. 5 INNIS DG (DG), (QRIH (4H, 8H)), RH (11H), 13/18H (13H), 17/21L (17L), A and SH.

BARROSA 4 March 1811, Peninsular War, 20 miles south-east of Cadiz in Spain. To support a besieged Spanish garrison in Cadiz, the Duke of Wellington (then Lord Wellesley) sent the British component of the garrison, comprising less than 4,000 men, by sea under Major-General Thomas Graham to land behind the French force of 8,000 under Marshal Victor. The French were finally defeated, and six guns and the eagle of the 8e Light Infantry Regiment was captured by the 2/87th Foot (Royal Irish Fusiliers) who had played a most important part in the battle. The 87th suffered 173 casualties. R IRISH (R IR F).

BLENHEIM 13 August 1704, War of Spanish Succession, 10 miles west of Donauwörth near Munich in Germany. The Duke of Marlborough and Prince Eugène forced a battle on Marshal Tallard, who commanded the Franco-Bavarian army, to solve the strategic impasse on the Danube front. Although without enough artillery to capture Munich, Marlborough attacked the French armies and achieved a complete victory, resulting in the saving of Vienna and the Allied conquest of Bavaria. More than 12,000 prisoners, 124 guns and 129 stand of colours were captured. The 8th Foot (King's (Liverpool) Regiment) lost four officers and the 16th Foot (Bedfordshire Regiment) sixteen – total soldiers' losses were 2,016. 'Within the memory of man there has been no victory so great as this.' (Marlborough to his wife, *John and Sarah: Duke and Duchess of Marlborough,* by S. J. Reid, John Murray, 1914.) KINGS (KINGS), R ANGLIAN (BEDFS HERTS).

BLIGNY 6 June 1918, Great War, south-west of Reims, France. 'On 6 June 1918, when the right flank of a British brigade [a composite brigade formed from the reduced battalions of the 56th and 58th infantry Brigades] was being seriously threatened by the progress of a heavy enemy attack, the 1/4th Battalion of the King's Shropshire Light Infantry, which had been held in reserve, was called upon to counter-attack an important position from which their comrades had just been ejected. With magnificent dash this battalion rushed the hill on which the enemy had established themselves, inflicting heavy losses on them and in the course of hand-to-hand fighting captured one officer and 28 other ranks. Thanks to this gallant and spirited recapture of the key to the whole defensive position, the line was completely restored. The dash, energy and intrepidity with which, on this memorable occasion, the 1/4th Battalion King's Shropshire Light Infantry carried all before it was largely responsible for the retrieval of a situation which had temporarily become critical.' *Special Order of the Day*, by Field Marshal Sir Douglas Haig, 26 September 1918. KSLI.

BOIS DES BUTTES 27 May 1918, Great War, France. The German attack on the Aisne in May 1918 was initially successful, but the city of Reims was able to hold out and the offensive came to a standstill on the line of Villers–Cotterets and Château Thierry on the River Marne. The 2nd Battalion of the Devonshire Regiment lost 23 officers (including the commanding officer) and 528 men killed or missing in this action. In addition to the unique honour of Bois des Buttes, the regiment was awarded the Croix de Guerre, the first British unit to receive this decoration. D AND D (DEVON).

CAMBRAI 20 November 1917, Great War, north-west France. Tanks were first used on a large scale at the battle of Cambrai (a few had been previously in action at Flers–Courcelette over unsuitable ground). More than 370 battle tanks attacked with no previous artillery bombardment, and the German trenches were overrun – in some places to a depth of four miles. The tank offensive was an immediate and immense triumph – the only time in the Great War when church bells were rung (in the Second World War they were rung for El Alamein). However, there were insufficient reserves to follow up the ground that had been gained – this was gradually lost to German counter-attacks. 'By 28 November we were back to where we had started. Many lessons were learnt at Cambrai regarding the use of tanks in open warfare, but the price paid in human lives was ghastly.' (*Machine-Gunner 1914–1918*, compiled by C. E. Crutchley, Bailey Brothers & Swinfen, 1975.) 'After many days, slowly and reluctantly the Press were informed of the failure of Cambrai,' (Lord Beaverbrook, *Men and Power 1917–1918*, Duell, Sloan & Pearce, 1956). Captain R. W. L. Wain (Tank Corps) was posthumously awarded the Victoria Cross. RTR (TANK CORPS).

CORUNNA 16 January 1809, Peninsular War, north-west Spain. During the retreat from Salamanca to Corunna, General Sir John Moore, with about 30,000 men, had been opposed by five times that number of French but was able to embark his army at Corunna. At Corunna, Moore's force, reduced by then to about 15,000, turned to face Marshal Soult's 16,000 troops, while awaiting the arrival of the British fleet for evacuation. After confused fighting, the 50th Foot and 42nd Foot met the French troops breaking through the village of Elvĩna, halted them, and then pursued them and drove them beyond the village, making the evacuation possible – although Moore was mortally wounded during the action. '[16 January] At about ½ past 3 pm. the French began an attack which lasted until dark at night. Sir John Moore desperately wounded and Sir D. Baird the same. When the action was over, returned to Corunna and attended Sir J. Moore in his last moments. He died precisely as the evening gun fired on board the Admiral's ship – 8 o'clock.' (Lieutenant-General Robert Long, *Peninsular Cavalry General*, ed. T. H. McGuffie, Harrap, 1951.) QUEENS (RWK).

DELHI 14 September 1857, Indian Mutiny. With 40,000 mutineer defenders, Delhi was besieged by less than 10,000 British and Indian troops. The siege lasted twelve weeks and resulted in more casualties than from the suppression of the Mutiny in the remainder of India. Thirty-two engagements were fought before the assault on 14 September. One column, including the 8th Foot (King's (Liverpool) Regiment), attacked a breach at the Water bastion on the northern side of the city walls, and another, including the 2nd Gurkha Rifles, attacked a breach at the Kashmir bastion: by 20 September, the city had fallen. The 8th Foot suffered 180 casualties, the 2nd Gurkha Rifles 316. KINGS (KINGS), 2GR.

DETTINGEN 27 June 1743, War of Austrian Succession, near Frankfurt in Germany. The brunt of the fighting in this battle fell on the British led by the Earl of Stair, their losses far exceeding those of their Austrian and Hanoverian allies. During the battle, the 3rd Hussars charged the massed French infantry three times, with all but two of their officers and more than half their men being killed or wounded. As a result of the battle, the French eventually withdrew over the Rhine. This was the last battle in which a reigning King of England (George II) was present in person, commanding the English/Austrian/Hanoverian/Hessian army: it was reported that he knighted Private Brown of the 3rd Hussars on the field for bravery. The 7th Dragoon Guards suffered 53 casualties and the 3rd Hussars 148. 4/7DG (7DG), QOH (3H).

EL ALAMEIN 23 October 1942 (to 4 November), Second World War, Egypt. At the start of the battle of El Alamein, the decisive action in the North African campaign, General Sir Alan Brooke (then CIGS) cabled to General Montgomery (GOC Eighth Army) 'You are engaged in the biggest thing in your life and I am confident you will pull it off.' As part of XXX Corps, the 2nd New Zealand Division had three armoured regiments of 9 Armoured Brigade in support of its two infantry brigades – 3rd The King's Own Hussars, the Royal Wiltshire Yeomanry and the Warwickshire Yeomanry; the 1st Armoured Division had three armoured regiments of 2 Armoured Brigade – The Queen's Bays, the 9th Royal Lancers and the 10th Hussars. In all, four divisions, with artillery support of a thousand guns, attacked the German and Italian forces in the north of the battle area while other divisions made diversionary attacks in the south. The attack of 9 Armoured Brigade in Operation 'Supercharge' resulted in the loss of 75 tanks out of 94 and of more than half of tank crews as casualties. Fighting continued for ten days, wearing down German and Italian strength, and on 2 November a major force assaulted the German defences, breaking through after heavy resistance and beginning the pursuit of the retreating Axis forces. During the retreat, General Ritter von Thoma was captured by the crew of a 10th Hussars' Daimler scout car. By the evening of 6 November, General Alexander (GOC-in-C) was able to cable to Winston Churchill, the Prime Minister 'Ring out the bells!' Total British casualties were about 14,500. QOH (3H), RH (10H, 11H).

ESLA 31 May 1813, Peninsular War, tributary of the River Douro in Spain. As the River Esla near Almendra was too deep for the infantry to ford, British Hussars each took a musket and the soldiers of the 51st Foot (King's Own Yorkshire Light Infantry) and the Brunswick Light Infantry each took hold of a stirrup and were dragged through the river. 'A Serjeant of the 15th Hussars conveyed two of us across . . . I held hold of the stirrup, the other held fast by the horse's tail.' (*The Letters of Private Wheeler*, ed. B. H. Liddell Hart, Michael Joseph, 1951.) Two days later at Morales, the 10th Hussars with the 18th Hussars in support charged two French dragoon regiments and took more than 200 prisoners. 15/19H (15H).

FEROZESHAH 21 December 1845, First Sikh War, 60 miles south of Lahore in India. The main assault on the Sikh entrenchments began just before dusk, but an attack by the British Fourth Division was checked and the 62nd Foot (Wiltshire Regiment) lost nearly 260 casualties in ten minutes. 'This was frightful indeed – I had never seen anything like it before!' (Sita Ram, *From Sepoy to Subedar*, ed. J. D. Lunt, Routledge & Kegan Paul, 1970.) That night, 'the enemy again opened a destructive fire in the dark: on this, the Governor-General [Sir Henry Hardinge] . . . called on the 80th Regiment . . . "My lads! No sleep for us until we take those guns." The battalion . . . drove a large band of Sikhs from their guns, which they spiked.' N. W. Bancroft, *From Recruit to Staff Serjeant*, 1885, reprinted Ian Henry, 1979.) The 80th (South Staffordshire Regiment) suffered 120 casualties. As a result of the battle, the Sikhs recrossed the frontier, having suffered very severe casualties and leaving 73 guns in British hands. The action has been described as one of the hardest fought of those engaged in by the British in India. STAFFORDS (S STAFFORDS), DERR (WILTS).

GALLIPOLI 25 April 1915, Great War. The attack on the Gallipoli peninsula was planned in the hope of achieving a quick success which might lead to the capture of Constantinople and to practical aid to the Russian forces on the Eastern front. The result proved a total disaster, owing chiefly to the inadequacies of the British naval and military commanders and the fierce resistance of the Turkish forces. In the first attack, two companies of the 2nd Battalion of the Hampshire Regiment had orders to land from the *River Clyde* on to Helles beach at Gallipoli, but were mown down by devastating Turkish fire from the shore. For more than an hour, attempts to land continued with fearful losses, and only a few troops finally gained the beach. R HAMPS (HAMPS).

GAZALA 12 June 1942, Second World War, 40 miles west of Tobruk, Cyrenaica. Although Wavell's offensive against the Italian forces in the Western Desert in December 1940 had resulted in the taking of 130,000 prisoners for less than 2,000 British casualties, the dispatch of his veteran divisions to Greece and the arrival of the German Afrika Korps under Rommel in Tripoli then totally altered the balance of power. The two disastrous British Operations 'Brevity' and 'Battleaxe' in May and June 1941 were followed by a lull in the desert fighting for both sides to build up their strength. Operation 'Crusader' in November allowed Tobruk to be relieved, but a renewed German offensive in January 1942 inflicted heavy losses on British armour and Auchinleck's troops fell back to the Gazala line. A major disaster for the Eighth Army on 12 June resulted from another German offensive, and the withdrawal from Gazala that was ordered was followed by the fall of Tobruk. QDG (KDG).

GHELUVELT 31 October 1914, Great War, east of Ypres in Belgium. A German attack with heavy reinforcements of fresh troops had succeeded in taking the village of Gheluvelt and nearly broke through the British Expeditionary Force to Ypres, as there were virtually no British reserves after the retreat from Mons. As a forlorn hope, the 2nd Battalion of the Worcestershire Regiment was ordered to counter-attack: one company advanced to a railway embankment to prevent the enemy advancing up the Menin Road and the rest of the battalion with lightened kit and extra ammunition advanced to the ridge at Polderhoek. The crest of the ridge was covered by enemy guns but, although over a hundred fell, the rest dashed down the slope and forced their way into the village and château. Surprised by the speed of the attack, the German troops, though far superior in numbers, gave way and the Worcesters linked up with the South Wales Borderers and the Welch Regiment who were still holding out. As a result of the action, the gap was closed, Ypres held and the Channel ports saved. RRW (WELCH), WFR (WORC R).

GLORIOUS FIRST OF JUNE 1 June 1794, French Revolutionary Wars, **Atlantic, 400 miles west of Ushant.** The naval ships making up Lord Howe's fleet at this memorable action carried the 2nd Foot (Queen's Royal Regiment) and the 29th Foot (Worcestershire Regiment) as marines. As HMS *Brunswick*, carrying 81 of the 29th into action, the Ship's Band, which included a drummer of the regiment, played *Heart of Oak*. Prizes taken by the fleet included two line-of-battle ships of eighty guns and four of seventy-four guns. QUEENS (QUEENS), WFR (WORC R).

GUADALOUPE 10 June 1759, Seven Years War, **West Indies.** In 1758, six foot regiments were embarked at Spithead for Barbados, where they were joined by two more. After a skirmish on Martinique, the naval force bombarded Basse Terre, the capital of the southern island of Guadaloupe: owing to the mortal illness of the C-in-C, Major-General Peregrine Hopson, little further action took place before his death on 16 February 1759. His successor, Major-General Barrington, however, leaving the 63rd Foot (Manchester Regiment) to hold Basse Terre, by a series of attacks forced the French to surrender on 1 May. The 63rd suffered 29 casualties in action. KINGS (MANCH).

IMPHAL 22 June 1944, Second World War, **Central Burma.** 100,000 Japanese had massed to launch a further drive on India, this time through the Imphal base in Manipur. After a fighting withdrawal to the 'Cat Fish' defensive box, the 1st and 2nd Battalions of the West Yorkshire Regiment were engaged for the next few months in the defence of Imphal. On the 259th anniversary of the formation of the regiment, the siege was raised and the advance of the division began. The 1st Battalion had suffered 344 battle casualties in six months. POW (W YORKS).

INKERMAN 5 November 1854, Crimean War. At early dawn in a thick fog, a large Russian force from Sevastopol surprised the outnumbered British and French troops in the trenches. After a furious struggle in which the Russians showed great gallantry, they were driven back with terrible slaughter. The 63rd Foot (Manchester Regiment) suffered 108 casualties. 'The Russians planned a victory and gained a defeat.' (Major-General Sir George Bell, *Soldier's Glory*, ed. B. Stuart, G. Bell, 1956.) KINGS (MANCH).

KHARTOUM 2 September 1898, Reconquest of the Sudan, **Central Africa.** The battle of Atbara had opened the road to Khartoum for Kitchener's army. On 2 September, after a gunboat bombardment of Omdurman, the Khalifa's army made three unsuccessful attacks on the advancing British and Egyptian troops. Then the 21st Lancers charged the mass of the enemy. 'At full gallop and in the closest order the British squadrons struck the fierce brigades with one furious shout. The collision was prodigious.' (Winston S. Churchill, *The River War*, Longmans Green, 1899.) The 21st Lancers suffered 71 casualties: Private T. Byrne, Lieutenant the Hon R. H. L. J. De Montmorency and Captain P. A. Kenna were awarded the Victoria Cross. 17/21L (21L).

KOHIMA 15 May 1944, Second World War, Burma. During the Japanese attempt to break through from Burma into India between March and July 1944, the defenders of Kohima held out until the arrival of reinforcements, when the British forces were able to go on the attack. KINGS (MANCH).

LADYSMITH 29 October 1899 to 27 February 1900, South African War, South Africa. During their four months' siege of Ladysmith, the Boers made only one attempt at assault – at Caesar's Camp – but there was always a greater chance of the garrison being forced to surrender from lack of supplies. However, on 27 February the mounted brigade commanded by General Sir Redvers Buller VC entered the city and raised the siege. Heaviest British casualties were at Caesar's Camp – 326 killed and wounded. The Manchester Regiment suffered 150 casualties during the siege: Private J. Pitts and Private R. Scott were awarded the Victoria Cross for the action at Caesar's Camp. KINGS (MANCH).

MAIWAND 27 July 1880, Second Afghan War, Afghanistan. The total defeat of a British and Indian Force at Maiwand by the Afghans led to the close investment of Kandahar. 'Some of the cavalry rode in from a flank to drive off a group of jehadis who had got into the rear of the 66th Foot . . . The 66th stopped the rush upon their front with one volley, but when the sepoy units collapsed the English soldiers too abandoned their ground.' (T. A. Heathcote, *The Afghan Wars*, Osprey, 1980.) The 66th Foot (Royal Berkshire Regiment) suffered 318 casualties, of which 286 were killed. DERR (R BERKS).

MEEANEE 17 February 1843, Scinde Campaign, Hyderabad (Scinde) in north-west India. After the First Afghan War, the Amirs of Scinde had entered into a treaty with the Indian Government to cover the costs of a British/Indian force in Scinde to safeguard the army's lines of communications. Sir Charles Napier was sent to Hyderabad (Scinde) to enforce respect for the treaty, but the Amirs' Baluchi forces attacked the Residency there. Napier then marched against the Amirs with 2,600 troops, including the 22nd Foot (Cheshire Regiment), the sole British battalion. After three hours' fighting, the Baluchis were driven off with considerable loss and the Amirs surrendered the next day. Napier's dispatch describing the battle is said to have been 'the first in modern English history that recognized the valour of non-commissioned officers and privates by name'. The 22nd Foot suffered 81 casualties. CHESHIRE.

MINDEN 1 August 1759, Seven Years War, on River Weser in Germany. Six British foot regiments, commanded by Duke Ferdinand of Brunswick, had been assisting Frederick the Great of Prussia in the campaign against the combined forces of France and Austria. At the battle of Minden, the British infantry, perhaps through mistaken orders, marched majestically against the French cavalry and defeated three attacks, after which the 1st Battalion RA changed the orderly retirement of the enemy into a disorderly rout. The action would have been an even greater success if Lord George Sackville (later Germaine), who commanded fifteen squadrons of British cavalry, had not refused to engage in the battle, but Hanover was saved. The 12th Foot (Suffolk Regiment) suffered 282 casualties, the 20th Foot (Lancashire Fusiliers) 321, the 23rd Foot (Royal Welch Fusiliers) 206, the 25th Foot (King's Own Scottish Borderers) 145, the 37th Foot (Royal Hampshire Regiment) 246 and the 51st Foot (King's Own Yorkshire Light Infantry) 108. R ANGLIAN (SUFFOLK), KOSB, R HAMPS.

MONS 24 August 1914, Great War, about 10 miles west of Mons in Belgium. Soon after noon, Brigadier-General Lisle, commanding the 2nd Cavalry Brigade, ordered the 9th Queen's Royal Lancers and part of the 4th Royal Irish Dragoon Guards to attack in flank the German troops advancing from Quivrain, if necessary by mounted attack. The 9th Lancers attacked at the gallop, but were badly mauled by the fire of nine German batteries. Eleven officers and some forty troopers then helped to save the guns of 119 Battery RFA, which had been under fire from three German batteries and a machine-gun at close range, by manhandling the guns and limbers out of action. Captain F. O. Grenfell, the senior officer of the 9th, was awarded the Victoria Cross, as was Lieutenant-Colonel E. W. Alexander, who commanded the battery. Captain Grenfell was killed at the end of May 1915. 9/12L (9L).

MOY 28 August 1914, Great War, west of Mons in Belgium. When German cavalry attempted to thrust into a 15-mile gap between I and II Corps of the British Expeditionary Force, the 4th Queen's Own Hussars and E Battery RHA checked the western column and the 5th Cavalry Division, commanded by Brigadier-General Sir Philip Chetwode, scored a brilliant success against the eastern column (Guard Cavalry Division). Near the village of Cerzy, a dismounted line of the Royal Scots Greys (2nd Dragoons) and J Battery RHA forced the Germans to dismount. The 20th Hussars and the 12th Royal Lancers (Prince of Wales's) were deployed to envelop the enemy: the 12th Lancers compelled another body of German horse to dismount by fire action, and one squadron charged, spearing seventy or eighty of the enemy for the loss of two officers and eight men. This is usually accepted as the last occasion when British regular cavalry used the lance in war. 9/12L (12L).

NORMANDY 6 June 1944, Second World War, north-west coast of France. In this great amphibious landing, five beaches were assaulted by two British divisions (3rd and 50th), one Canadian (3rd) and two American (1st/part 29th and 4th) supported by intense naval and air bombardment. During the next six days, a lodgment 80 miles wide by 10 miles deep was secured at the cost of 11,000 Allied casualties, while the landing of eight more combat divisions ensured the success of the invasion and, ultimately, the final defeat of Germany in the West. 4/7DG, 13/18H.

NUNSHIGUM 13 April 1944, Second World War, near Imphal. During bitter fighting at Imphal, the twin peaks of Nunshigum were held against severe Japanese counter-attacks. SCOTS DG (CARBS).

OATES Sunday 17 March 1912, Antartica. Captain L. E. G. Oates (1880–1912) had seen service with the 6th (Inniskilling) Dragoons in the South African War where he was wounded and mentioned in dispatches. In 1910, he joined an Antarctic expedition organized by Captain R. F. Scott, RN and took charge of the ponies to be used for sledge haulage. After establishing a base on Ross Island, the sledging party set out for the journey towards the South Pole: from the foot of the Beardmore glacier, the sledges were manhandled by a party of five, who tragically reached the Pole thirty-four days after Amundsen. Conditions were extremely bad for the return journey, although it was essential that the weakened party should reach each food depot before their own supplies of food and fuel were exhausted.

Suffering severely from frost-bitten feet, Oates could finally go no further: his request to be left behind was refused, but the next day (17 March) he walked out into a blizzard and never returned. The three survivors died a fortnight later when only eleven miles from the next food depot. Although Captain Scott's organization has been severely criticized, the bravery of the members of the expedition and the self-sacrifice of Captain Oates cannot be challenged. 5 INNIS DG (6D).

QUEBEC 13 September 1759, Seven Years War, Canada. On 27 June 1759, General Wolfe landed on Orleans Island just south of Quebec and sent Monckton's brigade to the right bank of the River St Lawrence and Murray's and Townsend's brigade to the left bank. The first brigade included the 15th Foot (East Yorkshire Regiment) and the second brigade the 35th Foot (Royal Sussex Regiment) and the 47th Foot (Loyal North Lancashire Regiment). After a determined attempt to assault the city had failed, the main English forces transferred to a position west of the citadel on the river's right bank. In a daring midnight move, the Heights of Abraham were scaled: after the death of Wolfe, Townsend carried on the siege vigorously, and General Ramesay, who had commanded the French troops after the death of General Montcalm, finally surrendered on 18 September. The 15th Foot suffered 132 casualties, the 35th Foot 111 and the 47th Foot 101. QUEENS (R SUSSEX), PWO (E YORKS), QLR (LOYALS).

RAMADI 28 September 1917, Great War, 40 miles north-east of Khan Baghdadi, Mesopotamia. A Turkish post at Ramadi on the River Euphrates, an outpost for a counter-attack on Baghdad, was attacked unsuccessfully in July 1917, but a further attack by a small force on 28 September was successful. 14/20H (14H).

RAMNUGGUR 22 November 1848, Second Sikh War, 50 miles north of Laore, north-west India. This was the first battle in the war, as General Gough marched from Lahore. The main position of the Sikh army, about 16,000 strong, was on the north bank of the River Chenab, with a deep nullah and an area of quicksands on the south side. The 14th Light Dragoons, commanded by Colonel William Havelock, charged into the nullah, perhaps through mistaken orders, and cleared the south bank of Sikh outposts and irregular horsemen. There were heavy losses on both sides, the 14th Light Dragoons having about 25 killed, including their Colonel. 14/20H (14H).

RORKE'S DRIFT 22/23 January 1879, Zulu and Basuto War, south-east Africa. After the fatal battle of Isandhlwana at which five companies of the 1st Battalion 24th Foot (South Wales Borderers) lost 416 killed and one company of the 2nd Battalion lost 183, the garrison at the commissariat store at Rorke's Drift valiantly resisted the repeated brave onslaughts of King Cetywayo's Zulu impis. That garrison of 139 men included 24 of the 1st Battalion (5 sick) and 99 of the 2nd Battalion (17 sick): British casualties were 15 killed and 10 wounded. In his dispatch to the Secretary of State, the GOC, General Lord Chelmsford, stated that 'The cool determined courage displayed by the gallant garrison is beyond all praise.' (*Lord Chelmsford and the Zulu War*, G French, Bodley Head, 1939.) Lieutenant N. J. A. Coghill and Lieutenant T. Melville (1st Battalion) were awarded the Victoria Cross after Isandhlwana; Corporal W. Allen, Lieutenant G. Bromhead, Privates F. Hitch, H. Hook, R. Jones, W. Jones and J. Williams (2nd Battalion) were awarded the Victoria Cross after Rorke's Drift. The reckless bravery of the Zulu impis, armed chiefly with spears, was recognized in 1990 when a special scroll as a bond of friendship, endorsed by Brecon town council, was presented to the Zulu nation. RRW (SWB).

SAHAGUN 21 December 1808, Peninsular War, near Corunna in north-west Spain. The 10th Hussars and the 15th Hussars had arrived near Sahagun before dawn to find the town occupied by General Debelle's French dragoons. The 10th Hussars marched straight to the town, while the 15th Hussars marched around it to cut off the enemy's retreat. A French patrol gave the alarm, however, so that Lord Paget, with 400 men of the 15th, was faced by a line of 600 dragoons. The 15th charged the French, broke their line and then followed them in pursuit. About 15 or 20 dragoons were killed and 13 officers and 154 men taken prisoner in an affair which lasted twenty minutes. Sahagun was then occupied by British infantry, and Debelle retired to Santerbas. 15/19H (15H).

SALAMANCA 22 July 1812, Peninsular War, 100 miles north-west of Madrid in Spain. This was the first large-scale battle fought by the Duke of Wellington who, with some 42,000 men (including 15,000 Portuguese), was opposed by Marmont with an equal number of French. In the early stages of the battle, the left wing of the French became separated from the centre through Marmont's decision to seize the height of Miranda and secure command of Wellington's line of retreat. After heavy fighting, the scale was turned by the attack of the 6th Division. 'In little more than an hour the enemy left was completely beaten and in retreat.' (*An Ensign in the Peninsular War: The Letters of John Aitchison*, ed. W. F. K. Thompson, Michael Joseph, 1981.) Wellington then brought up the Light Division, but the main body of the French army managed to escape across the River Tormes. The British suffered more than 5,000 casualties, while Marmont admitted to a loss of 6,000 apart from prisoners. Casualties to the 5th Dragoon Guards were 53, the 32nd Foot (Duke of Cornwall's Light Infantry) 137, the 44th Foot (Essex Regiment) 29, the 51st Foot (King's Own Yorkshire Light Infantry) 2, the 53rd Foot (King's Shropshire Light Infantry) 142 and the 68th Foot (Durham Light Infantry) 20. 5 INNIS DG (5DG), R ANGLIAN (ESSEX), LI (DCLI, KOYLI, KSLI, DLI).

SALERNO 9-16 September 1943, west coast of Italy, 50 miles from Naples. The day after the Italian government had surrendered, the Fifth Army under General Mark Clark made an amphibious attack on Salerno, with Naples as the ultimate objective. The British X Corps captured Battipaglia and Salerno, but after three days a strong German counter-attack recaptured Battipaglia and on 14 September were only two miles from the coast. After naval and air bombardment, troops under General Alexander halted the counter-attack and General Montgomery's Eighth Army from the south made contact, securing the beachhead. Naples fell on 1 October. QUEENS (QUEENS).

SEVASTOPOL 1854-5, Crimean War, Crimea, Russia. Every regiment which landed in the Crimea before the final storming of the Redan were awarded Sevastopol as a battle honour – this was also awarded to regiments with other Crimean War battle honours. The 50th Foot and the 97th Foot (Queen's Own Royal West Kent Regiment) had fought in the campaign since the first landing on 14

September 1854, taking part in the Battles of Alma and Inkerman and suffering many casualties in action. Members of the regiments were awarded eleven French Légions d'honneur and fifteen war medals, twenty Turkish Orders of Medjidieh and twelve Sardinian medals. QUEENS (RWK).

SOBRAON 10 February 1846, First Sikh War, 40 miles south of Lahore in India. This battle resulted in the final defeat of the Sikhs on the banks of the River Sutlej. Stacey's brigade, which included the 10th Foot (Royal Lincolnshire Regiment), the 53rd Foot (King's Shropshire Light Infantry) and the 80th Foot (South Staffordshire Regiment) carried the first line of Sikh trenches, though with heavy casualties. Meanwhile, the division led by Sir Harry Smith, which included the 31st Foot (East Surrey Regiment) and the 50th Foot (Queen's Own Royal West Kent Regiment) were also successful. 'The gallant soldiery of Stacey swarming in scarlet masses over the banks, breastworks, and fascines . . . driving the Sikhs before them within the area of their defences, over which the yellow and red colours of the 10th and 53rd were flying . . .' (N. W. Bancroft, *From Recruit to Staff Serjeant*, 1885, reprinted Ian Henry, 1979.) The British suffered appalling casualties – three generals and four brigadier-generals were killed, and the 10th lost 69 and the 31st 154. QUEENS (SURREYS), R ANGLIAN (LINCOLNS).

TALAVERA 27 July 1809, Peninsular War, 75 miles south-west of Madrid in Spain. At Talavera, the Duke of Wellington (then Sir Arthur Wellesley) with 20,500 British troops and 34,000 Spanish (who played no part in the battle) was faced with about 50,000 French under Marshal Victor. During the battle, the Brigade of Guards and the King's German Legion advanced too far and their line was broken. Deploying in the rear of the broken troops, the 48th Foot (Northamptonshire Regiment) under Colonel Donellan advanced, halted, broke into column to allow the Guards and Germans to pass through, wheeled into line again and poured a destructive fire upon the pursuing French: the band of the 48th – normally stretcher-bearers – laid their instruments aside and fought in the ranks. The Guards and Germans rallied and reformed on the 48th: the French halted, wavered and retired, suffering heavily from artillery fire. 'The 48th marched in beautiful order amongst the retiring crowds of our men, wheeling back in companies to allow them to pass at intervals, then again resuming line and marching upon the pursuing columns of the French, plying them with a destructive fire, and then closing upon them with a firm, yet regular step, which checked all forward movements. Our broken divisions, having rallied, were again moved forward, when a charge was made, and the enemy retired in disorder.' (*Autobiography of Andrew Pearson, A Peninsular Veteran*, ed. A. H. Haley, Bullfinch, 1987.) 'The battle was certainly saved by the advance, position and steady conduct of the 48th.' (Wellington, *Despatches*, IV, 510, John Murray, 1838.) The British suffered more than 6,250 casualties, the 48th 326. R ANGLIAN (NORTHAMPTONS).

WAGON HILL 6 January 1900, South African War, South Africa. Early in January 1900, the Boers attacked Caesar's Camp and Wagon Hill, two of the chief defensive positions of Ladysmith. Both attacks were beaten off after a courageous charge by the Devonshire Regiment. Lieutenant J. E. Masterson was awarded the Victoria Cross for this action. D AND D (DEVONS).

WATERLOO 18 June 1815, Hundred Days, 30 miles south of Brussels in Belgium. The Battle of Waterloo has probably been written about more than any other battle in British history before this century, yet 'There is one event noted in the world – the battle of Waterloo – and you will not find any two people agreed as to the exact hour when it commenced.' (Wellington to Lord Mahon, *Conversations with the Duke of Wellington*, by Earl Stanhope, OUP, 1947.) On 16 June, Napoleon attacked the Prussians at Ligny and the British at Quatre Bras, the Prussians being worsted and Quatre Bras being a doubtful action. The Allies fell back and agreed to make a further stand at Waterloo. On 18 June, the British army withstood the French attack until the effect of the Prussian advance had begun to be felt: by darkness the battle had been won. 'I never saw the British infantry behave so well.' (Lord Beresford in Wellington's *Despatches*, XII, 529, John Murray, 1838.) Battle casualties were heavy on both sides: the British at more than 11,500 were half of those of the entire Allied armies, while those of the French have been estimated at from 18,000 up to 30,000. The Royal Horse Guards lost 85, the Royal Dragoons 187, the King's Dragoon Guards 147, the 7th Hussars 184, the 30th Foot (East Lancashire Regiment) 260 – including 41 at Quatre Bras – and the 53rd Foot (King's Shropshire Light Infantry) 199. Waterloo was the first engagement for which the CB was awarded: The Royal Horse Guard, King's Dragoon Guards and 52nd Foot (Oxfordshire and Buckinghamshire Light Infantry) received one decoration each and the 30th three. RHG/D (RHG, ROYALS), QDG (KDG), SCOTS DG (GREYS), 5 INNIS DG, QOH (7H), Q LAN R (E LAN R), RGJ (OXF BUCKS).

YPRES 31 July 1917, Great War, north-west France. At the start of the Third Battle of Ypres, the North Staffordshire Regiment were given the task of capturing Jehovah Trench and the Jordan Trench, after which came Bulgar Wood. No man's land was about 1,000 yards deep, but there were German forward posts only 100 yards from the regiment's front line. 'We were to remain in our front trench, Image Crescent, till the barrage had blasted our first objective, Jehovah: only then were we to go over the top, not to charge at the double across No Man's Land as in the old tactics but to walk at a steady pace towards Jehovah till our watches told us the barrage was lifting to our second objective, Jordan. Then, and not till then, we were to charge on whatever might be left of Jehovah.' (B Martin, *Poor Bloody Infantry: A Subaltern on the Western Front 1916–1917*, John Murray, 1987.) The first two objectives were reached in spite of heavy casualties, but Jordan Trench was found to be waterlogged so that digging in was impossible, and the regiment was ordered to retire to the Jehovah line. Casualties were nearly half the regiment's strength. STAFFORDS (N STAFFS).

OVERSEAS ALLIANCES IN 1914

AUSTRALIA

1st Battalion New South Wales Scottish Rifles – Black Watch (Royal Highland Regiment)

CANADA

5th Royal Highlanders – Black Watch (Royal Highland Regiment)

6th Regiment, The Duke of Connaught's Own Rifles – Rifle Brigade (Prince Consort's Own)

12th Manitoba Dragoons – 12th (Prince of Wales's Royal) Lancers

13th Royal Regiment – Prince Albert's (Somerset Light Infantry)

15th Light Horse – 15th (The King's) Hussars

16th Light Horse – 14th (King's) Hussars; 16th (The Queen's) Lancers

18th Mounted Rifles – 18th (Queen Mary's Own) Hussars

25th Brant Dragoons – 6th (Inniskilling) Dragoons

48th Highlanders – Gordon Highlanders

52nd Regiment (Prince Albert Volunteers) – Oxfordshire and Buckinghamshire Light Infantry

57th Regiment 'Peterborough Rangers' – Duke of Cambridge's Own (Middlesex Regiment)

60th Rifles of Canada – King's Royal Rifle Corps

63rd Regiment 'Halifax Rifles' – King's Royal Rifle Corps

72nd Regiment (Seaforth Highlanders of Canada) – Seaforth Highlanders (Ross-shire Buffs, The Duke of Albany's)

77th Wentworth Regiment – Duke of Cambridge's Own (Middlesex Regiment)

78th Pictou Regiment (Highlanders) – Seaforth Highlanders (Ross-shire Buffs, The Duke of Albany's)

79th, Cameron Highlanders of Canada – Queen's Own Cameron Highlanders

91st Regiment (Canadian Highlanders) – Princess Louise's (Argyll and Sutherland Highlanders)

100th Winnipeg Grenadiers – Prince of Wales's Leinster Regiment (Royal Canadians)

101st Regiment 'Edmonton Fusiliers' – Royal Munster Fusiliers

104th Regiment (Westminster Fusiliers of Canada) – Royal Munster Fusiliers

105th Regiment (Saskatoon Fusiliers) – King's Own (Yorkshire Light Infantry)

106th Regiment (Winnipeg Light Infantry) – Durham Light Infantry

INDIA

1st King George's Own Sappers and Miners – Corps of Royal Engineers

2nd Queen Victoria's Own Sappers and Miners – Corps of Royal Engineers

3rd Sappers and Miners – Corps of Royal Engineers

NEW ZEALAND

1st Canterbury Regiment – Queen's Own (Royal West Kent Regiment)

2nd (South Canterbury) Regiment – Durham Light Infantry

3rd Auckland Regiment (Countess of Ranfurly's Own) – Suffolk Regiment

5th (Wellington) Regiment – York and Lancaster Regiment

6th (Hanraki) Regiment – Oxfordshire and Buckinghamshire Light Infantry

7th (Wellington West Coast) Regiment – Royal Irish Regiment

8th (Southland) Regiment – Manchester Regiment

9th (Wellington East Coast) Regiment –
Prince of Wales's Volunteers (South
Lancashire Regiment)
10th (North Otago) Regiment – Duke
of Edinburgh's (Wiltshire Regiment)
11th Regiment (Taraniki Rifles) – Duke
of Cambridge's Own (Middlesex
Regiment)
15th (North Auckland) Regiment –
Northamptonshire Regiment
16th (Waikato) Regiment – Prince of
Wales's Own (West Yorkshire
Regiment)

SOUTH AFRICA
Natal Carbineers, 1st and 2nd Mounted
Rifles – 6th Dragoon Guards
(Carabiniers)

OVERSEAS ALLIANCES AND ASSOCIATIONS IN 1990

AUSTRALIA

Adelaide University Regiment – Royal Irish Rangers

Armoured Regiment RAAC, 1st – Royal Tank Regiment

Australian Army Aviation Corps – Army Air Corps

Australian Army Catering Corps – Army Catering Corps

Australian Army Legal Corps – Army Legal Corps

Australian Intelligence Corps – Intelligence Corps

Hunter River Lancers, 12th/16th – Royal Scots Dragoon Guards (Carabiniers and Greys); 16th/5th The Queen's Royal Lancers

Light Horse, 10th – Royal Hussars (Prince of Wales's Own)

Light Horse (QMI), 2nd/14th – Queen's Royal Irish Hussars; 14th/20th King's Hussars

Melbourne University Regiment – Royal Green Jackets

Monash University Regiment – Light Infantry

Prince of Wales's Light Horse, 4th/19th – 4th/7th Royal Dragoon Guards

Royal Australian Armoured Corps – Royal Armoured Corps

Royal Australian Army Chaplains' Department – Royal Army Chaplains' Department

Royal Australian Army Educational Corps – Royal Army Educational Corps

Royal Australian Army Nursing Corps – Queen Alexandra's Royal Army Nursing Corps

Royal Australian Army Ordnance Corps – Royal Army Ordnance Corps

Royal Australian Corps of Military Police – Corps of Royal Military Police

Royal Australian Corps of Signals – Royal Corps of Signals

Royal Australian Corps of Transport – Royal Corps of Transport

Royal Australian Dental Corps – Royal Army Dental Corps

Royal Australian Engineers – Corps of Royal Engineers

Royal Australian Medical Corps – Royal Army Medical Corps

Royal Australian Regiment – Brigade of Gurkhas:

1st Battalion – Grenadier Guards

2nd/4th Battalion – Coldstream Guards; Irish Guards

3rd Battalion – Queen's Royal Irish Hussars; Scots Guards

5th/7th Battalion – Welsh Guards; Gordon Highlanders

8th/9th Battalion – Parachute Regiment

Royal Corps of Australian Electrical and Mechanical Engineers – Corps of Royal Electrical and Mechanical Engineers

Royal New South Wales Lancers, 1st/15th – 1st The Queen's Dragoon Guards; 15th/19th The King's Royal Hussars

Royal New South Wales Regiment – Queen's Regiment; Devonshire and Dorset Regiment; Royal Regiment of Wales; Black Watch (Royal Highland Regiment)

Royal Queensland Regiment – King's Own Royal Border Regiment; Black Watch (Royal Highland Regiment); Argyll and Sutherland Highlanders (Princess Louise's)

Royal Queensland Regiment, 25th Battalion – King's Own Scottish Borderers

Royal Regiment of Australian Artillery

– Royal Regiment of Artillery

Royal South Australia Regiment – Queen's Own Highlanders (Seaforth and Camerons); King's Regiment

Royal Tasmania Regiment – Royal Anglian Regiment; Queen's Lancashire Regiment

Royal Victoria Regiment:
2nd Battalion – Staffordshire Regiment (The Prince of Wales's)
5th/6th Battalion – Royal Regiment of Fusiliers; Gordon Highlanders

Royal Western Australia Regiment – Queen's Regiment; Gloucestershire Regiment; Queen's Own Highlanders (Seaforth and Camerons)

South Australian Mounted Rifles, 3rd/9th – 5th Royal Inniskilling Dragoon Guards; Queen's Own Hussars

Special Air Service Regiment – Special Air Service Regiment

Sydney University Regiment – Royal Green Jackets

University of New South Wales Regiment – Queen's Regiment

Victorian Mounted Rifles, 8th/13th – Queen's Royal Irish Hussars; 14th/20th King's Hussars

Western Australia University Regiment – Royal Green Jackets

Women's Royal Australian Corps – Women's Royal Army Corps

BARBADOS

Barbados Regiment – Royal Anglian Regiment

CANADA

Algonquin Regiment – Duke of Edinburgh's Royal Regiment (Berkshire and Wiltshire)

Argyll and Sutherland Highlanders of Canada (Princess Louise's) – Argyll and Sutherland Highlanders (Princess Louise's)

Armour Branch – Royal Armoured Corps

Black Watch (Royal Highland Regiment) – Black Watch (Royal Highland Regiment)

British Columbia Dragoons – 5th Royal Inniskilling Dragoon Guards

British Columbia Regiment (Duke of Connaught's Own) – Royal Green Jackets

Brockville Rifles – Royal Green Jackets

Calgary Highlanders – Argyll and Sutherland Highlanders (Princess Louise's)

Cameron Highlanders of Ottawa – Queen's Own Highlanders (Seaforth and Camerons)

Canadian Airborne Regiment – Parachute Regiment

Canadian Grenadier Guards – Grenadier Guards

Canadian Hussars (Princess Louise's), 8th – Queen's Royal Irish Hussars

Canadian Scottish Regiment (Princess Mary's) – Royal Scots (The Royal Regiment)

Chaplain Branch – Royal Army Chaplains' Department

Communications and Electronics Branch – Royal Corps of Signals

Elgin Regiment – Royal Regiment of Fusiliers

Essex and Kent Scottish – Queen's Regiment; Royal Anglian Regiment

Field Artillery Regiment RCA(M), 49th Sault St Marie – Royal Hampshire Regiment

Fort Garry Horse – 4th/7th Royal Dragoon Guards

Fusiliers de St Laurent – Royal Regiment of Fusiliers

Fusiliers de Sherbrooke – Devonshire and Dorset Regiment

Governor-General's Foot Guards – Coldstream Guards

Governor-General's Horse Guards – Blues and Royals (Royal Horse Guards and 1st Dragoons); 1st Queen's Dragoon Guards

Grey and Simcoe Foresters – Worcestershire and Sherwood Foresters Regiment (29th/45th Foot)

Hastings and Prince Edward Regiment – Queen's Regiment

Highland Fusiliers of Canada – Royal Highland Fusiliers (Princess Margaret's Own Glasgow and Ayrshire Regiment)

Highlanders of Canada, 48th – Gordon Highlanders

Hussars, 1st – Royal Hussars (Prince of Wales's Own)

Intelligence Branch – Intelligence Corps

Irish Regiment of Canada (Sudbury), 2nd Battalion – Royal Irish Rangers (27th (Inniskilling) 83rd and 87th)

King's Own Calgary Regiment – King's Own Royal Border Regiment

Lake Superior Scottish Regiment – Royal Anglian Regiment

Lanark and Renfrew Scottish Regiment – Black Watch (Royal Highland Regiment)

Land Electrical and Mechanical Engineering Branch – Corps of Royal Electrical and Mechanical Engineers

Legal Branch – Army Legal Corps

Lincoln and Welland Regiment – Royal Anglian Regiment; Duke of Edinburgh's Royal Regiment (Berkshire and Wiltshire)

Lord Strathcona's Horse (Royal Canadians) – 17th/21st Lancers

Lorne Scots (Peel, Dufferin and Halton Regiment) – Royal Regiment of Fusiliers

Loyal Edmonton Regiment (4th Battalion Princess Patricia's Light Infantry) – Queen's Lancashire Regiment

Medical Branch – Royal Army Medical Corps

Military Engineering Branch – Corps of Royal Engineers

North Saskatchewan Regiment – Light Infantry

Nova Scotia Highlanders (Cape Breton), 2nd Battalion – Cheshire Regiment

Ontario Regiment RCAC – Royal Regiment of Wales (24th/41st Foot)

Prince Edward Island Regiment – 9th/12th Royal Lancers (Prince of

Wales's); Black Watch (Royal Highland Regiment)

Princess Louise Fusiliers – Royal Irish Rangers (27th (Inniskilling) 83rd and 87th)

Princess of Wales's Own Regiment – Queen's Lancashire Regiment

Princess Patricia's Canadian Light Infantry – Royal Green Jackets

Queen's Own Cameron Highlanders – Queen's Own Highlanders (Seaforth and Camerons)

Queen's Own Rifles of Canada – Queen's Regiment; Royal Green Jackets; Brigade of Gurkhas

Queen's York Rangers (1st American Regiment) – Queen's Regiment; Green Howards (Alexandra, Princess of Wales's Own Regiment of Yorkshire)

Régiment Blindé du Canada, 12e – Royal Tank Regiment

Régiment du Maisonneuve – Light Infantry

Rocky Mountain Rangers – Green Howards (Alexandra, Princess of Wales's Own Regiment of Yorkshire)

Royal Canadian Dragoons – Blues and Royals (Royal Horse Guards and 1st Dragoons)

Royal Canadian Horse Artillery, 1st and 3rd Regiments – 1 and 3 Royal Horse Artillery

Royal Canadian Horse Artillery, 2nd Regiment – 2nd Field Regiment, Royal Artillery

Royal Canadian Hussars (Montreal) – Queen's Royal Irish Hussars; 13th/18th Royal Hussars (Queen Mary's Own)

Royal Canadian Regiment – Royal Regiment of Fusiliers; Gloucestershire Regiment

Royal Hamilton Light Infantry (Wentworth Regiment) – Light Infantry

Royal Montreal Regiment – Prince of Wales's Own Regiment of Yorkshire

Royal New Brunswick Regiment

(Carleton and York), 1st Battalion –
Prince of Wales's Own Regiment of
Yorkshire; King's Own Scottish
Borderers
Royal Newfoundland Regiment –
Royal Scots (The Royal Regiment)
Royal Regiment of Canada – King's
Regiment
Royal Regiment of Canadian Artillery –
Royal Regiment of Artillery
Royal Regina Rifle Regiment – Royal
Green Jackets
Royal 22e Régiment – Royal Welch
Fusiliers
Royal 22e Régiment (Châteauguay), 4e
Bataillon – Staffordshire Regiment
(The Prince of Wales's)
Royal Westminster Regiment – Royal
Regiment of Fusiliers
Royal Winnipeg Rifles – Royal Green
Jackets
Seaforth Highlanders of Canada –
Queen's Own Highlanders (Seaforth
and Cameronians)
Security Branch – Intelligence Corps
Sherbrook Hussars – Queen's Own
Hussars; Royal Anglian Regiment
South Alberta Light Horse – 15th/19th
The King's Royal Hussars; Queen's
Regiment
Toronto Scottish Regiment – Gordon
Highlanders
Voltigeurs de Quebec – Prince of
Wales's Own Yorkshire Regiment;
Duke of Wellington's Regiment (West
Riding)
West Nova Scotia Regiment – Queen's
Lancashire Regiment
Windsor Regiment (RCAC) – Royal
Scots Dragoon Guards (Carabiniers
and Greys)

FALKLAND ISLANDS
Falkland Island Defence Force – Prince
of Wales's Own Regiment of
Yorkshire

FIJI
Army Pay Corps – Royal Army Pay
Corps

Corps of Fiji Engineers – Corps of
Royal Engineers
Fiji Artillery – Royal Regiment of
Artillery
Fiji Infantry Regiment – Royal Green
Jackets

GIBRALTAR
Gibraltar Regiment – Royal Anglian
Regiment

HONG KONG
Pay Section, Royal Hong Kong
Defence Corps – Royal Army Pay
Corps
Royal Hong Kong Regiment (The
Volunteers) – Queen's Regiment

INDIA
Army Service Corps of India – Royal
Corps of Transport
Corps of Electrical and Mechanical
Engineers – Corps of Royal Electrical
and Mechanical Engineers
Corps of Signals – Royal Corps of
Signals
Indian Army Ordnance Corps – Royal
Army Ordnance Corps
Indian Engineers – Corps of Royal
Engineers
Lancers, 2nd – Royal Tank Regiment
Regiment of Artillery – Royal
Regiment of Artillery
Skinner's Horse (1st Duke of York's
Own Cavalry) – 13th/18th Royal
Hussars (Queen Mary's Own)

JAMAICA
Jamaica Regiment – Staffordshire
Regiment (The Prince of Wales's)

KENYA
Kenya Regiment, 3rd Battalion –
Gloucestershire Regiment
Kenya Rifles, 1st Battalion – Light
Infantry

LEEWARD ISLANDS
Antigua and Barbuda Defence Force –
Staffordshire Regiment (The Prince of
Wales's)

MALAYSIA

Malaysian Artillery – Royal Regiment of Artillery

Malaysian Electrical and Mechanical Engineers – Corps of Royal Electrical and Mechanical Engineers

Malaysian Engineer Corps – Corps of Royal Engineers

Malaysian Military Police – Corps of Royal Military Police

Malaysian Ordnance Corps – Royal Army Ordnance Corps

Malaysian Service Corps – Royal Corps of Transport

Malaysian Signal Corps – Royal Corps of Signals

Royal Malay Regiment: 1st Battalion – Royal Anglian Regiment; 2nd Battalion – Queen's Lancashire Regiment; 4th Battalion – Royal Welch Fusiliers; 5th Battalion – King's Own Scottish Borderers; 6th Battalion – Devonshire and Dorset Regiment

Royal Malaysian Armoured Corps, 2nd Regiment – 13th/18th Royal Hussars (Queen Mary's Own)

MAURITIUS

Mauritius Special Mobile Force – Light Infantry

NEW ZEALAND

Corps of Royal New Zealand Electrical and Mechanical Engineers – Corps of Royal Electrical and Mechanical Engineers

Corps of Royal New Zealand Engineers – Corps of Royal Engineers

New Zealand Scottish RNZAC, 1st and 2nd Squadrons – Royal Scots Dragoon Guards (Carabiniers and Greys); Black Watch (Royal Highland Regiment)

New Zealand Women's Royal Army Corps – Women's Royal Army Corps

New Zealand Special Air Service – Special Air Service Regiment

Queen Alexandra's Squadron RNZAC – 14th/20th King's Hussars

Royal New Zealand Armoured Corps – Royal Tank Regiment

Royal New Zealand Army Education Corps – Royal Army Educational Corps

Royal New Zealand Army Medical Corps – Royal Army Medical Corps

Royal New Zealand Army Ordnance Corps – Royal Army Ordnance Corps

Royal New Zealand Chaplains' Department – Royal Army Chaplains' Department

Royal New Zealand Corps of Signals – Royal Corps of Signals

Royal New Zealand Corps of Transport – Royal Corps of Transport

Royal New Zealand Dental Corps – Royal Army Dental Corps

Royal New Zealand Infantry Regiment: 1st Battalion – Royal Highland Fusiliers (Princess Margaret's Own Glasgow and Ayrshire Regiment); Royal Green Jackets

2nd/1st Battalion – 6th Queen Elizabeth's Own Gurkha Rifles

2nd Battalion (Canterbury Nelson Marlborough West Coast) – Queen's Regiment; Light Infantry; Royal Irish Rangers (27th (Inniskilling) 83rd and 87th)

3rd Battalion (Auckland (Countess of Ranfurly's Own) and Northland) – Royal Anglian Regiment

4th Battalion (Otago and Southland) – King's Regiment; Queen's Own Highlanders (Seaforth and Camerons)

5th Battalion (Wellington, West Coast and Taranki) – Queen's Regiment; Royal Hampshire Regiment

6th Battalion (Hauraki) – Royal Regiment of Fusiliers; Royal Green Jackets

7th Battalion (Wellington (City of Wellington's Own) and Hawkes Bay) – Queen's Lancashire Regiment; Duke of Edinburgh's Royal Regiment (Berkshire and Wiltshire); Queen's Own Highlanders (Seaforth and Camerons)

Corps of Royal New Zealand Military
  Police – Corps of Royal Military
  Police
Royal New Zealand Nursing Corps –
  Queen Alexandra's Royal Army
  Nursing Corps
Royal Regiment of New Zealand
  Artillery – Royal Regiment of
  Artillery
Waikato/Wellington East Coast
  Squadron RNZAC – 4th/7th Royal
  Dragoon Guards; Queen's Own
  Hussars

PAKISTAN

Army Medical Corps – Royal Army
  Medical Corps
Army Ordnance Corps – Royal Army
  Ordnance Corps
Army Service Corps of Pakistan –
  Royal Corps of Transport
Artillery of Pakistan – Royal Regiment
  of Artillery
Baluch Regiment:
  7th Battalion – Staffordshire Regiment
    (The Prince of Wales's)
  10th Battalion – Duke of Wellington's
    Regiment (West Riding)
  11th Battalion – Royal Highland
    Fusiliers (Princess Margaret's Own
    Glasgow and Ayrshire Regiment)
  14th Battalion – Light Infantry
Cavalry:
  12th (Sam Browne's Cavalry) –
    9th/12th Royal Lancers (Prince of
    Wales's)
  14th (Frontier Force) – 1st The
    Queen's Dragoon Guards
Corps of Military Police – Corps of
  Royal Military Police
Frontier Force Regiment:
  1st Battalion (Scinde) – King's
    Regiment
  5th Battalion – Royal Anglian
    Regiment
  9th Battalion (Wilde's) – Royal Irish
    Rangers (27th (Inniskilling) 83rd and
    87th)
  13th Battalion – Duke of Edinburgh's

Royal Regiment (Berkshire and
  Wiltshire)
  15th Battalion – King's Own Royal
    Border Regiment
Guides Cavalry – Royal Hussars (Prince
  of Wales's Own)
Lancers:
  6 - 13th/18th Royal Hussars (Queen
    Mary's Own)
  13 - Royal Tank Regiment
  15 - 4th/7th Royal Dragoon Guards
  19 - 15th/19th The King's Royal
    Hussars
Pakistan Electrical and Mechanical
  Engineers – Corps of Royal Electrical
  and Mechanical Engineers
Pakistan Engineers – Corps of Royal
  Engineers
Pakistan Remounts, Veterinary and
  Farm Corps – Royal Army Veterinary
  Corps
President's Bodyguard – Life Guards
Punjab Frontier Force – Argyll and
  Sutherland Highlanders (Princess
  Louise's)
Punjab Regiment:
  1st Battalion – Royal Irish Rangers
    (27th (Inniskilling) 83rd and 87th)
  8th Battalion – Queen's Lancashire
    Regiment
  12th, 14th, 15th and 17th Battalions –
    Queen's Regiment
  13th Battalion – Worcestershire and
    Sherwood Foresters Regiment (29th
    and 45th Foot)
Signal Corps – Royal Corps of Signals

PAPUA NEW GUINEA
Pacific Island Regiment Papua New
  Guinea – 7th Duke of Edinburgh's
  Own Gurkha Rifles

SINGAPORE
Singapore Voluntary Artillery – Royal
  Regiment of Artillery

SRI LANKA
Reconnaissance Regiment, 1st – 1st The
  Queen's Dragoon Guards

Signal Corps – Royal Corps of Signals

Sri Lanka Army Medical Corps – Royal Army Medical Corps

Sri Lanka Army Ordnance Corps – Royal Army Ordnance Corps

Sri Lanka Army Service Corps – Royal Corps of Transport

Sri Lanka Artillery – Royal Regiment of Artillery

Sri Lanka Corps of Military Police – Corps of Royal Military Police

Sri Lanka Engineers – Corps of Royal Engineers

ZAMBIA

Zambia Armoured Car Regimental – 14th/20th King's Hussars

Zambia Army Medical Service – Royal Army Medical Corps

Zambia Corps of Engineers – Corps of Royal Engineers

Zambia Corps of Signals – Royal Corps of Signals

ROYAL CONNECTIONS

In the past, many regiments were named after royalty, although only five have survived the 1958–1971 amalgamations (starred★ here). The royal personages and the regiments concerned may be of some historical interest. Regiments now amalgamated are shown in parentheses ( ).

Queen Catherine of Braganza (1638–1705), wife of Charles II – QUEENS★

Queen Caroline (1683–1737), wife of George II – (BAYS), (7H)

Queen Charlotte (1744–1818), wife of George III – (4H), (16L)

King George IV (1762–1830), as Prince of Wales – (3DG), (10H), (12L), (S LANCS)

Duke of York and Albany (1763–1837), second son of George III – (SEAFORTH)

Princess Royal (1766–1828), eldest daughter of George III – (7DG)

Queen Adelaide (1792–1849), wife of William IV – (9L), (RWK)

Princess Charlotte of Wales (1796–1817), only daughter of George IV – (5DG), (R BERKS)

Queen Victoria (1819–1901), as Princess (R IR F); as Queen (CAMERONS); as Empress of India (21L)

Albert, Prince Consort (1819–61), husband of Victoria – (11H)

Duke of Cambridge (1819–1904), second cousin of Victoria – (17L), (MX)

King Edward VII (1841–1910), as Prince of Wales – (N STAFFS), (W YORKS); as Duke of Cornwall – (DCLI)

Queen Alexandra (1844–1925), wife of Edward VII, as Princess of Wales – GREEN HOWARDS★; as Queen – (19H), QARANC★

Duke of Edinburgh (1844–1900), second son of Victoria – (WILTS)

Princess Louise (1848–1939), fourth daughter of Victoria – A AND SH★

Queen Mary (1867–1953), wife of George V – (18H)

King George VI (1895–1957), as Duke of York – (E YORKS)

Princess Margaret (b.1930), second daughter of George VI – RHF★

ABBREVIATIONS OF REGIMENTAL AND CORPS TITLES

(Amalgamated or disbanded units in parentheses [].)

AAC Army Air Corps

A AND SH Argyll and Sutherland Highlanders (Princess Louise's)

ACC Army Catering Corps

APTC Army Physical Training Corps

[BAYS 2nd Dragoon Guards (Queen's Bays)]

[BEDFS HERTS Bedfordshire and Hertfordshire Regiment]

[BORDER Border Regiment]

[BUFFS Buffs (Royal East Kent Regiment)]

BW Black Watch (Royal Highland Regiment)

[CAMERONIANS Cameronians (Scottish Rifles)]

[CAMERONS Queen's Own Cameron Highlanders]

CHESHIRE Cheshire Regiment

COLDM GDS Coldstream Guards

D AND D Devonshire and Dorset Regiment

[DCLI Duke of Cornwall's Light Infantry]

DERR Duke of Edinburgh's Royal Regiment (Berkshire and Wiltshire)

[DEVON Devonshire Regiment]

[3DG 3rd Carabiniers (Prince of Wales's Dragoon Guards)]

4/7DG 4th/7th Royal Dragoon Guards

INNIS DG 5th Royal Inniskilling Dragoon Guards

[6DG The Carabiniers (6th Dragoon Guards)]

[DLI Durham Light Infantry]

[DORSET Dorsetshire Regiment]

DWR Duke of Wellington's Regiment (West Riding)

[E LAN R East Lancashire Regiment]

[ESSEX Essex Regiment]

[E YORKS East Yorkshire Regiment (The Duke of York's Own)]

[FORESTERS Sherwood Foresters (Nottinghamshire and Derbyshire Regiment)]

GLOSTERS Gloucestershire Regiment

GORDONS Gordon Highlanders

2GR 2nd King Edward's Own Gurkha Rifles (The Sirmoor Rifles)

6GR 6th Queen Elizabeth's Own Gurkha Rifles

7GR 7th The Duke of Edinburgh's Own Gurkha Rifles

10GR 10th Princess Mary's Own Gurkha Rifles

GREEN HOWARDS Green Howards (Alexandra, Princess of Wales's Own Regiment of Yorkshire)

GREN GDS Grenadier Guards

[GREYS Royal Scots Greys (2nd Dragoons)]

GTR Gurkha Transport Regiment

[3H 3rd The King's Own Hussars]

[4H 4th Queen's Own Hussars]

[7H 7th The Queen's Own Hussars]

[8H 8th King's Own Irish Hussars]

[10H 10th The Prince of Wales's Own Hussars]

[11H 11th Hussars (Prince Albert's Own)]

[13H 13th Hussars]

13/18H 13th/18th Royal Hussars (Queen Mary's Own)

[14H 14th King's Hussars]

14/20H 14th/20th King's Hussars

[15H 15th The King's Hussars]

15/19H 15th/19th The King's Royal Hussars

[18H 18th (Queen Mary's Own) Hussars]

[19H 19th Royal Hussars (Queen Alexandra's Own)]

[20H 20th Hussars]

[HLI Highland Light Infantry]

IG Irish Guards

[INNISKS Royal Inniskilling Fusiliers]

INT CORPS Intelligence Corps
[KDG 1st (King's) Dragoon Guards]
[KINGS King's Regiment; King's
  Regiment (Liverpool)]
[KINGS OWN King's Own Royal
  Regiment (Lancaster)]
KING OWN BORDER King's Own
  Royal Border Regiment
KOSB King's Own Scottish Borderers
[KOYLI King's Own Yorkshire Light
  Infantry]
[KRRC King's Royal Rifle Corps]
[KSLI King's Shropshire Light
  Infantry]
[5L 5th Royal Irish Lancers]
[9L 9th Queen's Royal Lancers]
[12L 12th Royal Lancers (Prince of
  Wales's)]
9/12thL 9th/12th Royal Lancers (Prince
  of Wales's)
[16L 16th The Queen's Lancers]
16/5L 16th/5th The Queen's Royal
  Lancers
[17L 17th Lancers (Duke of
  Cambridge's Own)]
17/21L 17th/21st Lancers
[21L 21st Lancers (Empress of India's)]
[LEICESTERS Royal Leicestershire
  Regiment]
[LF Lancashire Fusiliers]
LG Life Guards
LI Light Infantry
[LINCOLNS Royal Lincolnshire
  Regiment]
[LOYALS Loyal Regiment (North
  Lancashire)]
[MANCH Manchester Regiment]
MPSC Military Provost Staff Corps
[MX Middlesex Regiment]
[NF Royal Northumberland Fusiliers]
[NORFOLKS Royal Norfolk
  Regiment]
[NORTHAMPTONS Northampton-
  shire Regiment]
[N STAFFS North Staffordshire
  Regiment (The Prince of Wales's)]
[OXF BUCKS Oxfordshire and
  Buckinghamshire Light Infantry]
PARA Parachute Regiment
PWO Prince of Wales's Own Regiment

of Yorkshire
QARANC Queen Alexandra's Royal
  Army Nursing Corps
QDG 1st The Queen's Dragoon
  Guards
QGE Queen's Gurkha Engineers
QG SIGNALS Queen's Gurkha
  Signals
Q LAN R Queen's Lancashire
  Regiment
QOH Queen's Own Hussars
QO HLDRS Queen's Own
  Highlanders (Seaforth and Camerons)
QRIH Queen's Royal Irish Hussars
[QUEENS Queen's Regiment; Royal
  Regiment (West Surrey)]
RA Royal Regiment of Artillery
RAC Royal Armoured Corps
RAChD Royal Army Chaplains'
  Department
RADC Royal Army Dental Corps
RAEC Royal Army Educational Corps
RAMC Royal Army Medical Corps
R ANGLIAN Royal Anglian Regiment
RAOC Royal Army Ordnance Corps
RAPC Royal Army Pay Corps
[RASC Royal Army Service Corps]
RAVC Royal Army Veterinary Corps
[RB Rifle Brigade (Prince Consort's
  Own)]
[R BERKS Royal Berkshire Regiment
  (Princess Charlotte of Wales's)]
RCT Royal Corps of Transport
RE Corps of Royal Engineers
REME Corps of Royal Electrical and
  Mechanical Engineers
[RF Royal Fusiliers (City of London
  Regiment)]
RGJ Royal Green Jackets
RH Royal Hussars (Prince of Wales's
  Own)
RHA Royal Horse Artillery
R HAMPS Royal Hampshire Regiment
RHF Royal Highland Fusiliers (Princess
  Margaret's Own Glasgow and
  Ayrshire Regiment)
[RHG Royal Horse Guards (The
  Blues)]
RHG/D Blues and Royals (Royal Horse
  Guards and 1st Dragoons)

[R IR F Royal Irish Fusiliers (Princess Victoria's)]

R IRISH Royal Irish Rangers (27th (Inniskilling) 83rd and 87th)

RMP Corps of Royal Military Police

[ROYALS Royal Dragoons (1st Dragoons)]

RPC Royal Pioneer Corps

RRF Royal Regiment of Fusiliers

RRW Royal Regiment of Wales (24th/41st Foot)

RS Royal Scots (The Royal Regiment)

[RSF Royal Scots Fusiliers]

R SIGNALS Royal Corps of Signals

[R SUSSEX Royal Sussex Regiment]

[RTC Royal Tank Corps]

RTR Royal Tank Regiment

[RUR Royal Ulster Rifles]

RWF Royal Welch Fusiliers

[RWK Queen's Own Royal West Kent Regiment]

SASC Small Arms School Corps

SAS Special Air Service Regiment

Scots DG Royal Scots Dragoon Guards (Carabiniers and Greys)

SG Scots Guards

[SEAFORTH Seaforth Highlanders (Ross-shire Buffs, The Duke of Albany's)]

[S LAN R South Lancashire Regiment (The Prince of Wales's Volunteers)]

[SOM LI Somerset Light Infantry (Prince Albert's)]

[S STAFFORDS South Staffordshire Regiment]

STAFFORDS Staffordshire Regiment (The Prince of Wales's)

[SUFFOLK Suffolk Regiment]

[SURREYS East Surrey Regiment]

SWB South Wales Borderers

[WARWICKS Royal Warwickshire Fusiliers]

WG Welsh Guards

[WELCH Welch Regiment]

WFR Worcestershire and Sherwood Foresters Regiment (24th/45th Foot)

[WILTS Wiltshire Regiment (Duke of Edinburgh's)]

[WORC R Worcestershire Regiment]

[W YORKS West Yorkshire Regiment (The Prince of Wales's Own)]

WRAC Women's Royal Army Corps

[Y & L York and Lancaster Regiment]

SELECT BIBLIOGRAPHY
(See main text for histories of individual regiments or corps)

ASCOLI, David. *A Companion to the British Army 1660–1983*, Harrap, 1983.

BAKER, Anthony. *Battle Honours of the British and Commonwealth Armies*, Ian Allan, 1986.

BARNES, R Money. *A History of the Regiments and Uniforms of the British Army*, Seeley Service (2nd ed.), 1951.

— *The Soldiers of London*, Seeley Service, 1963.

— *The British Army of 1914*, Seeley Service, 1968.

BOORMAN, Derek. *At the Going Down of the Sun – British First World War Memorials*, Boorman, 1988.

BRERETON, J. M. *A Guide to the Regiments and Corps of the British Army on the Establishment*, Bodley Head, 1985.

— *The British Soldier – A Social History from 1661 to the Present Day*, Bodley Head, 1986.

BRUCE, Anthony. *A Bibliography of the British Army, 1660–1940*, Saur, 1985.

CHANT, Christopher. *The Handbook of British Regiments*, Routledge & Kegan Paul, 1988.★

CHILDS, John. *The Army of Charles II*, Routledge & Kegan Paul, 1976.

— *The Army, James II, and the Glorious Revolution*, Manchester UP, 1980.

— *The British Army of William III, 1689–1702*, Manchester UP, 1987.

COOK, Hugh. *The Battle Honours of the British and Indian Armies*, Leo Cooper, 1987.

COOPER, Leonard. *British Regular Cavalry 1644–1918*, Chapman & Hall, 1965.

CROOK, M. J. *The Evolution of the Victoria Cross*, Midas/Ogilby Trusts, 1975.

EDWARDS, T. J. *Regimental Mascots and Pets*, Hutchinson, 1939.

FORTESCUE, Sir John. *The Last Post*, Blackwood, 1934.

— *History of the British Army* (13 vols.), (2nd ed.), Macmillan, 1935.

FREDERICK, J. B. M. *Lineage Book of the British Army*, Hope Farm Press (USA), 1969.

GRIFFIN, David. *Encyclopaedia of Modern British Army Regiments*, Patrick Stephens, 1985.

HIGHAM, Robin (ed.). *British Military History – A Guide to Sources*, Routledge & Kegan Paul, 1972.

JOSLIN, E. C., LITHERLAND, A. R., and SIMPKIN, B. T. *British Battles and Medals*, Spink, 1988.

LAVER, James (intr.). *The Book of Public School Old Boys, University, Navy, Army, Air Force and Club Ties*, Seeley Service, 1968.

LESLIE, Norman. *Battle Honours of the British and Indian Armies 1695–1914*, Leo Cooper, 1973.★★

MEYER, S. L., and KOENIG, W. J. *The Two World Wars – A Guide to Manuscript Collections in the United Kingdom*, Bowker, 1976.

NEUBURG, Victor. *Gone for a Soldier*, Cassell, 1989.

NORMAN, C. B. *Battle Honours of the British Army*, John Murray, 1911, reprinted David & Charles, 1971.

SMYTH, VC, Sir John. *The Story of the Victoria Cross*, Muller, 1963.

— *The Story of the George Cross*, Arthur Barker, 1968.

STANHOPE, Henry. *The Soldiers – An Anatomy of the British Army*, Hamish Hamilton, 1979.

STRAWSON, John. *Gentlemen in Khaki – The British Army 1890–1990*, Secker & Warburg, 1989.

SWINSON, Arthur (ed.). *A Register of the Regiments and Corps of the British Army*, Archive Press, 1972.

WHITE, A. S. *A Bibliography of Regimental Histories of the British Army*, Society for Army Historical Research, 1965, (2nd ed.), London, Stamp Exchange, 1988.

WINSTOCK, L. *Songs and Music of the Redcoats 1642–1902*, Leo Cooper, 1970.

WISE, Terence. *A Guide to Military Museums*, Athena, 1990.

The Register of the Victoria Cross, This England, 1981.

The Register of the George Cross, This England, 1985.

*Includes corps.   **From 1662.

INDEX